Conditioned
reinforcement

THE DORSEY SERIES IN PSYCHOLOGY

EDITOR HOWARD F. HUNT *Columbia University*

Conditioned reinforcement

Edited by

DEREK P. HENDRY, Ph.D.

Associate Professor of Information Engineering
and
Associate Professor of Psychology
University of Illinois
Chicago Circle

1969

THE
DORSEY
PRESS   Homewood, Illinois
Irwin-Dorsey Limited, Georgetown, Ontario

First Printing, August, 1969

Library of Congress Catalog Card No. 79–90237
Printed in the United States of America

FOREWORD

Werner K. Honig

Professor of Psychology
Dalhousie University

The definition of a reinforcer stresses its immediate past: A reinforcing event is one that strengthens the behavior which precedes it. But all psychological events, be they environmental or behavioral, have not only a past, but also a future. In the case of primary reinforcers, the future is seldom investigated at a psychological level. Most analyses of primary reinforcement concern the physiological consequences of reward; only one theory (Premack, 1965) provides an analysis couched in behavioral terms. For the moment, most psychologists involved in the experimental analysis of behavior are content to accept primary reinforcers as a boon to research, since they provide the principal source of experimental control over the organisms that we use for the research. Seldom do they ask what makes the reinforcer reinforcing.

With conditioned reinforcers, the situation is quite different: They have not only an immediate past in the behavior that they maintain, but also a future in the behavior over which they exert control, or in the stimuli with which they are associated. It is through this "future" that conditioned reinforcers acquire and maintain their strength as reinforcing events. If instrumental behavior is defined as behavior maintained by its consequences, then conditioned reinforcement can be defined as that class of consequences which owe their strength, in turn, to their own consequences. Conditioned reinforcement may be described as the process in which behavior is strengthened or maintained by "reinforced reinforcers."

The two terms contained in this bit of verbal dexterity suggest that there are two aspects to conditioned reinforcement which are discussed in detail in this book. First, it must be established that conditioned reinforcers are indeed effective. And we can ask, under what conditions of their presentation will they be most effective? What methods are most sensitive for demonstrating their potency? In what ways does their effectiveness differ from that of primary reinforcers? Second, the establishment of conditioned reinforcers must be investigated—the conditions of their own "reinforcement" must be studied in some detail. It is in this area that conditioned reinforcers are distinguished most strongly from primary reinforcers. Conditioned reinforcers are learned reinforcers. What is the learning process like? Can it be incorporated under the fundamental principles of learning, to the extent that these have been established? Can the process involved in the establishment of conditioned reinforcers provide new information on learning processes in general, information which has not been provided through other techniques involving either stimulus control or the "classical" association of two stimuli?

In any experiment on conditioned reinforcement, it must be established that the reinforcer is effective, and that its effectiveness is not some artifact of a correlation of the response in question with primary reinforcement. Thus the relationship of the conditioned reinforcer to its immediate past must be demonstrated. The necessity to do this stems in part from a long distrust of the strength of conditioned reinforcement; there is still a widespread belief that conditioned reinforcement is a "textbook phenomenon," which may be easy to describe, but hard to support. As Hendry points out in his introductory chapter, the traditional methods of examining secondary reinforcement—the "extinction method" and the "new response method"—while they precluded the confounding of conditioned and primary reinforcement, also assured that the conditioned reinforcer was decreasing in its effectiveness in the course of its presentation, since it was correlated with extinction. If psychologists had been more keenly aware of the fact that conditioned reinforcement was likely to obey the fundamental laws of learning, they would not have taken these methods so seriously. At any rate, Kelleher and Gollub (1962) and Kelleher (1966) described many studies in which the correlation between conditioned reinforcement and extinction could be avoided; in other words, in which primary reinforcement could be maintained in the situation. The methods, which, in part, they developed provided much of the basis for the research reported in this book.

The effectiveness of a conditioned reinforcer is generally demonstrated in the experiments reported in this book in several ways. Some experimenters, whose work is reported in the first group of chapters, use different patterns of responding to sort out the effects of the conditioned reinforcer and the primary reinforcer. Zimmerman shows that when primary reinforcement is made contingent on not responding, conditioned reinforcement will still maintain the criterion response at a steady, if rather low, level. Marr reviews second order schedules, in which the conditioned reinforcer clearly produces patterns of response appropriate to its contingency of presentation, such as a fixed-interval basis. Schuster shows that a fixed ratio production of conditioned reinforcement will lead to an increase in rate, and so, in a different context, does Schaub. All of these methods involve necessary control groups, or conditions which show that the conditioned reinforcer is necessary to maintain the response patterns in question, and/or that the primary reinforcer is not sufficient to do the same. There is a wealth of material in this book to demonstrate that conditioned reinforcers *are* effective; the traditional difficulties in previous attempts to demonstrate conditioned reinforcement seem to have lain in the methods used, not in the reality of the phenomenon.

A second method used to demonstrate secondary reinforcing power is the observing response method, where two different responses are required, one to turn on a cue, the other to gain primary reinforcement. Again, this amounts to a sorting out of two response patterns, which may of course be in competition. This method appears to be primarily used in studies devoted to the analysis of "informative" stimuli as reinforcers (Kendall, Dinsmoor) ; if the subject wants information, he makes it clear to the experimenter by performing a response different from responding for food. The classic study was performed by Wyckoff, and appears in this book at long last in published form. Due to the influence of this study, the observing response method has been used largely for the study of informative stimuli. But there is no reason why the separate response method, as we may call it, should be restricted to research with observing response. One could easily attempt to replicate many of the second order schedule effects with a similar method, permitting one response to produce the conditioned reinforcer plus food, and the other to produce the conditioned reinforcer alone. This method was actually used by Zimmerman in his original experiments, but has not been exploited by others for the same purpose.

A third method for demonstrating effects of secondary reinforcement is a preference method. Due perhaps to Autor's influential thesis, which also is published in this book for the first time, Concurrent Chain schedules have been used for preference studies. In this method, all of the evidence for a preference occurs in the first leg of the Chain; when the second (and final) component begins, the choice is over, and the animal can neither escape the second schedule nor prolong it. This method, like most preference methods, is very sensitive, and may be particularly appropriate for the study of weak conditioned reinforcers. It is a tool used not so much for the demonstration of conditioned reinforcers as for the analysis of the variables which govern their strength, e.g. their "informativeness" (Hendry), the density of primary reinforcement schedules in their presence (Autor), or the aversiveness (or attractiveness) of particular response requirements with which they are associated (Fantino).

As psychologists continue the experimental analysis of conditioned reinforcement, other ingenious methods will assuredly be devised, methods which are both sensitive and which provide measures unadulterated with the direct effects of primary reinforcement itself. All of the methods mentioned above involve either some competition between the responses producing conditioned and those producing primary reinforcement, or they limit the opportunity for choice to certain portions of the program. One might, for example, adopt concurrent responses with a change-over key, a technique used very effectively in other contexts by Catania, and described by him in some detail (Catania, 1966). The subject might be permitted to switch freely between one schedule involving food plus a conditioned reinforcer, and another in which conditioned reinforcers are scheduled alone as well. Or an observing response could be required which competed less strongly with the food response. The subject might, by standing in front of one key, depress the floor on one side of the box so as to produce a relevant cue, while standing in front of the opposite key would have the effect of producing irrelevant cues. This book shows what can be accomplished in the development of refined methods for the study of conditioned reinforcement; it will most likely provide a stimulus for the development of further methods that will overcome the remaining limitations of those described here.

But the most interesting questions, surely, concern not so much the "how" of conditioned reinforcement, but the "why." The action of conditioned reinforcers seems to be similar to that of their primary counterparts—this similarity is assured by the definition of reinforcement if for no other reason. Furthermore, there have been few studies of such variables as the "magnitude" of conditioned reinforcers, the delay of reward, and so forth, in which the action of the two classes of events could be compared. The critical difference between them is that conditioned reinforcers are, by definition, acquired in the course of an experiment. The "form" of the conditioned reinforcer is arbitrary, within the limits of the sensory capacities of the organism, but the primary reinforcers effective for a given species are restricted in number and quality.

In order to study the "why" of conditioned reinforcement, it is necessary to look at its "immediate future," rather than at its immediate past. Naturally, the final performance reflects the past experience of the subject with this "immediate future." We are interested in the succession of events following the presentation of an arbitrary stimulus necessary to provide the individual subject with a history that establishes it as a conditioned reinforcer.

This general question is discussed by Hendry in his introductory chapter, and its main issues need not be repeated here. Clearly, stimuli that are discriminative for some subsequent response can become conditioned reinforcers, although a *specific* response requirement for primary reinforcement may be shown to be mildly aversive (Fantino). Clearly, the temporal contiguity of a neutral stimulus with primary reinforcer can turn that neutral stimulus into a conditioned reinforcer, although the mediation of some response between the two stimuli can never be ruled out without the special procedures, such as curarization, which are now employed in other areas of associative learning. Clearly, two stimuli that provide differential information with regard to the availability of primary reinforcement can come to be preferred over noninformative stimuli, although it is not yet clear whether the presentation of only a stimulus that signals "bad news" will maintain an observing response. It is pointless to argue that one of these routes to conditioned reinforcement is the "most basic"; we should know by now that in the development of behavioral phenomena, alternate routes can lead to the same effect. Instead, we may ask what they have in common. In all cases, the conditioned reinforcer acts as a signal to some other event, or the two reinforcing stimuli serve as signals distinguishing two different events. Even when the reinforcer acts as a discriminative stimulus for a response, this response is maintained by some event which is of necessity correlated with the conditioned reinforcer, even though it may not be contiguous with its onset. What we mean by a "signal" is that its occurrence increases the predictability of some other, signaled event, and this increase in information may, as Hendry argues, be essential to the acquisition and maintenance of secondary reinforcing strength.

Many chapters in this book support this notion empirically; almost half are devoted to the explicit study of the relation between information and conditioned reinforcement. The methods used by Wyckoff, Hendry, Kendall, and others need not be detailed here, but it should be noted that in order to study this problem, they have used two different signals, each differentially associated with primary reinforcement, schedules of reinforcement, or some other aspect of the experimental situation. But we should remember that the single stimulus used in the typical demonstration of conditioned reinforcement carries information as well. After all, the absence of the conditioned reinforcing stimulus is correlated with the absence of its primary counterpart. The presence and the absence of the stimulus constitute two signals.

The whole question of the degree of association or correlation between a neutral "signaling" stimulus and the signaled event has been reopened and extended in the psychology of learning, due largely to the efforts of Rescorla and Solomon (1967) and their associates. But this extension has not yet been recognized in the area of conditioned reinforcement. It may be useful to indicate the direction that a comparable extension in the area of conditioned reinforcement would take. We can view the positive correlation of a signal with a primary positive reinforcer as only one point lying on two experimental "dimensions"; it is the only point that has been studied in detail in the area of conditioned reinforcement. One dimension is the degree of correlation between the two events. This can run from plus one through zero to minus one. Psychologists have not, for example, studied the reinforcing effectiveness of a neutral stimulus with a random temporal relation to a primary re-inforcer, in the manner suggested by Rescorla (1967) as a control procedure for classical conditioning.

The other dimension is the appetitiveness vs. aversiveness of the primary stimulus. Presumably, a stimulus that is negatively cor-related with an aversive event could become a positive conditioned reinforcer, since it signals the absence of such an event. Evidence on this matter is sparse, although there is some support for the notion (Dinsmoor and Clayton, 1966). Likewise, a signal correlated with shock becomes a conditioned punisher (Hake and Azrin, 1965). This line of reasoning also suggests that a signal of Extinc-tion (negative correlation with food) should take on punishing properties. In his chapter, Schaub points out that such an associa-tive effect may detract from the informative value of a stimulus that signals Extinction. A number of chapters in this book do sug-gest that since a stimulus correlated with an aversive condition carries informational value, it may be positively reinforcing, and there is a tradition of research (Lockhard, 1963) which indicates that animals prefer signaled to unsignaled shock. If this is the case, it would support the view that conditioned reinforcers have two sources of strength. One would be purely associative, or "emo-tional"; the conditioned reinforcer is established through a con-ditioning process and takes on the "sign" of the primary reinforcer. The other would be informational, or "cognitive," and would de-pend on the degree of correlation between two events. Such a value would always be positive, unless the correlation was zero. Now in most experiments on conditioned reinforcement, the positive values of the associative and informational aspects of conditioned rein-forcement are combined and confounded, since positive correlations with appetitive events are usually involved. An extension of re-search along the dimension that I have suggested would permit a separation of these two aspects, and the research reported here by Schaub and by Dinsmoor and his associates can be viewed as initial steps in this direction.

The research dimensions described above have been examined during recent years with regard to the effects of neutral stimuli on a baseline of ongoing behavior, both appetitive and avoidant. It is well established now that "safe" stimuli reduce avoidant behavior, and "danger" stimuli enhance it (Rescorla and LoLordo, 1965). Danger signals reduce appetitive behavior, in the form of conditioned suppression, and it appears that safe signals may enhance it (e.g. Hammond, 1966, 1967; Hendry, 1967; Hendry, Yarczower and Switalski, 1969). It is not well known whether conditioned stimuli that are correlated with positive reinforcers will affect a baseline of avoidant behavior. But it would certainly be of great interest to compare the reinforcing value of stimuli conditioned in these various ways with their effects on ongoing instrumental behavior. For example, a "safe" stimulus, while inhibiting an avoidant response occurring in its presence, might not be able to enhance a response which produces it, i.e. it might not function as a conditioned reinforcer. It might also be found, conversely, that while a signal for food can act as a conditioned reinforcer, it will not enhance an ongoing appetitive response occurring in its presence (Azrin and Hake, 1969).

The possible comparisons of conditioned reinforcers and conditioned stimuli, and the analyses that they would suggest, are numerous, and could become quite complex. Such experiments could indicate to what degree a conditioning process is a determinant of conditioned reinforcement, and to what degree other processes associated with the stimulus (such as chaining of behavior), or other values that it might assume (such as the informative one), contribute to the establishment of conditioned reinforcers. The comparisons with the effects of conditioned stimuli on an ongoing baseline of behavior provide a link between conditioned reinforcement as a phenomenon, and the general effects of an association between neutral and "primary" events on appetitive and avoidant behavior.

Just as every conditioned reinforcer has a past and a future in the temporal sequence of psychological events, so does the field of conditioned reinforcement itself. It has for many years been recognized in introductory texts as an important phenomenon, since it may provide the connective tissue between the dry bones of the experimental psychology of learning, and the living flesh of the behavior of "real people." It is obvious that men are reinforced by words and money as strongly as by food and sex, and the need for a mechanism which would link the primary reinforcement of the rat laboratory to the conditions governing human behavior is equally obvious. Unfortunately, most of the texts which have stressed the importance of conditioned reinforcement proceeded to provide very limited evidence for it, and to stress its evanescent character. This situation can now be corrected. By developing, and refining their research techniques, the workers in this area have found their efforts rewarded through systematic demonstrations of conditioned reinforcement. Much of the record of this development is to be found in this book.

While a worthy aim of experimental psychology is the exploration of phenomena that contribute to the understanding of "real people's" behavior, such phenomena, once established, tend to become objects of research in their own right. The manner in which reinforcement schedules and aversive control actually determine the behavior of people is not discovered in the pigeon or rat laboratory, but such phenomena are carefully studied with regard to the processes underlying them. In my opinion, much the same will happen with conditioned reinforcement. Its role as "connective tissue" will have to be determined *in situ,* that is, in working with "real people." Its importance as the outcome of a learning process will be increasingly recognized by experimental psychologists in the area of learning. In their analysis of the learning processes that underlie conditioned reinforcement, they will contribute to a general understanding of the manner in which events that are related to each other, particularly in their temporal association, come to control behavior.

REFERENCES

Azrin, N. H. and Hake, D. F. Positive conditioned suppression: conditioned suppression using positive reinforcers as the unconditioned stimuli. *Journal of the Experimental Analysis of Behavior,* 1969, 12, 167–173.

Catania, A. C. Concurrent operants. In Honig, W. K. (Ed.), *Operant behavior: areas of research and application.* New York: Appleton-Century-Crofts, 1966, 213–270.

Hammond, L. J. Increased responding to CS—in differential CER. *Psychonomic Science,* 1965, 5, 337–338.

Hammond, L. J. A traditional demonstration of the five properties of Pavlovian inhibition using differential CER. *Psychonomic Science,* 1967, 9, 65–66.

Hendry, D. P. Conditioned inhibition of conditioned suppression. *Psychonomic Science,* 1967, 9, 261–262.

Hendry, D. P., Yarczower, M. and Switalski, R. C. Periodic shock with added clock. *Journal of the Experimental Analysis of Behavior,* 1969, 12, 159–166.

Kelleher, R. T. Chaining and conditioned reinforcement. In W. K. Honig (Ed.) *Operant Behavior: Areas of research and application.* New York: Appleton-Century-Crofts, 1966, 160–212.

Kelleher, R .T. and Gollub, L. R. A review of positive conditioned reinforcement. *Journal of the Experimental Analysis of Behavior,* 1962, 5, 543–597.

Lockard, Joan S. Choice of a warning signal or no warning signal in an unavoidable shock situation. *Journal of Comparative and Physiological Psychology,* 1963, 56, 526–530.

Premack, D. Reinforcement theory. In D. Levine (Ed.), *Nebraska Symposium on Motivation.* Lincoln, Nebraska: University of Nebraska Press, 1965.

Rescorla, R. A. Pavlovian conditioning and its proper control procedures. *Psychological Review,* 1967, 74, 71–80.

Rescorla, R. A. and LoLordo, V. M. Inhibition of avoidance behavior. *Journal of Comparative Physiological Psychology,* 1965, 59, 406–412.

Rescorla, R. A. and Solomon, R. L. Two-process learning theory: Relationships between pavlovian conditioning and instrumental learning. *Psychological Review,* 1967, 74, 151–182.

PREFACE

In recent years, new evidence about reinforcement and conditioned reinforcement has been accumulating at an increasing pace. Even more impressive than the rapidity of the growth of knowledge has been the viability of the old theories of behavior in the face of what appeared to be fundamentally new phenomena. Three possibilities occurred to me: the remarkable survival of the old theories reflected either the genius and prescience of their founders, or a tenacious conservatism, or a lack of new theories. The time seemed ripe to bring together a group of young experimental psychologists who were actively investigating conditioned reinforcement. The object of such a meeting would be to acquaint the participants with the current work and thinking of their colleagues. Accordingly, a meeting was arranged and took place at Chicago Circle in October, 1967, as part of the centennial celebrations of the University of Illinois. Those who attended thought the meeting was successful in exposing them to a variety of provocative phenomena and ideas in the area of conditioned reinforcement. There emerged, however, no consensus on the most appropriate theoretical structure to encompass these phenomena, or even whether one was needed. The single new formulation in the last few years—the Information Hypothesis, attributable to Berlyne and to Egger and Miller—received a good deal of attention. The Information Hypothesis can accommodate many of the old ideas, and with progressive refinement and quantitative expression it may become the unifying conception of conditioned reinforcement.

This book is based on the Chicago Conference. Each author had an opportunity to revise his paper in the light of the reaction it had provoked at the Conference, whether adulatory, solemn, heated, or hilarious.

The results of Wyckoff and Autor are referred to over and over again in the literature on conditioned reinforcement. Yet these papers are not readily available. This was a fine opportunity to make these classic studies accessible and specially edited versions are printed here with the kind permission of the authors.

The chapters are grouped in three sections into those concerned mainly with schedules of conditioned reinforcement, those measuring conditioned reinforcement with Concurrent Chains, and those concerned with the reinforcing value of information in discrimination learning and performance. The groups seem to me to be internally cohesive and to represent the areas of most intense contemporary experimental effort in the study of conditioned reinforcement. However, some chapters are represented in more than one conceptual group. For example, Schuster's chapter develops concurrent-chains technology but incidentally uses a schedule (FR 11) of conditioned reinforcement, and produces results relevant to information interpretations of conditioned reinforcement. Chapter 12 is mainly concerned with information interpretations of conditioned reinforcement, but includes effects of varying the schedule of conditioned reinforcement (fixed ratios of observing responses) and several experiments use Concurrent Chains.

In a book such as this there is considerable overlap in what the contributors write. I have not edited the contributions to minimize redundancy or to arbitrate contradictions. Indeed, such is the interrelatedness of the contributions that the very detection of redundancy and inconsistency is a delightful and continuing intellectual task.

Reinforcement may be "primary" and "secondary"; or "unconditioned" and "conditioned." The more general term "conditioned" is favored over "secondary"; awkward terms like "tertiary," "quaternary," etc., are thereby avoided. However, the term "unconditioned" is itself a long, stilted, modified modifier that means unmodified. Thus we use the qualifiers "primary" and "conditioned," with apologies to linguistic purists.

I wish to thank those who helped in the preparation of this volume. The final product benefited from careful and penetrating criticism of an early version by Howard Hunt, the Dorsey editor of this series, and Evalyn Segal, my colleague in the University of Illinois. Mary Bailey Gruber, my research assistant at the University of Illinois, not only helped in conducting the experiments reported in Chapter 12, but efficiently dealt with many matters in composing this book. Rita Miller took effective charge of the myriad details in the preparation of the text, including the retyping that went on almost continuously for over a year.

I am indebted to J. O. de Lorge, E. Fantino, R. J. Herrnstein, R. T. Kelleher and to the Society for the Experimental Analysis of Behavior for permission to reprint some of the material in Chapters 2 and 7 that has appeared in recent issues of the *Journal of the Experimental Analysis of Behavior*. Specifically: Figure 2.3 originally appeared in Fixed-interval behavior maintained by conditioned reinforcement, *Journal of the Experimental Analysis of Behavior*, 1967, *10*, 271–276, by J. O. de Lorge (Copyright 1967 by the Society for the Experimental Analysis of Behavior, Inc.); Figure 2.4 originally appeared in Conditioned reinforcement in second-order schedules, *Journal of the Experimental Analysis of Behavior*, 1966, *9*, 475–485, by R. T. Kelleher (Copyright 1966 by the Society for the Experimental Analysis of Behavior, Inc.); Figures 7.5, 7.6, 7.7, 7.8 and 7.9 originally appeared in Secondary reinforcement and number of primary reinforcements, *Journal of the Experimental Analysis of Behavior*, 1968, *11*, 9–14, by E. Fantino and R. J. Herrnstein (Copyright 1968 by the Society for the Experimental Analysis of Behavior, Inc.); Figure 7.2, 7.3, 7.4 and Tables 7.1 and 7.2 originally appeared in Effects of required rates of responding upon choice, *Journal of the Experimental Analysis of Behavior*, 1968, *11*, 15–22, by E. Fantino (Copyright 1968 by the Society for the Experimental Analysis of Behavior, Inc.).

July, 1969   DEREK P. HENDRY

TABLE OF CONTENTS

poral and informative relations in extensions of the Estes-Skinner procedure. General implications. Note on terminology.

chapter 1

INTRODUCTION

Derek P. Hendry

University of Illinois, Chicago Circle

The purpose of this chapter is to provide basic information about the analysis of behavior and a conceptual framework to aid in understanding the remaining chapters.

First, I include a description of apparatus and general procedures that is designed to help the reader who has slight acquaintance with what is usually called "operant conditioning." Most of this information is available elsewhere, but it is convenient to have it in this volume. Even in this section, however, some of the statements are new and will not be universally accepted.

The next short section, on the definition of "operant," may also be regarded as controversial. That reaction would be refreshing, I think, because the cut-and-dried simplicity of the usual textbook definitions of operant and respondent seem to me very misleading.

The remainder of this chapter is devoted to the development of concepts and methods in the study of conditioned reinforcement. I believe these sections can be read with profit before reading any of the following chapters.

APPARATUS

Most of the experiments represented in this book were conducted in ways which are now fairly standard. Pigeons are confined to a chamber commonly called a Skinner box which varies little in essentials. It is about one foot cube and insulated from extraneous sights and sounds by an outer box of appropriate material. Such a box can easily be made lighttight, but sound-attenuation with ordinary materials in manageable mass rarely exceeds some tens of decibels. Therefore, a masking noise is often added, produced either by white noise delivered to a speaker in the box or, conveniently, by a ventilating fan. The isolation of the bird enables people in the laboratory to go about their business without disturbing the animal, even when the chamber is not in a separate room. A peephole for observing the bird is often provided.

The experimental chamber contains a "houselight" for general illumination, a feeder for controlling the birds' access to grain (water is rarely used), and one or more pigeon keys, which are designed to register pecking directed at them, and are, therefore, at a convenient height, some 9–10 inches above the floor. The feeder is a hopper that can be brought up to an aperture, allowing the bird to eat. The aperture is usually lit, and other lights are turned off, when the feeder operates. Each key, from the bird's point of view, is a disk of translucent plastic, about 1 inch in diameter. The key can be lit from behind by various colored lights, or have symbols projected onto it. In nearly all experiments the operation of the feeder depends upon pecking the key under specified conditions, such as when the key is blue. Most keys are lightly sprung levers which operate upon the application of 5–25 gm, a range which spans the impulsive force generated by the "natural" pecking of a pigeon. It is common to have the key connected to a relay in the chamber so that each peck produces a "click" audible to the experimenter and presumably to the bird. The relay is often referred to as a "feedback relay." In most experiments the feeder operates for 2–6 sec. About 50–150 such exposures (reinforcements) allow most pigeons to eat enough food to sustain them. Consequently, most experiments are performed with daily sessions of at most 50 reinforcements.

GENERAL PROCEDURES

Deprivation

Birds are first reduced to 60–80 percent of their weight as determined during free access to food and water. The chosen weight is maintained throughout an experiment (unless, of course, weight is an experimental variable, which it very rarely is). A pigeon should never be given free access to grain during the course of an experiment, after being deprived, because it can store several days' supply of grain in its crop. This ability also is responsible for a lack of precision in determining the bird's weight when not deprived.

Shaping

Birds must be brought to a condition in which they peck the key repeatedly. This is usually done by "shaping." The feeder is operated repeatedly until the hungry bird has learned to feed promptly from it. The operation of the feeder is then made to follow some identifiable aspect of behavior, such as orienting toward the key. The probability of this behavior increases, which is the process or the result of reinforcement. The position of the beak and the movement of the head vary, of course. On the basis of these variations, one selectively reinforces closer and closer approximations to a peck at the key. Eventually, the bird pecks the key, which should at this stage be arranged to operate the feeder automatically. After a few pecks have been reinforced, the probability of pecking will usually reach an asymptote quickly without further intervention by the experimenter.

The practice of having the experimenter actively engage in this initial shaping is probably an unnecessary and even undesirable legacy from an earlier time when apparatus was not so reliable, or it may be simply an archaic superstition of experimenters. Nearly every bird can be induced to peck the key in a reasonable time without the personal intervention of the experimenter. It is necessary to train the bird to eat from the feeder promptly when it operates. This is done by repeatedly (say 50–100 times over 1–2 hours) operating the feeder. If the key operates the feeder, too, in this initial period, many birds will learn to peck the key. For those birds which do not learn, the next step is to stop the repetitive operation of the feeder, leaving the bird in the chamber. Very few birds will fail to peck the key over a period of several hours—especially if the key is brightly lit. The process can be speeded by gluing a piece of grain to the key, or placing the grain next to the key so that the bird strikes the key in the act of pecking at the grain.

Intermittent reinforcement

The initial object of most experiments is to establish a moderate rate of key pecking. When reinforcements are given for every response, most of the session will be occupied by eating. It is one of the fundamental and most seminal discoveries in psychology that systematic performance can be maintained by intermittent reinforcement of a response. Indeed, it is perhaps not too farfetched to say that this discovery has led to a distinctive experimental analysis of behavior, independent of both the formulations of common sense and the confining strictures of the hypothetico-deductive method.

Base-line performance

The fact that performance can be sustained for relatively long periods has led to the concept of "base-line performance" or persistent behavior with some easily identifiable characteristics which have proved to be sensitive to a variety of experimental variables. It has thus become possible to investigate the effect of whatever variable in a single organism, over a reasonable period of time. The favored fundamental "design" of an experiment can be symbolized "BXB," where B means "base line," and X means "experimental variable." One establishes a base-line performance, changes the conditions to determine the effect of an experimental variable, then reestablishes the original conditions, usually reestablishing the base-line performance, and thus verifying that the change in performance was due to X. Many experimenters omit the return to base line, because the base-line performance is well-known and easily recognized, or because internal controls are substituted. On the other hand, when several variables, or many values of a single variable, are to be investigated, the most common design is $BX_1BX_2B - X_nB$, or, more rarely, $BX_1X_2 - X_nB$.

Response rate

The dependent variable in the analysis of behavior is almost always response rate or a closely related measure, such as latency or interresponse time. The interest in response rate has created a demand for a simple means of registering and portraying response rate. This demand is met in virtually all laboratories by the cumulative recorder. In a cumulative record each response displaces the recording pen a small distance—typically 0.25 millimeters—on paper drawn past the pen at a constant speed—typically 30 centimeters per hour. The resulting record of responses versus time is an irregular "staircase" whose slope is proportional to response rate.

Other recording devices are used, such as counters and running-time meters, but a cumulative response record contains all possible information about the occurrence of responses, and other response-operated recorders provide no information that could not, in principle, be extracted from the cumulative record. For example, one might use a counter to tally the number of responses that occurred within 10 sec of the previous response. This would give the total number of such responses but not the time at which these responses occurred, whereas a cumulative record of appropriate resolution would show exactly when each such response occurred.

Schedules of reinforcement

Reinforcements are usually delivered according to a criterion based on number of responses emitted or elapsed time, or a combination of these. In more unusual experiments reinforcement may depend on response force, a particular sequence of responses, the absence of a response, etc. Various schedules may be portrayed in a diagram analogous to a cumulative record, with time as the abscissa and cumulative responses as the ordinate. Various common schedules are shown in Figure 1.1. Assume that in each diagram, after every reinforcement, a line starts at the origin, moves right as time passes and up for every response. The reinforcer is delivered after the first response that occurs in the hatched region.

The second two schedules (3 and 4) are variations of the first two, simplest schedules. Instead of requiring a fixed number of responses or a fixed time since the last reinforcement, the number or the time is variable. The variability is signified by the double-ended arrow in the diagrams.

In schedule 5 (*FI* with limited hold) the reinforcement is available for a specified, limited, time after the end of the fixed interval.

Schedules 6 and 7 show ways of combining different schedules. In a Mixed or Multiple schedule (6) the reinforcement depends now on one requirement, now on another. There may be several components. In Multiple schedules different stimuli are associated with each component; in Mixed schedules the same stimulus is associated with all components. In an Alternative schedule (7) each reinforce-

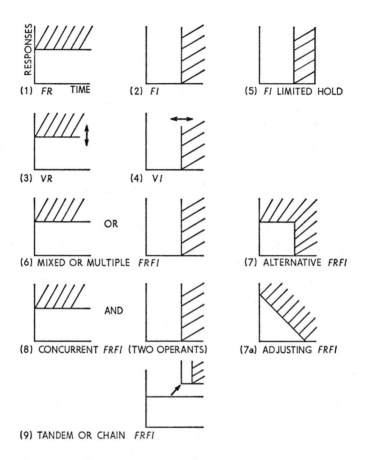

FIGURE 1.1. Various common schedules of reinforcement. All diagrams represent a schematic cumulative record of responses versus time, and symbolize the conditions under which a response will be reinforced (see text).

ment depends on one of two (or perhaps more) independent requirements. Where these requirements are not independent (7a) one talks of an Adjusting schedule.

Schedule 8 illustrates the programming of two schedules at the same time, or concurrently, on two keys. Schedule 7 might also be called a Concurrent, single-operant schedule.

Schedule 9 illustrates a method of portraying two common types of complex schedules—Tandem and Chain schedules. In these cases component schedules are programmed sequentially with the reinforcement occurring at the end of the final component. The transition from one component to another is here signified by an arrow. In Chain schedules different stimuli are associated with each component; in Tandem schedules the same stimulus is associated with all components.

Two special cases not shown in Figure 1.1 are reinforcement of all responses [FR 1 or continuous reinforcement (CRF)] and reinforcement of no responses [Extinction (EXT)].

Figure 1.2 illustrates those schedules defined by a rate criterion. The common way to specify a rate for scheduling purposes is to specify the reciprocal of momentary, response-by-response rate, which is simply interresponse time or IRT. Figure 1.2 shows differential reinforcement of low rate, of high rate, and of a rate within specified limits.

Characteristic performances are produced by FR, FI, VR, VI,

FIGURE 1.2.   Three schedules defined with respect to response rate. (1) Differential reinforcement of low rate; (2) differential reinforcement of high rate; (3) differential reinforcement of paced responding. Reinforcement is made contingent on a response occurring a specified time after the last response. The hatched region of the interresponse time (IRT) continuum indicates where a response may be reinforced. DRL specifies a minimum reinforceable IRT; DRH a maximum reinforceable IRT; and DRP a maximum and minimum reinforceable IRT.

DRL, and DRH schedules, as well as by many Mixed, Multiple, Tandem, Chain, and Concurrent schedules. The bulk of experimental work is done with these "standard" schedules providing baseline performance. Examination of the cumulative record is usually sufficient to inform the experimenter whether he has established adequate control over performance. The stability of performance is often sufficient to allow the experimenter to watch significant changes in performance as they occur. It is also true, however, that these basic schedules themselves are undergoing intensive analysis to throw light on behavioral mechanisms and to more precisely quantify characteristic performance.

Stimuli

One reason for the very general use of pigeons as experimental animals is their very keen vision. They are probably capable of spectral resolution that is comparable with that of man. It is easy to make the performance of pigeons depend upon visual stimuli. Complex performance can be controlled by colored lights projected on the response keys. The rough-and-ready laboratory rule is that if two colors can be distinguished by the normally sighted experimenter, they can be distinguished by the pigeon. This rule, perhaps too convenient, allows a large number of different stimuli to be used in an experiment. Commercial pigeon chambers usually have at least three different colors for each key. The three colors are phenomenally distinct but by no means pure spectral colors. It is possible without special equipment to produce about seven different "colors" —red, orange, yellow, green, blue, white, and dark (unlit). It is often assumed, with some justification, that it is not difficult to establish performances under these seven key colors which may be treated as independent. Loosely speaking, the birds will not confuse the stimuli to a degree which will seriously impair the assumption of independent performances, though the performances may interact for some other reason. A physicist, or even a psychologist, may voice reservations. For example, these colors are usually not monochromatic, so adjacent color stimuli usually have overlapping ranges of wavelength. Furthermore, even the corresponding spectral values are not equally spaced in wavelength. More important, perhaps, is the observation that under many different conditions, wavelengths are not distinguished at a behavioral level if the conditions of reinforcement do not encourage a distinction. In spite of such reservations, experimenters continue to conduct their experiments on the assumption that the colors they use are perfectly discriminable by the pigeon. In most cases it would be a simple, though tedious, matter to allow for imperfect discrimination but, in fact, this is rarely done. The main reason for the confidence of experimenters in the assumption of perfect discriminability is that they have repeatedly seen the assumption supported by behavioral results, where the schedule of reinforcement, signaled by a particular key color, has had a dominant influence on performance. Since the experimenter has no difficulty in discriminating certain performances emitted under different key colors, he infers that the bird, likewise, has no difficulty in discriminating the key colors. In other experiments, failure of the bird to discriminate the same colors cannot be due to a lack of sensitivity of its visual system. In fact, even without taking into account brightness and saturation, many experiments have shown that pigeons can very reliably distinguish monochromatic stimuli differing by only 20 nanometers.

Visual patterns are also used as stimuli. Pigeons discriminate easily the angle of a line projected on the key, which allows, estimating conservatively, 3–4 different stimuli. The size of dots on the key also provides, say, 3–4 possible stimuli. The number of other simple patterns that are discriminable, such as triangles and squares, is unknown. Clearly, the experimenter is not practically limited in the number of different, distinguishable conditions he can present to the pigeon. It is probable that this freedom largely explains the popularity of the pigeon as an experimental animal, despite the fact that all of the early work in operant conditioning was done (by Skinner) with the rat.

Study of individual organisms

Having a large number of distinctive stimuli available is important because of the flexibility and complexity of experiments that it allows. A characteristic of the experimental analysis of behavior is the dedication of its practitioners to the study of behavioral processes operating in individual organisms. Instead of applying different treatments to different groups of animals, all the treatments are applied, *seriatim*, to the same animals, in the $BX_1BX_2 - B$ design, or some variant of it. Suppose that the experimenter had a suspicion that performance in X_2 was affected by the residual influence of X_1. His design might be $BX_1BX_2BX_1BX_2, \ldots$, with the precaution that B, X_1, and X_2 were distinguished by different key colors. Eventually, the characteristic performance in B, X_1, and X_2 should emerge promptly on the change in key color and the experimenter can examine the history of performance for residual effects of X_1 on X_2. The results of a similar experiment with, say, rats, would probably have to be much more hedged with qualifications and reservations about the discriminability of the conditions. More likely, the experiment would be done with independent groups of rats (X_1 v. X_2 v. control) that would yield information about the effects of X_1 and X_2 but not about residual effects of experimental history.

The interest in laws whose operation can be seen in the individual organism leads to experiments which are relatively long and use relatively few animals. The ideal number of animals in an experiment is three—the same as the ideal number of wives, for somewhat similar reasons. Basing a conclusion on the performance of one animal is hazardous, since its performance may be peculiar, significantly influenced by some aspect of the animal's nonexperimental history. Therefore, any conclusion suggested by results with one animal may be checked against the results of a second animal. This will always reveal in what ways the results are uniform and in what ways they vary. Both these aspects of the results are important. However, in some cases an experimental variable will strongly affect performance, but in different ways in two animals, or a variable will affect one animal's performance and not another's. In such cases the performance of a third animal will often, as it were, settle the dispute between the other two. It is not simply a case of majority rule. The discrepancy in the results will establish a probability about which animal's behavior should be attended to in further behavioral analysis. The simple absence of an effect of an experimental treatment in one of these animals strongly suggests that the conditions of reinforcement have generated an unusual set of circumstances for that animal. The absence of an effect in two of the animals suggests that the animal that did show an effect was subject to unusual circumstances or a peculiar history. On the other hand, a monotonic effect of a variable in all three animals is sufficient evidence, for the time being, that the effect of the variable may be stated without reservations concerning individual differences.

The place of statistics

Descriptive statistics are widely used in the experimental analysis of behavior. Performance is described in terms of means, variances, and probabilities of response measures. However, such statistics usually refer to the performance of individual animals, rarely to groups of animals. One learns less, not more, about an animal by averaging its performance with that of another animal.

Since most inferential statistics require an assumption of independent measures, and measurements of the same animal's performance can hardly be independent, inferential statistics are sparingly used in the analysis of behavior. In addition to that theoretical impediment, however, experimenters prefer to demonstrate their conclusions by refining their control over performance in some relevant way. This kind of experimental analysis is in many cases an alternative, and an allegedly superior alternative, to statistical detective work. In many behavioral research labs there is a positive disdain for statistical inference, as a subterfuge unbefitting an experimental scientist.

WHAT IS AN OPERANT?

Behavior itself is not easy to define, though it seems to be understood well enough to be used in everyday discourse. The behavior of most interest to behaviorists seems to be the use of muscles in such a way as to produce the same effect in the environment. A refined notion of such behavior is the concept of operant. The basic notion of an operant is the modification of behavior by its consequences. This may be contrasted with respondent behavior controlled by its antecedents. Thus a respondent is behavior-elicited-by-a-stimulus, whereas an operant is behavior-controlled-by-its-consequences. The hyphens draw attention to the fact that movements, environment, and the relation between them are implicated in the definition. Having recorded only a movement, one does not know whether it is an operant or a respondent, no matter how precise the measurement. Some behavior appears to be both operant and respondent. For example, breathing is controlled by level of carbon-dioxide saturation in the blood, but anyone can stop breathing for a time if offered money to do so. In this example, operant behavior seems to correspond closely to "voluntary" behavior. While "voluntary" is a concept that serves well enough in everyday discourse, it is difficult to define to everyone's satisfaction.

Another example that illustrates how the "same" behavior can have different properties is laughter. Laughter as a consequence of being amused is respondent behavior. But one can be induced to laugh when not amused—every sensitive person laughs at his boss's jokes, whether they are funny or not. The laughing (or failure to laugh) is presumably controlled by its consequences. Thus, laughing, like breathing, may be a respondent or an operant. This is borne out in our clichés; one talks of "uncontrollable laughter" (respondent) and "forced laughter" (operant).

It is confusing to think of "laughing" as a behavior *element* which may be operant or respondent. The character of a bit of behavior should be decided by the lawful relations that it enters into, not its topographic character. It seems very perverse to stress the identity of movement involved in, say, saluting a superior officer and removing one's hat. That is perhaps why some authors have defined an operant as behavior that has the same reinforcing consequences, or, from a slightly different point of view, behavior that varies in probability as a consequence of the same reinforcing effects. Thus, in the context of conversation, smiling and nodding one's head may be the same operant—if the probability of each is affected in the same way by reinforcers given by the person one is talking to. These would be the same operants even though they involve quite different muscles, because the conditions of reinforcement affect them in a similar way.

While these matters are not settled, it is not seriously misleading to think of operant as "voluntary" behavior, whose probability depends on its consequences. The pecking of a pigeon is such behavior, and experimenters have considerable faith that it is representative of all operants, including those of man.

CONCEPTS OF CONDITIONED REINFORCEMENT

Two hypotheses

In one of the earliest systematic behaviorist treatments of learning that is still cited today, Hull (1943, p. 94 f.) stated the general principle that stimuli which occur in close temporal contiguity with a reinforcing state of affairs become (conditioned) reinforcers. According to Hull's principle, one stimulus acquires a property of another (the reinforcer) by being paired with it. We shall call this the *S-S hypothesis* to emphasize the operation (stimulus pairing) that is held to be crucial for the establishment of conditioned reinforcement. The *S-S* hypothesis was challenged by what came to be called the *discriminative stimulus hypothesis*, which may be attributed to Skinner (1938), and is most clearly stated by Keller and Schoenfeld (1950, p. 236). A *discriminative stimulus* is the counterpart, in instrumental performance, of the CS in classical conditioning. A discriminative stimulus does not "elicit" an instrumental response, but "sets the occasion" for it (Skinner, 1938, p. 241). A discriminative stimulus, therefore, was originally defined as a stimulus in whose presence an operant is reinforced. According to the discriminative stimulus hypothesis only discriminative stimuli become conditioned reinforcers. It is convenient to refer to the discriminative stimulus hypothesis as the *S-R hypothesis,* to indicate that according to the hypothesis a reinforced response has to occur in the presence of the stimulus to make the stimulus a conditioned reinforcer. The main difference between the *S-S* and the *S-R* hypothesis is that the *S-R* hypothesis implies that a stimulus has to gain discriminative control of a reinforced response as it becomes a conditioned reinforcer, whereas the *S-S* hypothesis implies no such conditions.

Evolution of the concept of discriminative stimulus

The original, simplest procedure for the defining of a discriminative stimulus was one in which all responses of a particular class were reinforced in one condition and no responses were reinforced in another condition. Such a procedure is a Multiple schedule, specifically MULT *CRF* EXT. By definition, the cue associated with *CRF* was a positive discriminative stimulus, or S^D, and the cue associated with EXT was a negative discriminative stimulus, or S^Δ. The development of operant conditioning technology permitted the study of more and more complex Multiple schedules, and the parallel evolution of the concept of discriminative stimulus. This evolution is schematically represented in Figure 1.3. While in early experiments on discrimination the required behavior was all-or-none, go/no-go, it soon became evident that the effective control of S^D over the reinforced response was hardly affected if an intermittent schedule of reinforcement (rather than *CRF*) were in effect in the presence of S^D. Therefore, the defining procedure for S^D was extended to a class of schedules, MULT *X* EXT, where *X* was any schedule of reinforcement. This is represented in the middle of Figure 1.3. In this case, since S^D meant the cue associated with *X* it could be most readily defined by exclusion, as "not-S^Δ." A further development in the concept of discriminative stimulus came with the acknowledgement that the restriction of one component of the Multiple schedule to Extinction was not a necessary condition for establishing a discrimination. This is represented at the bottom of Figure 1.3.

With the change in meaning of discriminative stimulus one is bound to ask whether the discriminative stimulus in its new sense has all the properties ascribed to it in its original sense. In particu-

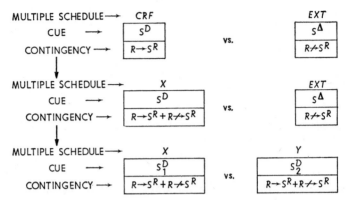

FIGURE 1.3. Schematic representation of the development of the concept of discriminative stimulus.

Each box represents a stimulus condition in the upper part and the associated contingency in the lower part. "$R \to S^R$" signifies that the response R produces reinforcement, and "$R \not\to S^R$" signifies that the response R does not produce reinforcement. "$R \to S^R + R \not\to S^R$" signifies partial or intermittent reinforcement.

lar, we have to consider whether a discriminative stimulus, in its contemporary sense, is a conditioned reinforcer.

A Multiple schedule need not include Extinction for its cues to be a source of conditioned reinforcement. For example, Kendall (1965a, 1965b) showed that cues associated with different fixed-ratio schedules would reinforce observing behavior. It seems reasonable to suppose that the discriminative stimuli created by the procedure MULT X Y, where X and Y are two schedules, are conditioned reinforcers. However, from considering special cases, such as $X = Y$, there must be certain restrictions on X and Y, or their relation, for the establishment of discriminative control and conditioned reinforcement. What are these restrictions? Assuming that both these presently unknown restrictions and resulting conditioned reinforcing effectiveness are matters of degree, what we seek are the experimental data that reveal conditioned reinforcing value as functions of various combinations of variations in X and Y.

The S-R hypothesis is inadequate

A great deal of evidence exists which is difficult to reconcile with the S-R hypothesis, as originally stated. The evidence most directly

relevant to the question whether or not stimulus control of a reinforced response is a necessary property of conditioned reinforcers
comes from experiments where the reinforcer is given to some extent independently of the organism's behavior.

A standard method to establish a stimulus as a conditioned reinforcer is by the use of chaining. In the simplest cases, responding in
one stimulus (S_2) produces another (S_1), and responding in that
stimulus produces a reinforcer. After training on such a schedule,
S_1 can be shown to be a conditioned reinforcer. Ferster (1953)
conducted several experiments with chains, with the innovation
that delivery of the reinforcer was not dependent on performance
of the same response as was required in S_2. In one experiment
(Experiment 4), pigeons pecked a key in S_2. After a variable
interval with a mean of 1 minute (VI 1) a key-peck produced S_1.
The appearance of S_1 initiated a delay of reinforcement of 1 minute
which was reset by every key-peck. In S_1 the birds had to engage in
behavior other than key-pecking for 1 minute; the schedule in S_1 is
referred to a "differential reinforcement of other behavior for 60
sec" (DRO 60). Under these conditions key-pecking was maintained in S_2 and suppressed in S_1. This result may be taken to show
that S_1 became a conditioned reinforcer (maintaining performance
in S_2) even though S_1 was not a discriminative stimulus in the
usual sense.[1]

Ferster also compared performance when there was a delay of
reinforcement of 1 minute in S_1, with performance when another
key-peck was required after 1 minute of S_1. The former, non-con-
tingent procedure produced much lower rates of key-pecking in S_1
than did the latter, yet the rates in S_2 were about the same for both
procedures. This result was also obtained in a similar experiment
by Ferster and Skinner (1957, p. 684 f). These results show that
under normal conditions it is unnecessary to specify what performance is required in S_1; the strength of S_1 as a conditioned reinforcer
probably depends on its association with reinforcement, not on its
control of a specific reinforced operant.

---

[1] It is possible, of course, that no pecks were emitted during DRO 60 because some incompatible response was being performed and, therefore, superstitiously reinforced. In that case, S_1 might still be regarded as a discriminative
stimulus. In fact, superstitious behavior was observed by Ferster. However,
even if stereotyped behavior had not occurred in DRO, the schedule still
strongly controlled performance and, therefore, the associated cue would be
regarded as a discriminative stimulus in the wider sense which closely corresponds to "informative stimulus," as developed later in this chapter.

Autor (1960), whose work is reprinted here in Chapter 6, used a procedure similar to Ferster's, comparing performance on two concurrent 2-member Chains (CHAIN *VI* 1 *VI* 15 sec and CHAIN *VI* 1 *VI x*, for various values of x). The relative response rate in the first member, which is essentially a measure of choice between the two Chains, and therefore a measure of relative reinforcing strength of the S_1s, increased with increasing relative frequency of reinforcement in the second member. The same result was obtained when a *DRO* schedule was substituted for the *VI* schedules in the second members, key-pecks in the second members being eliminated by punishing them with time-outs.

The results of these experiments (Autor, 1960; Ferster, 1953; Ferster and Skinner, 1957) show that the S-R hypothesis is untenable, or, at best, extremely implausible. There is no shortage of further examples of a stimulus being made a conditioned reinforcer by simply pairing the stimulus with a primary reinforcer (e.g., Bersh, 1951; Bower & Grusec, 1964; Egger & Miller, 1962, 1963; Estes, 1948; Jenkins, 1950; Marx & Knarr, 1963; Stein, 1958).

The S-S hypothesis is inadequate

The results mentioned above are all consistent with the S-S hypothesis. However, the adequacy of the S-S hypothesis has also been questioned recently. According to a proposal by Egger and Miller (1962), it is not sufficient for a stimulus to be paired with a reinforcer to become a conditioned reinforcer—it is necessary for the stimulus actually to be a reliable predictor of reinforcement. In one experiment (Egger & Miller, 1962) two stimuli (S_1 and S_2) ended at the same time, just before the presentation of food. S_1 lasted 2 sec, and came on 0.5 sec before S_2, which lasted 1.5 sec. For a second group of animals S_1 also occurred alone and then was not followed by food. Egger and Miller argued that in the first procedure S_1 was predictive and S_2 was redundant, while in the slightly different procedure with the second group S_2 was predictive. The stimulus conditions are shown in Figure 1.4. Egger and Miller found very tenuous evidence that S_2 was more reinforcing for the second group; at all events the differential effect of the procedures on the conditioned reinforcing value of S_2 was small. On the other hand, S_1 was a substantially stronger conditioned reinforcer for the first group (for which S_1 was a completely reliable predictor of rein-

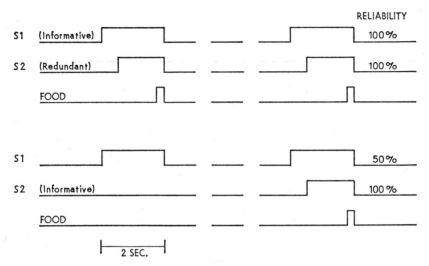

FIGURE 1.4. The arrangements used by Egger and Miller (1962) to vary the predictive relation of two stimuli to reinforcement.

forcement) than for the second (for which S_1 was a less reliable predictor of reinforcement).

These authors also performed another experiment designed to assess the reinforcing value of predictive and redundant pre-reinforcement stimuli (Egger & Miller, 1963). Rats were first trained to bar press, then given reinforcers after presentations of certain stimuli. The reinforcing effect of these stimuli was then assessed (during Extinction) by making the stimuli contingent on bar pressing. The essential result was that a pre-reinforcement stimulus, S_2, was a less effective conditioned reinforcer when it had been preceded, during training, by another stimulus, S_1. The presentation of S_1 made S_2 redundant, as in the previous study. If S_1 was given unassociated with the reinforcer as well as just before S_2 and the reinforcer, the conditioned reinforcing effect of S_2 was enhanced. The extra, unreinforced, presentations of S_1 made S_1 an unreliable predictor of the reinforcer, and therefore made S_2 a nonredundant predictor of the reinforcer. In this experiment S_1 was a single food pellet, S_2 was a flashing light, and the reinforcer was three food pellets. Egger and Miller interpreted their results as confirming their original hypothesis, namely, that stimuli must be informative for them to become conditioned reinforcers.

According to Egger and Miller's results the predictive relation to the primary reinforcer, rather than temporal contiguity, is crucial in determining the conditioned reinforcing value of the stimulus. Rescorla (1966, 1968) has shown similar effects with aversive conditioning: the conditioned aversive effect of a stimulus depends upon the probability of a primary aversive event in its presence, relative to the probability of a primary aversive event in its absence. Another striking demonstration of the importance of the predictive relation to primary reinforcement was given by Hendry and Coulbourn (1967). They showed a conditioned reinforcing effect of a stimulus that predicted reinforcement even when the same stimulus was systematically paired with nonreinforcement and a different, distinctive stimulus was paired with reinforcement.

For purposes of exposition we have until now refrained from clarifying the operation of "pairing" of stimuli. It has in fact been demonstrated that a stimulus must precede, rather than accompany, a reinforcer in order for it to become a conditioned reinforcer. When the stimulus coincides with eating, for example, it does not become a conditioned reinforcer, even when food and therefore the stimulus, is contingent on a response (Schoenfeld, Antonitis, & Bersh, 1950). This is also borne out by the results of Marx and Knarr (1963) who raised their subjects with exposure to different relations between the presentations of food and a light stimulus. The reinforcing effect of the light was subsequently tested. The light was an effective conditioned reinforcer if it had just preceded the presentation of food, and had no reinforcing value if it had accompanied the presentation of food. Similarly, Bersh (1951) found that the function relating strength of a conditioned reinforcer to the time between onset of the stimulus and presentation of food peaked at 0.5–1.0 sec, not 0.0 sec.

Insofar as these results show that to become a conditioned reinforcer a stimulus must precede reinforcement, they support the Egger/Miller hypothesis. Of course, in ordinary discrimination training as well, the presentation of the discriminative stimulus precedes the reinforced response.

The Information Hypothesis

Pre-reinforcement stimuli do not exhaust the meaning of "informative" stimuli. A stimulus may also be said to be informative if, in some sense, it reduces a number of possibilities. The concept of information is clearly relevant to situations in which response tendencies compete; controlling stimuli which resolve the competition in favor of one of the response tendencies can be said to be informative or to reduce uncertainty. Berlyne (1957, 1960) has cogently presented some of the implications of this point of view. If stimuli which resolve response competition are informative, it follows that the establishment of any discrimination generates informative stimuli. If different performances are brought under the control of two (or more) stimuli, these stimuli are informative. The hypothesis that stimuli which are informative in that sense are conditioned reinforcers is attributable to Wyckoff (see Chapter 9). Thus, although Wyckoff's procedure involved an S^D/S^Δ discrimination (MULT *FI* EXT), his formulation implies, more generally, that the differential control of behavior by any pair of cues is a source of conditioned reinforcement. This implication is supported by the results of Kendall (1965a, 1965b), already mentioned.

In Steiner's experiments (Steiner, 1967), monkeys and baboons were given the opportunity to produce discriminative stimuli, much as in Wyckoff's experiments. In Steiner's basic procedure the animal was presented with a Multiple *FI* EXT schedule. The discriminability of the discriminative stimuli (brightnesses) was varied from being easily discriminable to being identical. When the stimuli were identical, of course, the schedule of reinforcement was Mixed *FI* EXT. In addition, with another operant, or observing response, the animal could produce one of a pair of easily discriminable cues that signified the *FI* and EXT schedules—i.e., informative cues. Steiner measured both the relative reinforcing value of the informative cues (by finding the limit of the number of responses they would sustain in a progressive ratio schedule) and the efficiency of discrimination between *FI* and EXT (by calculating the proportion of responses emitted in the *FI* periods). Generally, the less efficient the discrimination between *FI* and EXT the more reinforcing the informative cues. One may express this by saying that the less redundant the information provided by the informative cues the more reinforcing they were. Alternatively, one may say that the less the cues reduced uncertainty the less reinforcing they were.

Steiner also found that the reinforcing value of the informative cues declined as the animal learned an easy discrimination (between *FI* and EXT).

Further, Steiner showed that the observing behavior was sus-

tained even when the reinforcer was presented "free." This probably indicates that the cues reinforced by virtue of predicting the
occurrence of a reinforcer rather than by virtue of resolving the
operant conflict "to press, or not to press. . . ."

So far we have considered two meanings of "informative stimulus."

1. Reliably predicting a reinforcer.
2. Controlling differentiated performances.

The general idea that information or reduction of uncertainty is
reinforcing is embodied in the Information Hypothesis, which we
shall regard as comprising two separate hypotheses, corresponding
to different sets of operations for generating information.

In one case stimuli occur in redundant sequences, so that it is
possible to predict a later stimulus from an earlier one. The early
stimulus or early part of the sequence gives a clue to the later
stimulus. We, therefore, refer to the idea that such predictive
stimuli are reinforcing as the *Clue hypothesis:* stimuli that reliably
predict a reinforcer become conditioned reinforcers. We use the
term *cue* specifically to mean a stimulus which controls performance. The hypothesis that cues are reinforcers was first proposed by
Wyckoff (Chapter 9). We call this the *Cue hypothesis:* stimuli that
control the rate of an operant are conditioned reinforcers. We
summarize our observations in the following way:

Information Hypothesis
(Uncertainty-reducing stimuli are reinforcing)

Clue hypothesis	Cue hypothesis
Operation: differential S-S relations	Operation: differential S-R contingencies
Clues signify what to expect	Cues signify what to do
Fore-runner: S-S hypothesis	Fore-runner: S-R hypothesis
Classic experiment: Egger and Miller (1962)	Classic experiment: Wyckoff (Chapter 9)

The crucial operation for generating conditioned reinforcement
was stimulus-pairing according to the S-S hypothesis and establishing an operant discrimination according to the S-R hypothesis.
From the standpoint of the Information Hypothesis, both these
operations may be used to generate uncertainty. However, the Information Hypothesis certainly does not imply that these opera-

tions are sufficient, without qualification, for establishing conditioned reinforcers.

The Cue hypothesis incorporates the S-R hypothesis, since all discriminative stimuli are cues, but is not equivalent to it. For example, the Cue hypothesis predicts that the stimuli of some Multiple schedules are conditioned reinforcers, so long as the Multiple schedule is still in effect. This prediction might be derived from the S-R hypothesis. The Cue hypothesis further predicts that the stimuli of a Multiple schedule will not be reinforcing when the components of the Multiple schedule are identical, so that the performances in the various components are identical. This prediction would clearly be difficult to derive from the S-R hypothesis, since the stimuli involved are still discriminative stimuli in the sense that responses are reinforced in their presence.

The two components of the Information Hypothesis may be related in at least two ways. A pre-reinforcement stimulus is predictive, but it may also be considered as a controlling stimulus in a discrimination paradigm. The absence of the pre-reinforcement stimulus acts as S^{Δ} and its presence acts as S^{D}. The behavior that comes under the control of the S^{D} are the responses that are preparatory to obtaining the reinforcer, such as approaching the magazine. This constitutes the normal course of "magazine training" and was noted at an early date by Skinner (1938, p. 82), who identified the reinforcing effect of the pre-reinforcement stimulus as the process of "adding an initial member to a chain." Therefore, even though we do not specifically arrange for the presentation of food to be contingent on a response, the use of a pre-reinforcement stimulus creates conditions in which we should ordinarily expect a discrimination to be formed. For establishing a pre-reinforcement stimulus as a conditioned reinforcer it may be less important that the stimulus is a reliable predictor of reinforcement, and more important that it controls the rate of "preparatory" responding. However, the results of Stein (1958) do not agree with this conjecture. Using brain stimulation as the primary reinforcer, Stein showed that a pre-reinforcement stimulus became a conditioned reinforcer; so far as is known there is no appropriate preparatory behavior for receiving reinforcing stimulation of the brain. In addition, experimenters who look for overt preparatory behavior during or after a pre-reinforcement stimulus often fail to detect it (e.g., Bower & Grusec, 1964).

On the other hand, the fact that a stimulus controls a particular performance may be a consequence of its predictive function. The stimulus might still have the same reinforcing function even if we eliminated the distinctive performance in its presence, as in the chaining experiments of Autor (1960) and Ferster (1953). The distinctive performance is an indication that the stimuli are affecting the animal, rather than a necessary condition for the stimuli to acquire significance for the animal.

It would be premature to try to decide whether we can carve nature better to the joint by regarding the predictive or the controlling criterion for informative stimuli as the more fundamental, but we should be aware of these possibilities.

Attention

Not all physical stimuli associated with a particular schedule of reinforcement come to control performance on that schedule. For example, when a *VI* schedule was signaled by two stimuli (triangle on a red key), as opposed to Extinction, also signaled by two stimuli (circle on a green key), one bird's *VI* performance was controlled by the triangle and another's by the red key (Reynolds, 1961b). As far as the experimenter could determine, both birds had been exposed to identical conditions, and both stimuli had been paired equally often with the primary reinforcer. From this (and many similar results) one is forced to conclude that the organism is not a passive receiver of environmental influences, but to some extent filters or selects these influences. When the organism exhibits selective sensitivity to certain stimuli we say it is "attending" to those stimuli. This viewpoint (generally held by the Gestalt psychologists) was not congenial with the *Zeitgeist* from about 1930 to about 1955. That period was dominated by a faith in operational constructs and explanation of behavior in terms of environmental and experiential factors and habit structures. After this long period of intellectual suppression, the concept of attention, which concedes to the organism some autonomy and incorporates, par excellence, the idea of organism-environment interaction, has again emerged as a respectable scientific concept.

Several independent series of experiments, in the fields of animal behavior, human performance, and neurophysiology, helped resurrect the concept of attention. Lawrence conducted experiments

(1949, 1950) on what was called "the acquired distinctiveness of cues." When a discrimination has been formed in one stimulus dimension (e.g., brightness) a subsequent discrimination based on that dimension is easier to establish. Apparently, the animal has learned to attend to brightness. In the area of human performance Broadbent (1958) conducted many experiments on selective perception, the results of which led to a characterization of the organism as a limited-channel-capacity processor of sensory data. This fundamental concept has since become widely accepted as a fruitful working hypothesis. In neurophysiological studies, changes in attention were shown to have correlates in brain function as changes in reactivity mediated by the reticular formation (e.g., Sharpless & Jasper, 1956; Hernández-Peón, Jouvet, & Scheerer, 1956; Galambos, Sheatz, & Vernier, 1956).

The concept of attention is closely related to the Information Hypothesis. The relation is expressed in a possible law, which, in its bare form, probably too simple to be accurate, we may state as:

Informative events are attended to.

There are certain mathematical or operational specifications of informative events, and there are certain behavioral and physiological criteria of attention. Even if there is not perfect correspondence of events attended to and informative events, there may be a simple mapping from one of these sets into the other.

The close relation of the concepts of information and attention is evinced by the fact that they give rise to certain virtually identical derivative concepts. Thus, reliability, redundancy, and relevance are attributes of cues upon which, so to speak, the concepts of attention and information converge.

Observing behavior has been regarded as "attentive behavior," but the role of attention in animal perception and learning surely goes beyond what can be exemplified in overt behavior. Thus, for example, a relevant element of a stimulus compound can be selectively responded to even when the elements are never presented separately (e.g., Wagner, Logan, Haberlandt, & Price, 1968). Such behavioral capacities bespeak the existence of a nervous system which contains appropriate processes for extracting signals from noise, where what is a "signal" is determined at a very high level of abstraction. Such central processes of attention will probably become more and more the concern of behavioral research, even though, at present, there scarcely exist any behavioral research methods suitable for such an undertaking. More information about experiments on attention in animal learning is given by Mackintosh (1965) and in the report of a recent symposium on discrimination learning (Gilbert, 1967).

Expectancy theory

It should be acknowledged that the view presented here of the organism's perceptual and behavioral capacity to be selectively reinforced by cues that predict reinforcement is an implication of the comprehensive behavior theory of Tolman and Brunswik (1935). The theory is generally referred to as "expectancy theory" and was more or less displaced by *S-R* reinforcement theory. Expectancy theory, as developed by Tolman, had a strong flavor of rationalism, since Tolman addressed himself to the general question: What behavioral functions must the organism possess if it is to have successful commerce with the environment? The shortest answer given to this question might be expressed as: The organism must be sensitive to the "causal texture" of the environment. In other words, the organism's behavior must come under the influence of regular sequences of environmental events.

". . . the environment is a *causal texture* . . . in which different events are regularly dependent upon each other. And because of the presence of such *causal couplings*, . . . actually existing in their environments, organism come to accept one event as a *local representative* . . . for another event. It is by the use of such acceptances or assertions of local representatives that organisms come to steer their ways through that complex network of events, stimuli and happenings, which surrounds them." (Tolman & Brunswik, 1935, p. 43.)

It follows that:

"the organism has [the task] of developing an adequate reception system which will tend to select reliable cues, rather than ambiguous, nonsignificant or misleading ones." (Tolman & Brunswik, 1935, p. 67.)

Perhaps this theory can be brought back to life by putting more empirical flesh on the rational skeleton.

METHODS FOR THE STUDY OF CONDITIONED REINFORCEMENT

One striking feature of the contributions in this book is the large number of different methods which are now used in the investigation of conditioned reinforcement. A listing of these methods is of interest in itself.

Extinction

In this, the oldest method, extinction is retarded when responses produce a conditioned reinforcer. The effectiveness of the conditioned reinforcer may be inferred from the prolongation of extinction. This method is criticized by several contributors, mainly on the ground that the conditioned reinforcer is changing in effectiveness during the test procedure, and the method is generally out of favor now.

Chain schedules

Here performance on one cued schedule is reinforced by transition to another cued schedule, the Chain eventually being terminated with primary reinforcement. Performance in an earlier schedule is reinforced by presentation of the cue associated with the next schedule. Variables of interest, which affect conditioned reinforcing value, pertain to the conditions of reinforcement in the final link. Investigations of Chain schedules were thoroughly described and analyzed by Kelleher and Gollub (1962).

Concurrent Chain schedules

This is an important extension of the simple Chain schedule, involving two Chains whose initial links are presented simultaneously, usually on different keys. The initial links are usually identical and have usually been variable-interval schedules. The final links contain the independent variable. Whereas in a single Chain schedule the dependent variable is simply the response rate in the initial link, in the Concurrent Chains procedure an apparently well-behaved dependent variable is relative rate in the initial links, a measure of choice. The first extensive study of conditioned reinforcement with concurrent chains was carried out by Autor (1960). His results are given in Chapter 6 and are referred to by several contributors. Autor discovered that relative rate of reinforcement in the final component determined choice of the first component. Herrnstein (1964a) extended and refined this generalization. If, in this context, we mean by "choice" the rate of responding on an option relative to the total rate on all options, Herrn-stein's analyses confirmed Autor's result that choice *matched* relative reinforcement rate. We refer to this important result as *Autor's law:* Preference for a stimulus matches the relative density of primary reinforcement in its presence.

Autor's law is a pinnacle of achievement in traditional reinforce-ment theory, but the boundaries within which it holds do not en-compass a vast area. Indeed, facts irreconcilable with Autor's law are described in most chapters in this book, notably those by Fan-tino (Chapter 7), Schuster (Chapter 8), Schaub (Chapter 13), and Hendry (Chapter 12). However, Autor's law probably does hold in cases where options differ only in density of primary reinforce-ment, and therefore it provides a context within which to evaluate the importance of all other factors that might affect the attractive-ness of different options.

There are many possible refinements of Autor's law. We need not be concerned with the precise meaning of "density" or with qualifi-cations that have to do with the temporal distribution of primary reinforcements. We should, however, be interested in generalizing Autor's law to the case of a "third link." Does the relative condi-tioned reinforcing value of a stimulus match the relative density of *conditioned* reinforcement in its presence?

Second-order schedules

Performance on one schedule can be reinforced by a conditioned reinforcer and this performance, treated as a "response," can pro-duce primary reinforcers according to another schedule. Such a procedure is called a second-order schedule (Kelleher, 1966a) and its effects are reviewed by Marr in Chapter 2. The dependent variable always relates to the pattern and persistence of the per-formance and the independent variable usually relates to the char-acter of the cue used as conditioned reinforcer.

An important concept associated with the use of second-order schedules is that of "schedule control." If a distinctive pattern of performance similar to that generated by a schedule of primary reinforcement is generated by an initially neutral stimulus sched-uled in the same way, one may infer that the stimulus is a condi-tioned reinforcer. Many instances of such schedule control are shown in Chapter 2. A brief stimulus which terminates the first-order component in a second-order schedule will be referred to as :*S*.

One great advantage of second-order schedules and like proce-dures is that variables affecting conditioned reinforcement give stable rather than shifting values of the dependent variable. In this respect second-order schedules are similar to observing-response procedures.

The development of second-order schedules has led to the emer-gence of a new method for the investigation of the conditions conducive to the establishment of conditioned reinforcement. Sec-ond-order schedules provide a convenient method of controlling the temporal association of a stimulus with primary reinforcement. Suppose a number (*FR* or *VR*) of first-order schedules has to be satisfied before primary reinforcement can occur. The stimulus delivered at the end of the first-order elements (:*S*) can be deliv-ered after all the elements, or after all the elements except the final one, which ends with primary reinforcement. Thus, :*S* can be paired or unpaired with reinforcement and the behavioral effects may be compared. Marr reviews some experiments which included such a comparison, and the results of De Lorge (Chapter 3) and Schuster (Chapter 8), whose procedures resembled second-order schedules in some respects, also allow such a comparison. In general, these comparisons show a marked attenuation of the ability of :*S* to maintain second-order schedule performance when the stimulus is not paired with the final primary reinforcer. One may conclude that pairing with a primary reinforcer has a large effect on the produc-tion of conditioned reinforcement, at least in the context of second-order schedules. However, one may be tempted to conclude that the results show that it is necessary for a stimulus to be paired with a primary reinforcer in order to become a conditioned reinforcer. In order for that conclusion to be rejected (in these experiments) it would be sufficient for there to be some conditioned reinforcing effect accruing to the stimulus when it was not paired with the primary reinforcer. This raises the question of a suitable control condition. One possible control condition is exactly the same sched-ule except for the removal of :*S*, the stimulus terminating each element. This may be referred to as the *tandem control* (cf., Kel-leher & Gollub, 1962). However, the tandem procedure, since it eliminates :*S* entirely, eliminates the discriminative or signaling function along with possible reinforcing effects. The change in performance in the Tandem schedule may be due to loss of discriminative control rather than loss of conditioned reinforcement within the Chain.

Even so, in the absence of conventions for measuring or expressing conditioned reinforcing value, noting a difference between experimental and control conditions is a crude way to assess or compare procedures. All that can be concluded is that certain inequalities obtain: A is more (or less) reinforcing than B.

Schedules of conditioned reinforcement with free primary reinforcers

It is not necessary to maintain performance on a schedule of primary reinforcement. To produce a conditioned reinforcer, it is sufficient, in some situations at least, to pair a cue with the presentation of a primary reinforcer. It is then possible to investigate conditioned reinforcement with virtually any method used to investigate primary reinforcement, without the complication of having to maintain complex behavior for the primary reinforcer. Zimmerman (Chapter 5) shows schedule control using a conditioned reinforcer established in this way.

Observing behavior

With chains the performance in the initial link may be reinforced by the opportunity to observe the cue associated with the final link. However, performance in the initial link is also instrumental in obtaining the final reinforcer. This might affect performance in the initial link, which therefore might not be wholly attributable to conditioned reinforcement. One may separate these two influences (conditioned and primary reinforcement) by using observing behavior. The observing response is different from the primarily reinforced response and therefore cannot in the ordinary way be directly affected by the primary reinforcement. However, when a primarily reinforced response follows an observing response the observing response may be affected by the (delayed) primary reinforcement. To minimize this effect a "change-over-delay" (*COD*) is often used. The *COD* is a specification that primary reinforcement may not occur within a given period after a specified response (in this case, the observing response). If the observed cues are systematically related to the availability of primary reinforcers (as they usually are), it is always possible to appeal to these relations and the possibility of maintenance of the observing behavior by primary reinforcement. A gap in time (such as a *COD*) between the observing response and reinforcement can be bridged, in theory, by "superstitious chaining." However, one can never prove the absence of superstitious chaining, so the appeal to the mechanism of superstitious chaining should not be made as a general rule, but only in particular cases where the evidence warrants it, in particular when specific (superstitious) behavior is repeatedly observed over a reasonable period of time.

In the *nondifferential control* procedure, used first by Wyckoff, all the response-produced stimuli are retained but the relation to reinforcement of any stimulus that formerly acted as a signal is the same as that of any other stimulus that formerly acted as a signal. The former signals are now uncorrelated with reinforcement—or, in effect, no longer signals. For example, in some cases in the experiments presented in Chapters 10 and 12 the signals for two *FR*'s were randomized so that they gave no information about the *FR* in effect. Yet of the relations among responses, stimuli and reinforcement, those often regarded as critical were unchanged by the randomization of signals. Responses were still intermittently reinforced in the presence of two particular stimuli; so, of course, these stimuli were still temporally contiguous with a primary reinforcer. Despite their contiguity with a primary reinforcer these stimuli lost their conditioned reinforcing effect.

Choice

Alternative behaviors which have similar or identical consequences in terms of primary reinforcement may be arranged to have different consequences in terms of other experimenter-controlled stimuli. Conditioned reinforcing value of these stimuli can then be inferred from preferences. This method is used in conjunction with other methods. The dependent variable in the concurrent chains method is relative rate of responding, or preference. A schedule with superimposed conditioned reinforcers may be offered on one key and the same schedule without the conditioned reinforcer on another key, as in some of Schuster's experiments (Chapter 8) or Hendry's (Chapter 12). In observing-response experiments the most obvious dependent variable may be regarded as preference. The subject may choose, by observing, to convert an uncued set of contingencies into the same set more differentiated, or cued. The proportion of opportunities on which he elects the cued option is a measure of the conditioned reinforcing value of the cues. This method is exemplified in Chapter 12.

Multiple schedule

Different sets of contingencies may be alternated, under stimulus control, in a Multiple schedule. The cues of the Multiple schedule signify the prevailing contingencies. Comparison of performance in the two (or more) components may be used to infer differences in conditioned reinforcing value. For example, De Lorge (Chapter 3) compared certain second-order schedules and their Tandem controls in Multiple schedules.

Critique of methods

These methods derive their appeal or validity sometimes from intuition, sometimes from analogy with the known effects of known reinforcers, and sometimes from internal experimental control. As an example of the latter, Schuster (Chapter 8) scheduled primary reinforcement instead of an initially neutral stimulus analogous to :S, in order to demonstrate the sensitivity of his procedure to reinforcing effects of :S. Although in particular cases one may raise questions about the validity of inferences concerning conditioned reinforcing effects, the methods seem generally appropriate. However, they all suffer the restriction that inferences have to be stated in terms of an *ordinal* scale. One has to say that conditioned reinforcing value of A is greater or less than that of B or that it is greater than zero. Because we have no way of measuring absolute conditioned reinforcing value, any more than absolute primary reinforcing value, which is to say we have no ratio scale with a zero point, we cannot compare results of experiments which used different methods. Does a relative rate of 0.7 imply 70 percent preference in discrete trials or other choice situation? The resounding reply, "not necessarily!," illustrated, for example, by Schuster's results, reflects both the rejection of premature attempts at quantification, which is a hallmark of the analysis of behavior, and a severe impediment in comparing results from different experiments.

What is needed is a metric or calculus of reinforcing value. In the absence of convertible measures, a standard method of comparing reinforcing value is required. Recently, Verhave (1963) proposed a general method for comparing reinforcers. He imposed certain schedules of reinforcement, giving the subject the option of switching to the more preferred. The behavioral "cost" of switching was adjusted so that it reached a steady value determined by the animal's persistence in choosing the more preferred schedule of reinforcement. Verhave's procedure appears capable of comparing any two reinforcers and, therefore, of generating a scale of reinforcement value. Moreover, it does not seem to distinguish primary from conditioned reinforcing value; it scarcely seems to matter whether we regard the reinforcing condition as the schedule or the cues associated with the primary reinforcement. Fantino's proposed procedure (see Chapter 7) has objectives similar to Verhave's. In order to quantify reinforcement or "distance to reward," both authors use a comparison, conflict or choice. The questions raised by this kind of endeavor are like questions of economics and decision theory. Is a large reward on a large FR equivalent to a small reward on a small FR? Is a trip to Bermuda equivalent to a second car in "utility?"

One of the difficulties that we encounter in evaluating theories of conditioned reinforcement and their evolution, is that statements about conditioned reinforcement are couched in terms which are too general. Both Hull's and Skinner's principles say that such and such conditions create conditioned reinforcers. This type of statement implies the form of experiment appropriate to establishing its own truth. Two sets of conditions are examined—one set conforms to those specified by the principle and the other (control) set of conditions departs from those specified in some important particular. The expected result is that performance will significantly differ in the two cases.

The control condition should produce zero conditioned reinforcement. However, paradoxically, the concept of zero conditioned reinforcement strikes a strange and false note and there is no accepted way of establishing that a stimulus has zero reinforcing power.

Even in a relatively recent review (Kelleher & Gollub, 1962) the question is put in these terms: "What are the necessary and sufficient conditions for the establishment of a conditioned reinforcer?" Yet the current experimental methods are not generally oriented toward establishing necessary and sufficient conditions. In experiments that seek to establish relations between independent and dependent variables the establishment of necessary and sufficient conditions implies two-valued dependent and independent variables.

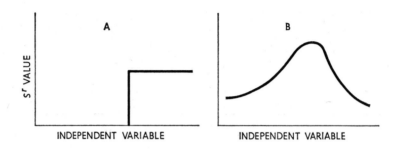

There is a translation from A, above, to a specification in terms of sufficient and/or necessary conditions, but not from B, since in B all the values of the independent variable produce some conditioned reinforcement.

Let us clarify the meaning of "necessary and sufficient conditions." Consider, for example, the statement that the necessary and sufficient condition for a stimulus to become a conditioned reinforcer is that it acts as S^D for some reinforced response. The four possible combinations of attributes are as follows:

	S^D	not S^D
S^r	1	2
not S^r	3	4

The claim that the necessary and sufficient condition for a stimulus to become a conditioned reinforcer is that it act as S^D implies that the class of S^Ds and the class of S^rs fall in boxes 1 and 4 *only*. No cases must occur in boxes 2 and 3. A case occurring in box 3 invalidates the specification "sufficient," and a case occurring in box 2 invalidates the specification "necessary." "All S^Ds are S^rs" implies that no cases fall in box 3, and "all S^rs are S^Ds" implies that no cases fall in box 2. The important restrictions implied by the "necessary and sufficient" terminology are:

1. The property of most interest (here S^r) is an all-or-none variable.
2. The defining property (here S^p) is an all-or-none variable.
3. A few negative instances force one to discard the generalization in spite of the fact of a possibly strong association of the two properties (S^p and S^r). However, negative instances are difficult to find since they require one to establish the *absence* of a property—S^p or S^r.

Though no research proceeds without a plan, there is a tendency for reviewers and systematizers in science to be too prescriptive about the direction of future research. Rather than saying what problems *should* be tackled, a judicious guess about what kinds of questions *will* be tackled, may be more useful. If such a guess proves to be wrong, the fault is clearly with the prognosticator, not the experimenters! Most future research in conditioned reinforcement, I venture, will separate easily into two categories. On the one hand, many studies, perhaps most, will use methods which are generally sufficient to sustain performance with conditioned reinforcers, thus allowing the establishment of a base-line performance. The statement of the problem of conditioned reinforcement in this case is: given conditions sufficient to sustain a conditioned reinforcer, how does the effectiveness of the conditioned reinforcer depend upon the variables in the situation? This way of stating the problem is reflected in the research strategy of most of the contributions in this book. On the other hand, the genesis of conditioned reinforcement is of interest, too, and there will be attempts to extend conditioned reinforcement theory to new situations as dictated by tentative generalizations about the conditions that produce conditioned reinforcers. The question here is: what (untried) conditions are sufficient to establish a conditioned reinforcer? This way of stating the question is reflected in the research strategy of some of the contributions in this book, notably Dinsmoor *et al.*'s.

Schedules of conditioned reinforcement

This section comprises four chapters concerned with the maintenance of performance by conditioned reinforcers, where some of the main variables are the schedules according to which the conditioned reinforcers are presented.

Marr reviews work on second-order schedules, which may be regarded as "schedules of schedules" of primary reinforcement, or as schedules of primary reinforcement overlaid with schedules of conditioned reinforcement. De Lorge's results give evidence as to the importance for the maintenance of second-order schedule performance of the temporal association of the conditioned reinforcer and the primary reinforcer.

Thomas' results show maintenance of performance by schedules of conditioned reinforcement, in spite of a consequent reduction in rate of primary reinforcement. This evidence that performance maintained by conditioned reinforcement is in some ways independent of primary reinforcement is added to by Zimmerman's extensive results, which show sustained schedule-controlled performance by a conditioned reinforcer long after discontinuation of the primary reinforcer.

SECOND-ORDER SCHEDULES

M. Jackson Marr[1]

Harvard Medical School

The recognition of the significance of intermittent primary reinforcement introduced a new era in the scientific study of behavior. Even casual observation of the behavior of any organism shows that continuous reinforcement is an exceedingly rare phenomenon. As Morse (1966, p. 53) has pointed out, "Only under intermittent reinforcement can the effects of reinforcement be fully manifested, and many characteristics of learned behavior are directly attributable to the dynamic interactions of variables which are necessarily in effect under intermittent reinforcement." These arguments apply equally well to conditioned reinforcement, yet the study of intermittent scheduling of conditioned reinforcement is a recent development. The early investigations concerned with schedules of conditioned reinforcement (see Kelleher & Gollub, 1962) were limited in that since the effects were studied during extinction the reinforcing properties of the scheduled stimulus were continually decreasing along with the behavior under study. It is thus of considerable interest to study conditioned reinforcement under stable experimental conditions. Second-order schedules permit the study of patterns of behavior controlled by the scheduling of a condi-

[1] On leave of absence from the Georgia Institute of Technology, 1967–68. Some of these experiments were carried out at the University of North Carolina at Chapel Hill and supported by U.S. Public Health Service Grant MH07534. Other experiments were carried out at Harvard Medical School and were supported by U.S. Public Health Service Grants MH02094, MH07658, and 5T1-MG-07084. The author wishes to thank Doctors R. T. Kelleher, W. H. Morse, and P. B. Dews for their helpful comments. Appreciation also goes to Miss Leona Delaney and Mrs. Catherine Jackson for assistance in conducting some of these experiments and to Miss Judy Brennan for help in preparation of this manuscript.

tioned reinforcer in a situation where responding is ultimately maintained by the scheduling of a primary reinforcer.

A second-order schedule is defined by Kelleher (1966a) as "one in which the behavior specified by a schedule contingency is treated as a unitary response that is itself reinforced according to some schedule of reinforcement." Second-order schedules can thus be considered as "schedules of schedules." Second-order schedules may be loosely divided into two principal subclasses depending upon how stimuli are introduced: brief stimulus procedures and chaining procedures. In the *brief stimulus procedures* a brief stimulus is presented under a schedule and the behavior engendered by this schedule is treated as a unitary response that is reinforced according to some schedule of primary reinforcement. The stimulus may or may not be temporally paired with the reinforcer, and responses in its presence have no scheduled consequences. As an example, consider the behavior under a fixed-interval of 1 min (FI 1) schedule as a unitary response which is reinforced according to a fixed ratio of 20 (FR 20) schedule of food presentation. This basic schedule would be denoted FR 20 (FI 1) (Kelleher, 1966a). Suppose further that the completion of each FI 1 component produces a brief presentation of, for example, an overhead light or a key color change. This schedule would be denoted FR 20 (FI 1:S). Since the stimulus terminates each FI 1 component, it will be paired with food presentation at the end of every 20th component. If, however, a brief stimulus were presented after completion of each of the first 19 FI 1 components but did not follow the terminal FI 1 component, the schedule would be a Tandem schedule, denoted TAND [FR 19 (FI 1:S)] [FR 1 (FI 1)]. In a more complex situation a Multiple schedule could comprise both of the above schedules. For example, in the presence of a red key light the schedule FR 20 (FI 1:S) could be in effect, while in the presence of a green key light the schedule TAND [FI 19 (FI 1:S)] [FR 1 (FI 1)] could be in effect. Such a Multiple schedule would be useful in comparing the effects of presenting a stimulus paired with a reinforcer with one which is not paired.

Many schedule combinations are possible with brief stimulus procedures, e.g., FI t (FR n:S), in which a brief stimulus follows n responses and the first FR n completed after t minutes is reinforced; or, FI t_1 (FI t_2:S), $t_1 > t_2$, wherein the first response after t_2 minutes produces a brief stimulus and the first FI t_2 completed after t_1 minutes is reinforced[2]; or *DRL t* (*FR n:S*) in which a brief stimulus follows n responses, but the first *FR n* completed after an initial pause of at least t minutes is reinforced. In addition, the designated unitary response may itself be a complex sequence. For example, consider the schedule *FR* n_1 (CHAIN *FI t FR* n_2:*S*) where the unitary response is taken as the behavior under a CHAIN *FI t FR* n_2, the execution of which produces a brief stimulus, and the n_1th completion of the CHAIN *FI t FR* n_2 produces primary reinforcement.

In *chaining procedures*, the second subclassification of second-order schedules, reinforcement terminates a sequence of component schedules associated with different discriminative stimuli. Consider the schedule CHAIN *FR* 3 (*FI* 2). This schedule may be shown schematically as

$$\boxed{\frac{S^D_3}{FI\ 2}} \rightarrow \boxed{\frac{S^D_2}{FI\ 2}} \rightarrow \boxed{\frac{S^D_1}{FI\ 2}} \rightarrow S^R.$$

Thus in the presence of S^D_3 a response after 2 min produces S^D_2; in the presence of S^D_2 a response after 2 min produces S^D_1; and (in the presence of S^D_1) a response after 2 min produces food reinforcement (S^R). In chaining procedures, unlike brief stimulus procedures, responses in the presence of a response-produced stimulus do have scheduled consequences. If no stimulus change occurs, then a Tandem schedule is defined which could be denoted simply as *FR* 3 (*FI* 2).

BRIEF STIMULUS PROCEDURES

Early experiments using the brief stimulus techniques include the percentage reinforcement studies of Ferster and Skinner (1957) and Zimmerman (1960), the response-sequence experiments of Ferster (1958b), and the token reinforcement studies of Kelleher (1957, 1958b). One of the first experiments using brief stimuli intermittently paired with reinforcement to maintain a schedule sequence was reported by Findley (1962). A pigeon performed on a three-component *FR* 10 Chain schedule with the

---

[2] Strictly speaking, the first *FI* t_2 *initiated* and completed after t_1 minutes should be reinforced. However, the author is not aware of any experiment studying this more stringent condition.

key light sequence blue, green, red. Completion of the terminal component of the Chain schedule resulted in the presentation of a 4-sec white key light after which the initial component was reinstated. Food was presented following the eighth presentation of the white light. In this schedule the behavior under a CHAIN FR 3 $(FR$ 10) can be considered as the unitary response, and the complete schedule may be denoted as FR 8 [CHAIN FR 3 $(FR$ 10) :S]. Performance under this schedule was compared with an ordinary three-component FR 80 Chain schedule with the same stimulus sequence. Although 240 responses were required to produce food presentation under each schedule, the response rate was higher under the brief stimulus schedule. About 40 to 50 reinforcements per session occurred under the brief stimulus schedule, while only 4 or 5 reinforcements per session occurred under the FR 80 Chain schedule. Findley and Brady (1965), Kelleher (1966a, 1966b), Thomas and Stubbs (1966), De Lorge (1967) and others have shown that when a brief stimulus, paired with food presentation is presented at the termination of each component schedule in a second-order schedule, considerable enhancement of responding may occur especially under conditions of low frequency of food presentation. Usually there is no enhancement when the brief stimulus is not paired with the presentation of a primary reinforcer.

The following experiments are concerned with the effects of presenting brief stimuli, paired or nonpaired, in second-order schedules. Two aspects of schedule performance are significant: (1) the overall rate and pattern of responding throughout the sequence of component schedules terminating in food presentation; and (2) the pattern of responding within each of the component schedules terminating with the presentation of a brief stimulus.

Using a second-order schedule in the pigeon, Marr and De Lorge (1966) compared the reinforcing effects of presenting a brief stimulus which was paired with food presentation with a brief stimulus not paired with food presentation. A Multiple second-order schedule was used. When the symbol "X" was projected on the key completion of 10 components, each a fixed interval of 2 min (FI 2), resulted in grain presentation. Completion of each FI 2 component produced a 0.5-sec presentation of an overhead light. At other times the experimental chamber was dark except for the key light or the magazine light which was present during grain presentation. In the 10th FI 2 component a response after 2 min produced the 0.5-sec houselight presentation followed by 10-sec access to grain. The brief stimulus was thus paired with primary reinforcement. This segment of the Multiple schedule can be denoted FR 10 (FI 2:S^r).

When the symbol "O" was projected on the key reinforcement also followed the completion of 10 FI 2 components. However, in components 1–9 a response after 2 minutes produced a 1,000 Hz tone of 0.5-sec duration. In the 10th component, as in the "X" condition, a response after 2 min produced the 0.5-sec houselight presentation followed by food presentation. The tone was thus never paired with food presentation. This section of the Multiple schedule can be denoted TAND [FR 9 (FI 2:S^n)] [FR 1 (FI 2:S^r)]. Figure 2.1 shows the final performance of two birds on this schedule.

The average response rate throughout the sequence of FI 2 components in the S^r condition was considerably higher than in the S^n condition. Generally, schedule performance in the FI 2 components terminating with the presentation of the paired stimulus was characterized by accelerated responding (scalloping), while presentation of nonpaired stimulus produced an erratic pattern characterized by long pauses and occasional short periods of rapid responding. Component fixed-interval patterns were seldom observed when the stimulus presented was not paired with reinforcement.

Figure 2.2 shows the response distribution throughout the sequence of 10 FI 2 components in the paired (S^r) and nonpaired (S^n) conditions. In all components responding which led to the paired stimulus exceeded that which led to the nonpaired stimulus.

Both subjects tended to respond less in the early than in the later components. As the minimum interreinforcement time (20 min) was substantial in these schedules, a pattern of overall accelerated responding might be expected. In fact, this seldom occurred, although a few exceptions are seen in Figure 2.1. The overall pattern of responding on schedules of this type will be discussed later.

De Lorge (1967) compared in the pigeon the effects of (1) presenting a brief stimulus paired with reinforcement with (2) a nonpaired stimulus, or with (3) no stimulus presentation at the termination of each component of a second-order schedule. The basic schedule was FI 18 (FI 3); i.e., the first FI 3 component completed after 18 min was reinforced. A red key light was present during the session except during a brief stimulus presentation and during food presentation. In one condition a 0.5-sec presentation of

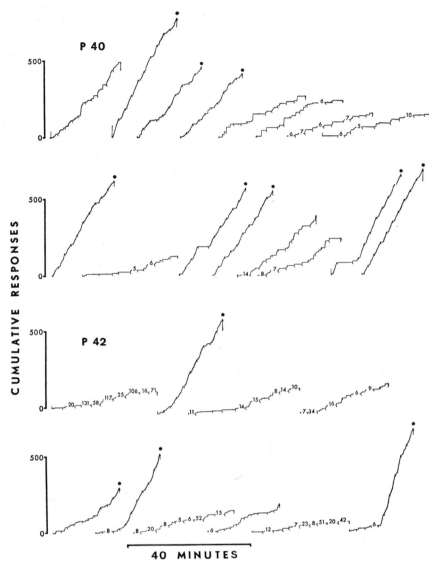

FIGURE 2.1. Representative cumulative records showing a portion of the final performance of pigeons P–40 and P–42 on a Multiple second-order schedule comparing the effects of presenting a brief stimulus paired, and a brief stimulus not paired with food presentation. In each section of the Multiple, the 10th *FI* 2 component terminated in food presentation. In the records marked with a dot a 0.5-sec presentation of an overhead light terminated each *FI* 2 component. In the records without a dot, a 0.5-sec presentation of a 1,000 *Hz* tone terminated *FI* 2 components 1–9, but did not terminate the 10th, reinforced component. The two sections of the Multiple second-order schedule occurred in an irregular sequence. The oblique marks of the response pen signify the presentation of a brief stimulus. Each record segment ends at food presentation and these segments have been displayed along the abscissa. The numbers denote the number of minutes during which no responding occurred that have been omitted from the record (Marr & De Lorge, 1966).

a yellow key light occurred at the completion of each *FI* 3 component including the one terminating in food presentation. The record
marked *Y* at the top of Figure 2.3 shows the performance in this
condition. The overall rate of responding was high, and responding
was accelerated within the FI 3 components.

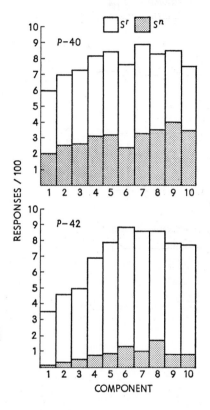

FIGURE 2.2.   The response distribution
throughout the sequence of 10 *FI* 2
components in the paired (*S^r*) and nonpaired (*S^n*) conditions. The ordinate
represents the mean number of responses
(in hundreds) per session in each *FI* 2
component over the final three sessions
(Marr & De Lorge, 1966).

The record marked *G* shows the effects of presenting a green key
light of 0.5-sec duration at the termination of each *FI* 3 component
except the one terminating in food presentation. In contrast to the
Y condition, the overall response rate decreased with fewer component scallops and longer post-reinforcement pauses. That scalloping
occurred at all may, in part, be due to the bird's history of responding under a schedule in which the green key light was a discriminative stimulus and had thus been associated with reinforcement. The
other records marked "Y" show reinstatements of performance
using the paired yellow key light. In the record marked *N* no

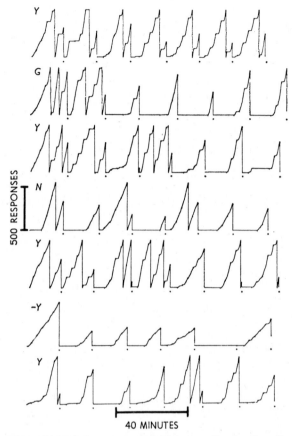

FIGURE 2.3. Sample cumulative records showing the terminal performance of a pigeon on the basic second-order schedule *FI* 18 (*FI* 3) under various brief stimulus conditions. *Y:* a yellow key light paired with reinforcement; *G:* green key light presented at the termination of each *FI* 3 component except that one preceding primary reinforcement; *N:* no stimulus presentation at the end of the *FI* 3 components; − *Y:* yellow key light occurred at the termination of all but the reinforced *FI* 3 component. The small dots mark the presentation of primary reinforcement (De Lorge, 1967).

stimulus change occurred at the termination of the *FI* 3 components; responding decreased and no component scallops occurred. The record marked −*Y* shows the effect after 14 sessions of no longer pairing the yellow key light with primary reinforcement; i.e., the yellow key light was presented at the completion of all but the terminal *FI* 3 components. This markedly decreased responding and there were few component scallops.

Kelleher (1966b) has investigated in the pigeon the pattern of responding within components of a second-order schedule, comparing the effects of a stimulus paired with food presentation with the effects of a stimulus not paired with food presentation. The basic second-order schedule was *FR* 15 (*FI* 4) ; i.e., completion of the 15th *FI* 4 component resulted in food presentation. In one condition a 0.7-sec white key light was presented at the end of each *FI* 4 component including the one immediately preceding food presentation. This schedule was denoted *FI* 15 (*FI* 4:*W*). In a second condition a 0.7-sec darkening of the key occurred at the termination of each of the *FI* 4 components with the exception of the final, reinforced component. This schedule was denoted TAND [*FR* 14 (*FI* 4:*D*)] [*FR* 1 (*FI* 4)]. In a third condition a red key light of 0.7-sec duration was substituted for the dark key in the above schedule.

Figure 2.4 shows the average distribution of response rates within individual *FI* 4 components. The first panel shows a comparison between the paired (*W*) and nonpaired (*D*) condition. When the stimulus was intermittently paired with food presentation the response rate increased throughout the interval; when the stimulus was not paired, the response rate was lower and relatively constant across the interval. The second panel illustrates the results of second and third replications of the paired condition. When a red key light was substituted for the dark key in the unpaired condition, the response rate was again lower, but responding tended to increase throughout the interval. This subject had a history of responding in the presence of a red key. A similar effect was seen in the experiments of De Lorge (1967) previously discussed. It appears that the effects of presenting an unpaired stimulus will be influenced to some extent by a history of exposure to that stimulus.

The above experiments show that pairing a brief stimulus with a primary reinforcer is sufficient to establish it as a conditioned reinforcer and that the scheduled presentation of such a stimulus can generate a pattern of responding similar to that generated by the presentation of a primary reinforcer under the same schedule. When the brief stimulus presented in a second-order schedule is not paired with a primary reinforcer the effects are more complex. Such a stimulus usually produces neither augmentation in rate of responding nor appropriate component schedule performance.

However, under certain circumstances an unpaired stimulus may serve to unify a complex response in a second-order schedule. The percentage reinforcement studies of Ferster and Skinner (1957) and Zimmerman (1960) demonstrated that the presentation of a stimulus not paired with reinforcement in a fixed-ratio schedule would generate appropriate fixed-ratio performance provided food followed a certain percentage of the ratios. Using a different procedure, Kelleher, Fry and Cook (1964) reported a similar effect with

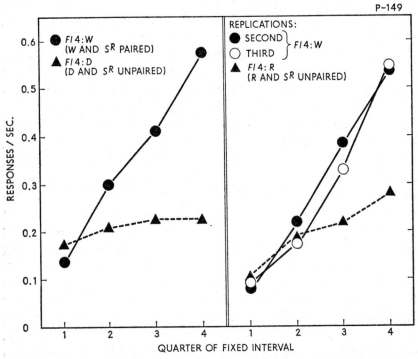

FIGURE 2.4. The effects of presenting a brief stimulus paired (white key light, W) and nonpaired (dark key, D or red key light, R) on the distribution of response rates within *FI* 4 components in a second-order schedule in which completion of the 15th *FI* 4 component produced primary reinforcement (after Kelleher, 1966b).

schedules of the form DRL (FR). For example, a squirrel monkey performed under the schedule DRL 60 $(FR$ 200) in which an initial pause of greater than 1 min when followed by 200 responses resulted in food presentation; an initial pause of less than 1 min when followed by 200 responses produced a 0.5-sec timeout with no food presentation. By the seventh session over 80 percent of the initial pauses were greater than 1 min. These pauses as well as those less

than 1 min were followed by a typical high-rate fixed-ratio performance, indicating that the *FR* 200 was acting as a unitary
response on a *DRL* 60 schedule. That such a performance could be
established without the brief stimulus is very doubtful.

A possible common factor in situations in which an unpaired
stimulus can unify a complex response is that the schedule producing this stimulus has fixed-ratio properties. Ratio schedules possess
a cohesive property not shared by other schedules (Mechner, 1958).
Support for this hypothesis comes from an experiment of Neuringer and Chung (1967). With pigeons as subjects, a schedule was
studied in which the behavior specified by a TAND *FR* 1 *FI* 5-sec
schedule was treated as a unitary response which was reinforced on
a *VI* 1 schedule. If the *VI* 1 had not terminated, the execution of a
TAND *FR* 1 *FI* 5-sec produced a 1-sec blackout period, a stimulus
not paired with reinforcement. In another condition, the component
schedule was an *FR* 11, also reinforced on a *VI* 1 schedule. Again, if
the *VI* 1 schedule had not terminated, a 1-sec blackout was scheduled on *FR* 11. Neuringer and Chung found that response rates on
these schedules were about twice those measured in an ordinary *VI*
1 schedule with about the same reinforcement frequency and substitution of food for the blackout did not appreciably change the
rate and pattern of responding. These investigators concluded that
the brief blackout periods had reinforcing characteristics, and that
the necessary conditions for the establishment of these reinforcing
properties "appear to be an identity between the required behavior
sequence leading to primary reinforcement and the required behavior sequence leading to blackout" (Neuringer & Chung, 1967, p.
52).

Neuringer and Chung also felt that the presentation of a blackout in their study led to an appropriate schedule performance. This
is difficult to evaluate, however, as the parameter values of the
schedules were exceedingly small. The average rates under the
TAND *FR* 1 *FI* 5-sec schedule ranged from 106–129 responses per
minute depending on the type and duration of the brief stimulus
presented. Under the *FR* 11 schedule, the average rate was 121
responses per minute, indicating that the rates on the two schedules
were essentially equal. In addition, further inspection of their data
suggests that the patterns of responding under the two schedules
were very similar—a pause followed by a high rate—characteristic
of fixed-ratio schedule performance. Thus, the possibility exists
that the ratiolike property of the schedule performance could be the

significant factor in determining the results of their experiments.

In the studies previously discussed concerned with the effects of presenting a nonpaired stimulus in a second-order schedule (De Lorge, 1967; Kelleher, 1966b; Marr & De Lorge, 1966;), the procedures satisfied the above Neuringer and Chung condition, and yet, in comparison with a paired stimulus, a nonpaired stimulus produced lower rates and did not generate appropriate schedule performance. Although Neuringer and Chung's stated condition for establishing a conditioned reinforcer is perhaps necessary, it is not sufficient. Substantially more research using a greater variety of schedules over a larger range of parameter values is needed to clarify the function of unpaired stimuli in second-order schedules.

If components in a second-order schedule can assume the properties of unitary responses, then the overall schedule performance might be similar to that in which single responses are reinforced under the same type of schedule. This was shown clearly in the study of Kelleher, Fry and Cook (1964), where the FR 200 acted as a unitary response on a DRL 60 schedule. In another experiment Kelleher (1966a) studied the performance of pigeons on the schedule FI 10 (FR 20:S) in which the completion of each FR 20 resulted in the presentation of a 0.5-sec white key light and the first FR 20 completed after 10 min produced the white key light followed by food. Performance under this schedule was characterized by progressively decreasing pre-ratio pauses throughout the 10-min interval, a feature comparable to the response distribution in an ordinary fixed-interval schedule. As the unitary property of the fixed-ratio schedule has been established, such a result may not seem unusual. It would be of interest if other schedules could also be shown to have unitary character. The following experiment demonstrates that responding under a fixed-interval schedule can perhaps assume unitary properties.

Figure 2.5 shows the performance of a pigeon on two second-order schedules in which the component schedules terminating in a brief stimulus presentation were the same (fixed interval) as was the minimum time between food presentations, but the schedules of components terminating in food presentation were different. In the record marked A the schedule was FR 20 (FI 1:S) in which completion of the 20th FI 1 component resulted in food presentation, and the execution of each FI 1 component terminated in the presentation of a 0.7-sec flash of a red key light. In the record marked B the schedule was FI 20 (FI 1:S) in which the first FI 1 component completed after 20 min was reinforced. Again, a response after 1 min in each component produced a 0.7-sec red key light.

The overall rate tended to be higher when the *FI* 1 components were reinforced by food according to a ratio (*FR* 20) than according to an interval (*FI* 20). In addition, in the *FI* 20 (*FI* 1:*S*) schedule lengthy pauses occurred in the early components followed

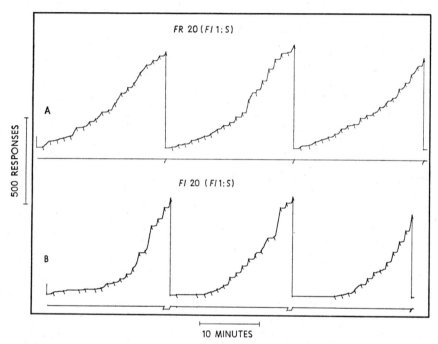

FIGURE 2.5. Cumulative records comparing performances on two second-order schedules in which the behavior under an *FI* 1 schedule is treated as a unitary response which is reinforced on a *FR* 20 (*A*) or a *FI* 20 (*B*) schedule. The brief stimulus terminating each *FI* 1 component was a 0.7-sec. presentation of a red key light. (Unpublished data kindly made available by Dr. R. T. Kelleher.)

by increasing rates of responding, showing a correspondence with an ordinary fixed-interval schedule. While low rates of responding occur in the early components of the *FR* 20 (*FI* 1:*S*) schedule the later components contain a high but variable number of responses. Kelleher (1966b) has pointed out a similarity of this pattern to the interresponse time (*IRT*) distribution in ordinary fixed-ratio schedules wherein the initial *IRTs* are long, but the later ones are short and variable.

The possibility that second-order schedules can be used to magnify certain performance characteristics of ordinary schedules of reinforcement is intriguing, yet there are many difficulties involved with such a notion. Perhaps the most fundamental problem involves the interaction between the component schedule terminating in a brief stimulus presentation and the schedule of components terminating in food presentation. For example, in a schedule of the form *FR n (FI t:S)* there may be a substantial minimum interreinforcement time resulting from the *FI* component contingency which would have a tendency to mask any fixed-ratio properties this schedule might have. Conversely, under a schedule of the form *DRL* t_1 *(FI t_2:S)* the *DRL* contingency could mitigate any tendency for accelerated responding within the fixed-interval components. Substantially more research is needed to determine the limitations of treating second-order schedule components as actual unitary responses.

CHAINING PROCEDURES

Chaining procedures involve schedules in which reinforcement is contingent upon the execution of a sequence of component schedules, each associated with a different discriminative stimulus. Tandem schedules in which one and the same stimulus is correlated with each component have been used as control procedures in the investigation of the discriminative and conditioned reinforcing properties of Chain schedule stimuli. Chain schedules have been exceedingly important in the experimental analysis of conditioned reinforcement as demonstrated in the comprehensive reviews by Kelleher and Gollub (1962) and Kelleher (1966a).

A salient feature of extended Chain schedules is the extremely low rate of responding which may occur in the initial components. This aspect of Chain schedule performance has been observed by several investigators (Findley, 1962; Gollub, 1958; Kelleher & Fry, 1962; Thomas, 1964; Thomas & Stubbs, 1967). These authors have suggested a combination of several factors to account for this behavior, including: (1) the decreasing conditioned reinforcing effectiveness of Chain schedule stimuli the more remote their position in relation to primary reinforcement, (2) the relation between the conditioned reinforcing effectiveness of a stimulus and the frequency of reinforcement in its presence, and (3) the association of the initial Chain schedule stimuli with periods of nonreinforcement (S^Δ property).

The distinctions between these factors are subtle and are difficult to differentiate experimentally. Factors (1) and (2) imply a gradient of conditioned reinforcement. If such a gradient could be extended "below zero," i.e., to stimuli associated with nonreinforcement, then all three factors would be equivalent, and factor (1) would emerge as the significant determinant of behavior in Chain schedules.

By using brief stimulus procedures, Marr (1965) has quantitatively evaluated the conditioned reinforcing effectiveness of Chain schedule stimuli in relation to their proximity to reinforcement. The schedule used was a complex Chain schedule, the initial section of which was a second-order schedule consisting of 10 FI 1 components. This initial section was called the test schedule. This was followed by a three-link Chain schedule consisting of FI 100-sec components. The stimulus sequence in the three-link Chain was red (S_3), green (S_2), and white (S_1). Presentation of food followed the first response after 100 sec in the presence of S_1 (white).

In the test schedule section of the complex Chain, either an orange key light or a blue key light was present except during a brief stimulus presentation. In the presence of an orange key light FI 1 components 1–9 terminated in a 0.5-sec presentation of the white key light (S_1), the stimulus associated with the terminal component of the three-link FI 100-sec Chain schedule. A response at the termination of the 10th FI 1 component produced a 0.5-sec presentation of the white key light followed by the onset of the red key light (S_3), the initial component of the three-link FI 100-sec Chain schedule. In the presence of the blue key light the above conditions in the test schedule were the same except that a response at the termination of each FI 1 component produced a 0.5-sec presentation of the red key light (S_3), the stimulus associated with the initial component of the FI 100-sec Chain schedule. When S_1 was presented in the test schedule, the complete schedule could be denoted CHAIN [FI 10 (FI 1:S_1)] [CHAIN FR 3 (FI 100 sec)]; when S_3 was presented the schedule could be denoted CHAIN [FR 10 (FI 1:S_3)] [CHAIN FR 3 (FI 100 sec)].

Figure 2.6 shows representative cumulative records of the performance of pigeon P-5. The initial (S_3) or terminal (S_1) stimulus presented in the test schedule is indicated above each record. Although responding in both the S_1 and S_3 conditions of the test schedule was erratic, the brief presentation of the white key light (S_1) maintained more responding than the presentation of the red

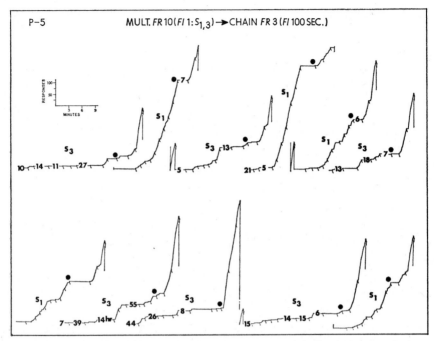

FIGURE 2.6. Cumulative records showing a portion of the final performance of pigeon P-5 on a complex Chain schedule, the initial segment being composed of 10 *FI* components in which either an orange or a blue key light was present, and a terminal segment composed of an ordinary three-link *FI* 100-sec chain schedule with the stimulus sequence red (S_3), green (S_2), and white (S_1). Food presentation followed the first response after 100 seconds in white. In the presence of the orange key light in the initial segment, a 0.5-sec presentation of S_1 (white) terminated each *FI* 1 component; in the presence of a blue key light a 0.5-sec presentation of S_3 (red) terminated each *FI* 1 component. The brief stimulus presented in the initial segment is marked over the records. The dots mark the beginning of the three-link *FI* 100-sec Chain schedule. The record has been collapsed and the response pen reset after 550 responses or at food presentation. (Marr, 1965).

key light (S_3). The S_3 condition is characterized by lengthy pauses occurring throughout the test schedule, while in the S_1 condition pauses generally occurred at the beginning of the test schedule followed by accelerated responding.

Figure 2.7 shows the mean number of responses over three sessions throughout the sequence of the 10 *FI* 1 components of the test schedule in both the S_1 and S_3 conditions. More responding occurred under scheduled presentation of S_1 than under S_3 in every component of the test schedule.

Figure 2.8 shows for bird P-5 the difference between the S_1 and

S_3 conditions as a function of the parameter value of the fixed interval in the three-link Chain schedule. The points on the ordinate are ratios of the number of responses when S_1 was presented (R_{1T}) to the number of responses when S_3 was presented (R_{3T}). As the figure shows, although there was little disparity between S_1 and S_3 at the 30- and 60-sec fixed-interval parameter values of the Chain schedule components, at 100-sec S_1 was considerably more effective in maintaining responding in the test schedule than

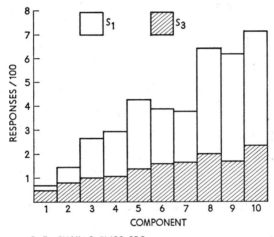

P–5   CHAIN 3 *FI* 100 SEC.

FIGURE 2.7.   The distribution of responses throughout the sequence of 10 *FI* 1 components of the test schedule when S_1 or S_3 was presented at the termination of each *FI* 1 component. The ordinate represents the mean number of responses (in hundreds) in each *FI* 1 component per session taken over the final three sessions (Marr, 1965).

S_3. The R_{1T}/R_{3T} index was an increasing function of the Chain schedule component parameter value indicating that as this value increased above some minimum level, the stimuli correlated with the initial and final component of the Chain schedule became relatively more disparate in their ability to maintain responding in the test schedule. Functions of this type might prove useful in comparing the conditioned reinforcing potency of Chain schedule stimuli as a function of different schedules of reinforcement. The brief stimulus method used in this experiment allows for the evaluation of the conditioned reinforcing effectiveness of a Chain schedule

stimulus in a manner relatively independent of the basic Chain
schedule itself and shows clearly that this effectiveness is dependent upon the proximity of the stimuli to reinforcement.

Several experiments have involved manipulations of Chain
schedules in an attempt to increase responding in the initial components. Findley (1962) found that by altering a five-component
Chain *FI* schedule to one in which the Chain length varied from one

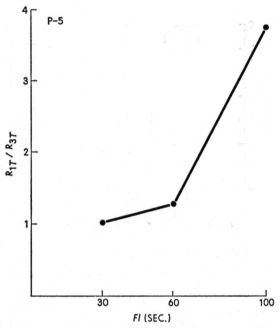

FIGURE 2.8.   The ratio of the number of responses in the test schedule when S_1 was presented
(R_{1T}) to the number of responses when S_3 was
presented (R_{3T}) as a function of the Chain schedule component parameter value (Marr, 1965).

to five components (with the same stimulus sequence), pausing was
abolished in the initial components and accelerated responding occurred in each component. Only when the component parameter
value was increased to *FI* 2 did significant pausing again return in
the initial components. Kelleher and Fry (1962) varied the sequence of stimuli in a three-component *FI* 1.5 Chain schedule so
that no stimulus was consistently correlated with food presentation.
Under these conditions behavior was well maintained in all compo-

nents. Marr (unpublished) investigated the effects of repeating
stimuli in a Chain schedule. The basic unit was a two-component *FI*
3 *FR* 30 Chain schedule. The behavior under this schedule was
treated as a unitary response that was reinforced on a *FR* 5; i.e.,
the fifth CHAIN *FI* 3 *FR* 30 completed resulted in food presentation. This schedule was denoted *FR* 5 [CHAIN *FI* 3 *FR* 30]. Figure
2.9 shows the performance of birds 354 and 237F. In the presence
of a red key light the first response after 3 min changed the key
color from red to blue. The 30th response changed the key color
back to red and reinstated the *FI* 3 schedule. This sequence was
repeated until the fifth presentation of the blue key light wherein
the 30th response produced food presentation.

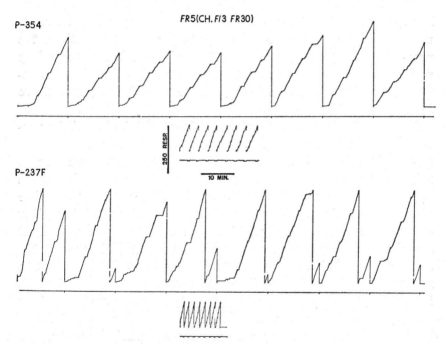

FIGURE 2.9. Performance of P–354 and P–237F on a repeated stimulus Chain
schedule in which every fifth completion of a CHAIN *FI* 3 *FR* 30 produced
primary reinforcement. The interval and ratio performances were recorded
separately and the recorders operated only during their assigned schedules.
The response pen reset at primary reinforcement or when 550 responses had
been emitted.

In the presence of the red key light (*FI* 3) responding was
positively accelerated, while in the presence of the blue key light

(*FR* 30) responding occurred at a sustained high rate. The consistency of performance throughout the sequence indicates that the blue key light by virtue of being intermittently paired with a primary reinforcer was established as an effective conditioned reinforcer capable of sustaining appropriate schedule performance in the early *FI* 3 components.

Byrd (1967) has investigated the effects of repeated stimuli in an extended Chain schedule consisting of seven *FI* 1 components. The key light sequence was white (S_7), green (S_6), white (S_5), blue (S_4), white (S_3), red (S_2), and white (S_1); i.e., the same key light color was present during the odd-numbered components. Although behavior was not well maintained in S_7 and S_6, accelerated responding occurred throughout the remainder of the components. Response rates tended to be higher in the odd-numbered components and occasionally considerable responding occurred in the presence of S_7 while long pauses occurred in S_6. More responding was maintained in this seven-component Chain schedule with repeated stimuli than in an ordinary Chain schedule composed of five *FI* 1 components.

In another schedule manipulation, Marr (1968) studied the performance of the pigeon under the following schedule: Responding under a *FI* 2 schedule was treated as a unitary response which was reinforced on a *FI* 8 schedule; i.e., completion of the first *FI* 2 component after 8 min was reinforced. Thus, the maximum number of components that could be executed was four. Each of these four components was associated with a different discriminative key light stimulus with the fixed sequence white (S_4), red (S_3), green (S_2), and orange (S_1). Because of the *FI* 8 contingency the bird could be reinforced in the presence of any one of the above stimuli depending on the amount of pausing. In a limiting case, for example, if the subject paused in the presence of the initial stimulus (white) for at least 8 min before emitting a response, then reinforcement would occur in the presence of the white key light (S_4). This schedule was termed a Sequence schedule and denoted SEQ. *FI* 8 (*FI* 2). The Sequence schedule has properties of an adjusting schedule (Ferster & Skinner, 1957; Kelleher, Fry, & Cook, 1964) in which the number of schedule components required to be executed is a function of the animal's performance.

Record *A* in Figure 2.10 shows several salient features of the performance on the Sequence schedule. First, sufficient responding

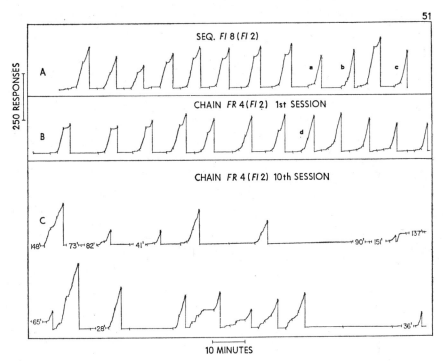

FIGURE 2.10. A comparison of the performance of P–51 on the Sequence schedule (record A) in which the first FI 2 component completed after 8 min was reinforced and an ordinary Chain schedule (records B and C) with the same stimulus order where reinforcement followed the completion of the fourth FI 2 component. Record B shows the first session on the Chain schedule following the Sequence schedule performance shown in record A. Record C shows the Chain schedule performance 10 sessions later. The numbers are minutes during which no responding occurred.

was maintained so that most reinforcements occurred in the presence of S_1. Exceptions are shown at a, b, and c where pausing in S_4 was lengthy enough so that reinforcement occurred in the presence of S_2.

The second feature of this schedule was that the response rates were often greatest in the presence of S_2, unlike an ordinary fixed-interval Chain where the rates are usually maximal in S_1. Perhaps the most interesting facet of this schedule was the clearly defined scallop pattern which occurred in S_1, again uncharacteristic of an ordinary extended fixed-interval Chain schedule. The high rates in S_2 and the distinct pattern of accelerated responding in S_1 can, in part, be accounted for by an interaction of the overall FI 8 schedule

and the component FI 2 schedule. The overall FI 8 schedule provided the possibility that food presentation might occur in the
presence of any one of the sequence of four stimuli, and also
increased the likelihood that an overall pattern of accelerated responding would occur. As reinforcement occasionally occurred in
the presence of S_2, this, combined with the accelerated responding
generated by the overall FI 8 contingency, could account for the
high rates seen in S_2. An additional factor is that responding in S_2
often produced S_1, presumably an effective conditioned reinforcer
which acted to maintain responding in S_2. The distinct scallop
pattern seen in S_1 can be accounted for, in part, by the fixed-interval schedule of food presentation in its presence. Possibly the rate
in S_1 is also affected by the high rate of responding in S_2, as a high
rate in a fixed-interval schedule tends to result in a lower rate in the
succeeding fixed interval (Ferster & Skinner, 1957). This lower
rate is manifested by longer pauses following the onset of the
interval. An additional factor contributing to the relatively low
rate in S_1 as compared with S_2 is that under a fixed-interval schedule the maximal rate may occur some time prior to the end of the
interval (Ferster & Skinner, 1957). As the Sequence schedule is a
fixed-interval schedule of components rather than individual responses, it may, as other second-order schedules discussed previously, amplify certain characteristics of the ordinary fixed-interval schedule.

The record marked B shows the next session after record A in
which the schedule was altered to an ordinary four-component FI 2
Chain schedule with the same stimulus order as in the Sequence
schedule. Rapid changes took place in this session so that at d the
response rate in S_2 had become substantially less than in S_1 and the
distinct scallop pattern seen in the sequence schedule in S_1 was no
longer present. The record marked C shows the 10th session under
the Chain schedule. Long pauses have developed in S_4 and S_3 and
although the response rate in S_2 is greater than that shown in B, it
is still less than S_1.

Although reinforcement rarely occurred in the presence of S_3 or
S_4, it occurred frequently enough to decrease considerably the
pause length over that observed in the comparable Chain schedule
(record B). However, low rates of responding also occurred in S_4
and S_3 of the sequence schedule. These rates resulted not only from
the low frequency of reinforcement in their presence, but also

resulted from the fixed-interval dependency of the schedule. More than one component was generally completed in the sequence schedule, just as more than a single response generally occurs during the ordinary fixed-interval schedule. That the completion of only a single component is possible is a significant feature in the maintenance of responding in the Sequence schedule as is the single response requirement in an ordinary fixed-interval schedule (Herrnstein & Morse, 1958).

The above experiments involving various manipulations of Chain schedules have shown that any alteration which leads to an intermittent placement of a Chain schedule stimulus in close temporal relation to primary reinforcement will increase its conditioned reinforcing effectiveness and thus enhance responding in the Chain schedule.

SUMMARY AND CONCLUSIONS

Second-order schedules are valuable for the study of the effects of intermittent scheduling of conditioned reinforcement under the relatively stable conditions where responding is ultimately maintained by primary reinforcement. Experiments using brief stimulus procedures have shown that pairing a stimulus with a primary reinforcer is sufficient to establish it as a conditioned reinforcer, and that presentation of a conditioned reinforcer under a schedule can generate a schedule performance similar to that generated by a primary reinforcer. Scheduled presentation of a brief stimulus not paired with reinforcement generally produces neither augmentation of rate of responding nor appropriate schedule performance, although under certain circumstances an unpaired stimulus may establish the unity of a complex response. This effect, however, is more easily realized when the stimulus is paired with reinforcement, and offers the possibility that second-order schedules may prove useful in magnifying certain aspects of ordinary schedules of reinforcement.

Many important variables remain to be investigated. Of considerable interest, for example, would be a systematic analysis of the function of the duration of the brief stimulus in the maintenance and pattern of responding in a second-order schedule. The designation of "brief stimulus procedures" has been used and yet the notion of "brief" remains undefined. The operations involved in pairing a stimulus with a reinforcer should be of particular concern. It is possible that the establishment of the reinforcing properties of the stimulus occurs as a result of respondent conditioning (Kelleher, 1966a); if so, these second-order schedule procedures may provide a productive link which can clarify the relations and interactions of respondent and operant behavior.

Chaining procedures have been used extensively in the experimental analysis of conditioned reinforcement, and much effort has been directed toward understanding the properties of Chain schedule stimuli. The various alterations of Chain schedules which have been studied suggest that the conditioned reinforcing effectiveness of Chain schedule stimuli is a function of their relative positions in relation to primary reinforcement.

Much attention has been directed toward the role of stimuli in relation to reinforcement in the analysis of patterns of responding in second-order schedules, but relatively little attention has been paid to the way in which these stimuli have been or can be scheduled. The particular component schedule terminating in presentation of a stimulus and the schedule of components terminating in the presentation of a primary reinforcer might under many circumstances prove to be considerably more important than any property of the stimulus per se. The manner in which events are scheduled in relation to ongoing behavior can be of greater significance in determining consequent behavior than the events themselves.

chapter 3

THE INFLUENCE OF PAIRING WITH PRIMARY REINFORCEMENT ON THE MAINTENANCE OF CONDITIONED REINFORCEMENT IN SECOND-ORDER SCHEDULES[1]

John de Lorge
University of South Alabama

INTRODUCTION

The present studies were designed to assess the effects of a briefly presented stimulus paired with a primary reinforcer. A briefly presented stimulus is one which is of shorter duration than the magazine cycle and generally is on the order of 0.5 sec to 1.0 sec. Such stimuli were here referred to as conditioned reinforcers when they were paired with the primary reinforcer. Although numerous investigations have been concerned with the variables influencing the formation of a conditioned reinforcer, only recently have studies investigated briefly presented stimuli (Kelleher, 1966b; Thomas & Stubbs, 1966; Zimmerman, 1963). Moreover, there has been a conspicuous lack of work, among the studies using brief stimulus presentations as conditioned reinforcers, comparing conditioned reinforcers, neutral stimuli (stimuli not paired with primary reinforcers), and primary reinforcers.

Traditionally, the investigation of conditioned reinforcers was carried out in experiments using extinction (Bugelski, 1938). Recently, within an operant conditioning paradigm, other techniques have been developed which vividly demonstrate the response

[1] These investigations were supported by Public Health Service Research Grant No. MH 13153 01 from the National Institutes of Health.

strengthening ability of a conditioned reinforcer. One of these techniques involved second-order schedules. "A second-order schedule treats a pattern of behavior engendered by a schedule contingency as a unitary response that is itself reinforced according to some schedule of reinforcement" (Kelleher, 1966b, p. 476). Kelleher used brief stimulus presentations to reinforce the component response patterns that made up the second-order schedule behavior (see Chapter 2).

In the present set of experiments second-order schedules in which brief stimulus presentations were used were further elaborated through the use of multiple schedules. Two experiments were conducted. They were of the same form but the second-order and primary reinforcement schedules differed.

GENERAL METHOD

Subjects

Two male White Carneaux pigeons approximately three years old at the start of Experiment 1 were used as subjects. They weighed about 60 percent–80 percent of their undeprived weight. They had previously been subjects in a red-green discrimination reversal experiment for 130 days, with a *VI* 1.5 schedule of reinforcement. In the present studies an interval of 90 days, during which the birds were given free access to food and water, intervened between the end of Experiment 1 and the beginning of Experiment 2.

Apparatus

The experimental chambers were three-key animal chests, model E3125AA–300, manufactured by Grason-Stadler. A three-watt houselight was added in the front upper left corner of each chamber and the original houselight aperture was covered with a piece of translucent red plastic. The houselight went on when an experimental session began and went off when the session terminated. In-line digital displays were mounted behind the keys and only the middle key was available to the birds. The other two keys were covered with metal plates. A Foringer multiple stimulus control panel, model 1166–4M1, was used to present sound stimuli in the first experiment. In the second experiment white masking noise was present during each experimental session. Also, in the second experiment the boxes were modified so that the food aperture could be illuminated by either one of two 7-watt lights, red or white. The regular houselight was also used in the second experiment. Water and grit were continuously available from cups mounted at the rear of the chamber. In Experiment 1 the birds were only removed from the chamber once a day for weighing purposes and obtained all of their food during an experimental session. In Experiment 2 the birds were removed overnight and received supplemental feedings. Two similar experimental chambers were used for the two animals. The animals were observed through a wide angle lens mounted in the top of the chest. Conventional relay and timing circuitry was used to program the experiments and responses were recorded on a Gerbrands cumulative recorder.

EXPERIMENT 1

Method

In this first study a two-component Multiple schedule was used to assess the effects of a briefly presented 0.5-sec stimulus (conditioned reinforcer) intermittently paired with the primary reinforcer (grain). Within the same study a comparison was made between the conditioned reinforcing stimulus and a briefly presented stimulus (neutral stimulus) never paired with the primary reinforcer. Another comparison was between the effects of presenting a conditioned reinforcer and the effects of having no stimulus-change. The final comparison was between the effects of a conditioned reinforcing stimulus and the primary reinforcer itself. The brief presentation of the stimuli was programmed to appear as a consequence of a response at the end of 1 min (FI 1). The number of FI 1 intervals presented prior to primary reinforcement was programmed on a variable ratio of 10 (VR 10). In other words, the primary reinforcer followed, on the average, the 10th presentation of the stimulus occurring at the end of FI 1. Table 3.1 is intended to clarify this procedure. Each of the different components of the multiple had a specific sound and key light as its correlated stimuli.

In the first comparison (phases A, C, and E of Table 3.1) performance in one component of the Multiple schedule was maintained with the stimulus paired with the primary reinforcer, VR 10

TABLE 3.1

Summary of Procedures for Experiment 1

Phase	Procedure	Number of Sessions	Paired Stimulus Compared with:
A	MULT [VR 10 (FI 1:W)] [TAND (VR 9 {FI 1:R}) (FR 1 {FI 1:W})]	49	Unpaired stimulus
B	MULT [VR 10 (FI 1:W)] [TAND (VR 9 {FI 1}) (FR 1 {FI 1:W})]	19	No stimulus
C	MULT [VR 10 (FI 1:W)] [as in A]	90	Unpaired stimulus
D	MULT [VR 10 (FI 1:W)] [FI 1]	68	Primary reinforcer
E	MULT [VR 10 (FI 1:W)] [as in A]	15	Unpaired stimulus

(FI 1:W). The other component showed performance under an identical schedule except the brief stimulus was never paired with the primary reinforcer, TAND (VR 9 {FI 1:R}) (FR 1 {FI 1:W}). The different components of the Multiple schedule were accompanied by different sounds and different letters on the key. The white light (W) used as a conditioned reinforcer was the food aperture light and the red light (R), used as the unpaired stimulus was located about 5 inches to the right of the response key. The Multiple schedule components alternated after every three primary reinforcers and sessions generally lasted until 24 primary reinforcers had been presented. Component duration and session length were generally the same under all conditions.

The second comparison was between performance maintained by the paired stimulus and by no stimulus at all, as in a Tandem schedule (phase B). In other words, the second component of the Multiple schedule in this case was identical to the first component except that no exteroceptive stimulus marked the end of one FI 1 and the beginning of the next. It was merely a VR 10 of FI 1's in which the completion of only the last FI 1 produced the white light followed by food. Food delivery in both parts of the Multiple schedule was always accompanied by illumination of the food aperture (W) as in all other conditions of the experiment.

The third comparison (phase D) was between performance maintained by the paired stimulus and by the primary reinforcer. In the first component of the Multiple schedule the paired stimulus occurred as before but in the second component the primary reinforcer was produced on completion of each FI 1. The primary reinforcement cycle was reduced from 18 sec to 3 sec in this case. The same *VR* program was used to generate both the number of paired stimuli (in the first component) and the number of food deliveries (in the second component). On the average, then, the number of food deliveries in the second component equaled the number of presentations of the conditioned reinforcer in the first component. The sessions generally lasted about four hours. The original schedule was reinstated following each of the other two comparison schedules.

Results

Figure 3.1 shows some representative cumulative records for

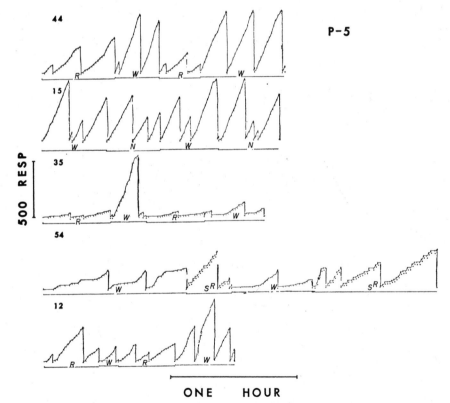

FIGURE 3.1. Typical sections from the cumulative records of P–5 in Experiment 1. The numbers refer to the session number. The letters refer to the stimuli at the end of each component schedule: *R* (a red light), *W* (the white feeder light), *N* (no stimulus), and S^R (the primary reinforcer). *W* was paired with the primary reinforcer, and *R* was not.

P–5. The records show behavior during the middle of a session, i.e., the records of the first and last six primary reinforcer presentations were removed. Dots beneath the records indicate when food occurred. *W* refers to the food aperture light and R refers to the red light. N means that no exteroceptive stimulus occurred at the end of *FI* 1 and S^R refers to the presentation of the primary reinforcer on the *FI* 1. The top record shows responding maintained by the paired stimulus W, and the unpaired stimulus, *R*. As

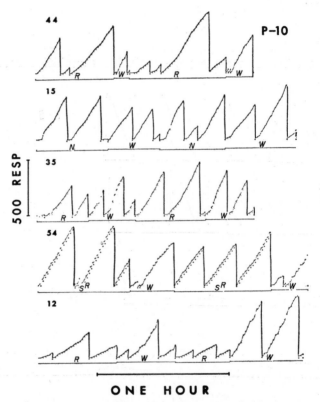

FIGURE 3.2. Typical sections from the cumulative records of P–10 in Experiment 1. The numbers refer to the session number. The letters and dots mean the same as in Figure 3.1.

seen in these records the response rate was higher when responding produced the stimulus associated with food delivery. The rate also tended to be relatively stable. In the second row of records it is seen that requiring the animal to meet the same schedule contingencies but with no FI 1 stimulus consequence produced the same or higher rates than responding for the paired stimulus. The third row of records illustrates session 35 of the reinstituted original schedule. Again it is shown that rates were higher for the paired stimulus. The fourth row of records illustrates a comparison between the primary and the conditioned reinforcer (paired stimulus). Running rates were higher and scallops more pronounced when responding produced a primary reinforcer. On the other hand, because of pauses after the primary reinforcer the amount of responding between primary reinforcers was lower than that between conditioned reinforcers on the previous schedules. The differences between the performances maintained by the paired and unpaired stimulus were recovered by returning the animal to the original schedule as seen in the last row of records.

Figure 3.2 shows similar records for P–10. Response rates were higher and scallops were more prominent with the paired stimulus (W) when compared with the unpaired stimulus (R) as in the case of P–5. No large differences appeared between the paired stimulus (W) and the no-stimulus conditions (N) except that response rates were somewhat higher in the no-stimulus portion of the schedule. However, in the comparison of the primary reinforcer with the paired stimulus there were smaller differences in response rate than in the case of P–5.

In general the paired stimulus maintained more responses per session than did the neutral stimulus, the same or fewer than did no-stimulus, and the same or fewer than did the primary reinforcer. Figure 3.3 illustrates these differences. The figure shows for both birds the difference in the mean number of responses per FI 1 for a stimulus paired with the primary reinforcer versus a stimulus not paired (R), no-stimulus (N), or a primary reinforcer (S^x). The plus sign on the ordinate indicates higher FI rates for the paired stimulus and the minus sign indicates higher rates in the comparison condition. Equal rates in both conditions are indicated by dots on the zero horizontal line. The top portion of the figure contains data for P–10 and the bottom portion contains data for P–5. Arrows on the abscissa and light lines in the body of the figure show where the conditions were changed. The small horizontal line in the data for P–5 indicates where it was removed for eight sessions for supplementary feeding. Although there were differences between the animals their response rates in relation to the

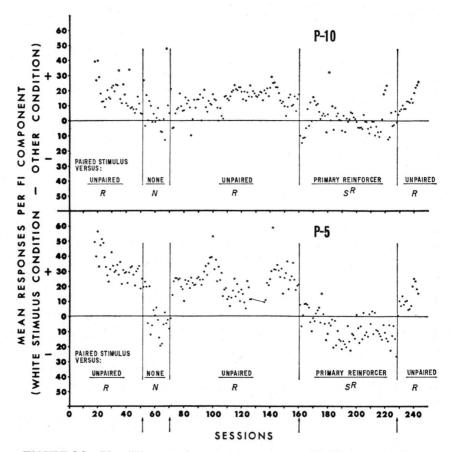

FIGURE 3.3. The differences in mean responses per *FI* 1 between each component of the Multiple schedule in Experiment 1 plotted over consecutive sessions. Dots above the horizontal line for both animals indicate more responding in the component of the Multiple schedule whose subcomponents terminated with the stimulus paired with the primary reinforcer.

experimental conditions were highly correlated. The figure also illustrates the reliable recovery of response rate differences maintained by the stimulus paired with the primary reinforcer and the stimulus not paired, as seen for both birds in the portions of the figure labeled *R*.

Experiment 1 demonstrated that pairing a stimulus with a primary reinforcer increased the rate of responses that produced the stimulus. In one arrangement of the schedule, with at least one bird, the conditioned reinforcer seemed to be as effective in maintaining performance as the primary reinforcer itself. Finally, another arrangement of the schedule demonstrated that merely the periodic response-contingent presentation of a stimulus not paired with the primary reinforcer was sufficient to maintain an animal's responding.

EXPERIMENT 2

Method

Experiment 2 followed the same sequence as Experiment 1 except that the Multiple schedule consisted of a different basic schedule. The basic schedule was FR 5 (DRL 10:W). With this schedule food reinforcement occurred following the completion of five consecutive DRL 10 components. The first response to occur after 10 sec of no responses in the presence of one letter on the key produced a 0.5-sec white illumination (W) of the food aperture, (DRL 10:W). In the second portion of the Multiple the first response to occur after 10 sec of no responses in the presence of a different letter on the key produced a 0.5-sec red illumination (R) of the food aperture, (DRL 10:R), in one procedure of the study; it produced no stimulus change, (DRL 10), in a second procedure; it produced a 3-sec access to grain, DRL 10, in the third procedure. When the fifth DRL component of each FR 5 sequence was completed grain was presented with the termination of the 0.5-sec white illumination of the food aperture. The food aperture was always illuminated by white light whenever food was presented both 0.5 sec before and during the food reinforcement cycle. (In this experiment the white and red illumination of the food aperture was reversed for the second animal.) A session was terminated after 36 primary reinforcers. The Multiple schedule components alternated every three primary reinforcers, and each of the different components had a correlated stimulus. The order of procedures and number of sessions in each procedure are shown in Table 3.2. The table shows that the original schedule was reinstated after each of the other schedules.

The first procedure (phrases A, C, and E in Table 3.2) compared responding when the paired stimulus (W) was contingent on the completion of a DRL component with responding when the un-

TABLE 3.2

Summary of Procedures for Experiment 2

Phase	Procedure (DRL in seconds)	Number of Sessions	Paired Stimulus Compared with:
A	MULT [FR 5 (DRL 10:W)] [TAND (FR 4 {DRL 10:R}) (FR 1 {DRL 10:W})]	36	Unpaired stimulus
B	MULT [FR 5 (DRL 10:W)] [TAND (FR 4 {DRL 10}) (FR 1 {DRL 10:W})]	32	No stimulus
C	MULT [FR 5 (DRL 10:W)] [as in A]	15	Unpaired stimulus
D	MULT [FR 5 (DRL 10:W)] [DRL 10]	40	Primary reinforcer
E	MULT [FR 5 (DRL 10:W)] [as in A]	14	Unpaired stimulus

paired stimulus (R) was produced on the completion of a DRL component. The difference in these stimuli was that the paired stimulus (W) always occurred 0.5 sec prior to and during food access whereas the unpaired stimulus (R) never accompanied food.

The second procedure (phase B in Table 3.2) allowed a comparison to be made between responding when the paired stimulus was contingent on completion of a DRL component and responding when no stimulus appeared at the end of a DRL component.

The third procedure (phase D in Table 3.2) allowed a comparison to be made between responding when the paired stimulus was presented at the completion of each DRL component and responding when the paired stimulus plus grain were presented at the completion of each DRL component. Food delivery occurred 15 times when the second unit of the Multiple schedule appeared in this procedure. Since food occurred so frequently here the food reinforcement cycle was reduced from 6 to 3 sec.

Results

In Experiment 2 the birds initially performed at very high rates, probably due to their history on other schedules, and therefore the schedule exerted little control. However, by the third week of this experiment, the rates for both animals had declined to about 10 responses per minute and they remained at about that level throughout the experiment.

There was very little variation in the rates of P–10 during the constant component of the Multiple schedule as seen in Figure 3.4. The abscissa indicates the sessions from which the data were obtained. The hatched bars represent the mean rates in the conditioned reinforcer portion and the unhatched bars represent the other component of the Multiple schedule: $X = RED$ indicates that the other component contained the unpaired (red) stimulus; $No\ X$ indicates that the other component had no stimulus appearing at the end of the DRL; and $X = REINF.$ indicates that in the other component food was produced on completion of each DRL. When the paired stimulus schedule was alternated with the unpaired stimulus schedule both animals always responded at higher rates in the paired stimulus component, as seen in this figure $(X = RED)$. Not seen in this figure was the fact that both birds also responded more and spent less time in the component with the paired stimulus than in the component with the unpaired stimulus.

Again, in the second procedure where no stimulus occurred at the end of the DRL $(No\ X)$, rates were higher in the component with the paired stimulus. Also, as in the former case, more responses occurred in that component, and less time was spent in it.

In the third procedure, where the effect of the paired stimulus was compared with that of the primary reinforcer itself $(X = REINF.)$, the primary reinforcer maintained higher rates. More responses were emitted in the portion of the session in which the primary reinforcer was scheduled but that portion also lasted longer. This could be an indication that the primary reinforcer actually exerted less control than did the paired stimulus on this schedule.

Figure 3.4 also shows that as the number of sessions increased the response rates in the conditioned and primary reinforcer portions of the Multiple schedule became less different. This also occurred in the case of the paired stimulus versus the unpaired stimulus.

It was difficult to discern differences in the cumulative records correlated with the different portions of the Multiple schedule after the animals had stabilized their responding in the DRL schedules. The rates were too low. However, observation of the cumulative records of one bird revealed initially higher rates and less time elapsed in the constant, paired-stimulus portion with a gradual decrease in rates as responding became stable. The other bird began

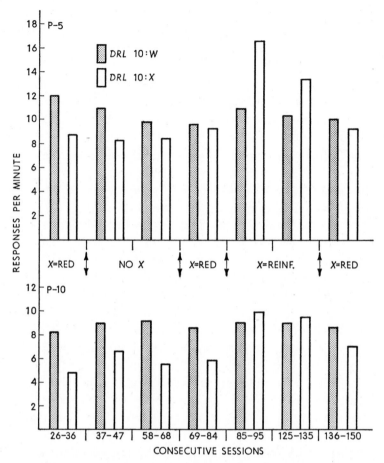

FIGURE 3.4. Mean response rates during each stimulus condition in the Multiple schedule in Experiment 2. The rates were obtained from the last 10 sessions and first 10 sessions under each condition except where otherwise indicated. (See text.)

with higher rates in the unpaired stimulus portion but by the fifth session there was a reversal and lower rates plus longer pauses after food appeared with the unpaired stimulus.

The cumulative records also revealed that when no exteroceptive stimulus appeared at the completion of a *DRL* longer pauses occurred after food. In fact, P–10 failed to respond in that condition after two alternations of the Multiple schedule during its first exposure to this procedure.

Rates were much higher initially in the condition where the

primary reinforcer was presented on the *DRL*, but gradually decreased in later sessions. The cumulative records of P–10 showed no consistent differences between the conditioned and primary reinforcer portions of the Multiple schedule.

The numbers of responses in consecutive *DRL* components tended to be lowest in the early parts of each *FR* 5 sequence and highest in the fourth and fifth components, especially under *FR* 5 (*DRL* 10:*W*). However, there was a great deal of variation as seen in Figure 3.5. The figure illustrates the mean number of responses

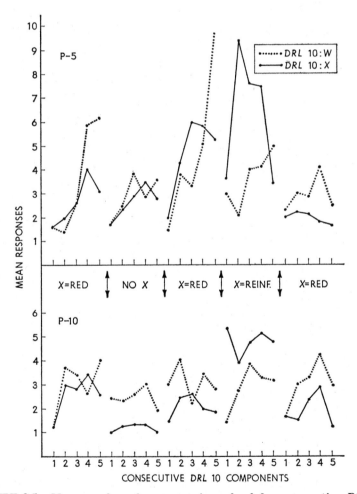

FIGURE 3.5. Mean number of responses in each of five consecutive *DRL* 10 components of representative sessions within each of the conditions of Experiment 2. (See text.)

occurring during *FR* 5 sequences of *DRL* components in sessions typical of the respective procedures. An *FR* 5 sequence of *DRL* components always terminated with the primary reinforcer. The dotted lines represent performance in the schedule with the paired stimulus and the solid line represents performance in the other schedules. The average curves seen in Figure 3.5 show greater acceleration from the first to the fifth *DRL* component than normally seen in an individual curve obtained from a single *FR* 5 (*DRL* 10) sequence. During the sessions in which an unpaired stimulus was scheduled on a *DRL* (*X* = *RED* in Figure 3.5) no consistent trend differences are seen. This was also true when no exteroceptive stimulus occurred (*NO X*). However, when food was presented at the completion of a *DRL* (*X* = *REINF.*) responding occurred at a fairly stable rate for P–10 and increased during the middle consecutive *DRL* components for P–5. These results seem to support the contention that the *DRL* 10 functioned in much the same way as other unitary responses reinforced on *FR* 5. There were exceptions, but in general the first *DRL* 10 component was preceded by a long post-reinforcement pause, which led to an average of approximately one to two responses in the initial component. Rates increased as the terminal *DRL* component and hence the primary reinforcer approached. This increment in rate disrupted *DRL* performance. Occasionally, rates showed some decrease in the fifth *DRL* component. The conclusion, then, is that due to the fixed number of *DRL* components and the 10-sec contingency of the *DRL*, the schedule had strong *FI* properties, as demonstrated by the accelerated rates from one primary reinforcer to another. This effect was less strong for P–10, but nevertheless it still existed. If the *DRL* requirements had been 1 second instead of 10, perhaps responding would have been more similar to typical *FR* 5 behavior. The *DRL* schedule used in this experiment actually was a poor device for discovering differences in the stimulus effects. Results tend to support the assumption, however, that it is responding and not pausing on a *DRL* that is controlled by the reinforcer. In almost all conditions response rates were higher when the paired stimulus or the primary reinforcer was contingent on completion of the *DRL*. If pausing was mainly under control of the reinforcer, then the rates should have been lower when the paired stimulus or primary reinforcers were presented.

DISCUSSION

The experiments in this chapter illustrate that pairing a brief stimulus with a primary reinforcer made the brief stimulus a conditioned reinforcer, enhancing its ability to sustain and control patterns of responding; that this ability waned if the stimulus was not paired; that Multiple schedules were effective means of comparing conditioned reinforcers with other stimuli; and that *DRL* schedules were relatively insensitive to the differences between conditioned reinforcers and other stimuli.

Although the results of this investigation may have been somewhat attenuated by the fact that the second-order schedules used were Chain schedules, several investigations support the outcome of this study (De Lorge, 1967; Thomas & Stubbs, 1966; Zimmerman & Hanford, 1966).

More questions have been raised than answered. It would be interesting to know why unpaired stimuli are as effective in sustaining behavior as they are. For example, Kelleher (1966b) found an unpaired stimulus to be an effective reinforcer for *FI* patterns of responding. Is this effect really due to the past experimental histories of the animals or is it due to the Chain schedule itself? Do the stimuli presented at the end of unitary responses in a second-order schedule acquire the character of a "count" or "tally?" It would also be interesting to discover if conditioned reinforcers always increase rates of responding regardless of the schedule when compared to other stimuli. Finally, if pairing a stimulus with a primary reinforcer is a sufficient method of producing a conditioned reinforcer then to what order can higher order conditioned reinforcers be obtained?

SUMMARY

Pairing a brief stimulus with primary reinforcement enhanced the effectiveness of the stimulus in reinforcing patterns of responding. The effects of a stimulus paired with primary reinforcement in one component of a Multiple schedule were compared in the other component with the effects of various response-produced stimulus conditions: namely, a neutral (unpaired) stimulus, no stimulus at all, and the primary reinforcer. The paired stimulus led to more responses per session than the unpaired stimulus, the same or fewer than no stimulus at all, and the same or fewer than the primary reinforcer. Multiple schedules with *FI* components proved to be effective means of comparing conditioned reinforcers with other stimuli, while Multiple schedules with *DRL* components were relatively insensitive to the differences between stimuli.

MAINTENANCE OF BEHAVIOR BY CONDITIONED REINFORCEMENT IN THE SIGNALED ABSENCE OF PRIMARY REINFORCEMENT[1]

John R. Thomas

University of Chicago

Recent research on positive conditioned reinforcement has suggested that the conditioned reinforcing function of a stimulus is directly related to the frequency of primary reinforcement with which that stimulus is associated (cf., Herrnstein, 1964a; Kelleher, 1966a; Kelleher & Gollub, 1962). However, the manner of associating stimuli with primary reinforcement and of introducing them in reinforcement schedules may be as important as frequency of primary reinforcement (cf., Kelleher, 1966a). Brief response-produced presentations of exteroceptive stimuli intermittently associated with primary reinforcement may enhance response rates in second-order and Concurrent schedules when the rate enhancement actually decreases the overall rate of primary reinforcement (Randolph, Thomas, & Sewell, in press; Thomas & Stubbs, 1967). Such brief stimulus presentations can also maintain responding for considerable time periods in the complete absence of primary reinforcement (Zimmerman & Hanford, 1967a).

A series of experiments is presented in which small fixed-ratio schedule requirements generated responding that was maintained by positive conditioned reinforcement in circumstances in which the maintenance of such behavior either decreased the rate of primary reinforcement or in which the fixed-ratio behavior was

---

[1] The research was supported by Grant NsG-450, National Aeronautics and Space Administration and conducted at the Institute for Behavioral Research.

maintained in the signaled absence of direct association with primary reinforcement.

In the following experiments, adult male white Carneaux pigeons maintained at approximately 80 percent of their undeprived weights performed in a standard single-key pigeon chamber (Ferster & Skinner, 1957). The response key used was designed for use with an In-Line Digital Display Unit (Ferster, Holtzman, & Leckrone, 1962). A feedback relay located behind the response key wall always operated with each recorded response. The chamber was illuminated during an experimental session by two houselights located on the top left and right corners of the response key wall. Directly below the response key a 2 inch by 2 inch feeder opening gave access to the grain hopper (Lehigh Valley Electronics) which could be raised into place to present the grain reinforcer.

Daily experimental sessions terminated after 50, 4-sec presentations of mixed grain. The key light and houselights went off simultaneously with the 4-sec operation of the grain feeder and illumination of the grain feeder light. Each session was preceded and followed by a blackout condition, variable in duration, during which all lights in the experimental chamber were off and responses had no programmed consequences.

The subjects initially performed on a two-component Multiple schedule. When a triangle was projected on the display unit, every 60th response (FR 60) produced grain reinforcement. When green light was projected on the unit, grain reinforcement was presented every 30 sec if no responses occurred on the response key (DRO 30). Each response during the DRO component reset the 30-sec grain presentation interval. The two components alternated every 2.75 min. Figure 4.1 shows an example of the performance on the MULT FR 60 DRO 30 sec base line for one subject. Behavior appropriate to the FR contingency occurred during the FR component and there was essentially no responding during the DRO component.

The Multiple schedule was changed such that every 10th response (FR 10) during the DRO component concurrently produced a brief presentation of the stimuli associated with grain reinforcement as well as reset the 30-sec DRO interval. The brief stimulus presentation consisted of a 0.3-sec operation of the feeder. The 0.3-sec operation allowed the feeder solenoid to be engaged but was not long enough to allow the hopper to swing up to the hole in the bottom of the reinforcement chamber. The hopper of the grain feeder was kept filled to ensure that the hopper was heavy enough not to swing up all the way during the brief operation. The brief operation of the solenoid presented the auditory stimuli associated with grain reinforcement without allowing access to grain. The key

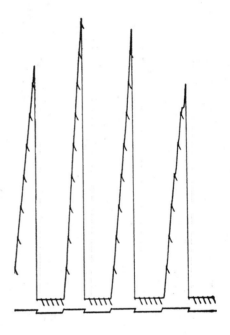

FIGURE 4.1.   Cumulative   response record of performance on MULT *FR* 60 *DRO* 30 schedule. Excursions of the recording pen while the event pen is up indicate performance on the *FR* 60 component and the segments while the event pen is down show performance on the *DRO* 30. Pips of the recording pen indicate the primary reinforcer.

light and houselights were turned off and the feeder light was illuminated for the 0.3 sec which presented the visual stimuli associated with the grain reinforcement.

When the *FR* 10 contingency was programmed during the *DRO* component, responding occurred in the component and often ratio-like performances were observed. Examples of the terminal performances with the *FR* 10 contingency programmed concurrently with the *DRO* are shown in Figure 4.2. Performance during the *DRO* component may be characterized by the types of variability in responding. At times the entire duration of the *DRO* component involved high rates of responding with no primary reinforcements as seen in the excursion labeled *B* in Figure 4.2. At other times the *DRO* contingency predominated as at *C* and *D;* no responses occurred and all primary reinforcers programmed were delivered.

Often, responding appropriate to both the *FR* and *DRO* contingencies could be observed during a *DRO* component, as in the excursion labeled *A*. In general, high response rates during the *DRO* component occurred infrequently, but were observed often enough to indicate control over responding by the *FR* 10 schedule of brief stimulus presentations. The most frequently observed behavior was a mixture appropriate to the two contingencies with some respond-

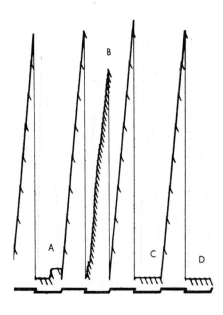

FIGURE 4.2. Performance on MULT *FR* 60 *DRO* 30 schedule with *FR* 10 contingency of conditioned reinforcement programmed concurrently with the *DRO* component. Event pen indications are identical to Figure 4.1. Pips of the recording pen during the *DRO* component indicate the primary reinforcer if no responses have occurred for 30 sec or the conditioned reinforcer if 10 responses have occurred.

ing throughout the component. There was enough responding maintained by the *FR* 10 contingency to reduce the overall primary reinforcement frequency during the *DRO* component from about 1.8 reinforcements per minute without the concurrent *FR* 10 schedule to about 0.7 reinforcements per minute with the concurrent schedule.

Following the above program of concurrent scheduling, the schedule that alternated with the *FR* 60 grain reinforcement schedule was changed to Extinction. While green light was projected on the display unit, responses had no programmed consequences. Responding rapidly declined during the green light component suggesting that responding during that component previously was due to the brief stimulus presentations.

The response requirement for grain reinforcement was increased from *FR* 60 to *FR* 120. The *FR* 120 component and the Extinction component of the Multiple schedule now alternated every 4 minutes. Performance on this schedule is shown in Figure 4.3. Discriminative control by the stimuli associated with each of the two components is indicated. Brief presentations of a neutral stimulus

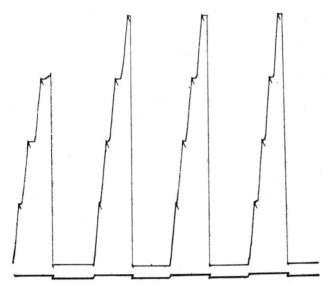

FIGURE 4.3. Cumulative response record of performance on MULT *FR* 120 EXT. The event pen is up during the *FR* 120 component and down during the Extinction component.

were then programmed according to various fixed-ratio schedules from *FR* 1 to *FR* 10 in the Extinction component. The neutral stimulus consisted of a 0.3-sec projection on the display unit of a red light. The ratio requirements for the neutral stimuli had no observable effects on the Multiple base line and the behavior looked essentially like that in Figure 4.3. The program was then changed so that the visual and auditory stimuli associated with grain reinforcement were again presented on a *FR* 10 schedule during the green light component. An example of the type of performance observed on the Multiple *FR* 120 (primary reinforcement) *FR* 10 (brief stimulus presentation) schedule is shown in Figure 4.4. The performance on the *FR* 120 schedule was essentially that observed without the brief stimulus presentations in the other component, although overall response rates were somewhat lower. The behavior during the *FR* 10 component consisted of relatively high response rates that often changed to periods of no responding. The behavior was appropriate to a small *FR* schedule and was quite similar to the types of behavior seen with small ratio requirements for primary

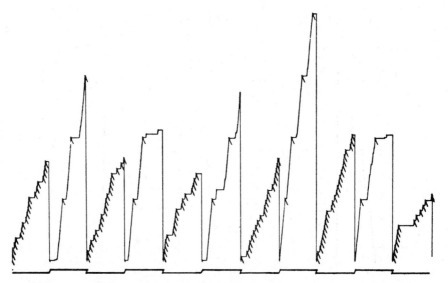

FIGURE 4.4.   Performance on MULT *FR* 120 *FR* 10, where *FR* 120 is a schedule of primary reinforcement and *FR* 10 is a schedule of conditioned reinforcement. Pips of the recording pen indicate primary reinforcements when the event pen is up and conditioned reinforcement when the event pen is down.

reinforcement. The pauses which occurred during the *FR* 10 component were almost exclusively pre-ratio pauses. The behavior indicated that the briefly presented stimuli, when programmed on a small ratio schedule, generated responding that was appropriate to the schedule. As the unpaired stimulus had no effects, it appears that a response-produced brief stimulus presentation must be associated with primary reinforcement in order to have these effects of maintaining behavior. The stimuli were capable of maintaining responding for a considerable time during a discriminated Multiple schedule component that did not include primary reinforcement. Such behavior has been maintained under several Multiple base-line procedures in our laboratories for extended periods when primary reinforcement was not associated with those components. Similar results have been obtained in other laboratories (Zimmerman & Hanford, 1967a).

Previous base lines have shown that the small ratio requirement could not be maintained under Extinction alone or by brief presentations of a neutral stimulus not directly associated with primary reinforcement. As it was possible that the behavior during the brief stimulus component might be chained to and maintained by the production of the fixed-ratio component associated with primary reinforcement, a 5-min blackout condition during which all lights in the experimental chamber were off was introduced between the two alternating components. This made the program a three-component Multiple schedule, with the 5-min blackout component following both the FR 120 component and the FR 10 component. The introduction of the blackout condition between the two alternating components had no effect upon the behavior during the FR 10 component. Performances were similar to those shown in Figure 4.4. It does not appear that the behavior during the FR 10 component was in any way maintained by the production of the FR 120 component associated with primary reinforcement. The blackout component remained in the Multiple schedule for the rest of the procedures to be described, except where indicated.

The FR 120 requirement for grain reinforcement was then reduced to FR 80 for a number of sessions. The FR 10 requirement for the brief stimulus presentations was removed from the green light component for a number of sessions (Extinction). Responding declined and a near zero rate of responding was obtained in the green light component. Figure 4.5 shows a segment of a session for the MULT FR 80 EXT. The FR 10 requirement for the brief stimulus presentations was then reintroduced into the green light (Extinction) component. The previous high response rates in the green light component were immediately reinstated by presenting the stimuli associated with grain reinforcement briefly several times at the onset of a component. The type of performance reinstated and maintained is shown in Figure 4.6. There was very little pausing during the green component and that pausing which did occur was almost always a pre-ratio pause.

The FR 10 requirement for the brief stimulus presentations was increased for one subject to FR 30 for a number of sessions and then returned to the FR 10. The performance on the FR 30 schedule indicated much weaker control by the conditioned reinforcers than on the *FR* 10 schedule and the overall response rates were lower. Figure 4.7 shows performances on the MULT *FR* 80 *FR* 30 schedule. During some of the green light components, severe ratio straining was evident and little or no responding occurred. The pre-ratio pausing was more extended and often multiple pausing occurred within a ratio. When the ratio requirement was returned to *FR* 10,

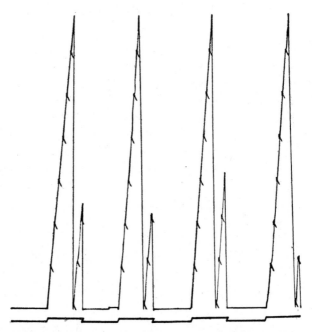

FIGURE 4.5. Cumulative response record of performance on MULT *FR* 80 EXT. The event pen is up during the *FR* 120 component and down during the Extinction component.

the performances during that component were much like those shown in Figure 4.6.

The *FR* 80 grain reinforcement component was then completely removed from the Multiple schedule. The *FR* 10 brief stimulus component alone alternated with the 5-minute blackout component. Performance on the *FR* 10 brief stimulus component alone is shown for one subject in Figure 4.8. The behavior was extremely variable and often was absent during a component. When responding did occur, it was similar to the responding in the brief stimulus components seen previously, with response rates and patterns of responding appropriate to the small fixed ratio requirement. This type of

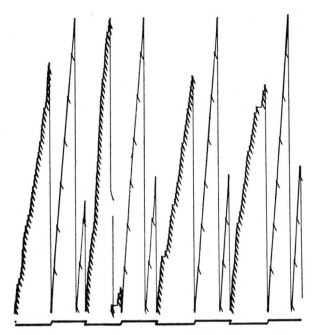

FIGURE 4.6. Performance on MULT *FR* 80 *FR* 10, where *FR* 80 is a schedule of primary reinforcement and *FR* 10 is a schedule of conditioned reinforcement. Event pen indications are identical to Figure 4.4

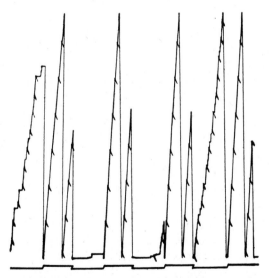

FIGURE 4.7. Performance on MULT *FR* 80 *FR* 30, where *FR* 80 is a schedule of primary reinforcement and *FR* 30 is a schedule of conditioned reinforcement. Event pen indications are identical to Figure 4.4.

behavior, in the complete absence of primary reinforcement, was maintained for over 20 sessions. No significant decline in behavior was observed over this time period. During components when responding did occur, it was always much like that shown in Figure 4.8. The maintenance of behavior over an extended number of sessions without primary reinforcements by brief presentations of

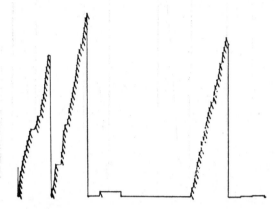

FIGURE 4.8. Cumulative response record of performance on *FR* 10 schedule of conditioned reinforcement alone. The *FR* 10 component alternated with a 5-min blackout period. The recorder paper drive did not run during the blackout components.

stimuli that had been associated with primary reinforcement has been demonstrated previously (Zimmerman & Hanford, 1967a).

The *FR* 80 component of the Multiple schedule was reinstated. Performances during the brief stimulus component, almost 60 sessions following the reinstatement of the *FR* 80 grain reinforcement component, are shown in Figure 4.9. This figure shows responding in the brief stimulus component for the last 13 occurrences of the component obtained during the last two sessions. Only the brief stimulus components are shown and the number below each component indicates the actual order in which it appeared. The behavior is characterized by a wide range of variability. During some components performance consists of little responding and excessive pausing. Although variable, behavior was maintained in the brief stimulus components over the extended number of sessions.

The brief stimuli intermittently associated with grain reinforcement were replaced with unpaired stimulus which consisted of a

1-sec presentation on the display unit of a red light. The *FR* 80 requirement for grain reinforcement remained in effect. Responding in the brief stimulus component soon declined to near zero rates, replicating the previous results with the unpaired stimulus. The program was then changed such that the red light was also presented 1 sec before as well as during the 4-sec grain reinforce-

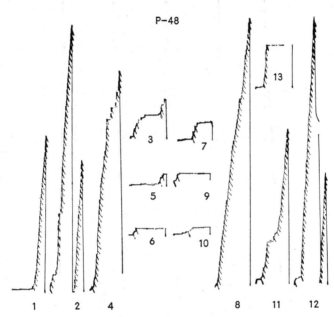

FIGURE 4.9. Performance maintained by *FR* 10 schedule of conditioned reinforcement. Only the conditioned reinforcement components are shown and the number below each indicates the order in which they were obtained.

ment cycle, associating the red light with primary reinforcement. Responding on the *FR* 10 schedule in the brief stimulus component was established and maintained under this procedure and was quite similar to the responding maintained previously by the other brief stimuli. Figure 4.10 shows performance on the schedule.

When the red light was no longer associated with grain reinforcement in the *FR* 80 component, responding declined in the brief stimulus component.

The subjects were again returned to the MULT *FR* 80 *FR* 10 base line. Then the ratio requirement was removed from the brief stimulus component, and instead 0.3-sec presentations of the stimuli associated with grain reinforcement were presented independently of behavior at the average rate at which the subjects had produced the stimuli by performing on the *FR* 10 schedule. The procedure investigated whether the occurrence of the behavior in

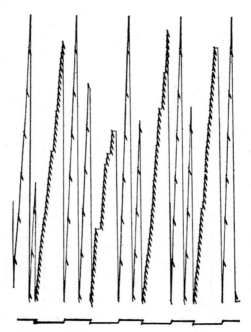

FIGURE 4.10.   Performance on MULT *FR* 80 *FR* 10, where *FR* 80 is a schedule of primary reinforcement and *FR* 10 is a schedule of conditioned reinforcement. Conditioned reinforcement during the *FR* 10 component was a 1-sec presentation of a red light which was also associated with the occurrence of the primary reinforcement.

the brief stimulus component was due to discriminative stimulus effects. Each brief stimulus presentation may have set the occasion for subsequent responding and may have been responsible for the maintenance of responding (Spradlin, Girardeau, & Hom, 1966). When the stimuli were presented independently of behavior, responding declined in the brief stimulus components. Performance on the Multiple schedule when the brief stimuli were presented independently of behavior is shown in Figure 4.11. Some minimal behavior still occurred, however, during the brief stimulus components, indicating that the stimuli did have some discriminative control of the behavior in the brief stimulus component.

In order to assure that the ratio behavior during the brief stimu-

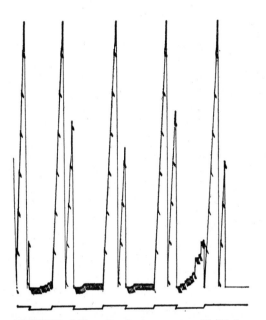

FIGURE 4.11.   Performance on Multiple schedule when the conditioned reinforcement was presented independently of behavior during the conditioned reinforcement components of the Multiple schedule.

lus components was not in any way due to induction from the ratio behavior maintained by primary reinforcement, the schedule in the primary reinforcement component was changed from fixed ratio to DRO. Grain reinforcement was presented every 20 sec if no responses occurred on the response key (DRO 20) during the primary reinforcement components. The brief presentations of stimuli associated with primary reinforcement were presented on a FR 10 schedule. Figure 4.12 shows terminal performance on this schedule. The fixed-ratio behavior maintained during the brief stimulus components was identical to that maintained previously when it alternated with a fixed-ratio schedule of primary reinforcement.

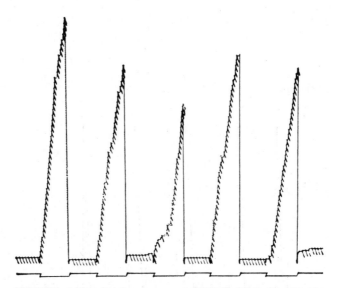

FIGURE 4.12. Performance on MULT *DRO* 20 *FR* 10, where *DRO* 20 is a schedule of primary reinforcement and *FR* 10 is a schedule of conditioned reinforcement.

SUMMARY

The series of experiments demonstrates that substantial behavior can be maintained in a Multiple schedule component that provides for no primary reinforcement. The maintenance of the fixed-ratio behavior indicates that the brief exteroceptive stimuli associated intermittently with primary reinforcement functioned as effective positive conditioned reinforcers. These effects were separated from those of unpaired stimuli as well as from discriminative aspects of the stimuli. In accord with recent literature, the present experiments suggest that in order to develop an effective conditioned reinforcer, association with primary reinforcement is all that is needed; the conditioned reinforcing stimulus does not have to be a discriminative stimulus. The present experiments show that conditioned reinforcing stimuli, in the signaled absence of primary reinforcement, can exert powerful control over behavior for extended time periods.

chapter 5

MEANWHILE . . . BACK AT THE KEY: MAINTENANCE OF BEHAVIOR BY CONDITIONED REINFORCEMENT AND RESPONSE-INDEPENDENT PRIMARY REINFORCEMENT[1]

J. Zimmerman

Indiana University School of Medicine

INTRODUCTION

A method of sustaining pecking in pigeons with conditioned reinforcement was described by this author in 1963 (Zimmerman, 1963). Concurrent but independent schedules of primary and conditioned reinforcement were programmed in a two-key experimental situation. Left-key responses intermittently produced access to grain while concurrently, right-key responses intermittently produced brief presentation of the set of stimuli which accompanied grain (0.50-sec magazine cycle). Under these conditions, Concurrent performances were differentially maintained. Grain-key rates were 5 to 20 times as high as rates generated on the right key. The lower rate, right-key performances were sustained indefinitely, however, and rates and patterns of this responding were appropriate to the particular schedule in effect on the right key.

Subsequent work in this laboratory showed that several related Concurrent procedures could similarly be employed to sustain performance with the 0.50-sec magazine cycle. Consequently, several studies were conducted in order to determine whether factors other

---

[1] These investigations were supported, in part, by Research Grant MH 10741 from the National Institute of Mental Health.

than the conditioned reinforcing function of the 0.50-sec magazine cycle could account for the observed long-term maintenance of behavior.

The possible contribution of infrequent magazine failures (which could have provided occasional, unprogrammed access to grain during or following the 0.50-sec magazine cycle) was both assessed and eliminated by the apparatus modification described by Leckrone, Zimmerman, and Hanford (1966). The aperture providing access to grain was covered with a transparent shutter. The shutter was displaced only when grain reinforcement was programmed. Following the introduction of the modified magazines (which have since been employed in all our work), the behaviors of subjects which had been performing in several different Concurrent schedule studies were not markedly altered and experimental results which had previously been obtained were successfully replicated.

Zimmerman and Hanford (1967a) examined the possible contribution of accidental grain reinforcement and of reinforcement by stimulus change, per se, to the long-term maintenance of right-key performance in the two-key situation. Employing experimental conditions similar to those of the 1963 study, these investigators found that right-key responding was sustained indefinitely as long as it intermittently produced the 0.50-sec magazine cycle (with the shutter in its resting, closed position). This performance was sustained in spite of the fact that each response postponed grain, if due, for 4 sec. In contrast, right-key performance was markedly weakened or extinguished whenever the 0.50-sec magazine cycles were removed, or replaced with 0.50-sec presentations of a set of novel (visual and auditory) stimuli never paired with grain. Therefore, the sustained right-key performance could be accounted for only on the basis of the conditioned reinforcing power of the 0.50-sec magazine cycle.

In the above study, Zimmerman and Hanford also observed that although each Concurrent performance was readily and appropriately influenced by the removal of its own response-produced consequences, (a) grain performance was not influenced by the manipulation of conditioned reinforcement, and (b) performance which produced conditioned reinforcement was less influenced by grain manipulation than by the manipulation of its own consequences. Indeed, after grain was completely removed and as long as it remained absent, two of four participating birds emitted right-key responding at rates which were only slightly lower than those previously generated with grain present. This behavior persisted long after concurrent performance on the grain key had extinguished. It persisted in one of the birds for periods of 13 and 23 days, respectively, over two separate exposures to the removal of grain. During its 23-day exposure to grain removal, a Multiple schedule of conditioned reinforcement and novel stimuli reinforcement was programmed on the right key and performance persisted only in the conditioned-reinforcement component. Similar results were obtained with the other bird over its single 44-day exposure to grain removal.

Zimmerman and Hanford (1966) described a related Concurrent schedule procedure which offers considerable promise as a tool for studying conditioned reinforcement effects. This procedure made use of only one key and the only immediate exteroceptive consequence of pecking was the intermittent production of conditioned reinforcement (the 0.50-sec magazine cycle with the shutter in its closed position). As with the two-key procedure, grain was intermittently available on a Concurrent but independent schedule. In contrast to the two-key procedure, however, grain was not produced by pecking, but instead delivered freely when scheduled. Zimmerman and Hanford (1966) observed that this one-key Concurrent schedule procedure sustained pecking indefinitely at rates of 3 to 8 responses per minute even though each peck postponed grain, if due, for 6 sec. This performance markedly weakened or extinguished whenever the conditioned reinforcer was removed or replaced with the set of novel stimuli. Zimmerman, Hanford, and Brown (1967) used this procedure to examine the effects of varying the scheduled frequency of conditioned reinforcement in one component of a two-component Multiple schedule. Rate of responding varied directly with conditioned-reinforcement frequency. Contrast effects (cf., Reynolds, 1961a) in the constant component were also observed. These results were strikingly similar (qualitatively) to those obtained in analogous Multiple schedules of primary reinforcement (cf., Ferster & Skinner, 1957; Nevin & Shettleworth, 1966).

Results obtained and characteristics of performance generated with the one-key procedure as a result of (a) programming different schedules of conditioned reinforcement, (b) varying the frequency of free grain presentation, and (c) removing grain from the experimental situation for extended numbers of sessions will be described here.

EXPERIMENT 1

Zimmerman (1963) showed that rates and patterns of responding on a key which produced conditioned reinforcement were appropriate to the particular schedule of conditioned reinforcement whether the schedule was fixed ratio, variable interval, or extinction. These results were obtained under conditions in which pecking at a second key intermittently produced primary reinforcement. They were also qualitatively similar to those obtained by Kelleher (1961) under conditions in which primary reinforcement was removed from the experimental situation. The present experiment examined the effects of programming conditioned reinforcement on different schedules under conditions in which a primary reinforcer was presented freely on an intermittent basis.

Procedure

Three adult, male, White Carneaux pigeons served as subjects. One (P–28B) served previously in the Zimmerman and Hanford (1966) study. One (P–23B) served previously in the Zimmerman, Hanford and Brown (1967) study. One (P–40B) served previously in both of those studies. Each of the birds was maintained at 80 percent of its undeprived weight and performed daily in the one-key box used in those two previous studies. Grain was automatically presented at variable intervals averaging 3 min. As in those studies, two-component Multiple schedules of conditioned reinforcement were programmed on the key. A blue light and a yellow light were projected on the key during the first and second components, respectively. The two components alternated every 24 min. A daily session was terminated after a bird was exposed twice to each component. A 1-min variable-interval (VI 1) schedule of conditioned reinforcement (0.50-sec magazine cycle with the shutter closed), was programmed in the second component throughout the study. In contrast, the schedule of conditioned reinforcement associated with the first component was varied. In that component, conditioned reinforcement was programmed on either a *VI* 1, *FR* 5, *DRL* 40, or *DRL* 60 schedule.

Each subject was exposed to a given Multiple schedule of conditioned reinforcement until rates in each component stabilized (no consistent trend observed) for four successive sessions. Table 5.1

TABLE 5.1

Multiple Schedules of Conditioned Reinforcement

Component		Number of Sessions		
1(X)*	*2(F)†*	*23B*	*28B*	*40B*
VI 1	*VI* 1	5	6	7
FR 5	*VI* 1	13	7	10
VI 1	*VI* 1	5	6	7
DRL 40	*VI* 1	17	11	18
DRL 60	*VI* 1	11	10	11
DRL 40	*VI* 1	8	9	7
FR 5	*VI* 1	12	12	13
VI 1	*VI* 1	11	11	9

* (*X*)—variable component.
† (*F*)—fixed or constant component.

presents the order and nature of each of the Multiple schedules together with the number of sessions for which each bird was exposed to each schedule.

The feeding procedure employed in the Zimmerman, Hanford and Brown (1967) study was employed throughout this study and was, therefore, common to each of the Multiple schedules of conditioned reinforcement. More specifically, 4-sec access to grain was presented intermittently via a 3-min variable-interval tape. To minimize the possibility of accidental grain reinforcement of key-pecking, grain made available by the tape was not presented unless or until no peck had occurred for at least 6 sec.

Results

Figure 5.1 summarizes the response rates obtained with each bird over the course of the study. Each open bar presents the median variable-component response rate (*X*), in responses per minute, based on the last five sessions of exposure to the Multiple schedule indicated on the abscissa. The adjacent closed bar presents the corresponding constant-component rates (*F*). Figure 5.1 shows that the behavioral effects of changing the X-component schedule were similar for all birds. Rates increased markedly each time the FR 5 schedule was introduced and remained elevated as long as this schedule was in effect. Rates decreased each time the FR 5 schedule was replaced with the VI 1 schedule. In addition, X-component rates (a) decreased when the DRL 40-sec. schedule replaced the VI schedule, (b) decreased further when the DRL value was increased from 40 to 60 sec, and (c) increased when the DRL value was

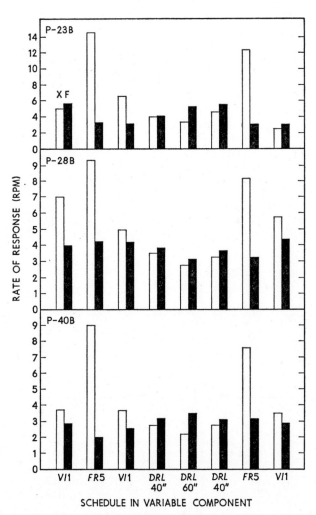

FIGURE 5.1. Response rates in each component of each Multiple schedule. Open bars and immediately adjacent closed bars present rates in the variable component (X) and constant (F) component, respectively.

decreased from 60 to 40 sec. Figure 5.1 also shows that F-component rates often increased or decreased following a change in the X-component schedule. Such changes in F-component rates were usually small in magnitude compared to X-component rate changes, however, and inconsistent in direction across birds.

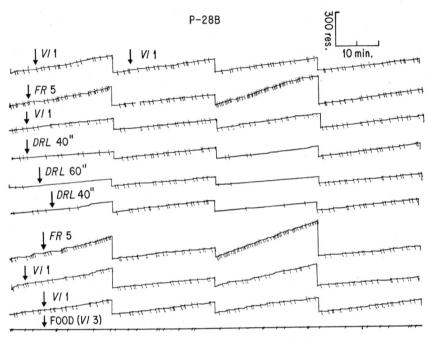

FIGURE 5.2. Cumulative response records of performance for P–28B under each of the multiple schedules arranged from top to bottom in order of exposure. Response pen resets at the termination of a component. Cumulative record pips indicate conditioned reinforcement. Bottom event line pips indicate grain presentation during the session from which the record immediately above was taken.

Representative results of Experiment 1 are further illustrated by the cumulative records presented in Figure 5.2 for P–28B. All but one of the records represent the performance for the entire last session or next to last session under the indicated Multiple schedule. The second record from the bottom shows performance in the first session which followed the final replacement of the FR 5 schedule with the VI 1 schedule. The bottom line is the event pen record which indicates the free presentation of grain during the session. Differential schedule control which developed under the MULT FR 5 VI 1 schedule is illustrated by the second and seventh records.

These show that rate and pattern of responding are appropriate to the schedule of conditioned reinforcement programmed in each component. The low, steady rate performances generated in the *F*-components were similar to those which were generated by the *VI* 1 schedule throughout the study. In contrast, the *FR* 5 schedule generated higher response rates and performances which were characterized by post-reinforcement pauses of variable duration, and fixed-ratio runs. A clear illustration of schedule effects is provided in the second record from the bottom. *X*-component performances in the session which immediately followed the removal of the *FR* 5 schedule show many instances of ratiolike bursts of responding. In contrast, such bursts are not seen in the corresponding *F*-component performances. The bottom cumulative record presents performance in the final MULT *VI* 1 *VI* 1 session. This record shows that performance in the final session of the study (the seventh session after the final removal of the *FR* 5 schedule) is similar to performance generated in earlier exposures to the MULT *VI* 1 *VI* 1 schedule, but infrequent instances of ratiolike bursts of responding are still in evidence in the second components. Finally, the three middle cumulative records show final performances generated under the *DRL* schedules. These records show that the *DRL* schedules generate performances which are not markedly different from those generated under the *VI* 1 schedule. The *DRL* schedules maintain responding at steady rates which are, however, slightly lower than the *F*-component (*VI* 1) rates. Also, occasional instances of short bursts of responding and locally higher rates are in evidence in the *DRL* components, as are occasional periods of extremely low rates. During these infrequent latter periods each of two or three successive responses are spaced widely enough in time to meet the interresponse-time contingency and produce conditioned reinforcement. The relatively low conditioned reinforcement frequencies under the *DRL* schedules (see Table 5.2 below) were a consequence of the maintenance of responding at low, steady rates rather than a result of the subject's failure to respond at all.

Qualitatively similar cumulative records were obtained for P–23B and P–40B throughout the study. Figure 5.3, for example, presents records obtained for each of these birds in the final MULT *FR* 5 *VI* 1 session of the study and in the initial MULT *VI* 1 *VI* 1 session which immediately followed. The differential schedule effects shown in these records are similar to those shown previously in the corresponding records of P–28B (second and third records from the bottom in Figure 5.2).

After the present study had been in progress for several weeks, the frequency of interresponse times (*IRTs*), in 10-sec *IRT* intervals, was recorded in each component. Figure 5.4 presents the relative frequency distributions of variable-component *IRTs* generated under each of the last five Multiple schedules to which P–28B was exposed. Each bar presents the median relative frequency in the indicated *IRT* interval (bin) based upon the final five sessions

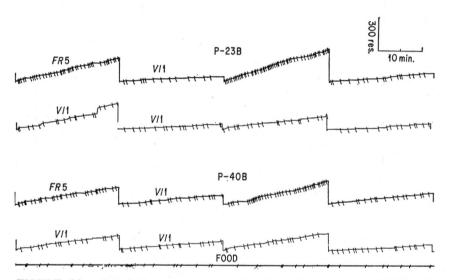

FIGURE 5.3.   Cumulative response records of performance for P–23B and P–40B in the final MULT *FR* 5 *VI* 1 session and in the MULT *VI* 1 *VI* 1 session which immediately followed.

under the indicated schedule. Adjacent bars in a given bin are presented from left to right in the order of exposure to the schedules. Figure 5.4 permits a within-bin comparison of relative frequencies generated by the various schedules. The relative frequency distribution generated under a given schedule can be seen by comparing like bars across bins. Figure 5.4 shows that the peak of each distribution except the *FR* 5 distribution occurred in the second bin. In contrast to all others, the *FR* 5 distribution is shifted toward shorter time intervals and has a marked peak in the first bin. Figure 5.4 also shows that in comparison with the *VI* 1 distribution, each of the *DRL* distributions is shifted to the right. Finally, the *DRL* 60 distribution is shifted to the right of both the *DRL* 40 distributions. This last result is most evident in the first, fourth, and fifth bins. Similar results were obtained with each of the other two birds.

Similar comparisons of the fixed-component *VI* 1 distributions showed that these were not markedly or consistently influenced by

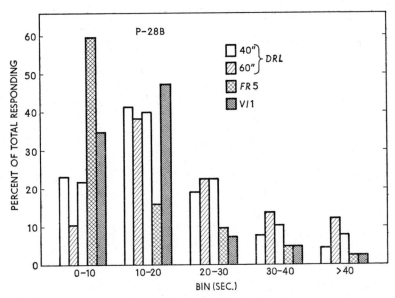

FIGURE 5.4. Relative frequency distributions of variable-component *IRT*s for the last five Multiple schedules to which P–28B was exposed, namely, MULT *VI* 1 *DRL* 40, MULT *VI* 1 *DRL* 60, MULT *VI* 1 *DRL* 40, MULT *VI* 1 *FR* 5, MULT *VI* 1 *VI* 1. Adjacent bars in a given 10-sec *IRT* interval (bin) are presented from left to right in order of exposure to the indicated schedules. A distribution generated under a given schedule can be seen by comparing like bars across bins.

changes in the variable-component schedule. For example, Figure 5.5 presents both variable-component and corresponding constant-component distributions generated under each of the last six schedules to which P–40B was exposed. The relative temporal positions of the various variable-component distributions are qualitatively similar to those which obtain for P–28B in Figure 5.4. The upper portion of Figure 5.5 shows that the corresponding constant-component distributions are, in contrast, strikingly similar to each other. Thus, a comparison of the variable and constant distributions presented in Figure 5.5 shows little evidence of an *IRT* induc-

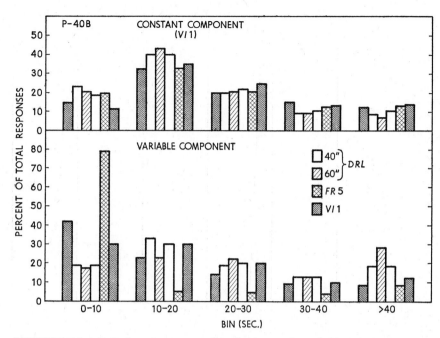

FIGURE 5.5.   Relative frequency distributions of variable- and constant-component *IRT*s for the last six Multiple schedules to which P–40B was exposed, namely, MULT *VI* 1 *VI* 1, MULT *VI* 1 *DRL* 40, MULT *VI* 1 *DRL* 60, MULT *VI* 1 *DRL* 40, MULT *VI* 1 *FR* 5, MULT *VI* 1 *VI* 1. See Figure 5.4.

tion from variable-components to constant-components. This last point is further illustrated by the sets of four distributions presented for each bird in Figure 5.6. The pair of distributions presented for each bird in the left columns is from final variable-component performances under the second exposures to the MULT *DRL* 40 *VI* 1 and the MULT *FR* 5 *VI* 1 schedules. Each of these pairs shows that variable-component *IRT*s shifted markedly to the left following the replacement of the *DRL* 40 schedule with the *FR* 5 schedule. The corresponding pairs of constant-component distributions presented for each bird in the right columns show that inductive *IRT* shifts were not obtained. As a matter of fact there was a definite contrasting shift in the opposite direction in the case of the *F*-distributions presented for P–23B and a slight shift in that direction in the case of the other two birds.

Since the rate of responding generated by *VI* schedules of conditioned reinforcement varies directly with conditioned reinforce-

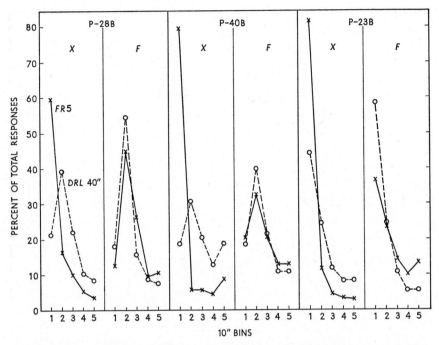

FIGURE 5.6. Relative frequency distributions of variable-component (*X*) and corresponding fixed component (*F*) *IRT*s from performances under the second exposures of each bird to the MULT *DRL* 40 *VI* 1 schedule and to the MULT *FR* 5 *VI* 1 schedule.

ment frequency (Zimmerman, Hanford, & Brown, 1967), some of the results of the present study may be accounted for, in part, by differences in the conditioned reinforcement frequencies generated under the different conditioned reinforcement schedules. Table 5.2

TABLE 5.2

Conditioned Reinforcement Frequencies Produced under Each Schedule

Schedule		Frequency per Minute					
		P–23B		P–28B		P–40B	
X-Component	F-Component	X	F	X	F	X	F
VI 1	*VI* 1	0.9	0.9	0.9	0.8	0.8	0.8
FR 5	*VI* 1	2.9	0.8	1.8	0.8	1.8	0.7
VI 1	*VI* 1	0.9	0.8	0.8	0.9	0.8	0.8
DRL 40	*VI* 1	0.3	0.8	0.2	0.9	0.5	0.8
DRL 60	*VI* 1	0.2	0.8	0.1	0.8	0.2	0.8
DRL 40	*VI* 1	0.4	0.8	0.3	0.8	0.4	0.8
FR 5	*VI* 1	2.5	0.8	1.6	0.8	1.5	0.8
VI 1	*VI* 1	0.7	0.7	0.9	0.9	0.8	0.8

presents the median frequency with which each bird produced conditioned reinforcement under each component based on the final five sessions of exposure to each indicated Multiple schedule.

Table 5.2 shows that the *FR* 5 schedule generated performances which produced conditioned reinforcement at frequencies which were two or more times as great as those produced by the *VI* 1 performances. In contrast, frequencies of conditioned reinforcement produced under the *DRL* schedules were markedly lower than those produced under the *VI* 1 schedule. Since the lowest frequencies of conditioned reinforcement were produced under the *DRL* 60 schedule, *X*-component conditioned reinforcement frequencies varied directly with *X*-component response rates (see Figure 5.1).

Table 5.2 also shows that each bird produced conditioned reinforcement across all *F*-components and within each homogeneous (*VI* 1, *VI* 1) Multiple schedule at relatively constant frequencies. The *F*-component response-rate data of Figure 5.1 thus indicate that contrast effects were sometimes observed in the present experiment. That is, when *X*-component response rates changed in a given direction because of a change in the *X* component, *F*-component response rates sometimes changed in the opposite direction. For example, in the case of both P–23B and P–40B, when *X*-component rates increased following the replacement of the *VI* 1 schedule by the *FR* 5 schedule, *F*-component response rates decreased. The *IRT* distributions presented in Figure 5.6 similarly indicated the occurrence of contrast effects (especially in the case of P–23B) following the replacement of the *DRL* 40 schedule with the *FR* 5 schedule. These effects and others in the opposite direction were observed following two, four, and five of the seven schedule changes in the case of P–28B, P–23B, and P–40B, respectively.

EXPERIMENT 2

The results of Experiment 1, together with results previously obtained in this laboratory, demonstrate that performances generated with conditioned reinforcement under Concurrent schedules are readily and appropriately influenced by changes in the schedule and/or frequency of conditioned reinforcement. In contrast to this demonstrated control of performance by *conditioned* reinforcement, Zimmerman and Hanford (1967a), using the two-key Concurrent schedule procedure, showed that such performance is relatively independent of *primary* reinforcement. The present study examined the effects of varying the scheduled frequency of grain presentation under conditions in which the schedule of response-produced conditioned reinforcement was held constant and primary reinforcers were delivered intermittently.

Procedure

Four birds served as subjects. They were P–23B, P–40B, P–28B (which were used in Experiment 1) and P–76R. [P–76R served previously in both the Zimmerman and Hanford (1966) and the Zimmerman, Hanford, and Brown (1967) studies. While the other three birds participated in Experiment 1, P–76R was being exposed to experimental conditions which were similar except that no grain was presented in the experimental situation (see "Persistence of Performance after Removal of Grain," below)].

Each of the four birds performed daily for 50 min in the one-key chamber employed in Experiment 1. Throughout the present experiment, pecking produced conditioned reinforcement on a *VI* 1 schedule. Concurrently, 4-sec access to grain was presented intermittently via a variable-interval tape. Each key peck postponed grain, if due, for 6 sec. The frequency of free grain was systematically varied over the study. Each bird performed with a given grain presentation schedule in effect until its pecking rate stabilized (no consistent trend) for four successive sessions. Table 5.3 presents the order and nature of the free grain schedules together with the number of sessions for which each bird was exposed to each schedule.

TABLE 5.3
Schedule of Free Grain Presentation

Schedule*	Number of Sessions			
	P–23B	P–40B	P–28B	P–76R
VI 1	7	6	6	7
VI 2	6	6	6	6
VI 4	8	9	7	7
VI 6	7	6	6	5
VI 12	12	7	9	5
VI 18	7	6	6	10
No grain	5	10	18	18
VI 18	16	8	5	8
VI 12	9	10	5	5
VI 6	7	10	16	12
VI 4	15	6	6	6
VI 2	14	14	10	10
VI 1	6	15	14	15

* The term *VI* usually implies that the reinforcer is response-produced. There is no generally accepted term that distinguishes the schedules referred to here, in which the food is presented aperiodically and independently of any operant. (Ed.)

Results

Figure 5.7 summarizes the results obtained with each bird over the experiment. Each circle presents the median rate of response based on the last five sessions of exposure to the free-feeding schedule whose *VI* value, in minutes, is indicated on the abscissa. The open circles present rates generated with conditioned reinforcement under each Concurrent free grain schedule over the ascending series of schedules with increasing *VI* values (decreasing frequen-

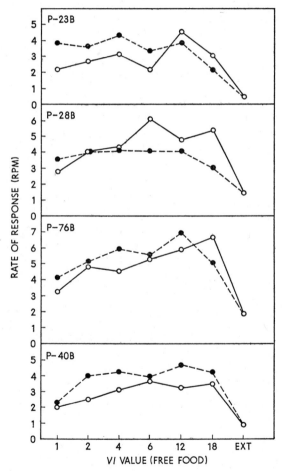

FIGURE 5.7. Response rates under the *VI* 1 schedule of conditioned reinforcement as a function of free grain frequency. Open circles and closed circles, respectively, present rates obtained during the ascending and descending series of grain schedule values. During the EXT condition, grain was not presented.

cies of grain presentation). The closed circles present similar rates generated over the descending series of grain schedules. Figure 5.7 shows that response rates increased during the ascending series as the VI schedule of grain increased in value from 1 to 18 min (P–76R), from 1 to 12 min (P–23B) and from 1 to 6 min (P–28B and P–40B). When grain was completely removed and subsequently reinstated on the *VI* 18 schedule, rates markedly decreased and increased, respectively, in the case of all birds. Each rate increased further when the grain schedule value was decreased from 18 to 12 min. Finally, over the remainder of the descending series, rates either decreased (P–76R and P–40B), or remained relatively stable (P–23B and P–28B) as the schedule value decreased from 12 to 1 min.

An overview of the results of Experiment 2 indicates that (*a*) responding was most weakly maintained in the absence of grain, (*b*) responding with grain present was usually most weakly maintained when grain was delivered most frequently (*VI* 1 schedule), and (*c*) responding was relatively insensitive to grain frequency over the wide middle range. These data suggest that under the present experimental conditions, in order to sustain responses by conditioned reinforcement at or near the maximum possible rate, one need not present grain more frequently than once every 18 min. Indeed, the data obtained during the ascending series of grain schedules suggest that one might be able to sustain responding at or slightly below maximum rates with even lower frequencies of free grain presentation.

PERSISTENCE OF PERFORMANCE AFTER REMOVAL OF GRAIN

In Experiment 2 it was observed that when the lowest rate of free grain presentation (*VI* 18) was first employed, responses which produced conditioned reinforcement were maintained at rates which were at or near the highest values generated in that experiment. When the rate of free grain presentation was subsequently set to zero, rates decreased markedly to the lowest values obtained. Not previously mentioned, however, was the observation that P–76R (one of the two birds exposed to 18 sessions without grain) responded at rates of from almost 2 responses per minute to over 4 responses per minute in 6 of the last 10 sessions during which grain was absent. Perhaps related to this latter observation were the observations of behavioral persistence in two birds follow-

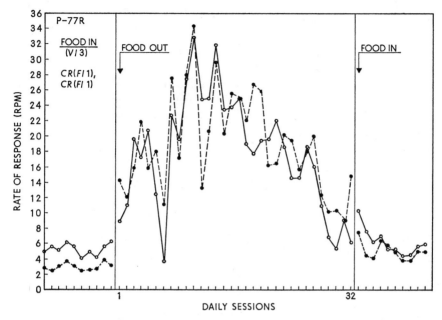

FIGURE 5.8. Daily response rates for P–77R in the first (open circles) and second (closed circles) components of the MULT *FI* 1 *FI* 1 schedule of conditioned reinforcement (*CR*).

ing the removal of grain in the Zimmerman and Hanford (1967a) two-key study. This section will be devoted to a detailed description of several similar observations made previously in this laboratory following the occasional removal of grain from the one-key experimental situation.

Following the termination of the study reported by Zimmerman and Hanford (1966), five birds with 7–16 months' exposure to the one-key concurrent procedure were exposed to the removal of grain. Immediately before this manipulation, each had been performing under conditions which were exactly the same as those employed in Experiment 1 (free food, with a Concurrent Multiple schedule of conditioned reinforcement), except that responses in each component of the Multiple schedule produced conditioned reinforcement on an *FI* 1 schedule. Three birds which responded at rates of 4–5 responses per minute with the Concurrent *VI* 3 schedule of free grain presentation performed at rates of ≦ 1 response per minute within 3–7 days following the removal of grain. In contrast, two birds continued to respond at rates which were usually equal to or greater than those previously generated with grain present. Responding which produced the conditioned reinforcer was maintained over the entire period during which grain was absent. Figure 5.8 partially summarizes the performance of P–77R. Figure 5.8 presents daily response rates generated under each component of the MULT *FI* 1 *FI* 1 schedule of conditioned reinforcement in each of the 32 successive sessions in which grain was absent and in each of the 10 previous and 10 subsequent sessions during which grain was presented freely on the *VI* 3 schedule. Before grain was removed, rates in each component were relatively stable across daily sessions and P–77R showed a rate bias which favored the first component. Following the removal of grain and throughout its absence, however, rates of responding were usually much higher than those generated previously or subsequently in the presence of grain, and were extremely variable across sessions and across components within sessions.

The performance of P–77R is further illustrated by the cumulative records presented in Figure 5.9. The top and bottom cumula-

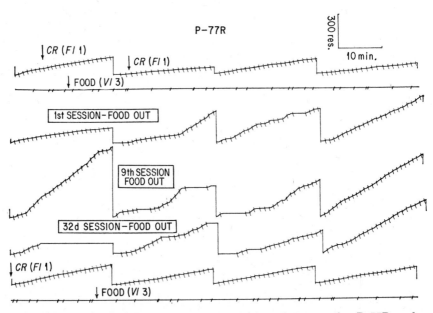

FIGURE 5.9. Cumulative response records of performance for P–77R under the MULT *FI* 1 *FI* 1 schedule of conditioned reinforcement (*CR*). The top record and the bottom record, respectively, present performance in the final session before and the first session after the period over which the *VI* 3 free grain schedule remained absent. The middle three records present representative performances in the absence of grain.

tive records are performances generated in the last session before
and the first session after the removal of grain, respectively. These
records are typical of the base-line records illustrated and discussed
in the Zimmerman and Hanford (1966) report. Responding occurred at low, steady rates and the temporal pattern of responding
usually generated under *FI* schedules was rarely in evidence between successive conditioned reinforcements. The three middle records in Figure 5.9 are representative of those obtained with grain
absent. They show that local rates varied markedly within such
sessions. Local rates were (*a*) sometimes higher than those previously generated in the presence of grain, (*b*) sometimes similar
to those previously generated, and (*c*) sometimes at or slightly
above zero. Finally, many instances of positively accelerated responding between reinforcements can be discerned in these records.
It should be noted, however, that such "scallops" are not constantly
in evidence. Figures 5.10 and 5.11 show that qualitatively similar
results were obtained from P–76R over the 24-day period with only
conditioned reinforcers scheduled.

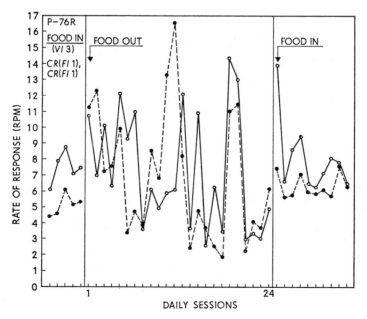

FIGURE 5.10.   Daily response rates for P–76R in the first (open circles) and
second (closed circles) components of the MULT *FI* 1 *FI* 1 schedule of conditioned reinforcement (CR).

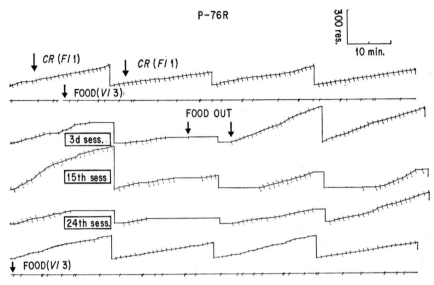

FIGURE 5.11. Cumulative response records of performance for P–76R under the MULT *FI* 1 *FI* 1 schedule of conditioned reinforcement (*CR*). The top record and the bottom record, respectively, present performance in the final session before and the first session after the period in which the *VI* 3 free-grain schedule remained absent. The middle three records present representative performances in the absence of grain.

The results obtained above with birds P–77R and P–76R were systematically replicated with P–76R, 11 months later (P–77R having died). After the end of the study reported by Zimmerman, Hanford, and Brown (1967), four birds were exposed once again to scheduled conditioned reinforcers with no primary reinforcers. Before this, the procedure had been the same as that at the beginning of Experiment 1, with a *VI* 1 schedule of conditioned reinforcement and a *VI* 3 schedule of response-independent presentation of grain.

When the *VI* 3 schedule of food presentations was discontinued response rates of three birds declined from 3–6 responses per minute to one response per minute (or less) in 4–12 sessions. In contrast, over the same period of time, P–76R responded at rates which were usually higher than those previously generated with grain present. As a consequence, while the other birds performed in Experiment 1, P–76R was exposed to some of the same conditions, but grain remained absent.

Table 5.4 presents the order and nature of the schedules to which this bird was exposed together with the number of sessions of

TABLE 5.4

Order and Nature of Experimental Conditions to Which P-76R Was Exposed and a Partial
Summary of Results Obtained under Each Condition

| Multiple Schedule of Conditioned Reinforcers | | Schedule of Grain | Number of Sessions | | | Final Rate (per min) | | | |
| X-Comp. | F-Comp. | | Total | Rate ≥ 3.8/Min | | Responses | | Conditioned Reinforcers | |
				X	F	X	F	X	F
VI 1	VI 1	VI 3	10	10	6	4.2	3.8	0.8	0.8
VI 1	VI 1	Out	13	11	10	9.3	8.4	0.6	0.5
FR 5	VI 1	Out	16	12	10	10.9	5.0	2.1	0.5
VI 1	VI 1	Out	10	2	5	3.3	3.9	0.3	0.4
FR 5	VI 1	Out	9	6	5	4.9	4.4	1.0	0.4
VI 1	VI 1	Out	7	5	5	5.0	7.2	0.5	0.6
DRL 40	VI 1	Out	21	3	8	1.5	2.0	0.1	0.3
FR 5	VI 1	Out	29	20	19	4.2	3.1	0.8	0.4
VI 1	VI 1	Out	22	5	6	3.5	2.6	0.3	0.3
VI 1	VI 1	VI 18	20	19	20	7.7	6.1	0.8	0.8

exposure and a partial summary of the results obtained. The X and F columns under the heading "Number of Sessions" present the number of sessions in which the response rate in the given component equaled or exceeded 3.8 per minute.[2] Response rates and reinforcement rates presented in the four rightmost columns are median values based on the final five sessions under each Multiple schedule.

Table 5.4 shows that P–76R was exposed to 127 successive sessions without grain. Table 5.4 also shows that rates equal to or greater than 3.8 responses per minute were often generated in one and/or the other component throughout this 127-day period. This was observed in most sessions under each exposure to the MULT FR 5 VI 1 schedule and under each of the first three exposures to the MULT VI 1 VI 1 schedule. Under the MULT DRL 40 VI 1 schedule, rates in DRL 40 rarely equaled or exceeded 3.8 responses per minute while rates in VI 1 did so in more than one third of the sessions. Finally, rates in one and/or the other component equaled or exceeded 3.8 responses per minute during one third of the sessions under the final exposure to the MULT VI 1 VI 1 schedule. During the 21-session exposure to the MULT DRL 40 VI 1 schedule and the 22-session final exposure to the MULT VI 1 VI 1 schedule rates were sometimes as low as or lower than 1 response per minute, but it should be pointed out that in the majority of these sessions, rates in one and/or both components exceeded 2 responses per minute.

The rest of the data presented in Table 5.4 shows that with respect to response rates and reinforcement frequencies, results obtained with P–76R over the 127-day grainless period were, in general, qualitatively similar to those obtained with the birds which performed under the Experiment 1 (grain present) conditions. Table 5.4 shows that the highest frequencies of conditioned reinforcement were produced under the FR 5 schedule, the lowest frequency was produced under the DRL 40 schedule and X-component response rates generally varied directly with reinforcement frequencies.

Performance characteristics are further illustrated by the cumu-

---

[2] This rate was chosen as a criterion because it was the lower of the two median component rates which were obtained during the final five sessions before grain was removed. As such it permits one to compare responding over the 127-day period without grain with responding maintained while grain was being delivered.

lative records for P–76R presented in Figures 5.12 and 5.13. The
top cumulative record in Figure 5.12 shows performance generated
in the session which immediately preceded the removal of grain.
This performance was typical of that generated in Experiment 1
under the MULT *VI 1 VI 1* conditioned reinforcement schedule.
Responding occurred at low, steady rates in each component.

The remaining cumulative records in Figure 5.12 and all but the

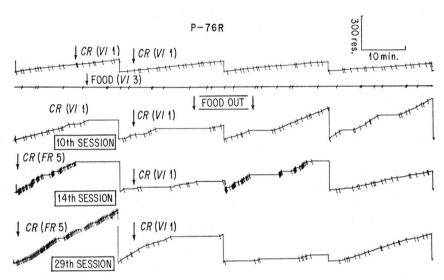

FIGURE 5.12. Cumulative response records of performance for bird P–76R
under the indicated Multiple schedules of conditioned reinforcement (*CR*).
The top record presents performance in the final session before the removal of
the *VI* 3 free grain schedule. The other records present representative performances in the absence of grain.

bottom cumulative record in Figure 5.13 are representative of those
obtained under the indicated Multiple schedules throughout the
127-day period during which grain remained absent. In contrast to
performances generated with the grain schedule in effect, these
records show that local rates within these sessions varied markedly.
Many "extinctionlike" periods of no responding and many periods
during which local rates are higher than those generated in the
presence of grain can be seen in these records. These performance
characteristics are similar to those seen previously in records presented for P–77R and P–76R in Figure 5.9 and Figure 5.11, respectively. In addition, schedule effects similar to those shown pre-

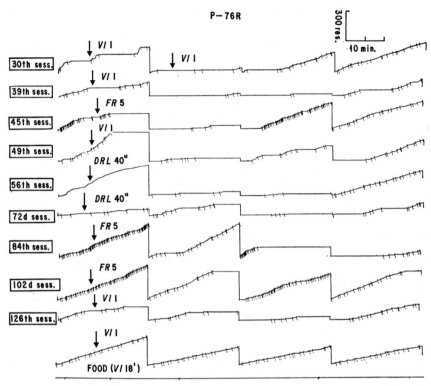

FIGURE 5.13. Cumulative response records of performance for P–76R under the indicated Multiple schedules of conditioned reinforcement. The bottom record presents performance in the third session after the reinstatement of grain on a free *VI* 18 schedule. The other records present representative performances in the absence of grain.

viously for the birds which participated in Experiment 1 can be seen in some of the present records. Performances generated under the *FR* 5 schedule are characterized by post-reinforcement pauses of variable duration, and fixed-ratio runs. Some of the pauses of extremely long duration were probably not schedule effects but rather represented behavioral effects observed in practically every session during which grain was absent. On the other hand, the control exerted by the *FR* 5 schedule can be inferred from the fact that most responses were emitted in runs of five with few isolated responses or runs of fewer than five responses occurring. In contrast, although local rates are extremely variable in the corresponding *VI* 1 components, ratiolike runs are rarely in evidence in these components.

Performances similar to those obtained in Experiment 1 were also obtained with P–76R in the sessions which immediately followed the first two replacements of the MULT *FR* 5 *VI* 1 schedule with the MULT *VI* 1 *VI* 1 schedule (top and fourth cumulative records in Figure 5.13). Performances in *FR* 5 in these sessions are characterized by many instances of ratiolike bursts of responding. Similar bursts are not seen in the performances in the *VI* 1 component.

The fifth cumulative record in Figure 5.13 presents performance generated in the first session of MULT *DRL* 40 *VI* 1. This record shows that even after being exposed to 55 grainless sessions, bird 76R responded throughout the first *DRL* 40 component at a rate which was too high to meet the reinforcement contingency. After several more sessions under the MULT *DRL* 40 *VI* 1 schedule, responding in the *DRL* component generally occurred at average rates which were lower than those obtained under any other schedule throughout the 127-day period. Typical performance under the *DRL* 40 schedule is shown in the sixth cumulative record. *DRL* performance was characterized by many periods during which no responding occurred and by occasional periods during which successive responses were spaced widely enough to produce the conditioned reinforcer. The conditioned reinforcement frequencies in the *DRL* schedule were lower than in any other schedule. Although this result was similar to that found in Experiment 1, in the present case it was more a consequence of the relatively long periods of time during which this bird failed to respond at all. The *VI* 1 performance in the *VI* 1 schedule shown in the sixth record of Figure 5.13 is representative of those generally seen under the MULT *DRL* 40 *VI* 1 schedule. Average rates in *VI* 1 were usually higher than those generated under the *DRL* schedule but lower than those generated in *VI* 1 when the other component was not *DRL*.

The second and third cumulative records from the bottom in Figure 5.13 show that even after grain had been absent from the experimental situation for over 100 successive sessions, appropriate performances were still being maintained with conditioned reinforcement. It should be pointed out, however, that neither of these records is typical of those generated under the final two schedules. Both illustrate relatively well-maintained performances under the respective experimental conditions, but response rates were typically lower than those shown.

Finally, the bottom cumulative record of Figure 5.13 shows performance generated in the third session following the reinstatement of free grain on a *VI* 18 schedule. Performance was similar to that previously obtained under the Concurrent *VI* 3 schedule of grain presentation except that the steady responding occurred at higher rates under the *VI* 18 schedule. This finding is compatible with the results obtained in Experiment 2 with P–76R.

DISCUSSION

Some results presented in this report systematically replicate results previously obtained with Concurrent schedules in this laboratory. In addition, some of the conditioned reinforcement effects described here are qualitatively similar to effects obtained by other investigators with (*a*) response-produced primary reinforcement under analogous experimental conditions and (*b*) response-produced conditioned reinforcement under other experimental conditions. Finally, some of the present results demonstrate that stimuli associated with a primary reinforcer can exert potent and durable behavioral effects.

The results obtained in Experiments 1 and 2 demonstrate that responding which intermittently produces a conditioned reinforcer can be sustained indefinitely under conditions in which free grain is concurrently presented on an independent schedule and in spite of the fact that each response postpones grain, if due, for 6 sec. We have similarly sustained responding with (*a*) the present one-key, Concurrent-schedule procedure (Zimmerman & Hanford, 1966; Zimmerman, Hanford, & Brown, 1967); (*b*) the two-key, Concurrent-schedule procedure (Zimmerman, 1963; Zimmerman & Hanford, 1967a; Zimmerman & Hanford, 1968); and (*c*) a three-key, complex-discrimination, Concurrent-schedule procedure (Zimmerman & Hanford, 1967b). In the last study, mismatching-to-sample performance intermittently produced a conditioned reinforcer in only one component of a two-component Multiple schedule. Each matching-to-sample sequence in both components produced a brief timeout. Concurrently, free grain was intermittently presented via a *VI* tape. Under these conditions, mismatching performance was sustained indefinitely and differentially with conditioned reinforcement in spite of the fact that every key peck postponed grain, if due, for 2 sec.

In Experiment 1, it was shown that rates and patterns of responding generated under the two-component Multiple schedules of conditioned reinforcement were appropriate to the particular schedule in effect in a given component. These results systematically replicate results obtained with the two-key, Concurrent-schedule procedure (Zimmerman, 1963). They are also qualitatively similar to results obtained by others (e.g., Ferster & Skinner, 1957) with Multiple schedules of primary reinforcement, and by Kelleher (1961) with schedules of conditioned reinforcement following the discontinuation of primary reinforcement.

Schedule control has also been generated under second-order schedules with brief exteroceptive stimuli. Kelleher (1966b) showed, for example, that the brief presentation of a visual stimulus associated with grain could generate typical fixed-interval response patterns in each interval component of a second-order schedule in which grain reinforcement was delivered on a fixed-ratio schedule of interval components. Findley and Brady (1965) and Thomas and Stubbs (1966) have similarly obtained schedule control using second-order schedules involving fixed-ratio components.

Like the extinction procedure employed by Kelleher (1961), both the second-order schedule procedures and the Concurrent-schedule procedures can be used to generate schedule control with brief presentations of exteroceptive stimuli associated with primary reinforcement. Unlike the procedure employed by Kelleher (1961), however, both of the latter procedures can indefinitely sustain conditioned reinforcement effects by virtue of the fact that primary reinforcement is not removed from the experimental situation. In contrast to performances generated under second-order schedules, however, performances generated with conditioned reinforcement under Concurrent schedules are *not* dependent on the maintenance of performance by primary reinforcement.

In Experiment 1, it was also shown that (*a*) rates of responding generated under various schedules of conditioned reinforcement correlated positively with frequencies of conditioned reinforcement produced by these schedules, and (*b*) contrast effects were often observed in performance in the unchanged component following a schedule change in the other component of the Multiple schedule. Both of these results were obtained in the study of Zimmerman, Hanford, and Brown (1967) which employed the one-key Concurrent-schedule procedure to examine the effects of conditioned reinforcement frequency under MULT *VI VI* schedules of conditioned reinforcement. The positive relation between reinforcement frequency and response rate obtained in that study was qualitatively similar to findings obtained by other investigators (e.g., Ferster & Skinner, 1957; Nevin & Shettleworth, 1966) with MULT *VI VI* schedules of primary reinforcement. The positive relation found in Experiment 1 may be accounted for, in part, by differential frequencies of reinforcement of different *IRT*s, which would obtain under the different schedules of conditioned reinforcement. That is, only long *IRT*s could have been reinforced under the *DRL* schedules. In contrast, the data presented in Figures 5.2–5.5 show that, with few exceptions, only short *IRT*s were reinforced under the *FR* schedule. Finally, one can certainly assume that all *IRT*s were reinforced with greater frequency under the *VI* schedule than were all but the shortest *IRT*s under the *FR* schedule and all but the longest *IRT*s under the *DRL* schedules.

The contrast effects frequently observed (Experiment 1) in the performances in the unchanged *VI* 1 component following a change of schedule in the other component of the Multiple schedule, and similar effects observed in the Zimmerman, Hanford, and Brown study, were qualitatively similar to those observed by other investigators (e.g., Bloomfield, 1967; Nevin & Shettleworth, 1966; Reynolds, 1961; Reynolds & Catania, 1961) with Multiple schedules of primary reinforcement. The contrast effects observed in both of the conditioned reinforcement experiments cannot be attributed to differential frequencies of free grain associated with the changed and unchanged components since in both studies each component of each Multiple schedule was associated with approximately equal grain frequencies. Thus, the results of both studies extend contrast findings previously obtained in Multiple schedules of primary reinforcement to Multiple schedules of conditioned reinforcement.

In Experiment 2 it was shown that as the programmed frequency of free grain was decreased from 1.0 to 0.055 per minute (*VI* value of grain schedule increased from 1 to 18 min), rates of responding which intermittently produced the conditioned reinforcer increased to a maximum. These results strikingly resemble results obtained by Zimmerman and Hanford (1967b) who examined the effects of varying the programmed frequency of free grain over the same frequency range, on performances sustained with the three-key, complex-discrimination, Concurrent-schedule procedure.

Qualitatively similar results have also recently been obtained by Zimmerman and Hanford (1968) with the two-key, Concurrent-schedule procedure. Right-key responses intermittently produced the conditioned reinforcer while, at the same time, left key responses produced grain on an *FR* schedule whose value was varied from 30 to 200, and subsequently on an *FI* schedule whose value was increased from 1 to 256 min. As grain presented under the *FR* or *FI* schedules decreased in frequency, response rates maintained by primary reinforcement decreased but response rates maintained by conditioned reinforcement increased to a maximum before decreasing.

One additional aspect of the results obtained in the two latter studies was similar to results obtained in Experiment 2. In all three studies it was found that responding sustained with conditioned reinforcement was insensitive to frequency of presentation of grain over a wide range. This result, when considered together with all previous findings in this laboratory, supports the observation (Zimmerman & Hanford, 1967a) that performance sustained with conditioned reinforcement under Concurrent schedules is readily affected by variables relating to the conditioned reinforcer but relatively insensitive to those relating to the primary reinforcer.

In Experiment 2, it was observed that in order to sustain performances with conditioned reinforcement at or near their maximum response rates, one need not present free grain more frequently than once every 18 minutes. This was confirmed with mismatching performances in the Zimmerman and Hanford (1967b) study. It might be noted that grain frequencies of the order of three presentations per hour are much lower than those typically employed to study performances generated under *VI* schedules of response-contingent primary reinforcement. One might speculate that a Tandem *VI* 18 *DRO* 6 schedule of grain reinforcement (a response-contingent schedule analogous to the *VI* 18 schedule of free grain used in Experiment 2 since no grain could be obtained sooner than 6 sec. after a response) might fail to maintain responding at rates as high as those maintained in Experiment 2 with conditioned reinforcement, or might fail to maintain responding at all.

Finally, several examples of the most unexpected results obtained over the course of our Concurrent-schedule work were presented in the previous section of this report. Following the removal of grain from the one-key, Concurrent-schedule situation, we observed that while in the majority of birds, behavior sustained with conditioned reinforcement markedly weakened or extinguished in 3–12 sessions, in the case of two birds this behavior persisted throughout the period in which grain was absent. That this persistent behavior was sustained on the basis of conditioned reinforcement, per se, is supported by the data presented in Figures 5.12 and 5.13 and Table 5.4 for P–76R. These data show that conditioned reinforcement exerted considerable schedule control over this persistent behavior. In many respects the performance of P–76R during the prolonged absence of grain strongly resembled performance generated in the birds which participated in Experiment 1 under similar conditions but with grain present.

That conditioned reinforcement, per se, maintained persistent behavior is also supported by the results obtained with birds 77R and 76R following an earlier grain removal. When these birds produced the conditioned reinforcer on an *FI* schedule in the presence of Concurrent free grain, *FI* patterns of responding were rarely obtained between conditioned reinforcements. In contrast, when presentations of grain were discontinued, responding persisted and frequent instances of *FI* "scalloping" were observed in the cumulative response records. As we suggested previously (Zimmerman & Hanford, 1966), the failure to generate *FI* patterns of responding with the *FI* schedule of conditioned reinforcement under the Concurrent-schedule conditions was probably a consequence of our use of the 6-sec, no-response contingency with respect to free grain delivery. This latter contingency, programmed in order to eliminate the possibility of adventitious grain reinforcement of key pecking, could also have served to inhibit positively accelerated behavior by virtue of the fact that such accelerated behavior would substantially lower delivery frequency of food. This analysis is supported by results of Ferster and Skinner (1957) who found that the typical response pattern generated by an *FI* 1 schedule of grain reinforcement was abolished and replaced by a linear response pattern when the *FI* contingency was modified by requiring that the reinforced response occur at least 6 sec after a previous response.

It might be argued that, contrary to our findings in Experiment 1, the above analysis suggests that the typical *FR* response pattern would not be generated with conditioned reinforcement under concurrent scheduling. It should be noted, however, that we employed an *FR* schedule of low value. As a consequence, conditioned reinforcement could be produced within a second or two with a short-ratio run. This is in marked contrast to the minimum period of time required to produce a conditioned reinforcer under an *FI* 1 schedule. Furthermore, studies of Holz and Azrin (1963) and Weiner (1963) suggest that when punishment is continuously applied on a response-contingent basis, it exerts its maximum effects on those responses which are least relevant to reinforcement. An analogous argument could certainly be applied to our differential *FI* and *FR* results. Every response is relevant to the production of each conditioned reinforcer under the *FR* schedule while only one response (and certainly *not* positively accelerated responding) is necessary to produce each conditioned reinforcer under the *FI* schedule.

Persistence of behavior has also been observed in two birds following the removal of grain in the two-key, Concurrent-schedule situation (Zimmerman & Hanford, 1967a) and in two birds following the removal of grain in the three-key, complex-discrimination, Concurrent-schedule situation (Zimmerman & Hanford, 1967b). That these persistent behaviors were sustained with conditioned reinforcement, per se, was also supported by the results obtained with each of these birds. The performance in the absence of grain was sustained with conditioned reinforcement but not with novel stimuli in the first two birds, and mismatching-to-sample performance similarly persisted and was differentially sustained with conditioned reinforcement in the case of the latter two birds.

The above observations strongly suggest that at least some environmental conditions can be arranged under which stimuli associated with primary reinforcement can be made into potent, durable conditioned reinforcers. That the performance of several birds has persisted without primary reinforcement following exposure to different Concurrent-schedule procedures suggests (but certainly does not prove) that some common characteristic of Concurrent-schedule procedures may be essential to produce this persistent performance. We know very little about the necessary and sufficient conditions for the generation of such persistent behavior. We have found that no bird has ever shown such persistence unless it has had at least six months' experience performing under a Concurrent schedule, but on the other hand, some birds with over three years of such experience have not persisted following grain removal.

It is possible that we might not have observed the "persistent-performance" phenomenon had we employed any other organism but the pigeon and any other response but the peck. Without further investigation we cannot assume that the phenomenon is more than a "pigeon-pecking" phenomenon. We are consequently starting to investigate the possibility of extending our Concurrent-schedule procedures to the study of bar pressing in the rat and pedal pressing in the pigeon. If we are not able to sustain these behaviors with conditioned reinforcement under concurrent but independent food reinforcement, all our findings might have to be considered peculiar to the pigeon and its pecking response. Even were this to be so, however, the use of the pigeon, the peck, and the Concurrent schedule would still offer the investigator a powerful biological preparation with which to study conditioned reinforcement.

Key pecking has now been sustained with conditioned reinforcement (under conditions in which grain is concurrently but independently available) in seven birds, four birds, and four birds, for periods of over two years, three years, and four years, respectively. In addition, pecking in a 16th bird was similarly sustained for over three years until it died. These results strongly suggest that such performance may be sustainable with Concurrent schedules over the entire experimental life of a pigeon.

Because of their potential ability to sustain performance with conditioned reinforcement over the life-span of a pigeon (or to be more conservative, because of their proven ability to do so for at least four years), our Concurrent-schedule procedures, as tools for the study of conditioned reinforcement, contrast markedly with procedures collectively referred to by Kelleher and Gollub (1962) as the Extinction procedure. The reinforcing function of stimuli is assessed with the Extinction procedure only after primary reinforcement has been removed from the experimental situation. Although this experimental paradigm eliminates the confounding effects of primary reinforcement, as pointed out by Kelleher and Gollub, among others, it also weakens the very stimulus function that it is assessing as the assessment proceeds. As a consequence, the Extinction procedure severely restricts the number of successive experimental sessions over which conditioned reinforcement effects can be examined. Because studies using the Extinction procedure have, as a consequence, failed to provide evidence for potent or durable conditioned reinforcement effects, many investigators have been led to de-emphasize the role of conditioned reinforcement in the maintenance of behavior or to seek alternative ways of accounting for effects usually attributed to conditioned reinforcement (see Kelleher and Gollub, 1962).

As Kelleher and Gollub demonstrated, an alternative approach to the Extinction method in the study of conditioned reinforcement involves the use of procedures which examine the conditioned reinforcing function of stimuli without removing primary reinforcement from the experimental situation. As examples of this approach, Kelleher and Gollub illustrated and suggested the application of Chain schedules and related procedures.

The Concurrent-schedule procedures employed in this laboratory are other examples of this general approach. Like the Chain-schedule procedures they can be used to examine conditioned reinforcement under chronic conditions. Unlike the Chain-schedule procedures, however, they generate and sustain behavior which does not eventually produce a primary reinforcer. Indeed, in our specific application of these procedures, responses which produce conditioned reinforcers also postpone the primary reinforcer. Since procedures with these characteristics can sustain behavior indefinitely with conditioned reinforcers, and since such sustained behavior persists in some pigeons even long after removal of the primary reinforcer, the role of conditioned reinforcement as an explanatory concept in the analysis of behavior should be reconsidered both by those investigators who have generally de-emphasized it, and by those who restrict its use to chaining phenomena.

SUMMARY

Free access to grain was intermittently provided via a variable-interval tape. Concurrently, key pecking intermittently produced 0.50-sec presentation of the exteroceptive stimuli paired with grain. Each response postponed grain, if due, for 6 sec. Performance sustained under these conditions was examined as a function of the conditioned reinforcement schedule and the frequency of free grain. *FR, VI,* and *DRL* schedules of conditioned reinforcement generated appropriate rates and patterns of responding. As the programmed frequency of free grain decreased from 1.0 to 0.055 per minute, rates of responding increased to a maximum. These rates were relatively insensitive to grain frequency, however, over a wide range. Finally, responses that produced conditioned-reinforcers persisted in two birds following discontinuation of the presentation of grain. Some of the results are similar to those obtained (*a*) with response-contingent primary reinforcers under analogous conditions, and (*b*) with response-contingent conditioned reinforcers under other experimental conditions. Some of the results demonstrate that conditioned reinforcement can exert durable if not potent behavioral effects.

SECTION II

Concurrent chains

This section includes three chapters on the Concurrent-chains technique for investigating conditioned reinforcement. The relative reinforcing values of different second links in two Chains are assessed by performance on identical, concurrent first links. The original investigation by this method was by Autor, whose work is here made generally available for the first time. Autor's work established what I have referred to as Autor's law: conditioned reinforcing value of a stimulus is proportional to the density of primary reinforcement in its presence.

Fantino's chapter establishes some boundaries to the area of the application of Autor's law. Specifically, the requirement of a particular rate of responding in a second link appears to diminish the relative reinforcing value of that link. Fantino offers a program of research based upon a new conception of "psychological distance to reward," applicable to Chains of all kinds.

Schuster uses Concurrent Chains to measure preference between a schedule of primary reinforcement and the same schedule with a superimposed FR 11 schedule of a brief visual and auditory stimulus. With some procedures the added stimulus may be regarded as a conditioned reinforcer for two reasons: first, because it is associated with the primary reinforcer; and second, because it exerts schedule control (FR 11), increasing the rate of responding. However, the schedule with the presumptive conditioned reinforcer is eventually not preferred, and in some cases avoided. Schuster's measure of preference is in some sense a relative rate, and Autor's measure of relative rate is in some sense a preference. Accordingly, Schuster's results place further limits on the area of application of Autor's law. Indeed, they support Schuster in his attempt to eliminate the concept of conditioned reinforcement itself.

chapter 6

THE STRENGTH OF CONDITIONED REINFORCERS AS A FUNCTION OF FREQUENCY AND PROBABILITY OF REINFORCEMENT

Sanford M. Autor

Somerville Guidance Center

INTRODUCTION

Most experimenters who have studied conditioned or secondary reinforcement have employed one of two basic procedures. One method is to pair an originally neutral stimulus with a primary reinforcer. This is followed by an attempt to condition some new response by substituting the previously neutral stimulus for the primary reinforcer. In a second method, a response is initially conditioned by means of a primary reinforcer. Paired with the latter is some neutral stimulus. The effect of conditioned reinforcement is measured by the increment in responding, if any, which occurs when the initially neutral stimulus is presented during Extinction. Many independent variables have been investigated with these two procedures, e.g., number of pairings of primary and neutral stimulus, interval between neutral and primary reinforcing

[1] The author wishes to thank Drs. B. F. Skinner, R. J. Herrnstein, and L. R. Gollub for their many suggestions, Dr. W. H. Morse for his helpful reading of the manuscript, and his wife, Sherry B. Autor, for her invaluable assistance.

This investigation was carried out during the tenure of a Predoctoral Fellowship from the National Institute of Mental Health, U.S. Public Health Service. The work was supported by a grant from the National Science Foundation, and was presented in partial fulfillment of the requirements for the degree of Doctor of Philosophy at Harvard University in 1960.

stimulus, amount of primary reinforcement, type of schedule of reinforcement, and degree of deprivation (Myers, 1958). The results of most of these studies have served mainly to emphasize the weakness and the transitory nature of the effects of secondary reinforcing stimuli.

Myers, in a review of the literature on secondary reinforcement, has summarized the problem in these terms:

> The secondary reinforcement literature yields few conclusions which can be substantiated by a number of experiments, and which are not contradicted by other experiments. There is no consistent picture of the effects of schedules of reinforcement, amount of primary reinforcement, satiation or irrelevant drives. . . . It is apparent that we have made only a tentative start towards an understanding of secondary reinforcement and the variables which affect its strength (1958, p. 297).

A different procedure which appears to be more promising than the earlier two involves Chain schedules of reinforcement, in which responding can be sustained at high rates by conditioned reinforcers. A two-link Chain schedule is one in which responding in the presence of a stimulus during the initial link is reinforced, according to a schedule, by the presentation of another stimulus. In the presence of the second stimulus, responding is reinforced, according to a second schedule, with a primary reinforcer. A Chain schedule can be extended to more than two links by the addition of links. Responding during the links of a chain prior to the one in which the primary reinforcer is received is controlled by the conditioned reinforcing properties of the stimuli produced by responding during these links. These stimuli serve as conditioned reinforcers because of their temporal contiguity to a primary reinforcer.

Ferster and Skinner (1957) provide basic data on Chain schedules, in which various schedules of reinforcement were links of the Chains. They showed that a performance emerges during each part of a Chain which is typical for the type of schedule in effect during that link. Gollub (1958) has extended their work by a systematic investigation of the variables which determine the maintenance of behavior during multi-link fixed-interval and variable-interval Chains. He found that responding was sustained during five-link *VI* Chains, whereas responding was not sustained during *FI* Chains with the same number of links, each of a duration equal to the mean of the *VI* links. For Chains consisting of *FI* links, the largest number of links during which responding could be maintained was a function of the length of the fixed interval during each link. For example, if the intervals were each 2 min, responding could not be well maintained during Chains of more than two links, while if the intervals were each 30 sec, responding was well maintained during three-link Chains.

The purpose of the present study was to investigate quantitative properties of conditioned reinforcement in Chain schedules. The relation between the strength of conditioned reinforcing stimuli and frequency of primary reinforcement was investigated. Frequency is defined as the mean number of food presentations delivered during a period of time. A second independent variable was probability of reinforcement. The probability of reinforcement for a single response is defined as the reciprocal of the mean number of responses required for a food presentation. This experiment examined the question: Is the strength of a conditioned reinforcer quantitatively related to frequency of reinforcement and to probability of reinforcement?

GENERAL METHOD

Subjects

The subjects were eight adult, male, White Carneaux pigeons. P–40, P–44, P–76, P–77, and P–108 were experimentally naïve at the outset of experimentation. P–267, P–270, and P–272 had experimental histories.

Seven subjects were maintained at approximately 80 percent of their free-feeding weights. P–76 was maintained at a 75 percent level, because it failed to behave effectively at 80 percent. Each bird was weighed before and after each session and, if necessary, was fed after the session an amount sufficient to maintain the required body weight. There were generally six sessions a week, and birds were maintained at their usual weights on the seventh day.

Apparatus

Two standard experimental chambers for pigeons were used. For a more detailed description of this type of apparatus, see Ferster and Skinner (1957) and the Introduction to this volume. The two response keys, 5⅜ inches apart at their centers, were adjusted for equal tension and excursion. A relay, located behind the panel equidistantly from the two keys, was operated by each response, providing auditory feedback.

One key could be illuminated with either green or yellow lamps, the other with white or red. The compartment could be illuminated from above by white or green houselights. Responding was recorded on Gerbrands cumulative recorders and electromagnetic counters; time durations were recorded on elapsed time meters.

General procedure

A general procedure consisting of a combination of Chain and Concurrent schedules of reinforcement was the basis for the specific procedures to be described in later sections. A two-link Chain schedule has already been described as one in which responding in the presence of one stimulus is reinforced, according to a schedule, by the appearance of a second stimulus. In the presence of the second stimulus, a response is reinforced, according to a second schedule, with a primary reinforcer. The stimulus for the second link is a conditioned reinforcer, because its response-contingent presentation controls responding during the first link of the Chain.

Concurrent schedules have been defined as "two or more schedules independently arranged but operating at the same time, reinforcements being set up by both" (Ferster & Skinner, 1957, p. 724). A variety of Concurrent schedules have been programmed for two keys (Findley, 1958; Herrnstein, 1958).

In the two-key situation described earlier, a two-link Chain schedule was programmed for each key. Each of the four links was correlated with either a different stimulus color on the key or a particular houselight color. The first links of each Chain were identical, independent, 1-minute variable-interval schedules (VI 1). The two VI 1 schedules were programmed concurrently.

Responding on either key during the Concurrent first links produced intermittently a new discriminative stimulus for that key, correlated with a particular schedule of food reinforcement (the second link of that Chain). At the same time, the two VI tapes which programmed the first links were stopped, so that the second link of the other Chain could not occur. After a specified period of exposure to the schedule of the second link, the Concurrent first links of the two Chains again came into force. This cycle was repeated until a fixed number of (5-sec.) food reinforcements had been presented during the second links.

In experiments to be described, the terminal (food) schedules were varied. Different types of schedules, different values of schedules, and different criteria for ending an exposure to a second link and returning to the Concurrent first links of the two Chains were examined.

EXPERIMENT 1: FREQUENCY OF REINFORCEMENT

Introduction

One variable which might influence the strength of a conditioned reinforcer is the frequency of primary reinforcement. (Frequency is defined as the mean number of food presentations delivered during a period of time.) Frequency is not to be confused with number of reinforcements, since the latter does not necessarily involve a temporal dimension. Myers (1958) has used frequency and number interchangeably in referring to the latter.

Variable-interval schedules can be used to determine the frequencies of food reinforcement associated with conditioned reinforcing stimuli. The problem arises: If the strength of a conditioned reinforcer is found to be related to frequency of reinforcement, is this relation to be attributed directly to the frequency of food presentations, or is it mediated by the responding sustained by these food presentations? In order to investigate this problem, the present experiment uses two procedures: one in which a food presentation is contingent upon the bird's responding, and a second in which food is presented only if the bird does not respond.

Under a two-link Chain, the stimulus which is the occasion for the intermittent presentation of food during the second link is also a conditioned reinforcer for responses during the first link. The relative frequency of responding during the concurrent first links of two Chains is a measure of the relative strength of the conditioned reinforcers which control this responding.

Procedure

VI in second link. Three birds, (P–44, P–77, and P–267) were used in a procedure in which responses produced food during the second links of two-link Chains programmed on two keys. The first links of the Chains, identical but independent *VI* 1s, were in force concurrently. A different colored light illuminated each key during these schedules: green on key *X* (left), white on key *F* (right). Each chain terminated in a *VI* schedule. The key color was then yellow on key *X*, or red on key *F*. The pigeon could be in only one

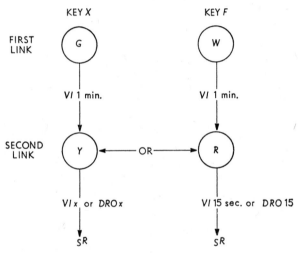

FIGURE 6.1. Diagram of the procedure. The first links of the two chains are programmed concurrently. Only one second link is in force at a time, and the other key is not illuminated. A second link ends after a specified period of time, and the first links again come into force. This cycle is repeated until a fixed number of food reinforcements have been presented during the second links. For some animals, the schedules in the second links were *VI*, and for other animals, *DRO*. Thus the schedules were CONC [(CHAIN *VI* 1 *VI* 15 sec) (CHAIN *VI* 1 *VI* *x*)] or CONC [(CHAIN *VI* 1 *DRO* 15) (CHAIN *VI* 1 *DRO* *x*)].

second link at a time. When one second link was in force, the other key was not illuminated and responding on it was never reinforced. Upon termination of an exposure to a *VI* food schedule, the first links were again in force. (See Figure 6.1 for a diagram of the procedure.) A white houselight provided general illumination.

The value of the second link schedule on key *F* was fixed (hence, "key *F*") at *VI* 15 sec (the standard value). The values of the second link schedule on key *X* were varied (hence, "key *X*") from *VI* 3.75 sec to 7.5 sec, 15 sec, 30 sec, and 1 min. For three of these values, 15 sec, 30 sec, and 1 min, the length of the exposure period was twice the mean value of the schedule. For example, the expo-sure period for *VI* 15 sec was 30 sec. For both *VI* 3.75 sec and *VI* 7.5 sec, 5 sec were added to twice the mean value of the schedule in order to compensate for the large portion of an exposure period taken up by the 5 sec food presentations. For *VI* 3.75 sec, the exposure time was therefore 12.5 sec, and for *VI* 7.5 sec, 20 sec. Since the longest interval of each *VI* schedule was slightly less than twice the mean interval of the schedule, at least one reinforcement was obtained during each exposure.

Each value of the second link on key *X* was continued until responding during the first links ceased to exhibit any progressive changes. About 30 sessions were generally required at each sched-ule value. The orders of presentation of the schedules were as follows: P–44: *VI* 15 sec, 1 min, 15 sec, 30 sec, 15 sec, 3.75 sec, 7.5 sec; P–77: *VI* 15 sec, 3.75 sec, 7.5 sec; P–267: *VI* 15 sec, 1 min, 15 sec, 30 sec, 1 min.

DRO in second link. A different procedure was used for three other birds (P–40, P–76, and P–270). Two-link Chains were pro-grammed for the two keys. The first links—identical, independent, *VI* 1 schedules—were in force concurrently. Key *X* was green, key *F* white; the houselight was not on. Responding produced intermit-tently the discriminative stimulus for a second link: a houselight of the same color as the key just responded on during the first links. In other words, a reinforced peck on key *X*, which was green, pro-duced a green houselight; a reinforced peck on key *F*, which was white, produced a white houselight. When either houselight was on, both keys were darkened. Food was then presented after a variable interval, provided no key peck occurred. Such a procedure is called *DRO* (differential reinforcement of zero responses, or other behav-ior). A response on either key turned off the houselight, blacking out the entire box and preventing the occurrence of further food presentations during that exposure period. The exposure time ter-minated as usual, and the first links were again in force.

The fixed *DRO* 15 schedule for key *F* corresponded to the fixed *VI* 15 sec schedule for key *F* in the first procedure and the *DRO* values for key *X* were identical to the *VI* values in the first procedure, as were the durations of the exposure periods and the *VI* programming tapes used. The criterion for changing the schedule of the second link for key *X* and the average number of sessions at each *DRO* value were also the same. The orders of presentation of the *DRO* schedules for key *X* were as follows: P–40: *DRO* 15 sec, 1 min, 30 sec, 15 sec; P–76: *DRO* 15 sec, 7.5 sec, 3.75 sec; P–270: *VI* 15 sec, 1 min, 15 sec, 30 sec, 15 sec, 7.5 sec, 3.75 sec. Each of the six birds obtained a fixed number of food presentations during a session. The number varied among subjects from 24 to 60, according to how many reinforcements a bird could receive without becoming overweight.

Results

The results for the response-dependent and *DRO* second-link procedures will be considered together. In each of the figures that follows, mean values of the *VI* or *DRO* schedules in the second link of the chain on key *X* are represented logarithmically on the abscissa. Equal distances on the abscissa represent equal relative increments in the mean frequency of reinforcement. Each point is the arithmetic mean obtained from the terminal five sessions for each value of the mean interval between reinforcements on key *X*. The corresponding mean interval between reinforcements on key *F* was always 15 sec. When values were replicated for a single bird, the point shown is the final replication. For each session, the mean frequency of food reinforcement actually obtained on each key was calculated by dividing the total exposure time to a schedule by the number of reinforcements received, and then compared to the programmed mean frequency of reinforcement. No substantial deviations between the two were noted.

Under the *DRO* procedure, responding during the second links of the two Chains was negligible. Occasionally, one or two responses were emitted on each key; usually, none was emitted. No further reference will be made to this responding.

Figures 6.2A and 6.2B present the overall mean rate of responding on both keys during the Concurrent first links of the two Chains for each value of the terminal *VI* or *DRO* on key *X*.

The total number of responses emitted on keys *X* and *F* is divided by the total time of the first links of the two Chains. Figure 6.2A represents the response-dependent procedure, with *VI* in the second link; Figure 6.2B represents the procedure with *DRO* in the second link. Variability in rate is evident among the six birds; the range for all birds extends from 25 to over 100 responses per minute. For two of three birds, responding during the first links of

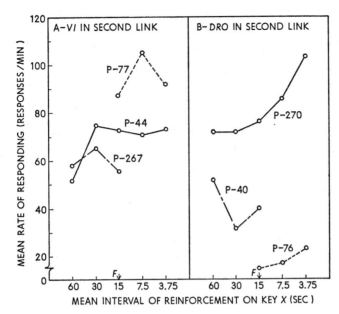

FIGURE 6.2. Overall mean rate of responding on both keys during the first links of the two Chains for each value of the second-link *VI* schedule on key *X*. The abscissa is a logarithmic scale. The value of the second-link *VI* or *DRO* schedule on key *F* is arrowed on the abscissa.

the Chains is sustained at lower rates when the second link is *DRO* than when it is *VI*. It is evident that responding is well maintained by conditioned reinforcing stimuli in this situation.

For any individual bird, the rate of responding is not constant over all of the schedule values. Changes in rate are frequent, and the direction of change coincides in some cases with the order in which the bird was exposed to the different values of the food *VI* or *DRO* for key *X*. P–76, P–77, and P–270 show an orderly increase in rate as a function of the order of presentation of the *VI* or *DRO* schedules. P–44's lowest rate is at *VI* 1, which was the first schedule to which it was exposed after an initial exposure to *VI* 15 sec (not shown). Rate changes, especially rate increases, are common during the course of extended observations.

The proportion of the total responses during the first links that was emitted on key *X* for each mean interval between reinforcements on key *X* is shown in Figures 6.3A and 6.3B for the *VI* second-link and *DRO* second-link procedures, respectively. This dependent variable is used as a measure of the relative strength of the two conditioned reinforcers which control responding during the first links. The points represented as squares are the values that would be expected if the relative frequency of responding on key X were to correspond to the relative frequency of primary reinforcement in the second links of the two Chains. For example, the reinforcement frequency of a *VI* 15-sec schedule is four times as great as the reinforcement frequency of a *VI* 1 schedule. If a bird's responses during the first links of the Chains were proportional to these frequencies, it would emit four times as many responses on the *VI* 15-sec key as on the *VI* 1 key. Consequently, 0.8 of its responses would be emitted on the *VI* 15-sec key, 0.2 on the *VI* 1 key.

The obtained values for each bird show that the relative strengths of the conditioned reinforcers which control responding during the first links are a function of the relative frequencies of reinforcement in the second links. As the mean interval between reinforcements on key X decreases (and the frequency of reinforcement increases) relative to the fixed-mean interval between reinforcements on key F, the relative frequency of responding on key X increases. At 30 sec and 60 sec, the obtained values deviate upward from the expected values, while at 3.75 sec and 7.5 sec, the obtained values deviate, in general, downward. In all instances, the ordering is preserved. For these four *VI* or *DRO* schedules, the obtained values, in general, do not attain the expected values, except at 7.5 sec. At *VI* or *DRO* 15 sec, when the frequencies of food reinforcement on keys X and F are equivalent, responding on each key is virtually equal. The two functions relating strength of conditioned reinforcers to relative frequency of reinforcement are negatively accelerated and do not markedly differ from each other at the values studied.

In spite of the variability among birds in overall concurrent rates, as shown in Figures 6.2A and 6.2B, the relative response rate functions are highly similar for all birds, as shown in Figures 6.3A and 6.3B. Replications of two of the *VI* and *DRO* schedules for key X (15 sec and 1 min) indicated that the patterns of responding during the first links were recoverable. The preferences for either key during the first links were not sufficiently prominent at any mean interval between reinforcements to cause deviations from an

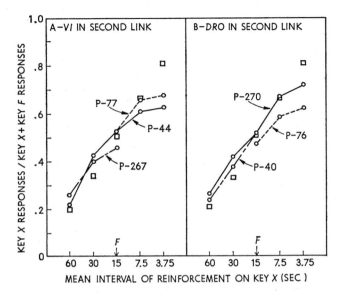

FIGURE 6.3.   Relative response rates on Key X during
first links for each mean interval between food reinforcements on Key X. The abscissa is a logarithmic scale. The
value of the second link VI or DRO schedule on key F
is arrowed on the abscissa.

approximately equal division of food reinforcements to the two
keys during individual sessions.

One means of assessing the generality of the obtained functions
is to use mean intervals of food reinforcement other than 15 sec as
the fixed value on key F. By this means some additional data were
obtained that bear on the general shape of the upper end of the
function relating relative response rate in the first link to value of
VI in the second link. P–267 was exposed to VI 3 schedules on both
keys during the second links of two chains. VI 1 was then introduced on key X. The proportion of the total responses during the
first links emitted on key X was 0.51 when the food schedules were
equivalent, and 0.71 when VI 1 was in force on key X. The last
value compares to an expected value of 0.75. P–77 received reinforcements according to VI 30 sec schedules on both keys during
the second links of two Chains. The schedule on key X was then
changed to VI 7.5 sec. When VI 30 sec was in force on each key, the
relative frequency of responding on key X during the first links
was 0.53. At VI 7.5 sec on key X, the obtained value was 0.72, as

compared to an expected value of 0.80. All obtained values are means of the last five sessions. The obtained values (0.71 and 0.72 for P–267 and P–77, respectively) fall below the expected values, and appear to confirm the general shape of the upper end of the function shown in Figure 6.3A.

The relative frequency of responding during the first links can be broken down into its component absolute rates. The rate of responding on each key for each value of the mean frequency between reinforcements on key X is shown for P–44 and P–270 in Figures 6.4A and 6.4B. The sum of the two rates is the overall concurrent rate. In general, changes in the relative frequency of response on key X are attained by the drawing apart of the individual rates on

TABLE 6.1

Relative Rate of Responding in First Links with Various *VI* Schedules in Second Links

Bird	Second Link *VI Schedule* Key X	Key F	Relative Rate of Reinforcement on Key X in Second Link	Relative Rate of Responding on Key X in First Link
267	3 min	3 min	0.50	0.51
267	1 min	3 min	0.75	0.71
77	30 sec	30 sec	0.50	0.53
77	7.5 sec	30 sec	0.80	0.72

each key from a virtual equality at *VI* 15 sec. For both birds, the rate on key X increases and the rate on key F decreases with increasing frequency of food reinforcement on key X. Exceptions to this are at the *VI* 1 value and the *VI* 3.75 sec for P–44 and at *DRO* 3.75 sec for P–270. Whereas the key X rate rises for each bird at *VI* 3.75 sec or *DRO* 3.75 sec, the key F rate remains relatively stable, instead of falling. Consequently, although the 3.75 sec schedule of the second link sustains a higher rate during the first link of the Chain on key X than does the 7.5 sec schedule, only a slight increase in the relative frequency of responding on key X results from changing the schedule to *VI* 3.75 sec or *DRO* 3.75 sec. The continued high rate on key F during the first link is probably due to the 15 sec schedule of food reinforcement in force during the second link. This high frequency of food presentation would be expected always to sustain a substantial rate during the first links.

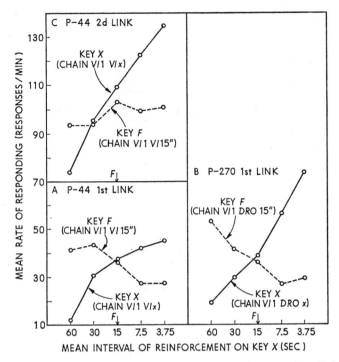

FIGURE 6.4. The rate of responding on each key during the first links of the two Concurrent Chains for each value of the mean interval between food reinforcements on key X is shown for birds P–44 and P–270 in A and B, respectively. The rate of responding during the second link of each Chain is shown for P–44 in C. P–44 had VI schedules in the second links and P–270 had DRO schedules. The abscissa is a logarithmic scale. The value of the VI or DRO schedule in the second link on key F is arrowed on the abscissa.

The rate of responding during the second link of each Chain is shown in Figure 6.4C for P–44, which was exposed to all of the VI food schedules on key X. The rate on key X increases with decreasing mean interval between reinforcements. The key F rate (i.e., on the VI 15 sec schedule) remains within a range of nine responses per minute. The key F curves in Figures 6.4A (first links) and 6.4C (second links) are dissimilar in shape, indicating either that they are independent of one another or that there is some variability.

In Figure 6.5, the rates during the first and second links of the Chains of each bird with VI schedules in the second links are presented together. The rates on the two keys are now shown as the ratio of the rate on key X to the rate on key F. The use of this ratio

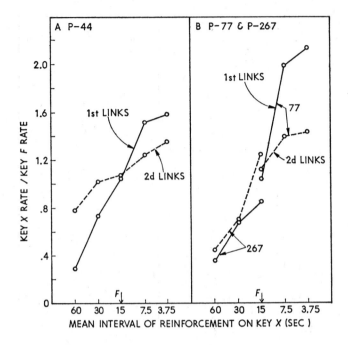

FIGURE 6.5. The ratio of the rates on the two keys during the first and second links of the Concurrent Chains for each value of the mean frequency between food reinforcements on key *X*. The data for P–44 are shown in A for P–77 and P–267 in B. All birds had *VI* schedules in the second links. The abscissa is a logarithmic scale. The value of the second-link *VI* schedule on key *F* is arrowed on the abscissa.

allows comparison between the rates during the first and second links, although the former were concurrent and the latter successive. The rate on key *F* was used as the denominator, because the schedule of food reinforcement for that key was held constant. For P–44 and P–77, when the ratio of the two rates during the first links is about 1, at *VI* 15 sec, the ratio of the two rates during the second links is approximately 1. In general, for all three birds, changes in the ratios of the rates during the first and second links covary, but the changes during the first links are of greater magnitude.

Figures 6.6A and 6.6B show how switching from one key to another during the first links is influenced by the mean interval between reinforcements in the second link of the chain on key *X*. The probability of a switch away from a given key is indicated on the ordinate, which is the number of times a switch is made from a

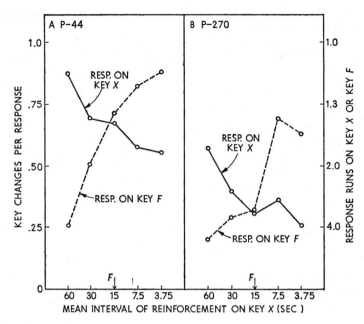

FIGURE 6.6. Switching from one key to another during the first links of the Chains as a function of the mean interval between reinforcements in the second link of the Chain on key X for P–44 and P–270. The abscissa is a logarithmic scale. The left and right scales of the ordinate are reciprocals. The plotted points show the mean number of consecutive responses on a particular key, as indicated. The value of the second-link VI schedule on key F is arrowed on the abscissa.

given key to the other key, divided by the total number of responses on the given key. For P–44, the probability of a switch away from key X decreases and the probability of a switch away from key F increases with increasing relative frequency of food reinforcement on key X. For P–270, this relationship is not so orderly. The reciprocal of the ordinate is the average number of responses on a key that occurs between a switch to a key and a switch away from it. In general, for both birds, as the relative frequency of reinforcement on key X increases, longer runs of responses on key X occur before a switch to the other key, while shorter runs of uninterrupted responses occur on key F.

Cumulative-response curves are presented in Figure 6.7. Responding on each key during each link of the Chain was recorded separately. During a single session, responding during either the first or the second links of the two Chains was recorded.

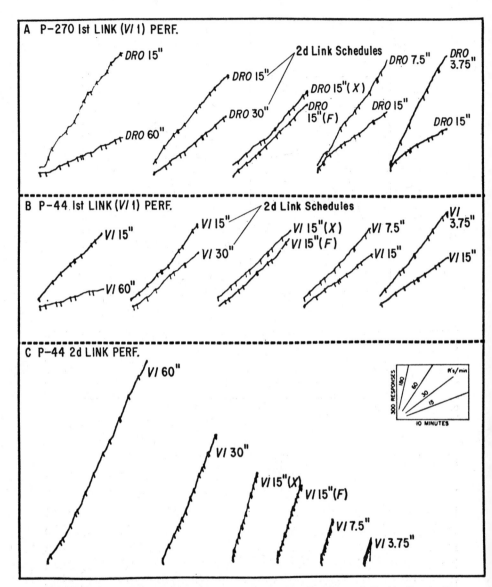

FIGURE 6.7. Cumulative-response curves for P–270 and P–44. In A the
schedule was CONC[(CHAIN *VI* 1 *DRO* 15 sec)(CHAIN *VI* 1 *DRO* *x*)].
Performance is shown on the first two links (*VI* 1) according to the schedule
in the second link. Pips indicate transitions to second links. B is the same as A,
except that the second-link schedules were *VI* rather than *DRO*. In C are
shown the performances of P–44 in the various *VI* schedules of the second link
on key *X* (except where indicated). Pips indicate reinforcements.

Figure 6.7 presents representative cumulative-response curves for two birds, P–270 and P–44. Each pair of curves in sections A and B is a complete record of responding during the first links during one of the last five sessions at each value of the schedule in the second link for key X. Section C of Figure 6.7 shows responding during the second links of the Chains for the same sessions shown in B for P–44. Responding is uniform, and the rate increases as the mean interval between reinforcements decreases.

DISCUSSION

The method used in this study provided a situation in which two operants, pecking on each of two keys, were sustained at high rates by the presentation of conditioned reinforcing stimuli. Considerable interbird variability in rate of responding occurred during the concurrent first links of the two Chain schedules. Rates ranging from 25 to 100 responses per minute were found for different birds. Despite this variability, a measure of the relative strengths of two conditioned reinforcers as a function of relative frequency of primary reinforcement was obtained which was in substantial agreement for the six birds used. The relative strengths of conditioned reinforcing stimuli were thus independent of the particular absolute rates of responding which prevailed.

The relative strength of a conditioned reinforcer was found to be a negatively accelerated function of relative frequency of food reinforcement. The range of relative frequencies of reinforcement studied was 1 to 16 reinforcements per minute, corresponding to VI values of 60 sec to 3.75 sec. Different procedures were used, in which food in the second link was dependent on key-pecking (VI schedules) or independent of key pecking (DRO schedules). Both procedures yielded essentially the same function relating relative conditioned reinforcing strength to relative frequency. Replications of two values of the mean frequency of reinforcement on key X indicated that points on the obtained functions were recoverable. The shape of the upper end of the function relating relative response rate in the first link to value of VI in the second link was confirmed by using two different standard values of the VI in the second link of the Chain on key F.

Wyckoff (1959) has formally derived functions for conditioned reinforcement based on data from "observing response" experiments. According to his model, conditioned reinforcing value would be a continuous and nondecreasing function of frequency of primary reinforcement, with positive acceleration in some region. The functions obtained in the present study were negatively accelerated, as have been many functions obtained in prior studies. For example, Bersh (1951) found that the function relating the strength of a conditioned reinforcer to the number of pairings between it and a primary reinforcer was negatively accelerated. The conditioned reinforcing strength of a stimulus was measured by its power to recondition a previously extinguished response. Miles (1956) confirmed Bersh's finding, using the number of responses emitted in Extinction as a measure of conditioned reinforcing strength. Miles also showed that the strength of a conditioned reinforcer was a negatively accelerated function of increasing hours of deprivation at the time of testing. There is the possibility, however, that the actual functions are S-shaped, in which case positive acceleration would be observed in a region of the curve, thus reconciling Miles's data with Wyckoff's theoretical model.

The strengths of conditioned reinforcers correlated with equivalent reinforcement frequencies were found to be equal. Deviations from equality were slight. This equality is a necessary precondition for the establishment of the functional relation demonstrated in this study.

The similarity of the functions for the relative strengths of conditioned reinforcers obtained with VI and DRO schedules in the second links indicates that the responding controlled by the conditioned reinforcers during the first links of the Chains is not necessarily determined by the responding during the second links. With the DRO schedules, the occurrence of the same operant during both parts of the Chain was not a necessary condition for the emergence of the relation between relative frequency of reinforcement and relative frequency of response. Therefore, the effective variable controlling relative response rates in the first links is frequency of food reinforcement in the second link.

Gollub (1958) pointed out that a stimulus that functioned as a discriminative stimulus did not necessarily serve as a conditioned reinforcer. This statement is in opposition to the widely accepted notion that a stimulus that is a discriminative stimulus is also a conditioned reinforcer (Dinsmoor, 1950; Schoenfeld, Antonitis, & Bersh, 1950). Gollub presented data which showed that while the initial stimulus of a two or three-link Chain controlled moderate rates of responding, it did not serve as a conditioned reinforcer for responses during an added preceding link.

Under the present procedure with *DRO* schedules in the second links, a stimulus clearly functioned as a conditioned reinforcer, but did not meet the usual requirement for a discriminative stimulus, at least with respect to the operant that produced the stimulus. The latter is defined as the occasion upon which a response is followed, usually intermittently, by reinforcement. Under the response-independent procedure, a stimulus became the occasion for the intermittent presentation of food without the intervening occurrence of a specified response (other than eating), but served nevertheless as a strong conditioned reinforcer. There is the possibility that some response or chain of responses, neither under the control of the experimenter nor measured, did become "superstitiously" reinforced, and occurred fairly consistently during the terminal parts of the two chains. Unfortunately, it was impossible to observe a bird's behavior during a session in order to obtain evidence concerning the possible existence of such superstitious behavior.

EXPERIMENT 2: PROBABILITY OF REINFORCEMENT

Introduction

In Experiment 1, a quantitative relationship was found between relative frequency of reinforcement and the relative strength of a conditioned reinforcer. As the frequency of reinforcement associated with a conditioned reinforcing stimulus was increased, the proportion of responding maintained by that stimulus during the Concurrent first links of two Chains also increased. In the present study, another independent variable, probability of reinforcement, is investigated. The question is raised: Is there a functional relation between probability of primary reinforcement and the strength of a conditioned reinforcer?

The problem can be approached through the use of variable-ratio (*VR*) schedules of reinforcement. (Under a *VR* schedule, reinforcements are programmed according to a random series of ratios. The particular number of responses required varies from reinforcement to reinforcement; the extreme values are chosen arbitrarily for an individual experiment.) A particular *VR* is designated by the mean number of responses required for reinforcement. The probability of reinforcement for a single response is the reciprocal of the size of the ratio. For example, in VR 100, when, on the average, one reinforcement is obtained for every 100 responses, the probability of reinforcement for a single response is 1/100th.

Ferster and Skinner (1957) have reported experiments in which VR schedules were studied. Their general finding was that these schedules, at low mean ratios of reinforcement, maintain responding at high, sustained rates of 3 to 8 responses per second. Pauses in responding tend to occur as the size of the mean ratio is increased; these pauses usually do not occur after reinforcement.

Procedure

Two birds (P–108 and P–272) were subjects. A two-link Chain was programmed on each of two keys. The first links of the Chains —identical, independent, VI 1 schedules—were programmed concurrently. Key X (left) was green, key F (right) white. During the second link of each chain, food was presented according to a VR schedule. Key X was yellow, key F red. When a VR schedule was in force on one key, the other key was darkened, and responding on it had no programmed consequence. An exposure to a VR schedule terminated after two food presentations, and the Concurrent first links again came into force. A white houselight provided general illumination. (The diagram of the procedure for Experiment 1, shown in Figure 6.1, applies if VR schedules are substituted for VI in the second links. Thus the schedule was CONC [(CHAIN VI 1 VR 40) (CHAIN VI 1 VRx)]. In addition, a second link now ends after two reinforcements.)

The second link of the Chain for key F was always VR 40. The values of the schedule in the second link for key X were VR 16, 28, 40, 57, 100. The orders of presentation were as follows: P–108: VR 40, 100, 40, 28, 16, 57; bird 272: VR 40, 100, 40, 57, 28, 16. Each VR value was continued on key X until responding during the initial links no longer exhibited any progressive changes. About 25 sessions were generally required. A daily session consisted of 40 reinforcements during the initial VR 40 and VR 100 values; the session length was increased to 52 reinforcements for the remainder of the experiment.

Results

The results for this experiment will be presented as in Experiment 1. In each of the following figures, the values of the VR schedule in the second link of the Chain on key X are represented logarithmically on the abscissa. Equal distances on the abscissa represent equal relative increments in the size of the variable ratio. Each point which is plotted is the arithmetic mean of data from the last five sessions for each value of the VR schedule on key X. The corresponding schedule on key F was always VR 40. The data obtained from two presentations of VR 40 on key X were similar, showing that the points were recoverable. The data from the second presentation are plotted in the figures.

The overall mean rate of responding on both keys during the first links for each value of the VR schedule on key X is presented for both birds in Figure 6.8A. The graph is a semilog plot. Total

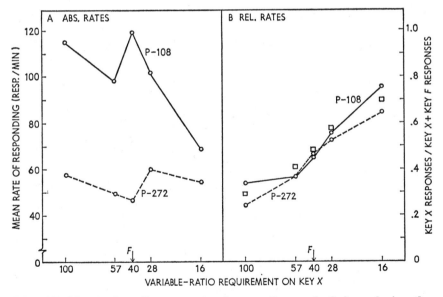

FIGURE 6.8. A. Overall mean rate of responding on both keys during the first links of the two Concurrent chains for each value of the VR schedule on key X. B. The relative response rate on key X during the first links for each value of the VR schedule on that key. The abscissa is a logarithmic scale. The value of the second link VR schedule on key F is arrowed on the abscissa.

responding on keys X and F during the first links is divided by the total time in these links in order to calculate the overall rate. The rate of responding maintained by the presentation of the conditioned reinforcing stimuli is high for each bird. P–108 has a higher rate, in general, than does P–272. The rate changes for each bird are not correlated in a systematic way with the order of presentation of the VR schedules on key X.

Figure 6.8B shows the proportion of the total responses during the first links that was emitted on key X for each value of the VR schedule on that key. The corresponding schedule on key F was held constant at VR 40. The points shown on the figure as squares indicate the values that would be expected if the relative frequency of responding on key X were to correspond to the relative probability of reinforcement in the second links of the two Chains. The agreement between the obtained and expected proportions is fairly close for both birds. The maximum deviation for P–108 is 0.06; for P–272, the maximum deviation is 0.05. The obtained values for P–272 are consistently below the expected values. The obtained values for P–108 deviate on both sides of the expected values: at VR 57, 40, and 28, the obtained are below the expected values, and at the ends of the function, above the expected values. The functions are negatively accelerated. The preference for either key during the first links was not sufficiently marked at any value of the VR schedule to cause deviations from an approximately equal division of food reinforcements to the two keys during individual sessions.

The results show that the relative strengths of the conditioned reinforcers which control responding during the first links are a function of the relative probabilities of reinforcement in the second links of the two Chains. As the probability of reinforcement on key X increases relative to the constant probability of reinforcement on key F, the relative frequency of responding on key X during the first links increases. This relative increase indicates an increment in the relative strength of the conditioned reinforcing stimulus that controls responding on key X. The relation between relative probability and relative strength is negatively accelerated, as is the relation between relative frequency and relative strength. When the schedules of food reinforcement on both keys X and F are VR 40, the frequencies of responding on each key are virtually equivalent. This shows that the strengths of the two conditioned reinforcers associated with these identical probabilities of food reinforcement are equal.

The rate of responding on each key during the first links for each VR schedule on key X is presented for both birds in Figures 6.9A and 6.9B. In general, a given relative frequency of response is attained by rate changes in opposite directions. For P–272, the rate on key X increases as a function of decreasing VR size in the second

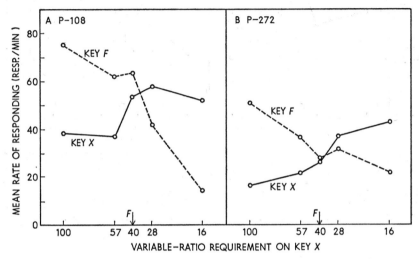

FIGURE 6.9. Rate of responding on each key during the first links of the two Concurrent Chains for each VR schedule on key X for P–108 and P–272. The abscissa is a logarithmic scale. The value of the second link VR schedule on key F is arrowed on the abscissa.

link on that key. For P–108, the corresponding curve is not monotonically increasing. The rate on key F tends to fall as a function of decreasing VR size for both birds, but there is a single reversal in each curve.

Figures 6.10A and 6.10B show how switching from one key to the other during the first links is influenced by the relative probabilities of reinforcement in the second links. The probability of a switch away from a given key is indicated on the ordinate, which is the number of times a switch is made from a given key to the other divided by the total number of responses on the given key. The abscissa is a logarithmic scale. The relationships are irregular, but

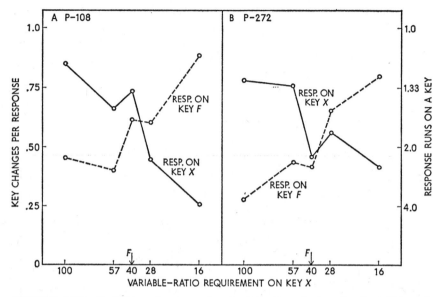

FIGURE 6.10. Switching from one key to the other during the first links of the Chains as a function of the variable-ratio requirement in the second link of the Chain on key X. The abscissa is a logarithmic scale. The left and right scales of the ordinate are reciprocals. The plotted points show the mean number of consecutive responses on a particular key, as indicated. The value of the second link VR schedule on key F is arrowed on the abscissa.

suggest that, in general, the probability of a switch away from key X decreases and the probability of a switch away from key F increases with increasing probability of food reinforcement on key X.

Figures 6.11A and 6.11B present the rates of responding during the second links of the chains for both birds. The schedule on key F is always VR 40; the values of the VR schedule on key X are represented logarithmically on the abscissa. The rates are uniformly high for each bird, ranging from more than two to over three responses per second. In calculating the rates shown, no adjustment was made for pausing during any of the VR schedules. For both birds, the rate on key X during the second link does not increase systematically as the size of the ratio is decreased. There is one reversal for P–272 and two reversals for P–108. The order of these rate changes does not appear to be correlated with the order in which each bird was exposed to the various VR schedules on key X. The key F rate, for which the schedule was always VR 40,

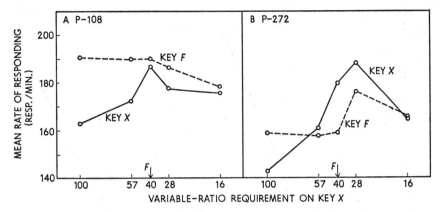

FIGURE 6.11.   Rates of responding during the second links of the two Concurrent Chains for P–108 and P–272. The schedule on key F was always VR 40; the values of the VR schedules on key X are represented logarithmically on the abscissa.

remains more uniform for P–108 than for bird P–272. For both birds, the key X and key F terminal rates appear to covary at some values.

The rates during the first and second links of the Chains are presented together in Figure 6.12. The rates on the two keys are now shown as the ratio of the rate on key X to the rate on key F. (The rate on key F was used as the denominator because the schedule of food reinforcement for that key was held constant.) The ratio of the two rates during the second links remains within a narrow range, while the ratio of the rates during the first links changes considerably.

Figures 6.13 and 6.14 present representative cumulative-response curves for P–108 and P–272, respectively. Each pair of curves in section A of each figure is a complete record of responding during the first links for one of the last five sessions at each value of the VR schedule on key X. The relations summarized in Figures 6.9A and 6.9B can be observed within single sessions.

Section B of each of Figures 6.13 and 6.14 shows responding during the second links under each value of the VR schedule on key X for the same sessions in section A. The middle two records are for keys X and F, when VR 40 was in force in the second link on each key. The remaining curves are responding on key X. Responding is sustained at high rates under all of the VR schedules, as

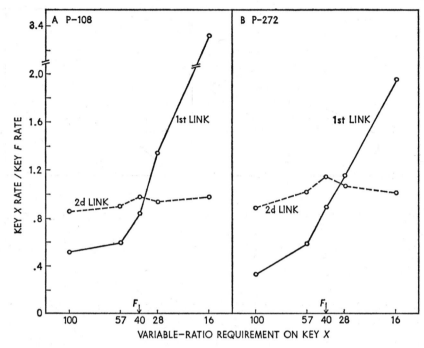

FIGURE 6.12. The ratio of the rates on the two keys during the first and second links of the Concurrent Chains for each VR schedule on key X for P–108 and P–272. The abscissa is a logarithmic scale. The value of the second link VR schedule on key F is arrowed on the abscissa.

summarized in Figure 6.11. For P–108 and P–272, some short pauses occur after reinforcements under VR 100. P–272 also pauses slightly during VR 57.

DISCUSSION

Responding was characteristically sustained at a high rate during the Concurrent first links of the two Chains. The relative frequency of responding on the two keys during the first links was used as a measure of the relative strength of the conditioned reinforcers which controlled this responding. In other words, the reinforcing strength of a stimulus, in this case a conditioned-reinforcing stimulus, was measured by the relative degree of responding which it maintained.

In Experiment 2, the influence of relative probabilities of rein-

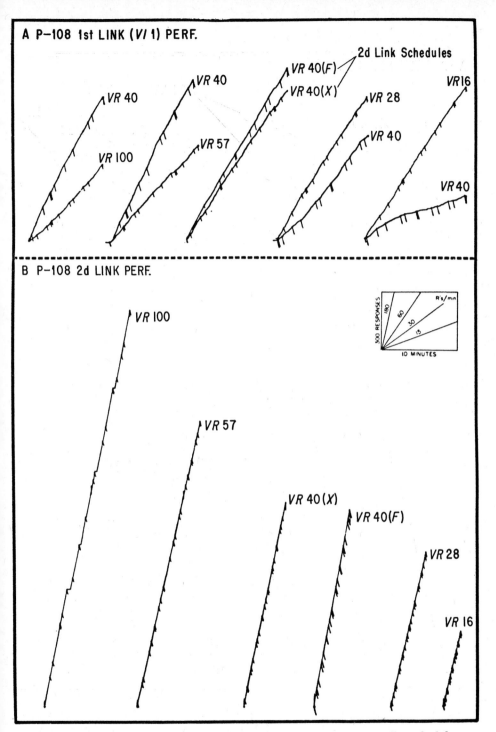

FIGURE 6.13. Cumulative-response curves for P–108. In A the schedule was CONC[(CHAIN VI 1 VR 40)(CHAIN VI 1 VR x)]. Performance is shown on the first two links (VI 1) according to the schedule in the second link. Pips indicate transitions to second links. In B are shown the performances in the various VR schedules of the second link on key X (except where indicated). Pips indicate reinforcements.

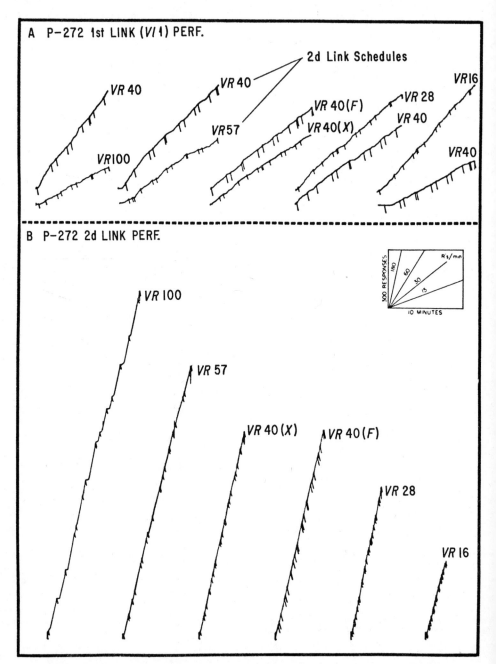

FIGURE 6.14. Cumulative-response curves for P–272. In A the schedule was CONC[(CHAIN *VI* 1 *VR* 40) (CHAIN *VI* 1 *VR* *x*)]. Performance is shown on the first two links (*VI* 1) according to the schedule in the second link. Pips indicate transitions to second links. In B are shown the performances in the various *VR* schedules of the second link on key *X* (except where indicated). Pips indicate reinforcements.

forcement on the relative strengths of conditioned reinforcers was investigated. It was shown that the strength of a conditioned reinforcer increased as a function of increasing probability of food reinforcement associated with it. In Experiment 1, it was shown that the strength of a conditioned reinforcer increased as a function of increasing frequency of food reinforcement. The values obtained for the strengths of conditioned reinforcers in Experiment 2 were in substantial agreement with the expected values. These expected values were calculated on the basis of the relative probabilities of reinforcement in the second links of the two Chains. The function relating relative strength to relative probability was negatively accelerated.

When the probabilities of food reinforcement in the second links of the Chains were the same, approximately equal numbers of responses were emitted on each key during the Concurrent first links. Therefore, the strengths of the conditioned reinforcers were equal under this condition. In Experiment 1, it was found that when the frequencies of food reinforcement in the second links were equal, the strengths of the associated conditioned reinforcers were also equal.

In order to compare the results of Experiments 1 and 2, it is possible to exchange abscissas for plotting the relative strength data. This can be done by the use of two simple transformations.

1. Under a variable-interval schedule, the average number of responses that a bird emits to obtain a food presentation varies with the length of the mean interval between reinforcements. In general, as the mean interval increases, so does the mean number of responses per reinforcement. This provides an independent variable comparable to a variable-ratio schedule, since a *VR* is specified by the mean number of responses required for a food presentation.

2. Under a variable-ratio schedule, the average number of seconds between food presentations varies with the mean number of responses required for a food presentation. In general, as the requirement increases, so does the mean number of seconds between food presentations. This provides an independent variable comparable to a variable-interval schedule, since a *VI* is expressed as the mean inverval between reinforcements.

The mean number of responses per reinforcement was calculated for each value of the *VI* schedule studied for P–44, P–77, and P–267. Each of these birds had to peck to obtain a food presentation (response-contingent procedure). The mean number of seconds between reinforcements was calculated for each value of the *VR* schedule studied for P–108 and P–272. The results of these calculations are used in Figure 6.15.

The ordinate of Figure 6.15 is the proportion of the total re-

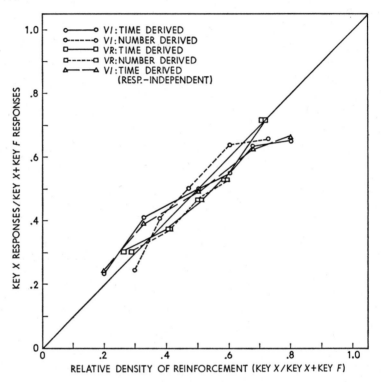

FIGURE 6.15. Functions for conditioned reinforcement, from both Experiments 1 and 2. See text for explanation.

sponses during the first links of the Chains emitted on key *X*. The values plotted are those shown in Figures 6.3A and 6.3B, but they are now the means for P–44, P–77, and P–267 and for P–108 and P–272. The mean data for P–40, P–76, and P–270 (*DRO* in second link) are also shown. The individual data are shown in Figure 6.3B.

The abscissa is the relative density of reinforcement on key *X*, where density can mean either frequency or probability. Five curves are shown:

1. *VI: Time-derived.*   The average data for the birds in Experiment 1 with *VI* schedules in the second link are plotted against the original relative frequency of reinforcement on key *X*.
2. *VI: Number-derived.*   These same data are plotted against the relative probability of reinforcement on key *X*. The abscissa was obtained from the transformation to mean number of responses emitted per reinforcement, averaged for the three birds.
3. *VR: Time-derived.*   The average data for the birds used in Experiment 2 are plotted against the relative frequency of reinforcement on key *X*. The abscissa was scaled according to the transformation to mean number of seconds between reinforcements, averaged for the two birds.
4. *VR: Number-derived.*   These same data are plotted against the original relative probability of reinforcement on key *X*.
5. *VI: Time-derived (Response-independent).*   The average data for the birds in Experiment 1 with *DRO* schedules in the second links are plotted against the original relative frequency of reinforcement on key *X*. A transformation to mean number of responses emitted per reinforcement is not possible, because each of these birds received food only when it did not peck.

The diagonal solid line which passes through the origin shows the function that would be obtained if the relative frequency of responding on key *X* were to match the relative density of reinforcement on that key. The five obtained functions correspond closely to the expected function. The *VR* time-derived and number-derived curves are virtually identical over the range of values studied. The *VI* number-derived curve is a somewhat better match to the expected function than is the *VI* time-derived curve.

Although both interval and ratio schedules were used to program the availability of food presentations, the choice of whether to select frequency or probability of reinforcement as the independent variable does not appear to be critical. Either seconds between reinforcements or responses per reinforcement can be used as the abscissa against which the relative response rates are to be plotted. This suggests that as far as conditioned reinforcement is concerned, there is no real difference between frequency and probability of reinforcement. In addition, the number-derived curves obtained with *VI* and *DRO* schedules in the second link in Experiment 1 are virtually identical. All of the findings suggest that the functions obtained for conditioned reinforcement in these studies are invariant under these different variations of procedure and independent variable.

Although the conditioned reinforcement functions obtained with the *VI* schedules in the second links in Experiments 1 and the *VR* schedules in Experiment 2 were very similar, other results did differ. In Experiment 2, the ratio of the rates on the two keys during the first links of the Chains changed widely over the values of the food reinforcement schedule on key *X*, but the ratio of the rates during the terminal variable-ratio schedules varied only slightly. It would appear that the patterns of responding during the first links were thus not determined in any obvious way by the patterns of responding during the second links. In Experiment 1, both ratios did covary. The changes in the ratio of the rates during the first links were of greater magnitude than the changes during the second links. The two conditioned reinforcement functions, which were based on the relative frequency of responding during the first links, were nevertheless similar. This suggests that the responding on the two keys during the second links did not determine the forms of the functions. In addition, with *DRO* schedules in the second links in Experiment 1, pecking did not occur during the second links. The function obtained was still virtually identical to the one obtained with the *VI* schedule in the second links, in which pecking did take place during the second links.

RELATED METHODS

The method used in the present study will be compared to those used in previous studies on conditioned reinforcement in Chain schedules.

The method reported by Findley (1954) used a two-link Chain schedule, programmed on one key. The first link of the Chain was always *VI* 4. The value of the *VI* in the second link was either 30 sec, 1, 2, 4, or 8 min. The rate of responding during the first link showed an orderly increase as a function of increasing frequency of food reinforcement in the second link. The rate increased by at least a factor of 10 for the three rats used. The results indicated that the strength of the conditioned reinforcer which controlled responding during the first link of the Chain increased as a function of increasing frequency of primary reinforcement in the second link.

One difficulty with Findley's study is that only extremely low rates of responding were maintained during the first link of the Chain. The maximum rates for the three rats during the first link when VI 8 was in effect in the second link were 0.5, 0.4, and 0.3 responses per minute. The highest rates attained, when the second link was VI 30 sec, were 4.6, 4.0, and 4.1 responses per minute. These low rates can probably be attributed to the comparatively long VI 4 in the first link, and do not provide an optimal base line for experimental manipulation. The fact that the rate during the first link changed by as much as a factor of 10 can probably be explained by the extremely low absolute rates which obtained. For example, an increase from 0.4 to 4.0 responses per minute represents a tenfold increase, while the absolute increase is only 3.6 responses per minute. In addition, the situation was one in which a conditioned reinforcer did not evidence sufficient strength to sustain responding at appreciable levels.

The question of whether responding during the first link of a two-link Chain is maintained by responding during the second link or by the reinforcements in the presence of the stimulus correlated with that link was studied by Ferster and Skinner (1957, pp. 684–85). A single bird was placed on a CHAIN VI 1 FI 1. The procedure was then changed so that reinforcement was independent of a response at the end of the FI 1. Since no requirement was added to limit responding during FI 1, this responding continued at a low rate because of accidental correlations between responses and reinforcement. Responding during VI 1 underwent no substantial decline during the response-independent procedure. Ferster and Skinner concluded that the conditioned-reinforcing property of the discriminative stimulus of the second link appeared to derive from its correlation with food, regardless of whether or not the bird was responding in the presence of this discriminative stimulus. This procedure should be repeated with additional subjects.

In the present study, a related question was investigated. It was found that the shape of the function relating the relative strengths of conditioned reinforcers to relative frequency of primary reinforcement was the same whether food presentations were dependent on responding or not responding. A comparison was not made between the two procedures with a single bird. It was observed, however, that responding during the first links of the Chains was well maintained in both cases.

There is one major difficulty with a procedure in which a two-link Chain schedule is programmed on one key in order to study the strength of the conditioned reinforcer which controls responding during the first link. The rate of responding during the first link serves as the dependent variable, but it may not be sufficiently sensitive to experimental operations. There is the possibility that a "locked rate" will develop. A locked rate frequently occurs after a long history of exposure to variable-interval schedules, and is characterized by the fact that it is not easily changed by any manipulation. This fact limits its usefulness as a dependent variable. Herrnstein,[2] however, has found that the relative frequency of responding during two Concurrent variable-interval schedules remains sensitive to experimental operations over long periods. The results of the present studies confirm Herrnstein's finding, and show that the relative frequency of responding during two identical Concurrent schedules is a sensitive measure of the strength of conditioned reinforcers.

SUMMARY

Two-link Chain schedules of reinforcement were used to study quantitative properties of conditioned reinforcers. Under a two-link Chain schedule, responding during the first link is controlled by the conditioned reinforcing properties of the stimulus for the second link. When appropriate schedules are programmed in both links, responding during the first link occurs at a high rate, and consequently provides an adequate base line for studying the strength of a conditioned reinforcer. In one experiment the frequency of food reinforcement associated with a conditioned reinforcer was varied, and in a second experiment the probability of food reinforcement was varied.

A two-link Chain schedule was programmed for each key in a two-key pigeon chamber. The first links of the Chains were independent, identical *VI* 1 schedules, programmed concurrently. Responding on either key produced intermittently a new stimulus for that key, correlated with a particular schedule of food reinforcement for the second link of the Chain. The second link of the Chain for the other key could not occur at the same time. After a specified period of exposure to a terminal schedule, the first links again came

---

[2] Personal communication, 1959.

into force. The relative strengths of the two conditioned reinforcers which controlled responding during the first links of the Chains were measured by the relative frequency of responding which each maintained.

In Experiment 1, *VI* or *DRO* schedules determined the frequencies of primary reinforcement associated with the two conditioned reinforcing stimuli. The value of the *VI* schedule in the second link on one key was held constant, while the value of the *VI* schedule in the second link on the other key was varied. Two procedures were used. (*a*) Food reinforcements were made contingent upon the bird's responding during the second link of the Chain. (*b*) Food reinforcements were presented only if the bird did not respond during the second link.

In spite of interbird variability in rate of responding during the first links of the Chains, the relative frequency of response measure was in substantial agreement for six birds. Both procedures yielded the same results: (1) the strengths of conditioned reinforcers correlated with equivalent frequencies of reinforcement were equal; (2) the relative strength of a conditioned reinforcer increased with increasing relative frequency of food reinforcement. Negatively accelerated functions were obtained under the two procedures. The occurrence of the same response (key pecking) during both the first and second links of the Chains was not a necessary precondition for the establishment of the functional relation between relative strength and relative frequency. This relation, then, can be attributed to the different frequencies of food reinforcement, and is not necessarily mediated by responding during the second links.

The effect of probability of food reinforcement on the strength of conditioned reinforcers was investigated in Experiment 2. Reinforcements during the second links of the Chains were presented according to variable-ratio schedules. The probability of reinforcement for any single response is the reciprocal of the value of the ratio. The value of the *VR* schedule on one key was held constant, while the value of the *VR* schedule on the other key was varied. The strengths of the two conditioned reinforcers were equal when the associated probabilities of food reinforcement were equal. As the relative probability of primary reinforcement increased, the relative strength of an associated conditioned reinforcer also increased. The function was negatively accelerated.

When food presentations are obtained by pecking, frequency

and probability of reinforcement can be interchanged by simple arithmetic transformations. When this was done, it was found that either could be satisfactorily used as the independent variable for Experiments 1 and 2. The relative strength curves were virtually the same, whether frequency or probability was the independent variable. This suggests that as far as conditioned reinforcement is concerned, there is no real difference between frequency and probability of reinforcement.

chapter 7

CONDITIONED REINFORCEMENT, CHOICE, AND THE PSYCHOLOGICAL DISTANCE TO REWARD[1]

Edmund Fantino

University of California, San Diego

The present paper discusses the strength of conditioned reinforcers in a choice situation. It discusses some experiments that used the choice technique to study the relation between conditioned reinforcement and the manner in which primary reinforcement occurs in its presence. This leads to an outline of a program for investigating some situations in which behavior is poorly maintained by conditioned reinforcement. In particular we are interested in quantifying a variable we will call "the psychological distance to reward."

Conditioned reinforcement has generally been studied in one of three ways. In one technique (Bugelski, 1938; Skinner, 1938), responses during training produce primary reward accompanied or preceded by an ostensibly neutral stimulus. When the response no longer produces primary reward (Extinction), the subject responds more often when the neutral stimulus is produced by its responses than when its responses are totally ineffective. This may be taken as evidence that the stimulus has acquired value as a conditioned reinforcer. One difficulty with this technique, however, is that stimulus generalization, and not conditioned reinforcement, may be responsible for the more persistent responding, since the difference between training and Extinction is less marked when the stimulus occurs occasionally. A second technique also omits pri-

[1] The research reported in this paper was primarily supported by NSF Grant GB-3626 to Yale University and by NSF Grant GB-6659 to the University of California, San Diego. The experiment done in collaboration with R. J. Herrnstein was also supported by NSF Grant GB-3121 to Harvard University.

mary reward but requires the subject to learn a new response which produces the stimulus (Miller, 1951). Conditioned reinforcement has been somewhat difficult to demonstrate using this procedure, perhaps because the potency of the conditioned reinforcer is itself waning in Extinction and is therefore not sufficient to reinforce the new response. The third technique maintains the effectiveness of the conditioned reinforcer by continuing to present primary reward in its presence. This is accomplished by using Chain schedules of reinforcement, which have been discussed extensively by Ferster and Skinner (1957), Kelleher and Gollub (1962), and by Kelleher (1966a). In a two-link Chain, for example, responses in the first link produce a different stimulus in the presence of which responses produce primary reward. This general procedure has at least one potential weakness, namely, that the effects of primary and conditioned reinforcement may be confounded. We shall discuss some evidence against this proposition later on. Now we shall turn to Autor's (1960) procedure for studying conditioned reinforcement with Concurrent-Chain schedules. Figure 7.1 depicts his general procedure, which is given in detail in Chapter 6.

This procedure has at least two important advantages. In the first place, the procedure keeps the number of conditioned reinforcements for responses in each first link fairly constant over a wide range of preference for pecking one key or the other. If a subject responds exclusively on one key, for example, all reinforcements would be delivered for those responses. However, because of the nature of concurrently available *VI* schedules, the subject produces a higher rate of reinforcement if it responds on both keys: the subject would be reinforced twice as often if it occasionally responded on each key. In practice, this assures that the number of reinforcers obtained on each key will be equal. Thus, the effects of number of conditioned reinforcements are not confounded with those of the independent variable. Moreover, this independence is achieved without resorting to the practice of forced trials which has been used in traditional experiments on choice to keep the number of trials or reinforcements for each alternative response equal. For example, after a rat chooses one of two sides of a *T*-maze, it is then run through with only the other side open. Thus, running to the only open side of the maze is considered as "equalizing" the effects of the rat's previous choice of one of two open sides. Similar, but more forceful, tactics have been employed with the jumping stand.

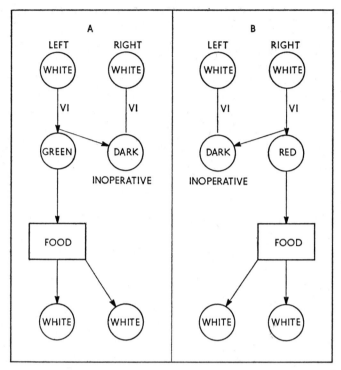

FIGURE 7.1. Pictorial representation of the Concurrent-Chains procedure. Figure 7.1A indicates the sequence of events when responses on the left key are reinforced. Figure 7.1B represents the analogous sequence on the right key. *VI* schedules program access to the stimuli of the second links. When such access is scheduled by either *VI* programmer, it stops operating, but the other *VI* programmer continues to operate. The next response on the appropriate key produces the second stimulus associated with that key and two additional events: (1) the *VI* programmer associated with the other key stops operating; (2) illumination is removed from the other key, which becomes inoperative. Pecks in the presence of either second stimulus produce food according to some schedule. Following food reinforcement, the first links are reinstated.

The second advantage concerns the study of conditioned reinforcement in a choice situation. The work of Catania (1963, 1966) and Herrnstein (1961) has shown the sensitivity of choice procedures to primary reinforcement parameters which do not always produce clear effects in single-stimulus experiments. This differential sensitivity may also hold for variables affecting conditioned reinforcement (for example, cf., Rachlin, 1967; Reynolds, 1963a).

In summary, then, with the Concurrent-Chains procedure we may study conditioned reinforcement: (1) in Chain schedules, where the problem of extinction of the conditioned reinforcer is avoided and (2) in a choice situation where responding seems to be maximally sensitive to experimental manipulations.

To bring us up to date, I shall now very briefly review some published experiments which have used the Concurrent-Chains design to study positive reinforcement. Autor (1960) varied the schedules of reinforcement in the presence of the conditioned reinforcer. He found that the distribution of responding in the first links was proportional to the rate (reinforcements/time) of reinforcement obtained in the second links. Herrnstein (1964a) extended and clarified this finding. Reinforcements in the presence of the second-link stimuli were obtained on variable-interval or variable-ratio schedules. He found that pigeons distributed their responses during the first links in the same proportion as reinforcements were distributed in the second links, they matched proportions of responses to proportions of reinforcements. For example, the rate of reinforcement on the right key was sometimes twice as great as the rate on the left key. In that case, the pigeon emitted twice as many responses on the right key as on the left key during the concurrently presented first links of the two Chains. Both Herrnstein (1964b) and Fantino (1967) studied the relation between conditioned reinforcement and the intermittency of primary reinforcement obtained in the presence of the conditioned reinforcing stimulus. In Fantino's study, primary reinforcement in one second link was always obtained on one fixed-ratio (FR) schedule, while either two or three FR values were possible in the other second link. Thus, the pigeons chose between a stimulus correlated with an FR schedule of food reward and one correlated with a mixed-ratio schedule. When the arithmetic mean of the mixed ratios equaled the fixed ratio, the stimulus associated with the mixed ratio was preferred, despite the fact that rate of reinforcement was generally *lower* in its presence. In other words, the simple equality between the proportion of responding in the first links and the proportion of reinforcements in the second links was disrupted. There was a suggestion, however, that the distribution of responding in the first links, i.e., choice, could be described by comparing the geometric mean of the reinforcement rates in the several mixed-ratio components with the reinforcement rates in the FR component. Finally, when the FR was sufficiently smaller than the arithmetic mean of the mixed-ratios preference shifted to it.

Each of these studies was concerned with describing the relation in a choice situation between the strength of a conditioned rein-

forcer and the rate of primary reinforcement occurring in its presence. We shall now turn to two studies in which the rate of reinforcement is kept constant and other variables are manipulated.
The first study investigates the effect upon choice of *requiring* a
particular response rate in the presence of the conditioned reinforcer. The second manipulates the number of primary reinforcers
obtained.

Herrnstein's (1964a) study had indicated that the distribution
of responses in the first links is not sensitive to the rates of *responding* in the second links, although he did not directly manipulate these rates of responding. This points to the possibility that
choice in this situation is determined solely by the rates of reinforcement. Premack (1965, pp. 159–61), for example, has predicted
that if different schedules of reinforcement yield the same probability and duration of the primary reinforcer, then the conditioned
reinforcing value of the stimuli associated with each schedule will
be the same. In the present study the schedule of reinforcement
associated with the second link of one Chain provides reinforcement only when the organism responds at a high rate, or, for some
subjects, at a low rate. The schedule associated with the other
second link does not require a particular rate of responding, but is
arranged to provide the same rate of reinforcement. Therefore, if
rate of primary reinforcement is the sole determinant of choice in
this situation, then the distribution of responses in the two first
links should not differ systematically.

Six White Carneaux pigeons, maintained at 80 percent of their
normal body weights, were used in this experiment. A standard
two-key experimental chamber (Ferster & Skinner, 1957) and
standard programming and recording equipment were used.

In the main part of the experiment, the birds were reinforced on
two Concurrent Chains: either CHAIN *VI* differential reinforcement of high rates (*DRH*) on one key concurrent with CHAIN *VI*
fixed-interval (*FI*) on the other or CHAIN *VI* differential reinforcement of low rates (*DRL*) on one key concurrent with CHAIN
VI FI on the other. At the start of a session on these Concurrent
Chains, each key was lit from behind by a white light. Identical, *VI*
1 schedules were associated with the first links of each key. In the
second link the left key was green and the right key was red. Pecks
in the presence of the green light were reinforced on the *DRH*
schedule (Pigeons P–14, P–16, P–19) or the *DRL* schedule (Pigeons P–1, P–17, P–18). Pecks in the presence of the second stimu-

lus on the right key were reinforced on a modified *FI* schedule of 15 sec. The *DRH* schedule had the following properties: (1) if the pigeon made at least a specified number of responses within 15 sec. of the onset of a green light, its first response after the 15 sec. had elapsed was reinforced with 4-sec. access to grain. Following reinforcement, the two white stimuli of the first links reappeared and both *VI* programmers began operating; (2) if the pigeon made fewer than the specified number of responses within the 15 sec., reinforcement did not occur, and the pigeon returned to the first links when the 15-sec. period terminated. The *DRL* schedule had analogous properties: (1) if the pigeon made fewer than a specified number of responses within 15 sec., its first response after 15 sec. was reinforced; (2) if the pigeon's number of responses equaled or exceeded the specified number, the pigeon merely returned to the first links when the 15-sec. period terminated.

It should be noted that the *DRL* and *DRH* schedules used in the present experiment differ from those generally used by other investigators (e.g., Staddon, 1965; Wilson & Keller, 1953) in that they do not explicitly reinforce selected interresponse times. A schedule which reinforces selected interresponse times may be viewed as the limiting case of the class of schedules used in the present study. The present *DRL* schedules, for example, reinforce the emission of fewer than n responses in t secs; in the more commonly used *DRL* schedules, $n = 1$.

The modified *FI* 15-sec schedule programmed reinforcements for the same percentage of trials as reinforcements occurred in the second link of the other Chain. For each subject, the number of reinforcements programmed on the *FI* key in a particular session was equal to the number obtained on the *DRH* or *DRL* key in the prior session. Thus, for each subject, in each part of the experiment, the number of reinforced trials on the *FI* key was equal to that on the *DRH* or *DRL* key. The sequence of *FI* reinforcement intervals was irregular. When an interval was to contain reinforcement, the first response after 15 sec produced reinforcement and the pigeon then returned to the first links. When the interval did not end in reinforcement, the first links were simply reinstated when the 15-sec period terminated.

After magazine training, each pigeon's pecks were shaped in the presence of the red and green lights. The Concurrent Chains procedure was then instituted with white lights and *VI* 1 in the first links and *FI* 15 sec in each (both red and green) second link. Each pigeon learned to respond in the first links without further shaping. After seven daily "pretraining" sessions, in which there was no systematic preference for either key, the *DRH* or *DRL* requirements were introduced in the second links of the left key. The first *DRH* or *DRL* value studied was the multiple of five which was closest to the average number of responses made during *FI* 15 sec on the left key in the final pretraining session. These values and the ones studied subsequently are shown in column (i) of Table 7.1. The number of sessions observed at each value is indicated in column (ii). A *DRH* or *DRL* value remained in effect until response rates appeared stable for at least 12 sessions with the additional provision that at least 28 sessions had been observed. Four values

TABLE 7.1
Order of Conditions and Number of Sessions

Bird Number	(i) DRH Requirement	(ii) Number of Sessions
16	25	43
	20	65
	15	32
	5	39
19	25	38
	20	64
	30	29
	35	38
14	40	38
	45–50	*
	35	43
	30	38
DRL Requirement		
17	15	42
	5	62
	2	31
	1	39
1	15	43
	20	51
	5	48
	10	39
18	15	42
	20	50
	5	45
	2	39

* Failed to sustain responding.

were studied for each subject. Following these determinations, each subject was studied with equal-valued *DRH* or *DRL* schedules in the second links of both keys. There was again no systematic preference for either key evident for either the *DRH* or the *DRL* group. Each daily session terminated after 40 presentations of the second link stimuli. For each pigeon, at every value studied, each second link stimulus was presented an average of 20 times per session, because, as we indicated earlier, Concurrent *VI* schedules keep the number of reinforcements on each key fairly constant over a wide range of preference. The number of primary reinforcements was, of course, determined by the pigeon's performance and could vary from 0 to 40 per session.

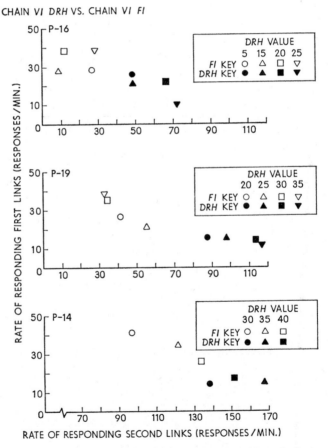

FIGURE 7.2. Absolute rates of responding in each first link plotted against absolute rates of responding in each second link for each *DRH* subject.

The absolute rates of responding in the first links are plotted against the absolute rates of responding in the second links in Figure 7.2 for each of the *DRH* subjects. These rates are the arithmetic means of data for the last four sessions of each procedure listed in Table 7.1. If the logic of the experiment were satisfied response rates in the *DRH* schedule should have exceeded those in the *FI* schedule. Figure 7.2 indicates that this was so for each pigeon. Thus all *DRH* data points in Figure 7.2 are to the right of all *FI* points. Was the dependent variable affected? Figure 7.2 indicates that each pigeon responded in the first links at a higher rate on the key producing the *FI* schedule than on the key producing the *DRH* schedule. Hence, for each pigeon, all *DRH* data points fall below all *FI* points.

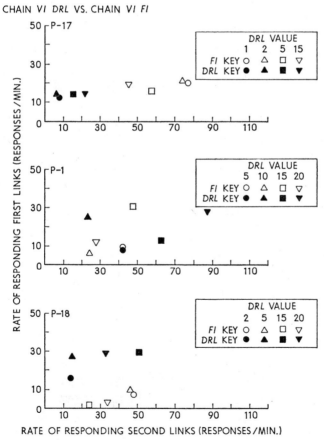

FIGURE 7.3. Absolute rates of responding in each first link plotted against absolute rates of responding in each second link for each *DRL* subject.

A different picture is obtained in Figure 7.3, which plots the corresponding data for the *DRL* subjects. Only P–17 satisfied the logic of the experiment; it always responded at a lower rate in the *DRL* schedule than in the *FI* schedule. Hence, the *DRL* data points fall well to the left of the *FI* points. This did not occur for either of the other subjects. They gave no evidence of discriminating between the *DRL* and interval requirements, in the sense that their rate and pattern of responding in the second links of each key did not differ systematically. P–17, like its *DRH* counterparts, responded at a consistently higher rate in the first link producing the *FI* schedule. Of the subjects which failed to discriminate between the two conditions, one bird, P–18, responded at a systematically higher rate in the first link producing the *DRL* schedule, while the other, P–1, displayed no systematic difference.

TABLE 7.2

Relative Rates of Responding (FI Key) and Percent Success on Each Key

| Bird | (i) DRH Requirement | Relative Rate of Responding (FI Key) | | (iv) Percent Reinforcement |
		(ii) First Links	(iii) Second Links	
P–16	5	0.53	0.33	98
	15	0.58	0.15	63
	20	0.63	0.14	27
	25	0.78	0.30	42
P–19	20	0.65	0.32	76
	25	0.59	0.36	71
	30	0.70	0.23	62
	35	0.76	0.23	65
P–14	30	0.74	0.42	87
	35	0.72	0.42	90
	40	0.60	0.47	90
	DRL Requirement			
P–17	15	0.57	0.67	100
	5	0.53	0.79	62
	2	0.59	0.92	54
	1	0.63	0.91	17
P–1	20	0.30	0.24	46
	15	0.71	0.44	23
	10	0.19	0.51	84
	5	0.55	0.50	3
P–18	20	0.08	0.49	93
	15	0.07	0.31	52
	5	0.28	0.77	70
	2	0.34	0.77	5

Several recent experiments (Chung & Herrnstein, 1967; Fantino, 1967; Rachlin, 1967) have analyzed choice in terms of relative rates of responding. Table 7.2 presents the relative rates of responding in each link for each condition. These rates were obtained as follows: (1) for each of the last four sessions of each procedure, the number of responses in the first link on the *FI* key was divided by the total responses in the first link on both keys; (2) the arithmetic mean of the four quotients for each procedure was then computed. The same procedure was followed for the second links. These data present a similar picture to the analogous data, in terms of absolute response rates, presented in Figures 7.2 and 7.3. Column (iv) in Table 7.2 presents the percentage of trials in which reinforcement was obtained. This percentage was a function of the pigeon's performance on the differential reinforcement schedules and was equal for the two keys. It can be seen that the relative rates of responding in the first links did not vary monotonically with the degree of the pigeon's success in obtaining reinforcements.

Figure 7.4A presents a sample cumulative record for P–16. While this bird responded at a higher rate during the *DRH* stimulus than during the *FI* schedule it can be seen that it responded at a higher rate in the first link producing the *FI* schedule; this is reflected by the steeper slope for the *FI* key. The cumulative records for the pigeons (P–14 and P–19), present the same picture. Table 7.1 notes that P–14 failed to sustain responding when the *DRH* requirement was raised from *DRH* 40 to either *DRH* 50 or *DRH* 45. Figure 7.4B illustrates the breakdown of the *DRH* behavior. In segment (*a*) the pigeon is generally satisfying the *DRH* 45 requirement. In segment (*b*), however, it misses several reinforcements in succession and its performance disintegrates. Although P–14 was easily shaped to recover its *DRH* behavior on *DRH* 40, several attempts at imposing a higher *DRH* requirement led to extinction. Thus it was not possible to obtain stable behavior from P–14 except on *DRH* schedules in which it generally achieved reinforcement.

Figure 7.4C illustrates the performance of P–17, a *DRL* bird. It responded throughout at a higher rate on the *FI* key. Figure 7.4D presents a sample record for P–18 showing that it failed to adequately discriminate the *DRL* requirement. This is evidenced by higher response rates during the *DRL* schedule than during the *FI*. P–18 responded throughout at a higher rate on the *DRL* key.

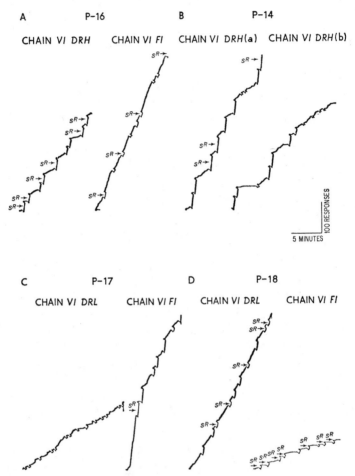

FIGURE 7.4. A. Sample cumulative record for P–16. In this session the *DRH* requirement was 20. Displacement of the recording pen indicates that the second link was in effect. Displacements marked by arrows indicate that reinforcement occurred before the first link was reinstated.
B. Sample records for P–14 on *DRH* 45. Segment (*a*) is from a session in which reinforcements are being obtained. Segment (*b*) from the next session, shows a disintegration of this performance.
C. Sample records for P–17 with a *DRL* requirement of 1.
D. Sample records for P–18 with a *DRL* requirement of 15.

Each of the four pigeons which discriminated between the differential rate and the *FI* schedules consistently responded at a higher rate in the first links that produced the *FI* schedule. This suggests that a conditioned reinforcer associated with a constraint on response rate is weaker than one which is not. For the *DRL* schedule, this conclusion is based on the data of only one pigeon, however.

This result refutes the prediction, derived from Premack (1965), that the pigeon would not systematically choose between these schedules of reinforcement since they yield the same probability and duration of primary reinforcement. Instead, the results suggest that the manner in which a particular rate of reinforcement is obtained affects choice. These results do not contradict Herrnstein's (1964a) previous finding, however, since he did not directly manipulate the rate of responding required. The present results do indicate that when response rates are directly manipulated the matching function between the distribution of responses in the first links and the distribution of reinforcements in the second links may be disrupted.

These *DRH* results also bear upon the possibility, raised most recently by Logan and Wagner (1965) and by Wike (1966), that the effects of primary and conditioned reinforcement are confounded in Chain schedules. Logan and Wagner, in discussing Herrnstein's experiment, caution that "the rate of pecking the keys during Phase I might be affected in anticipatory fashion by the rate that would later be appropriate on that key when the schedule changed" (p. 58). This is the potential weakness of the Concurrent-Chains procedure which we referred to earlier. Previous work with single response keys, however, has indicated that responding in the first links of Chain schedules is primarily maintained by conditioned reinforcement (Kelleher & Gollub, 1962). The present study extends this finding to the concurrent choice situation (CHAIN *VI DRH* v. CHAIN *VI FI* comparison) : although pigeons responded at a consistently higher rate in the second link of CHAIN *VI DRH*, they responded at a consistently higher rate in the first link of CHAIN *VI FI*. If the rate of responding in the first link were in "anticipation" of the rate of responding in the second link, the *VI* rate in the CHAIN *VI DRH* should have been the higher of the two *VI* rates.

The *DRH* data also suggest that a schedule which generates a high rate of responding for reinforcement may have aversive components, a fact that has been well documented only for fixed-ratio schedules (Appel, 1963; Azrin, 1961; Thompson, 1964). Indeed, an *FR* schedule is aversive even though it does not *require* a high response rate. These results raise the possibility that manipulations which generate a high rate of responding in the presence of a stimulus will weaken the stimulus as a conditioned reinforcer. This position is consistent with the provocative results collected by Richard Schuster at Harvard University, which are reported in the following chapter. In particular, Schuster fails to find preference for a second link in which a schedule of "conditioned reinforcement" is superimposed upon a schedule of primary reinforcement as opposed to a second link in which only the (same) primary reinforcement schedule is programmed. My position, which differs from Schuster's, is that the high rate of responding maintained by the superimposed schedule of conditioned reinforcement argues *for* the effectiveness of the conditioned reinforcement. However, since a high rate of responding is generated in that second link, the pigeon does not prefer it.

It should be noted that, although the probability of reinforcement on the *FI* schedule was successfully kept equal to that on the differential reinforcement schedules, in one respect the temporal distribution of reinforcements could differ for the *DRH*, *DRL*, and *FI* schedules. Since the pigeon responded at a higher rate on *DRH* than on the *FI* schedule its first response after 15 sec, i.e., the reinforced response, would tend to be emitted sooner. Hence the interval between the onset of the second link stimulus and reinforcement might be shorter for the *DRH* schedule. By the same token, for P–17, the reinforced response on the *DRL* schedule would tend to be emitted later than on the *FI* schedule. The data, however, indicate that this tendency was small. On the average, for P–17, reinforcements on the *FI* key occurred only 1½ percent sooner (about 0.2 sec) than reinforcements on *DRL*. It seems unlikely, therefore, that this variable was responsible for the preference for the *FI* schedule. For the *DRH* pigeons, reinforcements occurred only 2 percent sooner (about 0.3 sec) on the *DRH* schedule. This difference could not account for the obtained preferences which were, moreover, in the opposite direction.

Although each of the four pigeons clearly preferred the *FI* schedule, Figures 7.2 and 7.3 fail to indicate an orderly relation between the magnitude of this preference and the size of the differential reinforcement requirement. One factor which might account for this failure is the limited range of differential reinforcement values studied. This was most striking for P–14 whose responses were very frequently reinforced (87 percent to 90 percent) in the *DRH* 30 to *DRH* 40 range, but which extinguished at higher values.

This study demonstrates that, at least for the schedules studied in the present experiment, a conditioned reinforcing stimulus is stronger when it is not associated with a requirement of a particular rate of responding for reinforcement. The *DRH* data also indicate that a discriminative stimulus that occasions a high rate of responding need not be a stronger conditioned reinforcer than a discriminative stimulus occasioning a lower rate of responding. This finding supports previous work indicating that the conditioned reinforcing value of a stimulus need not covary with its value as a discriminative stimulus (Autor, 1960; Fantino, 1965; Gollub, 1958).

TABLE 7.3

Order of Conditions	Number of Primary Reinforcements per Cycle[a]		Number of Sessions
	Left Key	Right Key	
1	1	3	90
2	1	5	42
3	1	10	31
4	2	3	67
5	3	2	90
6	10	1	72
7	2	3	68

[a] Number of primary reinforcements in each cycle for each Chain. The right column lists the number of sessions for each condition. The schedule in the first links was always *VI* 1 while the primary reinforcements were always scheduled on a *VI* 15.

The second experiment was done in collaboration with R. J. Herrnstein. In previous experiments with Concurrent Chains absolute number of reinforcements was deliberately held constant throughout. In our experiment the number of primary reinforcements in each second link is varied while holding the rate of reinforcement in the second links constant. If number of reinforcements is a significant factor in its own right, the conditioned reinforcer associated with a greater number of primary reinforcements should maintain a higher rate of responding in the first link leading to it despite the fact that the rate of reinforcement in the presence of the conditioned reinforcer is constant.

The general procedure was the same as that in the response rate experiment, except that six different pigeons were employed. The first links were again *VI* 1 schedules. The schedule in each second link was *VI* 15 sec. The only difference between the two second links, in addition to the color of the associated key lights, was the number of primary reinforcers delivered on the *VI* 15-sec schedule before the first links were reinstated. Table 7.3 lists the number of food-reinforcements in each cycle on each key, and shows the order of experimental conditions and the number of sessions under each condition. A given pair of values remained in effect for a minimum of 28 sessions and until each subject's responding appeared stable for at least 12 daily sessions. Each session terminated after 60 reinforcements.

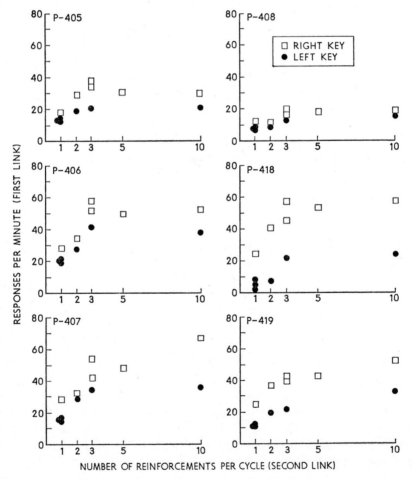

FIGURE 7.5. Responses per minute during the first link as a function of number of reinforcements during the second link, for each of the six pigeons.

With the rate of reinforcement constant at 4 reinforcements per minute in the presence of the second-link stimuli, did number of reinforcements exert any effect on responding in the first link? The answer is shown in Figures 7.5 and 7.6 for individual birds, and averaged data, respectively. In each figure, the number of reinforcements per cycle of the schedule is the abscissa and the rate of responding during the first link is the ordinate. Because all animals favored the right key, the rates for the two keys are plotted separately. The data for the fourth and seventh conditions (see Table 7.3) were averaged since these procedures were identical. In Figure 7.5, each of the six panels shows responses per minute for one

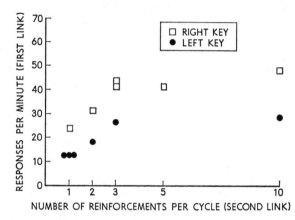

FIGURE 7.6. Responses per minute during the first link as a function of number of reinforcements during the second link, showing the mean rates of the six pigeons.

pigeon, averaged over the final four sessions under a given condition. The open squares show responding at the right key; the filled circles responding at the left key. Figure 7.6 shows the arithmetic means of the data of the six birds at each condition and appears to be a good summary of the individual results. It is evident that responding in the first link varies directly, but nonproportionally. with the number of primary reinforcements per cycle. No more precise characterization of the curves seems warranted by the data.

In contrast with responding during the first link, responding during the second link showed no systematic relation to the changes in the number of reinforcements. Figures 7.7 and 7.8 again show the individual and averaged data and were obtained from the same

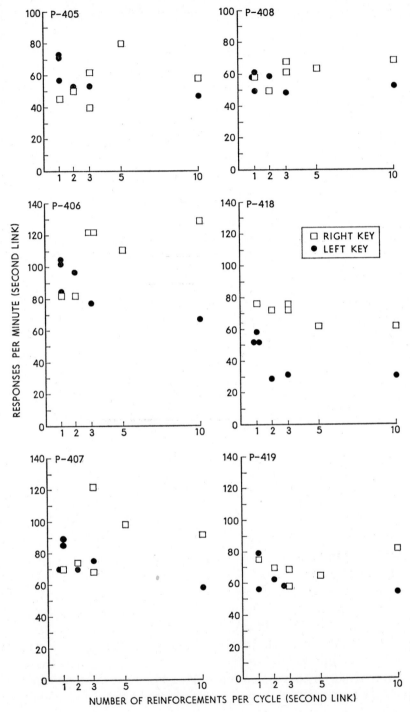

FIGURE 7.7. Responses per minute during the second link as a function of number of reinforcements during the second link, for each of the six pigeons.

sessions as were used for Figures 7.5 and 7.6. The bias in favor of the right key is evident here as well, although its relative magnitude may be smaller, perhaps because of the higher overall rates of responding during the second links. There is a slight upward trend in the curve for the right key and a slight downward trend for the left key. On balance, then, it appears that the variations in number of reinforcements did not materially alter the rates of responding during the second links.

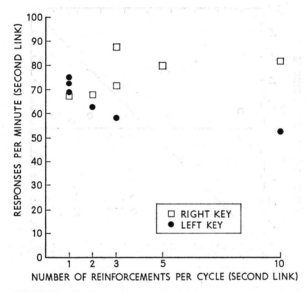

FIGURE 7.8. Responses per minute during the second link as a function of number of reinforcements during the second link, showing the mean rates of the six pigeons.

Thus the number of primary reinforcements is a significant factor in determining the potency of a conditioned reinforcer, as shown by the increasing rate of responding during the first link of a Chain with increasing number of primary reinforcements during the second link. Rate of responding in the second link, however, appears to be essentially independent of the number of reinforcers delivered during its course.

How do these results compare with those of Herrnstein (1964a) ? He found an approximate equality between the distribution of responding during the first links of Concurrent Chains and the distribution of reinforcements during the second link. In a plot of these relative quantities, of the type shown in Figure 7.9, the earlier data were well described by the 45-degree diagonal, indicating a linear function with slope = 1.0, i.e., a matching function. Figure 7.9 shows, however, that the present data don't fall on the matching diagonal. The points in Figure 7.9 are averages of the relative quantities for the six pigeons, with first-link rates of responding as filled circles and second-link rates of responding as

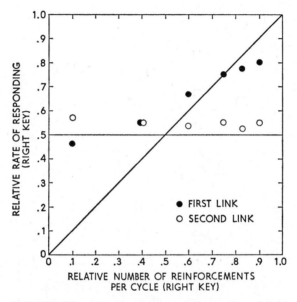

FIGURE 7.9. Relatives rates of responding (right key) as a function of relative number of reinforcements per cycle (right key) for first (filled circles) and second (open circles) links. Points are mean values for the six pigeons.

open circles. The position bias complicates slightly the interpretation of these data, but a satisfactory assessment is nevertheless possible. The second-link data show, by their horizontality, that rate of responding during the second link is independent of the number of reinforcements per cycle. The approximately 4 percent elevation of these points above the 0.5 level of the ordinate represents the bias in favor of the right key. The first link data also show the operation of the position bias, by the fact that the curve does not pass through the expected coordinates of (0.5, 0.5), but through something in the vicinity of (0.5, 0.6). The slope of the function indicated by these points is clearly and substantially less than 1.0.

It may therefore be concluded that in the case of number of reinforcements, unlike rate of reinforcement, a given change in the relative magnitude of the independent variable does not produce an equal change in the relative rate of responding during the first link. Over the range of values examined here, the relative change in responding is smaller than the relative change in number of reinforcements.

Still another indication that number of reinforcements does not affect the strength of a conditioned reinforcer in the same manner as rate of reinforcement is seen by examining data for certain values of the independent variable which were tested more than once. For the left key in conditions 1, 2, and 3, one reinforcement was scheduled in each cycle while reinforcements per cycle on the right key varied. Similarly, when three reinforcements were scheduled for each cycle on the right key either one or two reinforcements were scheduled for each cycle on the left. Was the rate of responding to obtain one second-link influenced by the number of reinforcements programmed in the other second link? If so, the three left key points at one reinforcement per cycle should differ from one another as should the two points at three reinforcements per cycle. Visual inspection of Figure 7.6 indicates that they did not differ substantially. Thus first-link responding on a given key appears to be largely independent of the number of reinforcements per cycle associated with the other key. As noted above, an analogous independence was not found by Herrnstein for rate of reinforcement.

If rate of reinforcement in the second links were exclusively in control of first link responding the data in Figures 7.5 and 7.6 would lie along a horizontal. Instead a positive relation is indicated for each of the six subjects and for each of the two response keys. This indicates that number of reinforcements is a determiner of the strength of a conditioned reinforcer. The present finding complements Herrnstein's (1964a) demonstration that rate of reinforcement in the second links controls first-link responding when number of reinforcements is held constant. The two studies indicate, however, that the two variables, rate and number of reinforcements, do not affect responding in the same way: the function relating first-link responding to rate of reinforcement is a proportionality while that relating first link responding to number of reinforcements is nonproportional.

Although the schedule of reinforcement associated with the second links was a *VI* 15 throughout the experiment, there is a point of view from which the present procedure did not fully eliminate rate of reinforcement as a variable. Let us consider, for example, what happened in the sixth experimental condition, when 10 reinforcers were given during the second link on the left key while just one was given during the second link on the right key. On the left key, 10 reinforcers were obtained in the second link after cycling only once through the first link. On the average, this required 1 min to get through the first link and $2\frac{1}{2}$ min to obtain the 10 reinforcers. Hence the overall rate of reinforcement was 10 reinforcements per $3\frac{1}{2}$ min = 2.86 reinforcements per minute. On the right key, where one reinforcer was obtained during the second link, the overall rate of reinforcement was one reinforcement per $1\frac{1}{4}$ min = 0.80 reinforcements per minute. In other words, rate of reinforcement calculated over total experimental time, instead of just the duration of the second link, is affected by the number of reinforcements per cycle. Although this variation in overall rate of reinforcement is a possible determinant of the positive functions as shown in Figures 7.5 and 7.6, this interpretation is refuted by subsequent experimentation.

Unlike previous experiments with Concurrent Chains, this subsequent study employed different *VI* schedules in the concurrently presented first links. The schedules for the left and right keys are CHAIN *VI* 30 sec *VI* 90 sec and CHAIN *VI* 90 sec *VI* 30 sec respectively. In other words, the conditioned reinforcer associated with the left key is obtained three times as frequently as that associated with the right key. In the second link of the Chain on the left key, however, the rate of reinforcement is one third of that in the second link of the Chain on the right key. Some implications follow. If the pigeon were indeed integrating rate of reinforcement over total experimental time, instead of just over time during the second link, it should not prefer either key since each provides an overall rate of reinforcement of 0.50 reinforcements per minute. If the pigeon's responding were maintained primarily by the density of conditioned reinforcement it should respond at a higher rate in the first link leading to the *VI* 30 sec schedule, i.e., the first link of the Chain on the left key. Finally, my position has been that the pigeon's responding is maintained primarily by the rate of primary reinforcement in the presence of the conditioned reinforcers; therefore, the pigeon should respond at a higher rate in the first link which leads to the *VI* 30 sec schedule in this second link, i.e., the first link of the Chain on the right key.

Although we have listed the three possible outcomes of the experiment and the hypothesis which each outcome would support, we have glossed over certain problems of interpretation. In the first place, consider the case in which the pigeon shows no preference for either key. This could mean either that the pigeon integrated rate of reinforcement over total experimental time or that the higher rate of conditioned reinforcement in the first link on the left key precisely offset the higher rate of primary reinforcement in the second link on the right key. If the pigeon preferred the left key this could be attributed to the richer rate of conditioned reinforcement or to the commensurately greater number of primary reinforcements attained on the left key. These two variables are confounded in this experiment: each time a conditioned reinforcer is obtained a primary reinforcer eventually follows. In other words, three times as many primary reinforcements occur on the left key (although these reinforcements occur at one third the rate) as on the right key. Thus, either of these first two outcomes would have required further experimentation to tease out the controlling variables.

Fortunately, the results, which were obtained in the same manner as those from the previous studies, unequivocally supported the third view: each of four pigeons showed a marked preference for the conditioned reinforcer of the right key. In other words, each pigeon responded at a higher rate in the first link of the CHAIN *VI* 90 sec *VI* 30 sec than in the concurrently available first link of the CHAIN *VI* 30 sec *VI* 90 sec. This preference for the right key occurred despite two features of the experimental design which favored the *left* key: (1) the greater number of conditioned and primary reinforcers obtained on the left; (2) the fact that *VI* 30 sec schedules normally maintain higher rates of responding than do *VI* 90 sec schedules. Moreover, the preferences were huge: the proportion of first-link responses on the right key for all four pigeons was above 80 percent; for three pigeons it was above 95 percent.

We shall return to an important implication of these results at the end of this paper. Their implication for studies using Concurrent Chains, in general, and for our study of number of reinforcements and choice, in particular, is straightforward: these data allow us to reject the possibility that the rate of reinforcement calculated over total experimental time is an important variable affecting choice.

The studies I have presented are consistent in showing (1) that the manipulations studied, namely required rates of responding and number of primary reinforcements, affect the strength of the conditioned reinforcer when the rates of reinforcement in the presence of the conditioned reinforcers are kept constant and (2) that neither manipulation exerts as much effect upon choice as do these rates of reinforcement.

Now I would like to indicate how I think the Concurrent-Chains technique will be valuable in trying to analyze a variable which may be more powerful than rate of reinforcement in affecting choice. This variable I will recklessly label "the psychological distance to reward," or the number of successive states (in terms of measurements I will speculate about shortly) that must be traversed on the way to reward. Perhaps we are talking simply about the number of links or the temporal length of the Chain. Gollub (1958) showed this to be a powerful variable in the maintenance of behavior. He showed, for example, that although behavior on an *FI* 5 schedule was well maintained, behavior on a Chain schedule of five successive *FI* 1's leading to a single reinforcement would disintegrate. At one point Gollub switched pigeons from a TAND *FI* 1 *FI* 1 *FI* 1 *FI* 1 *FI* 1 to a CHAIN *FI* 1 *FI* 1 *FI* 1 *FI* 1 *FI* 1. In the Tandem schedule, the same stimulus is present during each successive *FI* 1 and the animal does not respond very differently than it would on *FI* 5. When the pigeons were switched to the Chain schedule, however, their behavior changed dramatically. At first the pigeon performed well and continued to obtain close to the maximum rate of reinforcement. Then as stimulus control developed, the rates in the early components dropped drastically until the animal stopped responding altogether in the first component. This may be sharply contrasted with Kelleher's (1966b) more recent study in which a single reinforcement per hour was sufficient to maintain behavior, under proper stimulus and scheduling conditions.

I spent several frustrating but instructive months doing an experiment with rats which produced results reminiscent of Gollub's. I wanted to train rats to respond on four successive levers in order to obtain reward. They were required to press each lever five times, starting with the lever farthest from the pellet dispenser and ending with the lever closest to it. A light over the appropriate lever indicated where the rat should be working. The schedule was a (heterogenous) CHAIN *FR* 5 *FR* 5 *FR* 5 *FR* 5. Although the rats had no trouble with an *FR* 20 on a single lever, they did not master the four-lever Chain. A two-lever Chain was no problem. When the third lever was introduced, however, some rats had difficulty. The four-link Chain requirement was not impossible for the rats to *learn,* for several did. The most striking finding was that rats which seemed to be performing adequately would quit in subsequent sessions even when severely deprived. As in Gollub's experiment performance was achieved for a short time and then with an interesting exception, deteriorated permanently. This exception reliably occurred when the rats were studied after a layoff of several weeks. They would once again perform adequately for a short time before quitting.

A clever experimenter might come up with the proper apparatus, schedule and shaping details which would enable the rat to master Chains far more demanding than the four *FR* 5's on four different levers. My point is simply that a requirement of four successive *FR* 5 schedules is vastly inferior to a simple *FR* 20 in maintaining behavior. A stimulus in the presence of which reinforcement is sometimes obtained is obviously much more powerful in maintaining behavior than one which is once removed from reinforcement.

To give a sense of reality to my rambling about "psychological distance to reward," I will outline an experiment that is presently starting in my laboratory. It uses the Concurrent-Chains technique to sink some quantitative teeth into this distance problem. The first links are Concurrent *VI* 1 schedules. The second link of one key is CHAIN *FI* 30″ *FI* 30″. The second link of the other key is CHAIN *FI* X″ *FI* X″ *FI* X″. The object is to find the X which will produce no preference between the two sides, i.e., an indifference point. In other words, for each pigeon, that X is sought which will cause the pigeon to respond equally often in the two first (*VI*) links. Finding X for any given pigeon should be a straightforward matter. Once this equality between CHAIN *FI* 30″ *FI* 30″ and CHAIN *FI* X″ *FI* X″ *FI* X″ is established, we can see whether it is invariant under each of two types of transformations:

1. The length of the intervals is multiplied or added; for example, will CHAIN *FI* 1 *FI* 1 then be equal to CHAIN *FI* 2X″ *FI* 2X″

FI $2X''$? Or will CHAIN FI $40''$ FI $40''$ = CHAIN FI $(X + 10)''$ FI $(X + 10)''$ FI $(X + 10)''$?

2. The number of links is multiplied; for example, if an FI $30''$ is equal to a CHAIN FI X'' FI X'', will this indifference continue when CHAIN FI $30''$ FI $30''$ is compared to CHAIN FI X'' FI X'' FI X'' FI X''?

My guess is that the answer to the second and more interesting question is "no." I feel that increasing the number of links will have a profound effect upon preference and that X must be sharply reduced to preserve equality.

At least two other types of analyses should turn out to be fundamentally important in this program. One is to use the Concurrent-Chains procedure to compare Chain schedules with Tandem schedules; e.g., find X so that TAND FI X'' FI X'' = CHAIN FI $30''$ FI $30''$ for both two-link and longer Chains. The second analysis, which must be performed throughout, involves the actual rates of reinforcement occurring on each Chain or Tandem schedule. These actual rates may not covary with the programmed rates since behavior in the early links of the longer Chains may be severely disrupted, thereby lowering the associated rates of reinforcement.

This program of experimentation should enable us to map out "isopreference contours" with rate of reinforcement and number of links (distance) as parameters. In other words, these contours would describe various combinations of rates of reinforcement and number of links which produce equivalent preference proportions. These contours will indicate the relative weight of the roles played by these variables in determining choice.

The measure of "psychological distance" then would be the amount by which rate of reinforcement must be increased in order to compensate for a given increase in the length of the Chain. By appropriately manipulating these two dimensions, length and rate, a whole family of isopreference contours will be generated. This should represent a significant step toward the quantification of variables affecting the strength of conditioned reinforcement.

Finally, there is an additional sense in which the "distance to reward" is fundamentally involved in determining the strength of conditioned reinforcement. Up to now I have implied that the rates of primary reinforcement in the second links determine the distribution of responses in the first links. This is the formulation developed by Autor (1960) and Herrnstein (1964a), and supported by subsequent workers. Indeed, this well-established generalization that the distribution of responses in the first links matches the distribution of reinforcements in the second links is consistent with all of the relevant published data. It cannot, however, handle the huge preferences obtained in my recent experiment which was discussed above when we were considering the possibility that the pigeon integrated reinforcements over total experiment time. The matching hypothesis predicts that no more than 75 percent of the pigeon's responses should be made on the first link of the chain on the right key. If *fewer* than 75 percent were made the matching hypothesis would not be refuted since, as we indicated earlier, the experimental design contained two features favoring left key responses. Each pigeon, however, allotted *more* than 75 percent of its responses to the first link of the Chain on the right key.

Fortunately, there is an alternative model which is consistent with all of the earlier work and which predicts the huge preferences obtained in my experiment as well. This formulation stipulates that the critical variable determining the strength of conditioned reinforcement is the degree by which the conditioned reinforcer brings the organism nearer in time to primary reinforcement. Choice of one conditioned reinforcer over another should be a function of the shortening of the time to reward, signified by that conditioned reinforcer relative to the shortening of the time to reward signified by the other conditioned reinforcer. For example, if the shortening is twice as great for the left conditioned reinforcer as for the right, then the organism should allot two thirds of its first-link responses to the left key. We can make this formulation clearer by illustrating its application in our experiment with CHAIN *VI* 30 sec *VI* 90 sec and CHAIN *VI* 90 sec *VI* 30 sec. When the pigeon is in the first links how far away is it, in time, from reward? Summing over both *VI*s, on the average, it takes $22\frac{1}{2}$ sec to enter a second link, i.e., to obtain a conditioned reinforcer (since *VI* 30 sec = 2 reinforcement per minute and *VI* 90 sec = $\frac{2}{3}$ reinforcements per minute; $2\frac{2}{3}$ reinforcements per minute = 1 reinforcement per $22\frac{1}{2}$ sec). The probabilities that the second link is that of the left and right key are $\frac{3}{4}$ and $\frac{1}{4}$, respectively. The average times to reward for the left and right second links are 90 sec and 30 sec, respectively. Thus, once a conditioned reinforcer is obtained there are $[(\frac{3}{4})$ (90 sec) + $(\frac{1}{4})$ (30

sec)] = 75 additional sec, on the average, to obtain primary reinforcement. Hence, the pigeon begins $22\frac{1}{2}$ sec + 75 sec = $97\frac{1}{2}$ sec
from reward. When the conditioned reinforcer on the left is ob-
tained the pigeon is 90 sec, on the average, from reward. Thus its
lot has improved by only $7\frac{1}{2}$ sec, on the average. The conditioned
reinforcer on the right, however, signifies improvement of $97\frac{1}{2}$
sec − 30 sec = $67\frac{1}{2}$ secs. The model predicts that the pigeon will
allot the following proportion of its first-link responses to the
right:

$$\frac{67\frac{1}{2} \text{ sec}}{67\frac{1}{2} \text{ sec} + 7\frac{1}{2} \text{ sec}} = 0.90$$

This prediction is consistent with the data while the conventional
matching prediction of 0.75 or less is not.

We shall now present this formulation in more general terms
and compare it with its predecessor. Let R_L and R_R represent the
number of responses during the first link of the left and right keys
respectively; let t_L and t_R represent the average time to reward calculated from the onset of the second links of the left and right keys,
respectively. Finally, let T equal the average time to (primary)
reward calculated from the onset of the first links.

The older formulation ignores T and states:

$$\frac{R_L}{R_L + R_R} = \frac{\dfrac{1}{t_L}}{\dfrac{1}{t_L} + \dfrac{1}{t_R}} \tag{1}$$

Our new formulation, however, incorporates T and states:

$$\frac{R_L}{R_L + R_R} \begin{cases} \dfrac{T - t_L}{(T - t_L) + (T - t_R)} & \text{when } t_L < T, t_R < T \\ = 1 \text{ when } t_L < T, t_R > T \\ = 0 \text{ when } t_L > T, t_R < T \end{cases} \tag{2}$$

Of course, the case in which *both* t_L and t_R are greater than T is
impossible.

Of greatest interest is the implication that the rates of reinforcement in the second links do not, by themselves, determine the degree of preference. The size of the *VI*s in the first links are equally
important: these *VI*s help determine T but do not enter into (1).
Consider the conventional case in which the *VI*s of the second links

differ while those of the first links are equal. When the first link VIs are large relative to those of the second link, the proportion of responses in each first link should approach 0.50: the conditioned reinforcers of either key bring the pigeon a great deal closer to reward. On the other hand, when these first links VIs are very small (i.e., so that T is less than, say, t_R) the proportion of responses in the first link of the left key should approach 1: only one conditioned reinforcer brings the reward closer. Finally, only for a particular intermediate value should the distribution of responses in the first links match precisely the distribution of reinforcements in the second links. Of course, for a fairly wide band of values, approximate matching should occur; only values in this band have been used by previous workers. For these values (1) and (2) are indistinguishable. We are now working with values outside this band, however, i.e., with values for which the two formulations make very different predictions. The data which we have collected thus far unequivocally support the predictions made by our formulation (2).

SUMMARY

A conditioned reinforcer is stronger when it is not associated with a requirement of a particular rate of responding for reinforcement. Interval schedules are preferred over DRH and DRL schedules. A discriminative stimulus for a high rate of responding may not be a stronger conditioned reinforcer than one for a low rate of responding. The two variables, rate and number of reinforcements, do not affect responding in the same way: rate of responding in the first link of a Chain is proportionately related to rate of reinforcement and monotonically but not proportionately related to number of reinforcements. The concept of "psychological distance to reward," or the number of successive states (number of links or temporal length of the Chain) that must be traversed on the way to reward, is suggested as being useful in quantifying variables involved in conditioned reinforcement. Finally, a new model is developed to describe choice behavior in Concurrent-Chain schedules.

chapter 8

A FUNCTIONAL ANALYSIS OF CONDITIONED REINFORCEMENT[1]

Richard H. Schuster[2]
Harvard University

INTRODUCTION

Current theories of learning include the hypothesis that an arbitrary stimulus can become a reinforcer after pairings with a primary reinforcer (Hull, 1943, 1951; Keller & Schoenfeld, 1950; Mowrer, 1960; Skinner, 1938, 1953; Spence, 1956). These stimuli are known either as secondary reinforcers (Hull, 1943; Keller & Schoenfeld, 1950; Mowrer, 1960) or as conditioned reinforcers (Kelleher, 1966; Skinner, 1938, 1953). The concept of conditioned reinforcement, in turn, implies that a conditioned reinforcer, following a response, can reinforce the response in the same way as a primary reinforcer. Conditioned reinforcement has often been a very useful construct, since learning, in theory, would not always require primary reinforcement. Human behavior, for example, has often been explained with the help of conditioned reinforcement (Hull, 1951; Skinner, 1953).

The construct of conditioned reinforcement may be ragarded as embodying a two-factor behavior theory which is used to explain some types of learning (Mowrer, 1960). The first process or factor

---

[1] The research reported here was conducted while the author was a National Science Foundation trainee in the department of psychology, Harvard University, and was supported by National Science Foundation Grants GB 3121, GB 3723, and GB 6999 to Harvard University. The data reported here are based on a doctoral dissertation submitted to the department of psychology, Harvard University.

[2] Now at Johnson Research Foundation, University of Pennsylvania.

is simple association, according to which an arbitrary stimulus can function in the same way as a primary stimulus after the two are paired. The second process or factor is instrumental conditioning (Skinner, 1938), according to which a response increases in frequency if it is followed by a reinforcing stimulus. This is the venerable positive law of effect. In the case of conditioned reinforcement, the reinforcing property of a stimulus is supposed to be transferred to an arbitrary stimulus, after which the arbitrary stimulus can be used to reinforce responding. Although there is disagreement over whether the proper method of pairing involves classical (Hull, 1943; Mowrer, 1960; Kelleher; 1966a) or instrumental conditioning (Keller & Schoenfeld, 1950) the reinforcing property of conditioned reinforcers is widely accepted.

This theory, however, has posed theoretical and experimental problems which are interrelated. The experimental problem is that the theory is difficult to verify. The two most popular methods for demonstrating conditioned reinforcement, Extinction and Chain schedules, do not isolate conditioned reinforcement from the effects of primary reinforcement. In Extinction, conditioned reinforcement is introduced after pairings of the conditioned reinforcer with the primary reinforcer have been stopped. Without primary reinforcement a conditioned reinforcer is usually unable to sustain responding for more than brief periods. The other method, using a Chain schedule, continues primary reinforcement. For example, in a two-link Chain schedule, presentation of the conditioned reinforcer at the end of the first link is accompanied by the opportunity to obtain the primary reinforcer at the end of the second link. In this way, responding that is followed by an arbitrary stimulus (the conditioned reinforcer) can be maintained indefinitely. These results, taken together, illustrate a basic rule about behavior in general and about conditioned reinforcement in particular—that *behavior will extinguish unless primary reinforcement is continued* (Keller & Schoenfeld, 1950; Skinner, 1938).

The theoretical problem arises from the attempt of two-factor theory to overcome this stubborn rule by absorbing it. In so doing, the theory was forced to add a third process—decay. The reinforcing effectiveness of a *conditioned* reinforcer is said to decay after pairings with a primary reinforcer are discontinued (Keller & Schoenfeld, 1950).

The advantage of this decay factor is an apparent parsimony.

The contrasting effects of methods using Extinction and Chain schedules can be explained by a single theory. In exchange for this simplification, however, two disadvantages emerge. To save the two-factor theory, the complication of three factors is necessary— simple association, instrumental reinforcement, and a decay process. This complication, moreover, makes the theory difficult to disprove experimentally. Whether conditioned reinforcers can sustain responding or not, the two-factor theory of conditioned reinforcement is supported (Kelleher, 1966; Kelleher & Gollub, 1962; Miller, 1951; Myers, 1958; Wyckoff, 1959).

A remedy for these problems is suggested by an inconsistency within current learning theories. An arbitrary stimulus can influence responding whether it follows a response, as a conditioned reinforcer, or precedes a response. The stimulus can exercise considerable control over responding if it is arranged that a primary reinforcer be conditional upon the stimulus. This type of stimulus is called "discriminative" (Keller & Schoenfeld, 1950; Skinner, 1938; Terrace, 1966). The inconsistency is in the type of analysis used to explain the effects of these two stimulus arrangements. When analyzing the effects of discriminative stimuli on subsequent responding, the two-factor model is not used; that is, the stimuli are not endowed with any eliciting power corresponding to the reinforcing power ascribed to conditioned reinforcers, even though both kinds of stimuli derive their effects from association with a primary reinforcer. Instead, the analysis of discriminative stimuli is entirely descriptive and functional. A discriminative stimulus is said to control responding because of, and appropriate to, the reinforcement contingencies that are cued by the stimulus (Terrace, 1966).

A functional analysis of discriminative stimuli was necessitated by the inability of Pavlovian methods to generate discriminative control. The classic study by Brogden, Lipman, and Culler (1938) may be cited. They compared the Pavlovian and instrumental methods to see which would produce discriminative control over responding. Under the Pavlovian paradigm, a stimulus was consistently paired with electric shock whether or not a running response occurred during stimulus presentations. In this case, pairing had little influence on the frequency of running. Under the instrumental paradigm, however, the stimulus had a discriminative function—a response during stimulus presentations allowed the animal to avoid the shock, which meant that the stimulus was paired with shock only when a running response did *not* occur. In this case, running increased markedly during stimulus presentations.

This raises the question of why the effects of response-produced arbitrary stimuli are not similarly analyzed in completely functional terms, without adding that such stimuli are transformed into reinforcers. There is considerable evidence that some kind of stimulus function is served by effective conditioned reinforcers. One difference between Extinction and chaining procedures in the study of acquired functions of a stimulus resides in the functional relation between the stimulus and the primary reinforcer. In fact, Extinction and chaining procedures in the study of conditioned reinforcement, are roughly analogous, respectively, to the Pavlovian and instrumental paradigms in the Brogden *et al.* (1938) study. During Extinction tests, when the stimulus (the possible conditioned reinforcer) is programmed without primary reinforcement, the stimulus no longer is cueing the primary reinforcer, and the previously reinforced behavior is not maintained. In Chain schedules, on the other hand, the stimulus continues to cue primary reinforcement. The stimulus in this case is capable of maintaining both response rates and choice behavior appropriate to the cued reinforcement conditions (Herrnstein, 1964a; Kelleher, 1966; Kelleher & Gollub, 1962).

Thus, both a functional analysis and two-factor theory can explain the results of Extinction and of chaining procedures in the study of conditioned reinforcement. But a functional analysis offers some advantages. One is the opportunity for consistent treatment of the effects of arbitrary stimuli with a single type of analysis based on conditions of primary reinforcement, whether the stimuli precede or follow an instrumental response. Presently, many theorists are in the uncomfortable position of applying a two-factor model to conditioned reinforcers and a functional model to discriminative stimuli, even though the same stimulus can serve both functions in a Chain schedule (Kelleher & Gollub, 1962). A second advantage is simplicity. Instead of two or three factors, a functional analysis requires only one—the relation between the stimulus and primary reinforcement.

The purpose of this chapter is to offer a functional analysis of conditioned reinforcement, and to evaluate it against current two-factor theory. This will be accomplished in two parts. The next section will include a report of some conditioned reinforcement experiments which represent an explicit attempt to decide between the two types of explanations. In the same section, similar experiments will be critically reviewed. In a final section, the functional approach will be considered more generally, and applied both to the results reported here and to the results of the traditional Extinction and chaining methods.

Effects of response-produced cues in Concurrent schedules

The possibility of a functional analysis of conditioned reinforcement requires that experimental methods be chosen with care. It was outlined in the Introduction how chaining and Extinction methods are both inappropriate for resolving the issues raised here, since their effects are predicted from both two-factor theory and functional relations. In a Chain, the final-link stimulus is a cue for reinforcement which is also continually paired with the reinforcer; in Extinction, the stimulus formerly associated with the primary reinforcer is no longer a cue for reinforcement and is no longer paired with the reinforcer.

A critical test of conditioned reinforcement theories should emerge from experiments in which a stimulus and a primary reinforcer are continually paired even though the stimulus is not a cue for reinforcement when it is programmed as a conditioned reinforcer. In this situation alone, two-factor theory and a functional analysis predict different effects. If pairings are sufficient to generate conditioned reinforcing power, a stimulus being paired with a primary reinforcer should remain an effective conditioned reinforcer when response-produced. If, instead, a stimulus must reliably cue a primary reinforcer, and not merely be paired with a primary reinforcer, the stimulus should become ineffective as a conditioned reinforcer. This approach, incidentally, is analogous to that of Brogden et al. (1938), for testing the control exerted by a stimulus which precedes responding.

These conditions are satisfied by using the technique of Concurrent schedules (Herrnstein, 1961; Skinner, 1950), first applied to conditioned reinforcement by J. Zimmerman (1963). In any Concurrent-schedule situation, two different reinforcement schedules can be programmed simultaneously but independently; the subject is free to switch between them. In a Concurrent-schedule situation with conditioned reinforcement, one of the schedules provides conditioned reinforcement alone. But instead of ending primary reinforcement, as in Extinction, the experimenter programs a schedule of primary reinforcement as the other schedule, and the conditioned reinforcer can be continually paired with the primary reinforcer. In this way, conditioned reinforcement is isolated from primary reinforcement, as in Extinction, but pairings can be continued indefinitely. The critical feature of this method is that the arbitrary stimulus that might serve as a conditioned reinforcer, though paired on one schedule, is not a cue for reinforcement on the other schedule. The experimental question of interest is whether reinforcementlike effects of this Concurrent schedule of an arbitrary stimulus can be sustained indefinitely.

Concurrent schedule effects: A. Rate measurement

When the effects on response rate of a Concurrent schedule of an arbitrary stimulus paired with a primary reinforcer have been measured, low but sustained response rates have been found (Zimmerman, 1963; Zimmerman & Hanford, 1966; Zimmerman, Hanford, & Brown, 1967). This sustained effect has been construed as showing that the arbitrary stimulus had become a conditioned reinforcer. The fact that rates generated by Concurrent schedules of conditioned reinforcement have been relatively low may reflect only a preference for the stronger, primary reinforcer, on the alternative schedule. For example, Zimmerman (1963), in one procedure, used two response keys, programming a primary reinforcer on one and a stimulus associated with the primary reinforcer on the other. In another procedure (Zimmerman & Hanford, 1966) only one key was used, programmed so that responding produced the reinforcement-associated stimulus and periods of no responding were necessary to produce the primary reinforcer itself. The ability of the reinforcement-associated stimulus to sustain any responding at all in these situations is strong evidence for its being a conditioned reinforcer.

Increased response rates alone, however, do not compel a reinforcement interpretation, since rates can be increased by a variety of methods which do not involve reinforcement; increased food deprivation and emotion-inducing situations are two examples. Moreover, when used as an index of reinforcement, rate has not varied consistently with parameters of reinforcement such as amount (Catania, 1963; Neuringer, 1967), delay (Ferster, 1953), and intensity of intracranial stimulation (Hodos & Valenstein, 1962). In particular, we can pose the question whether rate increases produced by a Concurrent schedule of a response-produced stimulus provide evidence for its being a reinforcer.

If we describe the functions of the arbitrary response-produced stimulus in a Concurrent-schedule situation, an alternative to its being a conditioned reinforcer is suggested. As noted previously, the stimulus on one schedule is always associated with the primary reinforcer; on the other schedule, the same stimulus is unassociated with the primary reinforcer. A variety of experiments has shown that withholding the primary reinforcer from a previously reinforced response is sufficient to generate response rate increases, and furthermore, that stimuli can control increased rates when correlated with nonreinforcement. When a procedure changes from reinforcement to Extinction, there is often a transient increase in response rates that later gives way to a declining response rate (Skinner, 1938). Similarly, the force of bar-pressing undergoes a transient increase at the beginning of Extinction (Notterman, 1959). Skinner (1950) regards these as emotional by-products of nonreinforcement, sometimes referred to as "frustration."

Rate increases produced by withdrawing reinforcement can apparently be sustained for long periods when nonreinforcement and reinforcement are alternated. One example occurs in a Multiple schedule of reinforcement. In general, the rate of reinforcement during one component of the Multiple schedule may influence the rate of responding during another component. In particular, when reinforcement during one stimulus is discontinued, the rate of responding during another stimulus may increase. This is known as "positive contrast" (Reynolds, 1961). Moreover, conditioned reinforcement in this situation seems to function like nonreinforcement. When a conditioned reinforcer was substituted for the primary reinforcer at the end of some components of a Multiple schedule, positive contrast appeared (Hamm & Zimmerman, 1967).

Another sustained rate increase produced by nonreinforcement is known specifically as a "frustration effect" (Amsel, 1958; Spence, 1960). This is an increase in running speed in a straight alley following nonreinforcement. In two runways placed in tandem, so that the goal box for the first runway is the start box for the second runway, running speed was consistently elevated in the second alley whenever nonreinforcement occurred in the first goal box (Amsel & Roussel, 1952). This effect was enlarged by adding the stimuli in the first goal box to the first alley (Amsel & Hancock, 1957). These stimuli are conventionally regarded as conditioned reinforcers, since they are associated with a primary reinforcer.

Rate increases have also been produced by interposing "time-outs from positive reinforcement" during a schedule of positive reinforcement (Ferster, 1958a; Ferster & Skinner, 1957). A "time-out" is a signaled period during which responses are ineffective. This increase in response rate, moreover, can be brought under stimulus control. When an arbitrary stimulus precedes time-out from positive reinforcement, response rates may increase during presentation of the stimulus (Herrnstein, 1955; Leitenberg, 1966). Leitenberg (1966) views the increase as a type of frustration effect.

A Concurrent schedule of an arbitrary stimulus may therefore produce increases in response rate, not because it is reinforcing by virtue of its association with the primary reinforcer on one of the schedules, but because it is frustrating by virtue of its association with nonreinforcement on the other schedule. Lott (1967) pointed out the similarity of some so-called conditioned reinforcement procedures to other so-called frustration procedures. For example, in Amsel's frustration paradigm, the same stimuli in the first goal box are sometimes followed by the reinforcer and sometimes not; in the Concurrent conditioned reinforcement situation, the same stimuli are sometimes followed by the reinforcer and sometimes not. Both procedures produce increases in response rate following nonreinforcement. Yet Amsel refers to the effects of nonreinforcement while Zimmerman (1963) refers to the effects of conditioned reinforcement. It is also curious that Zimmerman cited nonreinforcement in the contrast study mentioned above (Hamm & Zimmerman, 1967), but conditioned reinforcement in the experiments with Concurrent schedules (Zimmerman, 1963; Zimmerman & Hanford, 1966), even though the same event, a brief presentation of the grain hopper, was used in both cases. Again, rate increases were shown in both cases. In short, measurement of response rate alone does not offer a clear distinction between the predictions of two contradictory interpretations—the effect of a stimulus sometimes associated with a primary reinforcer either as reinforcement or nonreinforcement.

It is possible to rely on response rate as an index of reinforcement with certain qualifications. For example, some inferences may be made from rate changes rather than absolute rates. The predictable effects of nonreinforcement are a transitory increase, whereas reinforcement produces a change in rate appropriate to the schedule in effect. For example, a *DRL* schedule (which delivers reinforcers for responses emitted at a low rate) might show whether a stimulus will act as reinforcer or nonreinforcer. Unfortunately, Concurrent experimental situations have always been arranged so that the conditioned reinforcement schedule will *increase* rates if the stimulus were reinforcing, so that the possible effects of reinforcement and nonreinforcement are confounded.

Another way to determine if a stimulus is reinforcing is to look at the patterning of responses over time (Kelleher, 1966a). Reinforcement should generate response patterns appropriate to the schedule in effect, such as fixed-interval "scallops" or fixed-ratio "break-and-run" behavior (Ferster & Skinner, 1957), whereas nonreinforcement should produce a more disorderly rate increase. In the Concurrent experiments, patterning has been absent (Zimmerman & Hanford, 1966) but, since the subject is switching to and from the primary reinforcement schedule, no definitive conclusion can be drawn from this fact.

Concurrent schedule effects: B. Rate and choice measurement compared

The studies to be reported were designed to separate reinforcing effects and possible "frustrative" effects on response rate by taking separate measures of response rate and preference. While response rate is not always a sensitive indicator of reinforcement, measures of choice have been sensitive to parameters of reinforcement such as frequency (Herrnstein, 1964a), immediacy (Killeen, 1968), amount (Catania, 1963; Neuringer, 1967), delay (Chung & Herrnstein, 1967), and number (Fantino & Herrnstein, 1968). Moreover, choice and rate measures can be obtained in the same experiment to examine the effects of primary reinforcers (Herrnstein, 1964) and stimuli other than positive reinforcers, such as brief electric shocks (Rachlin, 1967). Four experiments will be reported at this point, two dealing with response rate alone, and two with both response rate and preference. A fifth study will be reported later.

In all studies, the primary reinforcer was available for responses on each of two keys. On one of these keys was sometimes programmed a separate, Concurrent schedule of presentation of an arbitrary stimulus, called S^E, which was superimposed on the schedule of primary reinforcement. This key was programmed like the single-key Concurrent procedure of Zimmerman and Hanford (1966). On the other key only the schedule of primary reinforcement was programmed.

The logic of the experiments was simple. The schedules of primary reinforcement on the two keys were identical; the only asymmetry lay in the superimposed S^E schedule on one key. From previous studies, the S^E schedule was expected to produce a rate difference when S^E was paired with the primary reinforcer (Zimmerman, 1963; Zimmerman & Hanford, 1966). The additional experimental question was how these rate changes would be related to measures of choice. Measures of choice were obtained by offering subjects a choice between the opportunity to respond on one key for primary reinforcers alone, or on the other key for both primary reinforcers and S^E presentations. Studies with primary reinforcement have shown that, in a similar choice situation, the schedule with the higher frequency of primary reinforcement is preferred (Autor, 1960; Herrnstein, 1964; Killeen, 1968). If the S^E are reinforcing, the key with the additional schedule of S^E should be similarly preferred to the key with primary reinforcers alone.

The two superimposed schedules on one key, the schedule of S^E and the schedule of primary reinforcement, will be called the S^E condition; the primary reinforcement schedule alone on the other key will be called the non-S^E condition. These two conditions, in turn, were presented to two different groups of subjects. One group was the traditional conditioned reinforcement group, or paired group. For this group, every occurrence of the primary reinforcer on either key was paired with the arbitrary stimulus, S^E. For the other group, the unpaired group, the S^E was never paired with the primary reinforcer but the schedules of S^E and primary reinforcement were the same. Thus, the paired group was used for a comparison between the S^E paired and the non-S^E paired conditions, where the difference between the two conditions was the presentation of a Concurrent schedule of S^E during one condition; the unpaired group was used for the same comparison except that S^E was never paired with the reinforcer. The conditions corresponding to the S^E paired and non-S^E paired when the S^E was not paired are called the *S^E unpaired* and the *non-S^E unpaired* conditions.

For the paired group, the pairing procedure is diagrammed in Figure 8.1. Whenever primary reinforcement became due, the next response produced a 4.7-sec presentation of S^E; the primary reinforcer, S^R, was presented during the last 4 sec. The interval of 0.7 sec between the presentations of S^E and S^R was selected because Jenkins (1950) and Bersh (1951) displayed a maximum condi-

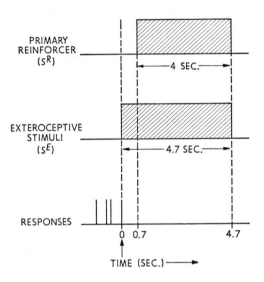

FIGURE 8.1. Schematic diagram of the relations among responses and stimuli during pairings of the primary reinforcer, S^R, and a set of arbitrary stimuli, S^E. The experimental subjects received such pairings whenever primary reinforcement occurred; control subjects never received pairings.

PRIMARY REINFORCER (s^R)

4 SEC.

EXTEROCEPTIVE STIMULI (s^E)

4.7 SEC.

RESPONSES

0 0.7   4.7

TIME (SEC.) ⟶

tioned reinforcing effect in Extinction when, during pairings, the stimulus preceded the primary reinforcer by about 0.5 to 1 sec. For the unpaired group, responses produced only the primary reinforcer, S^R, for 4 sec whenever the primary reinforcer became due.

The set of arbitrary stimuli, S^E, consisted of a buzzer, a change of both key lights to white (the functional key changed from either red or orange; the other key was previously unlit), and a dimming of the houselights. Unlike the conditioned reinforcer in the Zimmerman studies, the S^E stimuli did not include any stimuli directly involved in the presentation of the primary reinforcer, such as the hopper light or the sound of the hopper operating. For the unpaired group, whenever the 4-sec primary reinforcer occurred, both response keys were darkened and nonfunctional. Otherwise, there was no other stimulus change except for the hopper stimuli, which were the same for both groups.

The S^E and non-S^E conditions are diagrammed in Figure 8.2 for subjects in the paired group, showing one possible sequence of presentations of S^E and the primary reinforcer, S^R, that would occur for the same pattern of responding. The two schedules comprising the S^E condition were selected to minimize changes in the obtained frequency of primary reinforcement in consequence of changes in response rate, so that the S^E and non-S^E conditions could not influence preference through variations in reinforcement frequency. The schedule of primary reinforcement, which was the same on both keys, was a VI 30-sec schedule with a minimum interreinforcement interval of 5 sec and a maximum interval of 75 sec. A VI schedule was selected because the obtained rate of primary reinforcement is insensitive to changes in response rate over a very wide range; only a virtual failure to respond would have significantly affected the rate of primary reinforcement. On the other hand, the S^E schedule was selected so that the frequency of S^E presentations would depend on the rate of responding. The superimposed S^E schedule, was therefore a fixed-ratio schedule of 11 responses (FR 11), as shown in Figure 8.2, bottom.

The FR 11 schedule was superimposed on the VI schedule so that S^E was presented briefly for every 11th response. Concurrently, the primary reinforcer was produced by the first response that occurred after the reinforcer became due by the VI schedule. If primary reinforcement happened to occur for the 11th response after the previous S^E presentation, that presentation of S^E alone was cancelled. Instead, the primary reinforcer was produced, either paired with S^E (for paired, experimental subjects) or alone (for unpaired, control subjects).

The S^E presentations on the FR 11 schedule were for 0.7 sec, the duration by which S^E onset preceded every primary reinforcer for experimental subjects. This 0.7-sec duration is analogous to other conditioned reinforcers such as hopper lights, hopper magazines, and goal boxes, which serve to cue the presentation of primary reinforcers. The keys remained functional during the 0.7-sec presentations of S^E when presented alone or preceding the primary reinforcer; the keys were inoperative only during presentations of the grain hopper, and calculations of response rate excluded only hopper presentation time.

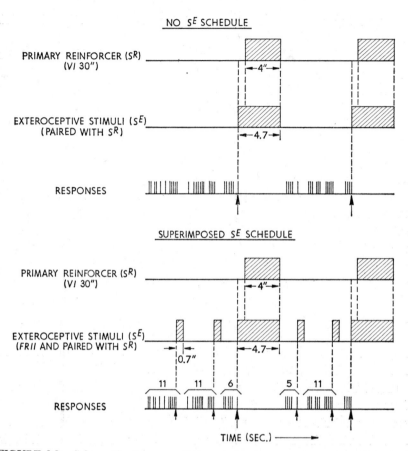

FIGURE 8.2. Schematic diagram of the relations among responses, the set of arbitrary stimuli (S^E), and the primary reinforcer (S^R) during the *non-S^E condition* (top) and the *S^E condition* (bottom). The same *VI* 30 sec schedule of primary reinforcement, paired with S^E, was programmed during both components for paired subjects; the S^E condition also included a superimposed *FR* 11 schedule of 0.7 sec presentations of S^E alone. Subjects in the unpaired group received the same schedules of S^E and S^R presentations, except that S^E and S^R were not paired on the *VI* 30-sec schedule.

In all experiments to be reported, hungry pigeons were reinforced with grain in a typical operant chamber (Ferster & Skinner, 1957; *cf.*, Introduction to this volume). The box was equipped with two 1-inch diameter keys mounted on one wall, side by side, and separated by about 2 inches. When functional, the left key was orange and the right key red, except during S^E presentations, when both keys were white.

RATE EXPERIMENTS

In Experiments 1 and 2, only the effects of the S^E condition on response rate were studied. The technique was to alternate the S^E and non-S^E conditions in a Multiple schedule. A Multiple schedule consists of different reinforcement schedules programmed successively, each schedule correlated with a different exteroceptive stimulus (Ferster & Skinner, 1957). In the present instance, the two conditions were correlated with the red and orange keys. When one condition was in effect on one key, the other key was darkened and pecks on it were ineffective. Each exposure to each condition lasted until two primary reinforcers were obtained, as shown in Figure 8.2; the other condition then went into effect. Sessions terminated after 48 reinforcements, i.e., 12 exposures to each condition.

Experiment 1

In Experiment 1, the superimposed FR 11 schedule of S^E presentations was added to one key after the non-S^E condition had been programmed as a base-line condition on both keys; the S^E condition on that key remained in effect for a minimum of 30 days and until response rates were stable. Both paired and unpaired subjects were used.

The result, shown in Figures 8.3 and 8.4, is that the S^E condition produced a large increase in response rates which lasted for the duration of the experiment, but only when S^E was paired. The bars are medians from the last seven days before and after the S^E schedule was added.

The increase produced by the S^E paired condition confirms previous findings (Zimmerman, 1963; Zimmerman et al., 1967) that a Concurrent schedule of arbitrary stimuli can sustain increased rates of responding when the stimuli are paired with a primary reinforcer. In the present experiment, the rate increases were quite large, whereas rates of less than 10 responses per minute were usually obtained by Zimmerman (1963) and Zimmerman & Hanford (1966). The large increase may be explained, in part, by the selection of S^E and primary reinforcement schedules which did not place responding for S^E in competition with responding for primary reinforcement.

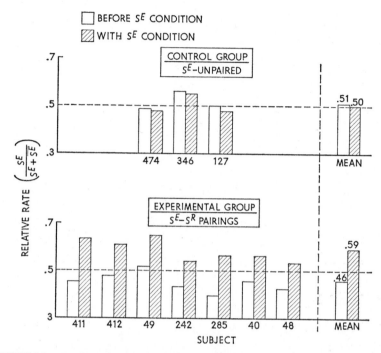

FIGURE 8.3. Median relative rates during the component of a MULT *VI* 30-sec *VI* 30 sec schedule in which a Concurrent schedule of S^E presentations was programmed. Rates are from the final seven sessions at each condition in Experiment 1. The means are averages of the medians.

Figure 8.4 also shows that, in five of seven birds, the rate produced during the unchanged *VI* 30-sec component did not change substantially after the S^E paired schedule (S^E schedule with S^E-S^R pairings) was added during the other component of the Multiple schedule. In the remaining two birds, the rate showed a marked increase. These rate increases were probably unrelated to the addition of the S^E schedule on the other key. P–40 was accidentally exposed to the S^E schedule on the wrong key during one entire session; the rate on this key quickly increased and never returned to the base-line level. (P–49 was exposed to the same error but the rate increase was only transient.) In P–48, the much larger increase in both components seems to have resulted from a shift in response topography during the experiment. Whereas most pecks were missing the key when the non-S^E condition was on both keys, the proportion of misses decreased markedly about two weeks after

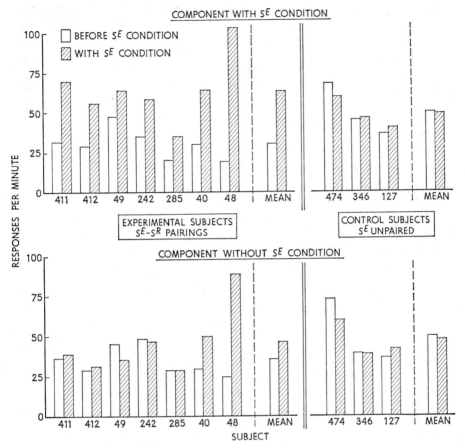

FIGURE 8.4. Median response rates during both components of a MULT *VI* 30 sec *VI* 30 sec schedule in which a Concurrent schedule of S^{E} presentations was added to one component. Rates are from the final seven sessions at each condition of Experiment 1. The means are averages of the medians.

the S^{E} condition was added. This shift in topography increased rates sharply on both keys.

A consistent finding in all seven S^{E} paired subjects was that the rate during the unchanged component *did not decrease* after the S^{E} schedule was added to the other component. This finding is inconsistent with the negative contrast effect produced by changes in the rate of *primary* reinforcement in a Multiple schedule. When the rate of primary reinforcement during one component of a Multiple schedule is increased markedly, the rate of responding during other components often shows a decrease, even though the schedule of reinforcement remains unchanged (Reynolds, 1961a). A similar decrease was not obtained here when a schedule of stimuli associated with the primary reinforcer (S^E) was added to one component of a Multiple schedule. This inconsistency was probably not due to the low frequency of S^E presentations, since the high response rates resulted in a rate of S^E presentations as high as five times the frequency of primary reinforcement. Much lower increases in the rate of primary reinforcement can produce contrast effects.

Experiment 2

In order further to examine the possibility of contrast produced by the S^E schedule, the same two-key, two-component Multiple schedule was continued in Experiment 2, except that the superimposed S^E schedule was successively added to and removed from a key. In addition, the S^E schedule was not confined to one key but, following each return to the base-line condition, the S^E schedule was moved to the other key. Only paired subjects were used. Each exposure to a base-line or S^E condition was for about 15 days, except that P–40 and P–242 were first exposed to the S^E condition on one key for over 30 days in Experiment 1. The procedure can be summarized as 15+ days of base line (no S^E schedule on either key), 15 days with the S^E schedule on one key, 15+ days of base line, 15 days with the S^E schedule on the other key, 15+ days of base line, etc.

To demonstrate contrast, we are interested only in the rate during the condition without the S^E schedule and how it is affected by adding the S^E schedule to the other component. A negative contrast effect like that produced by adding primary reinforcement to one key would be a decreased rate during the other (constant) component. One measure of contrast would therefore be the ratio of rates during the constant component without the S^E schedule after and before the S^E schedule is added to the other component (Reynolds, 1961a). A negative contrast effect would be shown if this ratio were less than 1.0.

Figure 8.5, showing ratios from successive five-day blocks during exposure to the S^E condition, indicates that reliable contrast effects did not occur. Only bird 246 showed any contrast, but the effect disappeared by the third 15-day period with the added S^E schedule.

Similar small and unreliable contrast effects with a conditioned

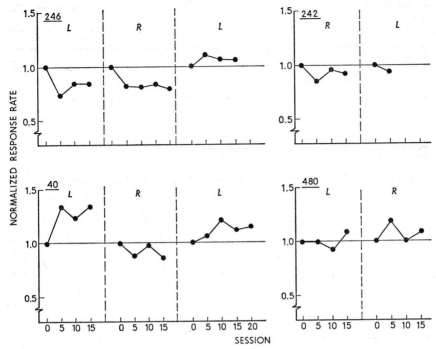

FIGURE 8.5. Changes in response rates during one component of a MULT *VI* 30 sec *VI* 30 sec schedule of primary reinforcement produced by adding a Concurrent schedule of S^E presentations to the other component. S^E was paired with every primary reinforcement. Each point is the ratio of two five-day median response rates during the non-S^E component—the rate *while* the S^E schedule was programmed during the other component divided by the rate *before* the S^E condition was added. At abscissa points 0, rate ratios are necessarily equal to 1.0. The key on which the S^E condition was programmed is indicated by L (left) and R (right).

reinforcer have been reported by Zimmerman, Hanford, and Brown (1967). When the frequency of conditioned reinforcement was varied during one component of a Multiple schedule, small contrast effects were reported in only two of four birds. In one, the rate change was between about 3 and 4 responses per minute, and in neither bird did the magnitude of the change vary with the frequency of conditioned reinforcement.

To summarize Experiments 1 and 2, the S^E schedule with S^E-S^R paired produced increased response rates, consistent with previous reports that conditioned reinforcement can augment responding either temporarily, as when programmed in Extinction, or permanently, when programmed concurrently with primary reinforcement. The same schedule, however, failed to generate contrast effects which are associated with changes in the frequency of primary reinforcement in Multiple schedules. This combination of results suggests that the rate increase is not a true reinforcement effect. Before considering the reinforcement question further, the effects of the same S^E schedule on the sensitive measure of choice will be described.

RATE AND CHOICE EXPERIMENTS

To measure the effects of the superimposed S^E schedule on preference, the schedule of primary reinforcement with and without S^E schedule were offered as alternatives in a choice situation. The two conditions were available on separate keys, as in Experiments 1 and 2. Now, however, the conditions were programmed so that the subjects had to respond in order to present one or the other condition. By offering the opportunity to produce either condition at the same time, a measure of preference between the two conditions was obtained. To accomplish this, the two conditions were programmed as terminal links of two separate two-link Chain schedules. This is the Concurrent-Chains method for measuring preference for one schedule over another, as well as performance while the schedules are in effect (Herrnstein, 1964a).

In general, the two experiments to be reported here examined choices between the identical S^E and non-S^E conditions programmed in Experiments 1 and 2. (Figure 8.2). In these previous studies, however, the two conditions alternated under the control of the experimenter, regardless of the subject's behavior; in the choice situation to be described now, the two conditions were produced according to the subject's choice behavior. Thus, although a combined total of 24 exposures to both conditions was again required to complete a session, the proportion and sequence of exposures to each condition were variable, dependent on the subject's performance.

The entire choice procedure is diagrammed in Figure 8.6. Although the description of this method is complicated, the main features are straightforward. As in any choice situation, the procedure could be in one of three states, shown as separate boxes in the figure. One state is the choice period; the remaining two are the conditions between which the subject is choosing. In the present

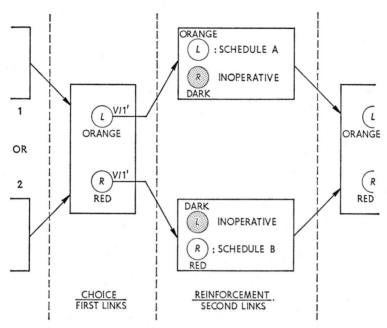

FIGURE 8.6. Diagram of the Concurrent Choice Chain procedure for choosing between two schedules of reinforcement. The two schedule alternatives, shown as Schedules A and B, are programmed as terminal links of two two-link chain schedules; the initial links were separate, concurrent VI 1 schedules. During the initial links, the subject could occasionally produce either Schedule A or B by responding on the appropriate key. When a response did not produce a schedule, both keys were darkened for 1 sec before the next choice response was possible.

case, these were usually the presence and absence of the S^E schedule. The choice period is signaled by illuminating both keys simultaneously. A peck on one key sometimes produces the condition available on that key. When this occurs, the chosen key remains illuminated and the other key is darkened until the requirements of the chosen condition are fulfilled. The choice procedure is thus analogous to a T-maze which offers a choice between two conditions visible at the choice point. But instead of choosing between simple reinforcement conditions, the subject is choosing to "remain in the goal box" for a stipulated period until certain conditions are fulfilled. When the requirements are fulfilled, the subject is returned to the choice point.

In the present experiments, the choice period was programmed like the Concurrent-Chains procedure of Autor (Chapter 6) and

Herrnstein (1964a) instead of like the typical T-maze. The initial links of the Concurrent Chains were VI 1 schedules (see Figure 8.6). However, the usual procedure was slightly modified by introducing a discrete-trials procedure in which a response on either key in the first link produced a 1-sec blackout of both keys before they were reilluminated for the next choice. Responses during blackouts were ineffective. Thus, only one choice response was permitted each time that both keys were lit, although many choices might be necessary before the next condition was produced. Discrete trials were used because opportunities to make a choice response were signaled by the red and orange keys correlated with the different terminal links. Free responding during the choice period would have confounded choices with the tendency to respond on a given key at a given rate. This discrete trials Concurrent Chain will therefore be called a Concurrent *Choice* Chain procedure. This procedure thus combines the advantages of a discrete choice response, like that in a T-maze situation, with the intermittent availability of the alternatives, like that in the standard Concurrent-Chains situation with VI schedules in the initial links.

Two choice experiments will be reported at this point. In one, choices were measured only after many sessions of experience with the alternatives, the presence or absence of the S^E schedules. In the second, choices were measured throughout exposure to both conditions. Thus, short- and long-term effects of the S^E schedule on choice were examined separately.

Experiment 3

In Experiment 3, subjects were offered a choice between the presence and absence of the S^E schedule, after these conditions had been experienced for at least 30 days in Experiment 1. In effect, these birds were exposed to both terminal links prior to being asked to express a preference between them.

The results are shown in Figures 8.7, 8.8, and 8.9. Figure 8.7 shows both median relative choices for the S^E schedule and median relative rates during exposure to the S^E schedule, for the first seven choice sessions. Although response rates were still *higher* (in the final link) during exposure to the S^E schedule (see Figures 8.3 and 8.4), the schedule of primary reinforcement alone, without the S^E schedule, was immediately preferred by all five birds. Figure 8.8

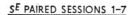

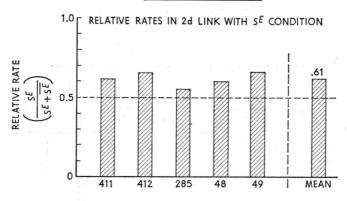

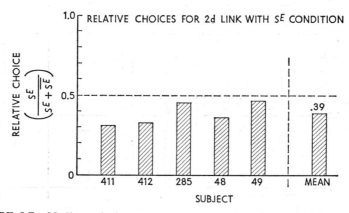

FIGURE 8.7. Median relative response rates during the terminal link of the Concurrent Choice Chain schedule with the superimposed S^E schedule (top), and median relative choices for this schedule (bottom), when S^E was paired with primary reinforcement. Data are from the first seven sessions of Experiment 3. Subjects had at least 30 days' pre-exposure to both terminal links before choices were measured. Means are averages of the medians.

(first bars) shows that after 30 or more days of continued choosing, the S^E schedule was avoided to an even greater degree than at first by four of the five birds; the fifth, P–285, showed an equally strong preference for the S^E schedule. This result is shown in the first bar for each bird. (The behavior of P–285 was peculiar in other respects. Figure 8.9, showing the response rates during both terminal links, indicates that P–285 responded more slowly than other birds during both terminal links.)

The aversion from the S^E schedule condition was contrary to the

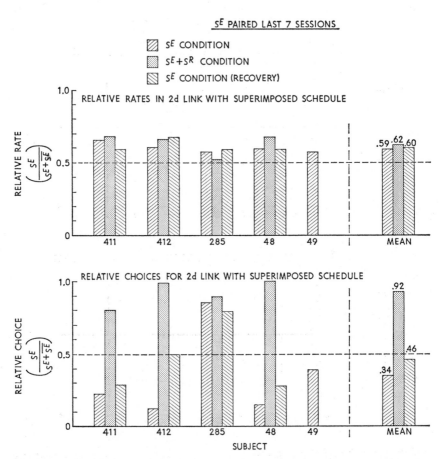

FIGURE 8.8. Median relative response rates during the terminal link of the Concurrent Choice Chain schedule with the superimposed S^E schedule (top), and median relative choices for this schedule (bottom), when S^E was paired with primary reinforcement on the *VI* 30 sec schedule (bars 1 and 3) and when S^E was paired with primary reinforcement on both the *VI* 30 sec and superimposed *FR* 11 schedules (bar 2). Data are from the final seven sessions at each condition of Experiment 3. Subject 49 was exposed to the first S^E condition only. Means are averages of the medians.

effects of a higher frequency of *primary* reinforcement during one terminal link (Autor, 1960; Herrnstein, 1964a). If S^E, when paired with primary reinforcement, was reinforcing, birds should have preferred the combination of S^E and primary reinforcement schedules to primary reinforcement alone. Therefore, as a check on the difference between S^E and primary reinforcement in this choice situation, the Concurrent S^E schedule was changed to a Concurrent

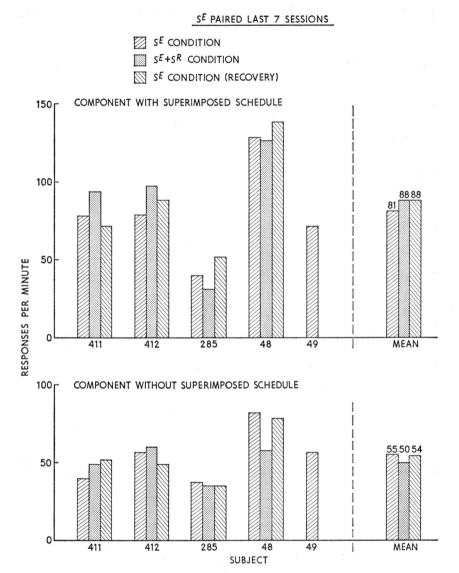

FIGURE 8.9. Median response rates during both terminal links of the Concurrent Choice Chain schedule, when S^E was paired with primary reinforcement on the VI 30 sec schedule (bars 1 and 3) and when S^E was paired with primary reinforcement on both the VI 30 sec and FR 11 schedules (bar 2). Data are from the final seven sessions at each condition of Experiment 3. P–49 was exposed to the first S^E condition only. Means are averages of the medians.

schedule of primary reinforcement on one key. This was accomplished by pairing every presentation of S^E, on both the VI and FR 11 schedules, with primary reinforcement. This is labeled the $S^E + S^R$ *condition* in Figure 8.8 (second bars). The effect was an immediate and strong preference for the key with the Concurrent schedule, in agreement with Herrnstein (1964a) and Autor (1960). Thus, given the same FR 11 Concurrent schedule on a key, opposite choice effects were produced by conditioned and primary reinforcement. Bird 49, due to an apparatus failure, was not exposed to this step. (Further indication of the aberrant behavior of P–285 is shown by the effects of the $S^E + S^R$ condition on response rate, shown in Figures 8.8 and 8.9. Rates in the non-S^E condition and the $S^E + S^R$ condition were equal, even though the latter included an extra FR 11 schedule of primary reinforcement. Pigeons typically respond at much higher rates on FR than on VI schedules (Ferster & Skinner, 1957), especially when the rate of reinforcement is three to five times higher on the ratio schedule.)

As a further check on the effects of S^E presentations, the four birds exposed to the $S^E + S^R$ condition were reexposed to the original choice between the presence and absence of the S^E schedule. The result, shown in the third bar for each bird in Figure 8.8, was virtual recovery of the results in the first part: aversion for the S^E schedule in P–411 and P–48, a reduction to complete indifference between the two conditions in P–412, and retention of the preference for the S^E schedule in P–285.

The behavior of control subjects summarized in Tables 8.1 and 8.2, indicates that the S^E schedule, when S^E was unpaired with S^R,

TABLE 8.1

Experiment 3. Median relative rates of birds during terminal link of the Concurrent Choice Chain procedure with superimposed S^E schedule when S^E and S^R were unpaired.

Subject	Relative Response Rate	
	First 7 Sessions	Last 7 Sessions
P-127	0.50	0.48
P–474	0.50	0.54
P–346	0.51	0.53
MEAN	0.50	0.52

was exerting no consistent effect on either response rate or choice. Although, by the end of the experiment, birds were not choosing equally between the presence and absence of the S^E schedule, the results do not indicate the aversion for the S^E condition that was shown when S^E was paired with S^R. The initial result during the

TABLE 8.2

Experiment 3.   Median relative choices of birds for second link of the Concurrent Choice Chain procedure with superimposed S^E schedule when S^E and S^R were unpaired.

| Subject | Relative Choice | |
	First 7 Sessions	Last 7 Sessions
P–127	0.54	0.61
P–474	0.43	0.31
P–346	0.50	0.67
MEAN	0.49	0.53

first seven choice days was indifference between the two conditions.

Experiment 4

In brief, Experiment 3 showed that the schedule of S^E when paired with S^R was avoided after long exposure. In numerous Extinction experiments, however, stimuli associated with S^R have been briefly preferred (Armus & Garlich, 1961; D'Amato, Lachman, & Kivy, 1958; Hall, 1951; Klein, 1959; Nevin, 1966; Saltzman, 1949; Stein, 1958). In Experiment 4, therefore, choices between the presence and absence of the S^E schedule, with S^E paired with S^R, were determined throughout an extended exposure to both conditions. A base-line condition was imposed first, in which the Concurrent S^E schedule was absent during both terminal links.

The results, plotted in Figure 8.10, are consistent with both the previous experiment and with the effects of conditioned reinforcement in Extinction. Immediately after the S^E schedule was introduced in one terminal link, that link was preferred by all birds. This is consistent with results of the Extinction procedure in the study of conditioned reinforcement where preferences for the stimuli previously associated with the primary reinforcer are examined

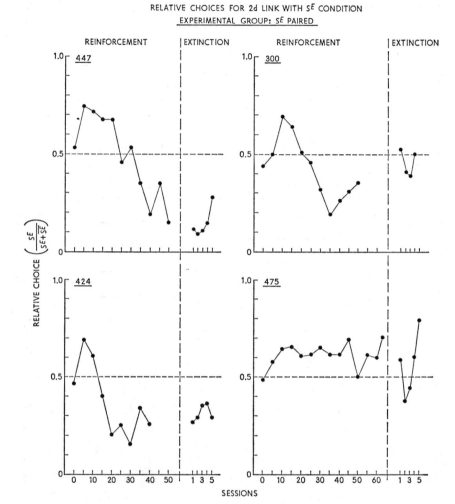

RELATIVE CHOICES FOR 2d LINK WITH S^E CONDITION
EXPERIMENTAL GROUP: S^E PAIRED

FIGURE 8.10. Changes in relative choice for the S^E schedule during primary reinforcement and Extinction in Experiment 4, when S^E was paired with primary reinforcement (before Extinction). Each point during reinforcement is the median from five successive sessions; each point during Extinction is from a single session. The points plotted at abscissa points 0 are from the final five sessions before the Concurrent S^E schedule was added to one terminal link. The choice procedure was the Concurrent Choice Chain.

when the stimulus is first presented alone. With continued exposure, however, the S^E schedule was eventually avoided by three of four birds; the fourth, P–475, like P–285 in the previous experiment, continued to prefer the S^E schedule. Thus, combining Experiments 3 and 4, seven of nine birds eventually displayed a strong aversion for the S^E schedule. Control subjects with the same S^E schedule but without the final pairing of S^E and S^R, once more showed no consistent effect of the S^E schedule on choice (Table 8.3).

In a terminal Extinction procedure, the VI 30 sec schedule of primary reinforcement was withdrawn from both terminal links, leaving only the FR 11 schedule of S^E presentation during one terminal link. Figure 8.10 shows that the preferences remained almost unchanged. Two birds still avoided the S^E schedule, and bird 475 still showed a preference for the S^E schedule; bird 300, on the other hand, was suddenly indifferent to the presence and absence of the S^E schedule. This indifference had previously occurred in one

TABLE 8.3

Experiment 4.   Median relative choices of S^E schedule in the Concurrent Choice Chain procedure when S^E and S^R were unpaired.

| | Relative Choice | | |
| | Base Line | S^E Schedule | |
Subject	Last 7 Sessions	First 7 Sessions	Last 7 Sessions
P–457..........0.37		0.37	0.37
P–41...........0.62		0.58	0.47
P–423..........0.50		0.54	0.53
MEAN.........0.50		0.50	0.46

bird, 412, in Experiment 3, after a long history of exposure to the S^E schedules.

Summary of Experiments 1–4

To summarize the results of Experiments 1–4, a Concurrent schedule for presenting an arbitrary stimulus, S^E, produced contrasting effects on response rate and preference when S^E was repeatedly paired with the primary reinforcer:

1. The effect on response rate was a sustained increase over the rate produced by primary reinforcement alone, as in all previous Concurrent schedule experiments;
2. The effect on preference changed with continued exposure to the S^E schedule:
a) After the S^E schedule was added to one alternative of a choice situation, the S^E schedule was preferred for several sessions;

b) After continued exposure to the S^E schedule, it was avoided by 7 of 9 birds.
3. The effects of the S^E schedule depended on the pairing of S^E and S^R. When S^E was not paired with S^R, there was no effect of the S^E schedule on response rate or choice.

A FUNCTIONAL ANALYSIS OF CONDITIONED REINFORCEMENT

The effects of the Concurrent S^E schedule on preference were similar to the familiar effects of conditioned reinforcement in Extinction. Initially, adding the S^E schedule was like adding extra primary reinforcement to one choice alternative (Herrnstein, 1964a)—the S^E schedule was preferred. This resembles the reinforcementlike effects temporarily produced by conditioned reinforcement in Extinction. Eventually, the S^E schedule was not preferred, an effect inconsistent with the hypothesis that S^E was sustained as a reinforcer. This effect is also reminiscent of the long-term effect of conditioned reinforcement in Extinction, namely, loss of behavior, which is also quite unlike an effect of primary reinforcement.

To explain these effects of the S^E schedule in behavioral terms, I favor a functional analysis over current two-factor theories which claim that stimuli such as S^E can become reinforcing. The functional approach will also be applied to the results of the more common Extinction and Chaining experiments on conditioned reinforcement. In the discussion that follows, it will be convenient to deal separately with the short- and long-term effects of conditioned reinforcement.

Long-term effects of conditioned reinforcement

In the Introduction, it was suggested that Extinction and Chain schedule methods of programming conditioned reinforcement produce long-term effects consistent with both two-factor theory and a functional analysis. The long-term effects of a Concurrent conditioned reinforcement schedule reported here, however, do not support the two-factor theory. In Experiments 3 and 4, S^E did not continue to produce reinforcementlike effects even though S^E was repeatedly paired with the primary reinforcer. This result contradicts the part of two-factor theory that claims continued pairings can sustain the reinforcing strength of an arbitrary stimulus.

This failure to sustain reinforcement effects suggests that we look to the cue function of response-produced arbitrary stimuli for the origin of their effects. In this discussion, the term "cue" will be used as a general term for any stimulus which is presented to a subject and reports a set of conditions for the subsequent occurrence or nonoccurrence of primary reinforcement. It should be noted that this usage says nothing about discriminative control or response requirements for primary reinforcers. This is because Chain schedules have clearly shown that the effects of conditioned reinforcement are not determined by such response requirements but only by the parameters of primary reinforcement correlated with the conditioned reinforcer (Autor, 1960; Herrnstein, 1964a; Kelleher & Gollub, 1962). A discriminative stimulus is thus one type of cue which, in addition, "sets the occasion" for the emission of a specific response which is required for producing primary reinforcement (Keller & Schoenfeld, 1950; Skinner, 1938; Terrace, 1966). The relevance of cue function for explaining conditioned reinforcement is being proposed here because both Concurrent and Chain schedule methods continue pairing of the exteroceptive stimulus with the primary reinforcer under a given schedule of reinforcement. Yet Experiments 2, 3, and 4 showed that reinforcementlike effects cannot be sustained with a Concurrent schedule of conditioned reinforcement, whereas a Chain schedule can sustain reinforcementlike effects on both response rate and choice behavior (Herrnstein, 1964a; Kelleher, 1966a; Kelleher & Gollub, 1962).

This difference in effects seems to be due to the different cue functions of the conditioned reinforcing stimulus in the two methods. In a Chain, the conditioned reinforcing stimulus is usually a reliable cue for the occurrence of primary reinforcement. In a Concurrent schedule, the conditioned reinforcing stimulus is never a cue for reinforcement, as in Experiments 1–4, where the only difference between the S^E paired condition (Figure 8.2, bottom) and the non-S^E paired condition (Figure 8.2, top) consisted of the Concurrent schedule of S^E presentations which were never followed by primary reinforcement. This Concurrent schedule produced an eventual preference for the condition without the Concurrent schedule, which is consistent with the view that one type of punishing event is the withholding of primary reinforcement (Skinner, 1953). The S^E schedule also generated rate increases like those produced with explicit procedures of nonreinforcement (Ferster,

1958a; Leitenberg, 1965, 1966; Reynolds, 1961a) or with the procedures which intermittently correlate a stimulus with nonreinforcement (Amsel & Roussel, 1952). If we include the Extinction method of conditioned reinforcement in which the long-term behavioral effect is loss of responding, it is possible to conclude that an arbitrary stimulus cannot produce a sustained reinforcementlike effect when it is not a cue for primary reinforcement.

This suggests that cues for reinforcement are still candidates for being conditioned reinforcers with a true reinforcing property since they alone seem capable of sustaining reinforcementlike effects. Such a theory could be offered as a modified form of two-factor theory in which Pavlovian conditioning is replaced by cue function as the method of association required for creating a conditioned reinforcer, such as in the "discriminative stimulus hypothesis" of Keller and Schoenfeld (1950). One argument against such a theory is that it is unnecessary. If the functional approach is correct, that a sustained reinforcementlike effect with an arbitrary stimulus is only possible when the stimulus is itself a cue for primary reinforcement, there is little to be gained by adding that the stimulus is itself reinforcing. By not doing so, there is the additional advantage that conditioned reinforcers could be combined with discriminative stimuli (Terrace, 1966) as arbitrary stimuli whose effects on responding can be explained entirely by their functional relation to primary reinforcement.

Single, extended Chain schedules also expose the weakness of any form of two-factor theory as an explanation for response-chaining. During initital links, responding all but disappears (Kelleher & Gollub, 1962). This behavior is explained by the discriminative control exerted by the first few discriminative stimuli in the Chain, since they signal that reinforcement is far away in time. Yet when responding begins to accelerate during later links, it has not been thought sufficient to cite only the cue function of the later stimuli in the Chain, the stimuli reporting that reinforcement is closer. Instead, the later stimuli are also called conditioned reinforcers, from which it is concluded that not all discriminative stimuli can be conditioned reinforcers (Kelleher, 1966a; Kelleher & Gollub, 1962). This is not very useful, though, if increased responding is the only evidence for conditioned reinforcement. A more consistent view can explain all changes within an extended Chain by correlating the ability of each succeeding discriminative stimulus to maintain responding with the reinforcement conditions cued by that stimulus.

Second-order Chain schedules (see Chapter 2) also produce effects which are not easy to reconcile with two-factor conditioned reinforcement theory. In a second-order schedule, behavior appropriate to a given schedule, say *FI* 4, is itself reinforced on another schedule, say *FR* 15, producing an *FR* 15 (*FI* 4) schedule. On this schedule, when the primary reinforcer is not delivered after an *FI* 4 link, some other exteroceptive stimulus can be substituted. Kelleher (1966), for example, has studied the effects of presenting stimuli paired with the primary reinforcer at the end of unreinforced links of an *FR* 15 (*FI* 4) schedule. The results partly contradict two-factor conditioned reinforcement theory. Although the same conditioned reinforcer was presented at the conclusion of every *FI* 4 link, the amount of responding was much higher as the time for reinforcement approached. Furthermore, responding during the first link of the Chain was minimal, even though the stimulus had just been paired with a primary reinforcer during the immediately preceding (terminal) link. Thus, a temporal discrimination seems to be exerting most of the control over responding. It is true that a stimulus paired with the primary reinforcer in this schedule can produce higher response rates than a stimulus not paired (Kelleher, 1966). But the S^E schedule in the experiments reported here revealed that a response-produced arbitrary stimulus may increase rates because of an intermittent association with primary reinforcement, and not because the stimulus is, itself, a reinforcer. This situation also exists in a second-order schedule.

To conclude this section, diverse methods for programming response-produced arbitrary stimuli produce long-term effects which only occasionally resemble the effects of primary reinforcement. Yet all effects can be predicted from the function of the stimuli in cuing or not cuing primary reinforcement. This supports the idea that phenomena traditionally explained with the hypothesis of conditioned reinforcement can be conveniently analyzed in functional terms, and that the additional hypothesis of conditioned reinforcement is of little value for the long-term effects of response-produced stimuli.

Short-term effects of conditioned reinforcement

A two-factor theory of conditioned reinforcement receives more support from transient, short-term effects of conditioned reinforcing stimuli, such as those produced in Extinction, because reinforcementlike effects usually precede the eventual effects of nonreinforcement. Experiment 4, reported here, also reproduced the familiar transient reinforcementlike effect. Yet it will be argued in this section that short-term effects are also more properly analyzed in completely functional terms, without the hypothesis of a reinforcement process. Support for this will concentrate along two lines. First, the inference will be criticized that a reinforcement effect can be supported by reinforcementlike effects which are undergoing Extinction. Second, it will be suggested that a functional analysis offers more help in analyzing short-term effects of conditioned reinforcement.

One problem, alluded to earlier, is that the acquired reinforcing power of a stimulus in two-factor theories is an inference rather than a reliable result. In all cases in which short-term effects are used as evidence for a reinforcing effect, the stimulus is called a reinforcer only for the short time that it acts as a reinforcer. In the case of Extinction tests, an attempt was made to sustain the validity of the original inference by ascribing the Extinction to a decaying conditioned reinforcer. But the only evidence ever offered to support the decay hypothesis has come from the very Extinction effects for which the hypothesis was created.

The results of Experiment 4 make this problem even more troublesome, for the decay hypothesis can not explain why S^E should have lost its reinforcing strength if pairings were never terminated. On the other hand, if S^E became ineffective only because it was not reliably cuing primary reinforcement, then this explanation should also suffice for the loss of reinforcing effects in Extinction. It would no longer be necessary to hold onto the decay hypothesis as an explanation of extinctionlike effects. And without an operation to explain why an alleged reinforcer should lose its effectiveness, it becomes more difficult to propose that a reinforcer is created in the first place.

Let us consider the common case when a subject is reinforced for responding, and reinforcement is then terminated. The behavioral events comprise a period of sustained or enhanced responding usually followed by a gradual decrease in response rates until responding is completely extinguished. When only primary reinforcers are involved, this sequence of changes is analyzed by considering only two processes—reinforcement and nonreinforcement (Keller & Schoenfeld, 1950; Skinner, 1938). These processes are correlated with the stable, "asymptotic" performances—reinforce-ment with responding, and nonreinforcement with Extinction. The lag between the change of conditions and the adjustment of behavior to the change is not explained with a separate reinforcement process. Instead, the transition state is regarded as a temporary period of instability which inevitably occurs when reinforcement conditions are abruptly altered. This two-stage view is not aban-doned just because the transition state can be prolonged, as in the classic case following intermittent reinforcement (Keller & Schoen-feld, 1950; Mowrer & Jones, 1945; Skinner, 1938). Instead, the magnitude of resistance is traced to the change from reinforcement to Extinction, and the relation between them. One hypothesis, for instance, predicts the amount of resistance to Extinction from the difference between reinforcement and Extinction stimulus condi-tions. This is known as the "discrimination hypothesis of Extinc-tion" (Mowrer & Jones, 1945). The central idea underlying this hypothesis is that Extinction will be retarded by conditions which make it difficult for a subject to detect that reinforcement has been terminated. This hypothesis, incidentally, has been applied to some conditioned reinforcement effects on the assumption that a condi-tioned reinforcing stimulus can increase the similarity of reinforce-ment and Extinction conditions (Bitterman, Feddersen, & Tyler, 1953). The value of this somewhat vague hypothesis is not at issue here. The point is that increased resistance to Extinction does not require an additional process intervening between reinforcement and Extinction conditions. Thus, even though a conditioned rein-forcing stimulus can retard Extinction, a functional analysis still requires only two processes to account for all the effects of present-ing arbitrary stimuli. Responding would be correlated with pre-senting a cue for primary reinforcement, and Extinction with pre-senting a stimulus which no longer cues reinforcement. There would be no need for the third process, reinforcement by an arbi-trary stimulus.

A functional approach also suggests that reinforcementlike ef-fects and discriminative effects of a stimulus should be correlated. This has been shown by examining changes in behavior both preceding and following each presentation of a conditioned rein-forcer. This correlation has been noted in Chain schedules where strength of reinforcing and discriminative effects of a stimulus both depend upon the position of the stimulus relative to the primary reinforcer (Kelleher, 1966b; Kelleher & Gollub, 1962). In Extinction studies, unfortunately, discriminative effects have not often been measured along with conditioned reinforcement effects. One reason is that, in simple pairing situations, the behavior after the stimulus consists only of approaching and consuming the reinforcer. This behavior is usually not quantified. When responding has been measured both before and after the conditioned reinforcer, conditioned reinforcement and discriminative effects have been related. Dinsmoor (1950) observed that a given stimulus can show either effect, depending on which effect experimental conditions permit. More convincing is the case when a Chain schedule is extinguished in one step, by withholding primary reinforcement at the end. Behavior weakens throughout the Chain, as the arbitrary stimulus seems to lose its discriminative and conditioned reinforcing effects together (Keller & Schoenfeld, 1950; Skinner, 1938). A similar effect was shown by D. W. Zimmerman (1959) in an Extinction test. A conditioned reinforcer was first established as a discriminative stimulus for running down an alley. Then, during Extinction, bar pressing produced the stimulus and allowed access to the alley. Extinction of the running response down the alley presaged extinction of the bar press. (See Wyckoff, 1959, for a review of cue functions related to conditioned reinforcement effects.) [3]

The correlation between discriminative and conditioned reinforcing effects also suggests one possibility which, while damaging to a two-factor account of conditioned reinforcement, would be consistent with a functional approach. This is the possibility that conditioned reinforcing effects of a stimulus can be abolished by reducing the discriminative control of the stimulus, even though it has been properly paired with a primary reinforcer. This may have been accomplished in an Extinction study by Keehn (1962). Rats were first trained to approach the reinforcer when a discriminative

---

[3] Sometimes, conditioned reinforcing effects occur without discriminative effects, as Ratner (1956) has shown. In his test of conditioned reinforcement, however, a bar was inserted at the beginning of Extinction. Although the conditioned reinforcer produced by bar pressing had been a cue for reinforcement, the bar itself was likely to be a cue for non-reinforcement. This might have reduced dipper approaches. Also, it should be noted that, in Chain schedules, the discriminative effects of a given stimulus are necessarily measured closer in time to reinforcement than are the conditioned reinforcing effects of the same stimulus.

stimulus was presented. One of two responses was required—running or climbing over a partition. Later, the discriminative stimulus was was tested for its conditioned reinforcing effects in Extinction by attempting to condition a bar press which was followed only by the stimulus. For some subjects, however, the original goal response was changed. Former runners were faced with a barrier to climb, and former climbers had a free path. For these subjects, there was an abrupt loss of both conditioned reinforcement effects and goal approaching. A similar effect was shown recently by Myers and Morningstar (1968).

The two-factor theory is unable to explain why a history of pairings could not produce a conditioned reinforcement effect, because there is nothing in the theory to explain why conditions *after* presenting a conditioned reinforcer should influence the effect. A functional analysis, on the other hand, can predict both Keehn's result and more traditional conditioned reinforcement effects. In Keehn's study, the discriminative control of the stimulus originally associated with reinforcement was probably reduced before it was ever made contingent on a new response in tests. In most other studies, including Experiment 4 reported here, there was no attempt to reduce the discriminative control of the stimulus before it was presented.

Experiment 5

Because Keehn's results strongly support a functional analysis, a similar experimental approach was attempted using Concurrent-schedule procedures. The intention was to show, again, that a paired stimulus will have minimal conditioned reinforcing effects if it is not an effective discriminative stimulus. The procedure was very different, however. In Keehn's study, the response leading to reinforcement was manipulated; in Experiment 5, the relation of a cue to the primary reinforcer was changed.

Experiment 5 can best be understood by recalling Experiment 4. In the latter, subjects first experienced pairings of S^E with every primary reinforcer *before* S^E was ever presented alone on the Concurrent FR 11 schedule; that is, S^E was a cue for primary reinforcement before it was first used as a (possible) conditioned reinforcer. This produced a transient reinforcementlike effect on choice (Figure 8.10). In Experiment 5, S^E was programmed alone on the Concurrent *FR* 11 schedule *before* it was ever paired with the primary reinforcer; that is, the unpaired S^E and non-S^E conditions preceded the paired S^E and non-S^E conditions as choice alternatives in the Concurrent Chain schedule. In all likelihood, S^E was not a cue for primary reinforcement before it was paired. The logic of the experiment is that if cuing primary reinforcement is the key to conditioned reinforcement, then prior exposure to the S^E unpaired with S^R should reduce conditioned reinforcement at the time pairings are initiated. If S^E can become a reinforcer owing merely to pairings with a primary reinforcer, even for a brief time, then prior exposure to the S^E unpaired with S^R should not reduce the eventual conditioned reinforcement effect after pairings are started.

The results, shown in Figure 8.11, were against the hypothesis that pairing with S^R was the crucial operation sufficient for establishing an arbitrary stimulus as a conditioned reinforcer. There was no transient preference for the S^E schedule after pairings were started. Instead, three of four birds showed little or no change in preference over 25 or more sessions of pairing, and one showed a rapid and sustained aversion from the S^E condition. This is in marked contrast to the results of Experiment 4 (Figure 8.10) in which transient preference was exhibited.

These results raise a new problem because of an effect not encountered earlier. The prior exposure to the S^E schedule, with S^E and S^R unpaired, not only eliminated the transient preference for the S^E schedule, but the aversion as well, in three of four birds. Experiments 3 and 4 did not point strongly to the aversion as a temporary effect although two birds, 411 (Experiment 3) and 300 (Experiment 4) ended up with no preference after several manipulations. If the aversive effects reflect an emotional state generated by the shift to nonreinforcement (Amsel, 1958; Skinner, 1950; Spence, 1956), then the possibility is raised that this emotion, like many others, is temporary. Moreover, two other effects produced by correlating a stimulus with nonreinforcement have been shown to be temporary, though long-lasting in comparison with the other transient effects mentioned previously. One is the contrast effect; the other is the peak shift in generalization gradients (Terrace, 1966).

RELATIVE CHOICES FOR 2d LINK WITH S^E CONDITION
S^E INITIALLY UNPAIRED

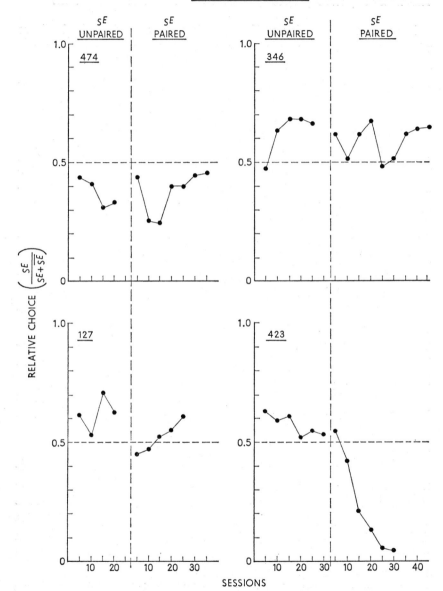

FIGURE 8.11. Changes in relative choice for the S^E schedule before and after pairings of S^E with primary reinforcement. Each point is the median from five successive sessions. The choice procedure was the Concurrent Choice Chain.

The new-response procedures of conditioned reinforcement

In fairness to two-factor theory, there are some transient effects which readily support a reinforcement interpretation. These are changes in behavior generated by conditioned reinforcement which were apparently not generated by presenting primary reinforcement. Two varieties may be cited. One such effect is the result sometimes obtained with the "new-response" procedure (Kelleher & Gollub, 1962; Wike, 1966) in which a stimulus formerly paired with a primary reinforcer is programmed to follow a response which was not previously followed by the primary reinforcer; another such effect may be obtained with a variation of the new-response procedure and may be called the "new-schedule" procedure, in which conditioned reinforcement is programmed on a schedule not used for programming pairings of the conditioned and primary reinforcers (Kelleher, 1961). D. W. Zimmerman (1959) combined both variations in a single Extinction experiment. Since programming conditioned reinforcement under new conditions should reduce, not increase, the similarity between reinforcement and Extinction conditions, the success of these procedures is said to be strong evidence for an acquired reinforcing function of the stimulus paired with the primary reinforcer (Kelleher, 1961; Myers & Myers, 1962).

One argument against a conditioned reinforcement explanation is that these effects can also be predicted from the discriminative control of the stimulus over goal responding. The Keehn (1962) study, in fact, used a new-response procedure, and the Concurrent experiments are examples of a new-schedule procedure. Discriminative control can also explain why intermittent schedules of conditioned reinforcement can prolong Extinction responding. After a stimulus ceases to be a cue for reinforcement, the rate at which its discriminative control over behavior decays is likely to depend on the number of presentations without reinforcement, and not on the number of Extinction responses or the time since the last primary reinforcement. If number of presentations is critical, Kelleher's (1961) and D. W. Zimmerman's (1957, 1959) results are more comparable to other extinction results. Another problem is that new response procedures base part of their reinforcement claim on the ability to increase the likelihood of a response without primary reinforcement. Given the results here, however, we must be wary of assuming that increased responding is always evidence of reinforcement.

New-response results also seem less convincing as evidence of a reinforcement effect if viewed as a special instance of Extinction, namely extinction of a two-link Chain schedule. In a typical two-link Chain, both links are first reinforced and then extinguished together. The same is true of the most frequent type of Extinction test, in which the same response is first conditioned with primary reinforcers paired with a stimulus, and extinguished later with the stimulus alone. New-response procedures resemble such a Chain, but one in which the links are introduced separately. The second link is formed first, when a stimulus is established as a cue for reinforcement. Then, the initial link is added by programming some new behavior to produce the cue. But this second step is accompanied by the beginning of Extinction, so that, in effect, a Chain is formed at the same time that Extinction is begun. By this temporal juggling, it looks as if a response is being "shaped" by conditioned reinforcement alone. But this is not sufficient to secure the claim that the stimulus is reinforcing. As Keehn (1962) showed, the success of the new-response procedure can be traced to the influence of primary reinforcement, since it is primary reinforcement that gives a stimulus its discriminative control. Since this control is necessary to produce a reinforcementlike effect on responding, a functional approach can also predict the success of new-response procedures.

CONCLUSIONS

To summarize this discussion, a functional analysis was proposed to explain the short- and long-term effects of stimuli associated with a primary reinforcer. At the same time, the current two-factor approach to conditioned reinforcement, which hypothesizes that arbitrary stimuli can be converted into reinforcers, was rejected. The obtained results supported the generalization that constituted the functional analysis, as follows: *When an arbitrary stimulus is programmed to follow a response, the effects of that stimulus on responding are a function of the conditions of primary reinforcement being cued by the stimulus.* Although we do not know all the factors which determine cue function, the important facts for conditioned reinforcement seem to be whether or not the presentation of a stimulus will presage primary reinforcement, and what the correlated conditions of primary reinforcement are. Moreover, to acquire discriminative control or cue function, it does not seem to matter whether this stimulus is merely paired, in Pavlovian fashion, with a set of reinforcement conditions, or is used as a discriminative stimulus for those conditions. Only the cued parameters of reinforcement seem to matter.

The following considerations support a functional analysis of conditioned reinforcement: (1) Sheer contiguity between a stimulus and reinforcement is not a sufficient explanation. This was shown here when a Concurrent schedule of conditioned reinforcement did not maintain reinforcementlike effect. In addition, Egger & Miller (1962, 1963) showed that a redundant stimulus, though paired, will not be an effective conditioned reinforcer, and Keehn (1962), as noted above, showed that changing the conditions leading to reinforcement can reduce the effects of conditioned reinforcement. (2) The effects of a stimulus associated with the reinforcer in Extinction and Chain schedule experiments also support a functional analysis; (3) The hypothesis that an arbitrary stimulus can acquire the power to reinforce, and the related hypothesis that this reinforcing power can decay, are logically unsound and difficult to verify with experiments; (4) Stimuli must first be cues for reinforcement in order to produce reinforcementlike effects when scheduled as conditioned reinforcers (Schoenfeld, Antonitis, and Bersh, 1950) ; (5) Discriminative and conditioned reinforcing effects of stimuli are closely correlated in time; (6) A functional analysis of conditioned reinforcement closely parallels current explanations of the effects of discriminative stimuli and primary reinforcement; (7) A wide range of effects can be produced with paired response-produced stimuli, only some which are reinforcementlike. To be compatible with the reinforcement hypothesis, a complex theory is required in which reinforcers are created and allowed to decay. A one-step functional analysis is simpler and can account for the whole range of effects.

Finally, if a functional analysis is to be accepted, a problem of terminology arises for discribing the process of presenting an arbitrary stimulus following an instrumental response. If what has heretofore been referred to as conditioned reinforcement is not a process of reinforcement, a new term is in order. Although the effects of such stimuli correlate well with cue function, this cannot properly be used to describe a process which produces its effect before the stimulus is presented (Terrace, 1966). In operant theories, unfortunately, stimuli presently can be given either a cue or a reinforcing function (or both), suggesting that arbitrary stimuli have been called reinforcers partly because the discriminative tag was completely inappropriate.

One solution to this semantic dilemma is suggested by recent experiments on "information" (Hendry, Chapter 12; Schaub, 1967). "Information" is described as a report about reinforcement conditions, and these experiments have studied the effects of making information conditional on responding. Procedurally, information turns out to be the presentation of a cue or discriminative stimulus which is not accompanied by any change in the conditions of reinforcement. In this way, these experiments resemble observing-response experiments (Hendry & Dillow, 1966; Wyckoff, 1952).

At present, information has been incorporated within the framework of conditioned reinforcement theory by proposing that "information" is reinforcing. One improvement over classical conditioned reinforcement theory is that Pavlovian pairings are not considered; informative stimuli are stimuli which cue reinforcement. But information as reinforcement introduces the same problem as conditioned reinforcement theory, namely, that the "reinforcing" effect of information may be completely a function of the information being conveyed about reinforcement, so the unqualified generalization that information is reinforcing is not true. For example, (Chapter 14) some stimuli that are informative about punishment are not reinforcing, although there is evidence that information about nonreinforcement can increase response rates (Hendry & Dillow, 1966; Schaub & Honig, 1967). In the latter instance, however, one problem is the effect of "frustrative" stimuli on response rate; inferences about reinforcing effects based solely on increases in response rate are hazardous because such increases may be due to a frustrative effect of nonreinforcement.

Nevertheless, the term "information" is useful, for it conveys the sense of producing a stimulus which reports something about the conditions of reinforcement. One solution for the semantic dilemma is therefore to broaden the notion of "information" to describe any situation in which an arbitrary stimulus is produced by an instrumental response. Furthermore, the conclusion of this paper would apply, so that the effects of producing an informative stimulus can be said to depend on which conditions of reinforcement are correlated with the stimulus.

Thus, an informative process is being proposed as a replacement for the traditional process of conditioned reinforcement to describe any behavioral situation in which an arbitrary, nonreinforcing stimulus follows a response. This proposal is offered because, given the wide range of effects produced, a purely functional analysis seems to offer more help than a theory in which arbitrary stimuli are said to become reinforcers.

SUMMARY

According to one hypothesis, an arbitrary stimulus can itself become a reinforcer after pairings with a primary reinforcer. This chapter proposes as an alternative a functional analysis of the effects of presenting stimuli, including those that might serve as conditioned reinforcers. According to a functional viewpoint, *the effects of arbitrary stimuli which follow a response, like the discriminative effects of stimuli which precede a response, can be predicted from the reinforcing consequences being cued by the stimulus*. To test the implications of this viewpoint, a set of stimuli was sometimes paired with, but also presented independently of, primary reinforcement. This was accomplished by superimposing a schedule of brief stimuli on a schedule of primary reinforcement on one response key; on another key, the identical schedule of primary reinforcement was programmed alone. Using a Concurrent-Chain procedure, preference for one schedule over the other was measured, in addition to performance while the schedules of brief stimuli were imposed. Although the superimposed schedule of brief stimuli increased response rates, this schedule was eventually chosen less often. This result was consistent with a functional analysis, since, on the key with the superimposed schedules, the brief stimuli were correlated more often with nonreinforcement. A functional interpretation of conditioned reinforcement was also found to fit the results with traditional Chain and Extinction procedures in the study of conditioned reinforcement.

SECTION III

Discrimination and information

This section comprises six chapters concerned mainly with the analysis of conditioned reinforcement in discrimination learning and performance.

The observing-response technique, in which presentations of discriminative stimuli are produced by an operant distinguishable from the primarily reinforced operant, was originated by Wyckoff and has since been widely used. The experimental part of Wyckoff's dissertation is widely referred to, and is here made generally available for the first time. Wyckoff's results show that the set of discriminative stimuli is a source of conditioned reinforcement that can sustain observing behavior. Kendall's experiments extend Wyckoff's method to the study of reinforcing effects of trace discriminative stimuli—those that are not temporally contiguous with the primary reinforcer. Crossman's results are included here because they show discriminative effects of a trace discriminative stimulus.

Hendry's experiments use the observing-response method and Concurrent Chains to test the hypothesis that the set of discriminative stimuli are reinforcing by virtue of their informative function. The results consistently show that relative rate of primary reinforcement is not an important variable in determining performance in these situations. The interpretation of the set of discriminative stimuli as informative is taken further by Schaub (Chapter 13) and Dinsmoor and his colleagues. Schaub provides evidence that the stimulus associated with Extinction will act as a conditioned reinforcer in appropriate circumstances. Schaub's results lead him to propose that the conditioned reinforcing effect of a stimulus is the algebraic sum of values based on its associative and informative relation to primary reinforcement. Dinsmoor *et al.* extend the notion of informative stimuli to the case of stimuli associated with presence and absence of a schedule of punishment, and provide evidence for a conditioned reinforcing effect of such stimuli.

chapter 9

THE ROLE OF OBSERVING RESPONSES IN DISCRIMINATION LEARNING[1]

L. Benjamin Wyckoff, Jr.

Department of Education, State of Georgia

INTRODUCTION

An observing response may be defined as a response which results in exposure to a pair of discriminative stimuli. The tendency for an observing response to occur, and changes in this tendency, may be expected to have a profound effect on discrimination learning. The effectiveness of discriminative stimuli is revealed by the degree to which they control performance. Therefore, we put forward the following general hypothesis regarding changes in the probability of an observing response.

General hypothesis: Exposure to discriminative stimuli will have a reinforcing effect on an observing response to the extent that the subject has learned to respond differently to the discriminative stimuli produced by the observing response.

The present experiment was designed to test the following specific hypotheses which are implied by this general hypothesis:

1. Under conditions of differential reinforcement the probability of an observing response will increase to some stable value, since the degree of differential performance will tend to increase to a stable value under this condition. It must be assumed that the probability of an observing response is initially greater than zero.

2. Under conditions of nondifferential reinforcement, the probability of an observing response will decrease to a low, stable value,

---

[1] Based on Part II of doctoral dissertation, Indiana University, 1950. Part I appeared in *Psychological Review*, 1952, 59, 431–42.

since the degree of differential performance will tend to decrease under this condition.

3. When a well-established discrimination is reversed, the probability of an observing response will decrease temporarily and then recover a high value. This hypothesis follows from the fact that when a discrimination is reversed, differential performance is eliminated as the original discrimination vanishes, and then reappears as the new discrimination is formed.

4. If, before a discrimination is formed, the probability of an observing response is low, discrimination formation will be retarded for some time but may finally occur quite rapidly. The extent of differential performance will increase very slowly at first because the subject will be exposed to the discriminative stimuli only a small proportion of the time. Then as the extent of differential performance becomes sufficiently great to bring about an increase in the probability of observing behavior the entire process will be accelerated.

Certain difficulties arise in devising a direct experimental test for these hypotheses. The most serious difficulty is encountered in obtaining a measure of the probability of observing behavior. To measure the familiar observing responses of orienting the head or fixating the eyes would be extremely difficult. We would always be confronted with the problem of identifying a response such that exposure to the discriminative stimuli would occur if, and only if, this response occurred. A subject might be exposed to an overhead stimulus even though it did not raise its head, etc.

One solution to this problem lies in selecting some response which is readily measurable and arranging the experimental situation so that this response is placed in the role of an observing response. In the present experiment the discriminative stimuli were presented if, and only if, the subject pressed a pedal in the floor of the apparatus. Thus, the pedal-pressing response, occurrence of which can readily be counted, falls within our definition of an observing response. There is no reason to believe that the learning processes affecting this response would differ in any crucial way from the processes affecting other, more familiar observing responses. This technique was used to obtain direct measures of an observing response under conditions of differential reinforcement, nondifferential reinforcement, and discrimination reversal.

A free operant experimental situation was used. The subjects were pigeons and the effective response was striking a translucent key, with a rate measure being recorded. The discriminative stimuli were colored lights (red and green) projected on the back of the key. The discriminative stimuli were withheld, and the key was lighted white, until the bird made the observing response of depressing a pedal on the floor of the compartment. The use of the pedal-pressing response enabled us to satisfy the following requirements:

1. The response was easily measured and recorded.

2. We can be reasonably certain that the bird was exposed to the discriminative stimuli if the observing response occurred, and that the bird was not exposed to the discriminative stimuli if the observing response failed to occur.

3. The observing response was relatively independent of the effective response of key-pecking. Pedal pressing was not a necessary complement of the effective response, nor was it in competition with the effective response.

4. The initial probability of an observing response could be adjusted, by the placing of the pedal, to obtain a value which would ensure learning within a reasonable time, but which could also increase.

The bird worked in a compartment equipped with a key which it could strike with its beak, a pedal on the floor of the compartment below and slightly to the right of the key, and a feeding mechanism to the left of the key (details given below). The experiment was conducted in continuous sessions of 75 min. However, it will be convenient to refer to 30-sec intervals within the session as "trials." Each trial was designated as positive or negative. Positive and negative trials were presented in a predetermined, mixed sequence. On each positive trial one key-pecking response was reinforced at the end of the 30-sec interval. Hence, key pecking was reinforced after a fixed interval of 30 sec (*FI* 30") on positive trials. The reinforcer consisted of access to a dish of grain for a short interval of fixed duration. No reinforcement occurred on negative trials; that procedure is formally referred to as Extinction (EXT). The rate of responding during each 30 sec gives an independent measure of response tendency for both positive and negative trials.

The pedal response affected the stimulus conditions during positive and negative trials, but had no effect on the reinforcement schedule. When the pedal was not depressed, the key was lit with white light regardless of whether the trial was positive or negative. When the pedal was depressed the key was lit with the positive color on positive trials, and with the negative color on negative trials, and these colors remained on the key so long as the pedal continued to be depressed.

The discriminative stimuli were not present throughout the trial, but were presented only when the observing response occurred. In a more familiar situation involving the observing response of orienting the head, we can see that essentially the same conditions hold. Even though in these other experiments the discriminative stimuli may be present throughout the trial, the subject will be exposed to them only if it makes the proper orienting responses. Otherwise it will be exposed to irrelevant stimuli.

Reinforcement was contingent on key pecking, but was independent of the pedal-pressing response. In a sense, the subject gained nothing but information by making the observing response. Increases in observing behavior under these conditions can be taken as evidence that exposure to discriminative stimuli is sufficient to bring about learning of the observing response, even though the final reinforcement is not contingent on this response. The results of this experiment show that this is the case.

METHOD

Apparatus

The apparatus for this experiment consisted of four duplicate Skinner boxes with accompanying operating and recording circuits. Each box was equipped with a key, a feeding mechanism and a foot pedal. The key was placed on the upper right, and the feeding mechanism on the lower left of the front panel. The foot pedal was placed on the floor, below and slightly to the right of the key. The inside dimensions of the compartment were 12 inches x 12 inches x 12 inches. The 1-inch diameter lucite key was $8\frac{1}{2}$ inches above the floor and $3\frac{1}{2}$ inches from the right wall.

The feeding mechanism consisted of a box of grain with a 1-inch circular hole in the top. The hole was normally covered by one of three metal fins which were mounted on a Telechron motor. When the feeding mechanism was operated the metal fin moved to the right exposing the grain for a period of 4 sec, after which another fin slid across the opening, and the motor was automatically stopped until the next operation. The food box was placed behind the front panel and the bird had access to it through a square hole in the panel. The hole was 2 inches x 2 inches and was placed 2 inches above the floor and 3 inches from the left wall. A 7-watt light placed directly over the food box, behind the front panel, was turned on during the 4-sec reinforcement period. The operation of the feeding mechanism was also accompanied by a loud buzzing sound.

The foot pedal was constructed in such a way that it became virtually part of the floor of the compartment. It was 10 inches long and 2 inches wide, and was placed perpendicular to the front panel, $\frac{1}{4}$ inch above the floor, with its left edge directly below the center of the key. Hence, if the bird stood to the right of the key it would be standing on the pedal. The position of the pedal was decided on the basis of preliminary experimentation in which an attempt was made to find a position such that the base level of pedal pressing would be high enough to ensure discrimination formation, but low enough so that increases in pedal pressing could occur. This arrangement also ensured that the bird would leave the pedal at the time of reinforcement, since the food box was on the opposite side of the compartment.

The stimulus lights were enclosed in a fan-shaped light house behind the translucent key. Three 7-watt, frosted white bulbs were in separate subcompartments at the back of the light house. Red and green color filters, constructed of lucite and cellophane, were placed in front of two of the lights. A ground-glass panel between the lights and the key effectively eliminated any directional effect which might have been produced by the placement of the lights. The intensity of the lights was rendered equal to the nearest $\frac{1}{10}$th of a footcandle, as measured by a photoelectric light meter. Light intensities were adjusted by placing strips of masking tape in front of the individual lights. At any given time only one of the three lights was lighted.

Performance was recorded graphically. The graphic record was then converted into number of key pecks to the nearest 5 responses, and duration of pedal pressing to the nearest 6 sec.

Procedure

Birds, reduced to about 80 percent of their undeprived weight, were first trained to peck the key when white, red, or green. A preliminary conditioning session of 45 min was given before the beginning of the experiment proper. In this session the bird was placed in the closed box and was trained to peck at the white, red, and green stimuli under a reinforcement schedule similar to that used for the condition of nondifferential reinforcement in the experiment proper; the only difference being that the pedal had no effect on the stimulus lights at this time. For the first 15 min the key was white. For the remaining 30 min the red and green lights were present in 30-sec trials in a mixed sequence. Key-pecking responses were reinforced at the end of one half of the trials, and equally often in the presence of each of the colors. Hence, during this session white, red, and green stimuli were presented for 30 trials each; and key pecking was reinforced at the end of one half of the trials for each stimulus. Pedal pressing was recorded during this session, but had no effect on the presentation of stimuli.

Each session after the preliminary one lasted 75 min, composed of a mixed sequence of 30-sec positive and negative trials (i.e., trials ending with reinforcement or nonreinforcement, respectively).

With the differential reinforcement procedure the key color produced by the observing response was correlated with positive versus negative trials, whereas with the nondifferential reinforcement procedure key color and positive versus negative trials were uncorrelated.

Experiment design

To test hypotheses 1 and 2, two groups of subjects (Groups I and II) were placed on nondifferential and differential reinforcement, respectively, for five 75-min sessions. According to the hypotheses we would expect the amount of pedal pressing to decrease or remain low for Group I and to increase or remain high for Group II.

After five sessions of differential reinforcement Group II birds were assigned at random to three subgroups:

Group II-a was continued on the initial discrimination.
Group II-b was placed on reversed discrimination.
Group II-c was placed on nondifferential reinforcement.

Group I was continued on nondifferential reinforcement. All birds were given seven additional sessions. The transition to new conditions for Groups II-b and II-c was made at the end of the first 15 min of session 6. The transition was made during a session so that its effects would not be confounded with the possible effects of spontaneous recovery which might occur at the beginning of a session. The design of the experiment is outlined in Table 9.1.

According to hypothesis 2 observing behavior (measured by du-

TABLE 9.1

The Design of the Experiment

Group	Sessions[a]	
	1–6*	6*–12
I (no discrimination) $n = 4$	Nondifferential reinforcement	Nondifferential reinforcement
II-a (discrimination) $n = 6$	Differential reinforcement	Differential reinforcement continued
II-b (discrimination reversal) $n = 5$	Differential reinforcement	Differential reinforcement with reversed discrimination
II-c (discrimination extinction) $n = 5$	Differential reinforcement	Nondifferential reinforcement

[a] In column heads, 6* denotes the end of the first 15 min of session 6.

ration of pedal pressing) should decrease or remain low for Group I throughout the experiment, and should decrease for Group II-c when the procedure is changed from differential to nondifferential reinforcement. According to hypothesis 3 observing behavior should decrease temporarily and then recover a high value for Group II-b when the discrimination is reversed. Hypothesis 4 applies only if at some point the probability of observing behavior is low and a discrimination is poorly established. This might occur at the beginning of the experiment for Group II or following reversal for Group II-c. Here we would expect discrimination formation to be retarded for some time and finally to occur at a relatively rapid rate.

RESULTS

The mean session-by-session rates of key pecking and relative durations of pedal pressing are presented in Figure 9.1, 9.2, 9.3 and

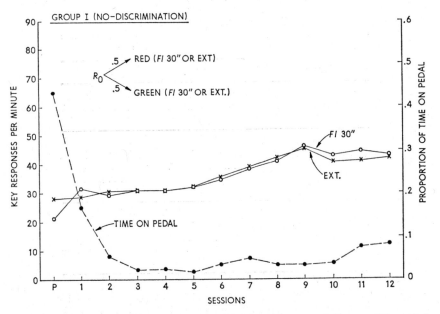

FIGURE 9.1. Group I means of rate of key responses and time on the pedal for birds on nondifferential reinforcement throughout. On any trial an observing response (R_o) was equally likely to produce a red or a green key, and each trial was equally likely to end with reinforcement.

The first session (marked P) was a control session in which pedal responses had no consequences.

9.4 for groups I, II-a, II-b, and II-c, respectively. The data of individual birds are given in the Appendix, Tables 1–4.

The major comparisons relating to the hypotheses under investigation are the comparisons between pedal pressing during initial discrimination, immediately after the change in conditions, and after reversed discriminations have been formed in Group II-b. For this purpose performances in the following sessions were compared. (*a*) The first five sessions for Group II; (*b*) the second

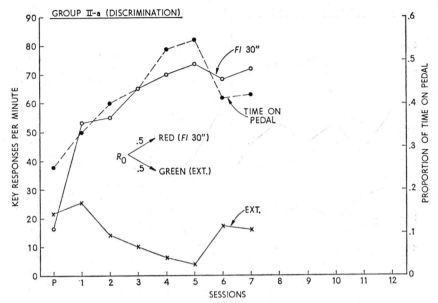

FIGURE 9.2. Group II-a means of rate of key responses and time on the pedal during discrimination formation. On positive trials an observing response (R_o) produced a red key, correlated with *FI* 30″; on negative trials an observing response produced a green key, correlated with EXT.

The first session (marked P) was a control session in which pedal responses had no consequences.

portion of session 6 combined with session 7, which immediately followed the change in conditions for Groups II-b and II-c; (*c*) sessions 11 and 12 which were the last two days of the experiment proper. The means for all groups for these three sets of data are presented in Appendix, Table 5.

The significance of differences between Groups II-a, II-b and II-c in sessions 6 and 7 was tested by means of analysis of covariance, using the mean total duration of pedal pressing in the first five sessions as the covariant. This analysis showed overall differences in the amount of pedal pressing by the various experimental groups in sessions 6 and 7 (see Appendix, Table 6).

The significance of differences in pedal pressing between groups in the various sessions (*a, b,* and *c,* above) was tested by means of tests for independent measures. The significance of changes in pedal pressing between sessions (*a, b,* and *c* above) was tested by means of *t*-tests for related measures. The results of these tests are presented in Appendix, Table 7.

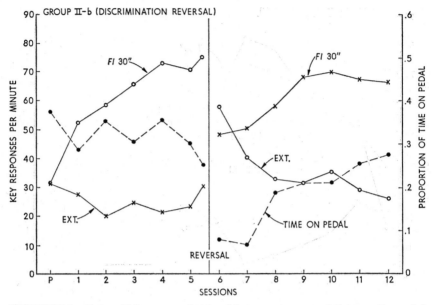

FIGURE 9.3. Group II-b means of rate of key responses and time on the pedal during initial discrimination formation and discrimination reversal. Up to session 6 the *FI* 30 sec schedule was correlated with a red key and the EXT schedule was correlated with a green key, if an observing response (pedal pressing) occurred. After session 6 the schedule/key color correlation was reversed.

The first session (marked P) was a control session in which pedal responses had no consequences. Reversal occurred during session 6, so two points are plotted for that session.

Inspection of the data indicates the following:

1. Time on the pedal during preliminary training (session P) was high for all groups, but decreased for birds in Group I, with nondifferential reinforcement, while it increased or remained high for birds in Group II, with differential reinforcement. (See Figures 9.1, through 9.4).

2. After the transition to reversed discrimination and nondifferential reinforcement, Groups II-b and II-c both showed a decrease in pedal pressing to a level significantly lower than the previous level for the same birds, and also significantly lower than Group II-a (on differential reinforcement) in the same sessions (see Figures 9.2, 9.3, and 9.4).

3. Pedal pressing recovered to a high value for Group II-b birds, and this recovery occurred at about the same time that the reversed discrimination appeared in the key-pecking response. Pedal press-

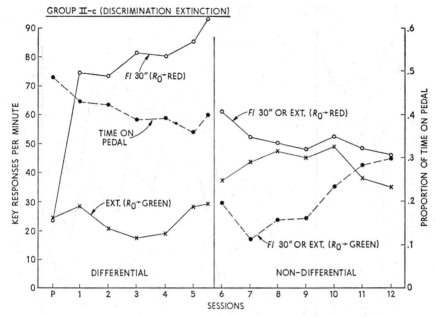

FIGURE 9.4. Group II-c means of rate of key responses and time on the pedal during initial discrimination formation and after the change to nondifferential reinforcement. Up to session 6, the *FI* 30 sec schedule was correlated with a red key and the EXT schedule was correlated with a green key, if an observing response (pedal pressing) occurred. After session 6 the schedule and the key color were uncorrelated.

The first session (marked P) was a control session in which pedal responses had no consequences. The change in conditions occurred during session 6, so two points are plotted for that session.

ing increased to a level only slightly below the level obtained during the initial differential reinforcement training.

4. The appearance of the reversed discrimination, and the recovery of pedal pressing occurred quite abruptly for some of the birds. This abrupt change is obscured in the group-average data since it did not occur at the same time for all birds. Of the five birds in Group II-b, four showed a relatively abrupt increase in pedal pressing. This change occurred on the third session for two of the birds (P–30, P–5), on the fourth session for one (P–38) and on the seventh session for the fourth (P–47). Figure 9.5 and 9.6 show relevant data for birds P–30 and P–38, which are fairly representative of the performance of the birds in Group II-b. The results in Figures 9.5 and 9.6 show that pedal pressing dropped sharply when the discrimination was reversed, remained low for some period up to several sessions and recovered a high value rather abruptly at

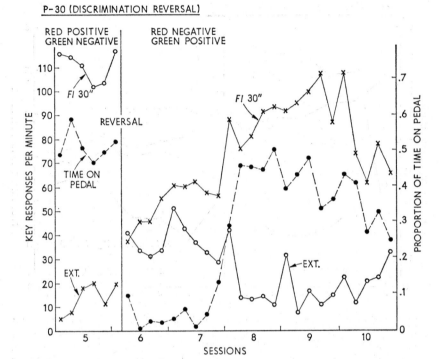

FIGURE 9.5. Food-reinforced response rate (key responses per minute) and observing behavior (proportion of time on pedal) of one bird, showing discrimination reversal. Each point is a measure of performance over a 15-minute interval. Up to the line indicating reversal the *FI* 30 sec schedule was correlated with a red key and the EXT schedule was correlated with a green key, if an observing response (pedal pressing) occurred. After the line the schedule/ key color correlation was reversed. Performance during the initial four sessions of differential reinforcement is not shown.

about the same time that the reversed discrimination appeared in the key-pecking response.

5. Although pedal pressing decreased sharply when the procedure was changed to nondifferential reinforcement, it recovered to some extent for almost all birds in later sessions as this procedure was continued. This gradual increase in pedal pressing appeared in both Group I and Group II-c (Figures 9.1 and 9.4), though the increases in pedal pressing were not statistically significant (Appendix, Table 7).

6. Relatively low durations of pedal pressing were always associated with relatively poor differentiation of performance on positive and negative trials. When pedal pressing decreased the degree of discrimination decreased accordingly. The converse was not al-

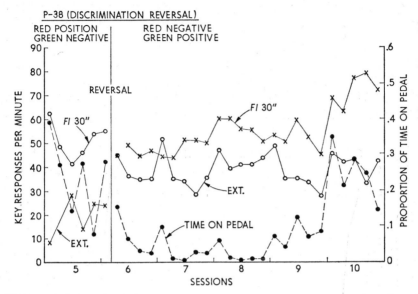

FIGURE 9.6. Food-reinforced response rate (key responses per minute) and observing behavior (proportion of time on pedal) of one bird, showing discrimination reversal. Each point is a measure of performance over a 15-min interval. Up to the line indicating reversal the *FI* 30 sec schedule was correlated with a red key and the EXT schedule was correlated with a green key, if an observing response (pedal pressing) occurred. After the line the schedule/key color correlation was reversed. Performance during the initial four sessions of differential reinforcement is not shown.

ways true. Increases in pedal pressing were not always accompanied by increases in the degree of discrimination. For example, in Group II-c pedal pressing tended to increase with continued nondifferential reinforcement, while the degree of discrimination remained low. However, whenever birds were given differential reinforcement, increases in pedal pressing were accompanied by increases in the degree of discrimination. This is shown in the initial differential reinforcement sessions for Group II and in the reversed discrimination sessions for Group II-b. (Figures 9.2, 9.3 and 9.4.) In most cases the initial discrimination formed rapidly, as soon as differential reinforcement was instituted. However, in a few cases the amount of pedal pressing was initially low at the beginning of differential reinforcement. Then pedal pressing increased rapidly as the initial discrimination was formed. An example of initial failure to establish the discrimination is given in Figure 9.7, which clearly illustrates the relation between pedal pressing and the degree of discrimination.

These results are in essential agreement with the hypotheses. In the comparison between Groups I and II we see that the time on the pedal was approximately six times as great for birds on differential reinforcement as for birds on nondifferential reinforcement. Time on the pedal for Group II-c was less than half as great after the change from differential to nondifferential reinforcement. Thus it is apparent that differential reinforcement of key-pecking re-

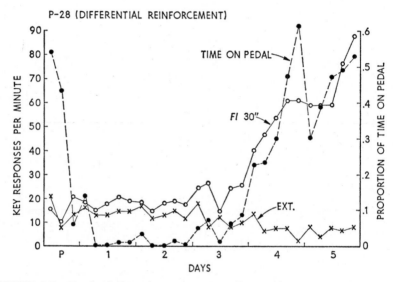

FIGURE 9.7. Food-reinforced response rate (key responses per minute) and observing behavior (proportion of time on pedal) of one bird, during differential reinforcement, illustrating an initial failure to establish the discrimination. Each point is a measure of performance over a 15 min interval. The first session (marked *P*) was a control session in which pedal pressing had no consequences.

sponses supports the pedal response well above the level obtained under nondifferential reinforcement.

The marked drop in pedal pressing when birds were placed on reversed discrimination is in accordance with the third hypothesis. The expected recovery of pedal pressing occurred within seven sessions for four of the five birds in the group, though, on the average, pedal pressing did not increase significantly from session 6–7 to session 11–12 (see Appendix, Table 7).

The fourth hypothesis regarding relatively abrupt onset of discrimination under certain conditions was not amenable to statistical test in the present experiment. However, the results of some birds in session 1–5 and most of the results of birds exposed to reversed discrimination give reasonably good support for the hypothesis. (Figures 9.5, 9.6, and 9.7).

Thus, the obtained data support the four hypotheses in a reasonably convincing way. In all cases where differences are predicted by the hypotheses, differences were obtained in the expected direction, and all but one of these differences were statistically significant at the 5 percent level of confidence or better.[2]

DISCUSSION

The results give reasonably good support to the four hypotheses presented, and thus support the general hypothesis that "exposure to discriminative stimuli will have a reinforcing effect on the observing response to the extent that the subject has learned to respond differently to these discriminative stimuli."

In the present experiment the frequency of reinforcement for the effective response was not changed by the occurrence or nonoccurrence of the observing response. One interpretation of the findings is that conditioned reinforcing value attained by the positive stimulus served to strengthen or maintain the observing response during differential reinforcement. A more detailed discussion of the operation of this mechanism is presented in Part I (see Wyckoff, 1952). As a possible alternative to this interpretation it could be suggested that the rate of occurrence of the effective response would be greater when the subject was exposed to the positive stimulus, and that therefore reinforcement would occur more promptly when the observing response occurred. This explanation is not plausible in the present experiment since reinforcement was always withheld during the first 30 sec of the trial. The difference in delay of reinforcement resulting from differences in rates of responding would be negligible compared to this constant 30-sec delay. Hence, the conditioned reinforcement interpretation is the more plausible.

---

[2] The gradual increase in pedal pressing, following an initial decrease, for many of the birds on nondifferential reinforcement (see Figure 9.4 and Appendix, Table 4) was not predicted. If this result is not due to chance, and it was not statistically significant (see Appendix, Table 7), it can probably be attributed to some extraneous factor such as postural changes, and does not imply any serious shortcoming of the present formulation.

If we adopt this interpretation it can be seen that the present formulation is quite generally applicable. In any particular experiment it is not necessary to show that reinforcement is directly contingent on the occurrence of an observing response. If an observing response is involved and if some effective response is differentially reinforced on the basis of the discriminative stimuli, the mechanism discussed above will operate to strengthen the observing response.

The obtained results make it apparent that the magnitude of changes in the probability of an observing response may be extremely great, and that these changes may occur quite rapidly. The corresponding effect on performance in discrimination learning will be profound. Observing responses may play a part in determining performance in a wide variety of experimental situations. Whenever visual stimuli are used, observing responses of orienting and fixating will be involved, with the possible exception of these cases where general illumination is used as a discriminative stimulus, or where stimulus cards occupy a large portion of the subject's visual field. In the case of pattern discrimination, it has been demonstrated that relatively precise fixation of the stimulus is required (Ehrenfreund, 1948).

As for other sense modalities, reception of tactual stimulation may depend on the subject's moving into contact with the stimulus object, or on some response such as stroking a surface; olfactory reception depends on the appropriate kind of breathing; and it is likely that auditory reception is affected by orienting responses. In addition to these identifiable responses it is possible that some unobserved reactions such as "attending responses" operate in a similar way to determine which of the stimuli in the environment will control the subject's behavior. Berlyne (1951) has suggested that attention be treated within reinforcement learning theory as an intervening variable. If we include this type of unobserved reaction it is reasonable to expect that the same mechanisms which control other observing responses will operate to control these. It would of course be necessary to derive a more explicit definition for such a variable, in terms of measurable aspects of effective responses. Theoretical considerations regarding this problem are discussed elsewhere (Wyckoff, 1952).

The consideration of the possible operation of unobserved reactions is, at this point, sheer speculation and no assumptions regarding such reactions are necessary to the present discussion.

The present investigation reveals certain functional relations between observing responses and discrimination learning, and serves to suggest a way of accounting for the learning of these responses within the framework of reinforcement learning theory. Further investigation of the role of such reactions may serve to clarify many issues regarding the relations among "sensory activity," "learning set," stimulus generalization and other phenomena which have previously not been integrated into a unified theoretical formulation.

SUMMARY

For purposes of the present discussion we define an "observing response" as a response which results in exposure to a pair of discriminative stimuli. In the present experiment a pedal-pressing response was placed in the role of an observing response and direct measures of its occurrence were obtained during discrimination learning (differential reinforcement), discrimination reversal, and nondifferential reinforcement. The major findings were:

1. Differential reinforcement maintained the probability of observing behavior at a level well above that obtained under nondifferential reinforcement.

2. When discrimination was reversed the probability of observing behavior decreased sharply and, for most subjects, recovered a high value as the reversed discrimination was formed.

3. When the probability of observing behavior was low at the beginning of the initial discrimination training, or following discrimination reversal, discrimination formation was retarded for some time but then occurred at a relatively rapid rate.

These findings can be subsumed under the general proposition that "exposure to discriminative stimuli has a reinforcing effect on the observing response to the extent the subject has learned to respond differently in the presence of the discriminative stimuli." This proposition can be related to reinforcement learning theory by employing the principle of conditioned reinforcement.

The present findings suggest that changes in the probability of observing behavior may have a profound effect on discrimination learning in a wide variety of experimental situations. Further analysis of the role of such responses may serve to clarify the interpretation of phenomena in several apparently diverse areas of psychology.

APPENDIX

TABLE 1

Mean Total Duration of Pedal Pressing per Session for Each Bird in Units of $\frac{1}{15}$ of 1 Percent of Maximum Possible Duration

Group	Bird	P	1	2	3	4	5	6 (0–15 min.)	6 (15–75 min.)	7	8	9	10	11	12
I.........	4	540	040	026	020	006	016	030	000	004	004	024	044	052	074
	29	800	210	224	032	030	006	070	010	052	084	076	126	118	110
	33	420	334	024	036	056	062	020	070	172	080	028	058	228	240
	1	923	380	052	010	048	080	070	097	038	038	070	024	034	036
	39	450	092	032	044	012	022	040	025						
II-a......	13	863	744	630	670	718	842	790	275	150					
	2	413	350	736	700	892	894	560	825	970					
	14	1,123	988	850	908	838	920	900	972	836	804	888	1,072	938	
	32	913	302	694	834	932	898	830	740	730	724	720	660		
	25	580	584	674	730	780	802	560	325	490	494	396	796	960	1,064
	28	513	048	012	092	554	648	590	517	714	576	722	578	426	328
II-b......	30	773	980	874	862	744	760	790	055	092	650	604	510	532	584
	38	496	168	642	408	508	346	040	017	050	022	118	372	516	276
	6	696	598	728	630	726	576	680	305	172	652	784	674	700	774
	47	456	350	220	174	250	266	100	087	018	004	004	002	086	354
	48	426	048	130	182	408	250	240	122	168	030	002	004	002	012
II-c......	26	716	054	006	028	028	040	070	040	034	014	008	002	010	018
	15	683	724	854	784	730	816	890	425	182	164	390	396	526	412
	27	666	854	488	326	598	488	590	230	026	012	024	038	110	064
	45	813	862	1,028	1,056	986	922	700	252	090	298	194	556	686	976
	5	555	724	796	736	682	488	800	582	522	700	638	762	832	774

TABLE 2

Rate of Key Pecking during Initially Positive Trials for Each Bird (Responses per 10 Minutes)

Group	Bird	P	1	2	3	4	5	6 (0–15 min.)	6 (15–75 min.)	7	8	9	10	11	12
I	4	222	230	189	137	218	224	393	351	379	359	368	350	354	390
	29	218	532	398	306	298	348	227	308	316	289	347	337	297	280
	33	311	191	176	158	170	222	528	454	452	534	694	577	623	663
	1	155	316	263	316	373	392	262	300	386	460	429	465	494	486
	39	169	228	333	451	381	345								
II-a	13	149	696	569	708	695	725	906	553	691					
	2	119	306	755	761	794	781	612	718	709					
	14	291	786	577	816	785	652	647	503	583	566	644	531	567	657
	32	223	707	881	1,056	1,012	1,192	1,250	1,088	1,025	713	1,165	1,200	478	564
	25	006	525	381	380	429	396	408	364	491	464	489	523	653	
	28	157	184	185	235	524	678	944	786	863	725	895	662	467	459
II-b	30	224	606	734	1,072	1,016	1,097	1,156	344	387	192	171	224	196	123
	38	254	376	630	546	508	503	544	372	369	422	357	415	202	209
	6	228	667	630	644	922	617	700	393	428	295	254	220	205	192
	47	388	628	543	604	478	457	487	445	473	334	412	443	387	321
	48	481	361	364	458	750	764	793	528	291	383	349	384	432	403
II-c	26	116	350	363	426	490	777	921	546	437	571	515	394	278	265
	15	094	563	514	993	999	973	936	587	289	196	275	277	236	267
	27	207	800	723	720	669	744	1,164	944	569	359	412	538	515	427
	45	395	947	1,000	874	982	967	557	479	611	977	689	626	522	481
	5	402	1,074	1,098	1,075	929	852	1,050	564	671	417	512	744	857	876

TABLE 3

Rate of Key Pecking during Initially Negative Trials for Each Bird (Responses per 10 minutes)

Group	Bird	P	1	2	3	4	5	6 (0–15 min.)	6 (15–75 min.)	7	8	9	10	11	12
I	4	256	285	198	156	341	225	364	380	374	391	326	319	308	268
	29	173	360	361	278	283	330	293	322	322	293	344	336	280	275
	33	231	173	173	209	201	236	528	470	490	536	667	529	573	629
	1	333	324	278	349	373	445	154	381	359	440	424	452	467	514
	39	395	275	367	421	387	316								
II-a	13	235	429	252	128	133	061	340	400	424	000	041	068	031	363
	2	157	188	090	148	051	047	377	052	031	255	176	255	462	041
	14	397	218	061	033	050	008	067	000	024	204	256	220	071	141
	32	270	317	263	151	072	072	250	211	214	172	158	128	100	
	25	082	241	032	019	009	022	014	245	200					
	28	140	144	141	119	077	075	147	161	135					
II-b	30	252	200	190	185	073	126	192	463	591	857	955	763	757	797
	38	258	261	168	226	088	245	238	462	477	554	513	704	621	542
	6	350	199	046	144	177	201	331	472	585	601	932	921	879	801
	47	386	330	244	345	228	124	208	479	801	437	512	526	511	559
	48	366	346	293	321	494	430	554	492	231	407	443	497	531	531
II-c	26	201	312	322	221	290	550	408	481	466	552	497	411	265	296
	15	118	254	163	128	171	209	192	326	242	193	259	332	245	275
	27	142	302	405	443	279	226	321	342	579	381	410	577	575	454
	45	408	385	088	073	145	095	423	494	518	912	851	804	592	475
	5	374	198	081	055	134	404	208	254	344	333	256	289	261	237

TABLE 4

Group Mean Rates of Key Pecking (Responses per 10 minutes) during Initially Positive Trials (+), and Initially Negative Trials (−), and Proportion of Time on the Pedal (Ped) in Units of $\frac{1}{15}$ of 1 Percent of Maximum Possible Duration

Group	P	1	2	3	4	5	6 (0–15 min.)	6 (15–75 min.)	7	8	9	10	11	12
I	+ 213	317	292	308	306	327	353	378	383	410	460	432	442	433
	− 283	283	295	314	311	332	335	388	386	415	440	409	407	422
	Ped...648	254	083	031	037	043	050	051	067	052	050	063	108	115
II-a	+ 158	534	558	659	707	738	804	669	727					
	− 217	256	140	100	065	047	200	178	171					
	Ped...877	503	599	656	786	834	705	609	648					
II-b	+ 315	528	580	665	735	700	736	416	390	325	308	337	284	250
	− 323	267	188	244	212	225	305	474	497	571	671	682	660	646
	Ped...569	429	519	451	527	440	370	117	100	272	302	312	367	400
II-c	+ 244	666	678	734	739	774	926	624	489	484	461	497	454	469
	− 229	277	220	200	215	297	310	379	402	459	432	450	364	320
	Ped...727	644	634	586	605	551	610	306	171	238	251	351	433	449

TABLE 5

Mean Total Duration of Pedal Pressing per Session for Each Bird (in Units of $\frac{1}{15}$ of 1 Percent of Maximum Possible Duration) for Sessions Selected for Statistical Analysis

Group	Bird	Sessions a*	Session b*	Session c*
I............................	4	022		
	29	100	007	063
	33	102	061	114
	1	114	135	234
	39	040	032	035
	mean	089	059	112
II-a...........................	13	721	213	
	2	714	898	
	14	901	904	
	32	732	735	
	25	714	408	
	28	271	616	
	mean	675	629	
II-b..........................	30	844	074	556
	38	414	034	396
	6	652	239	737
	47	252	053	220
	48	204	145	007
	mean	473	109	384
II-c...........................	27	551	128	087
	45	971	171	831
	5	685	552	903
	26	031	037	014
	15	782	304	469
	mean	604	238	441

* a—Session 1–5.
  b—Session 6 (last 60 min) and session 7.
  c—Sessions 11–12.

TABLE 6

Summary of Analysis of Covariance* of Mean Total Duration of Pedal Pressing in Session 6 (Last 60 Minutes) and Session 7 of Groups II-a, II-b, and II-c

Source of Variance	Sum of Squares	df	F	p
Within groups.........	5,247.43	12		
Between groups.......	6,581.10	2	7.5	< .01
Total...............	11,828.53	14		

* The effect of differences in performance in sessions 1–5 was controlled by using a performance measure in these sessions as covariant.

TABLE 7

Differences in Mean Total Duration of Pedal Pressing per Session (Units of 1/15 of 1 Percent of Maximum Possible Duration) for Selected Sessions

A. Comparisons between Sessions*

	Group						
	I		II-a		II-b		II-c	
Sessions*	Diff.	t	Diff.	t	Diff.	t	Diff.	t
a v. b.............	−031	1.3	−047	0.4	−365	3.0†	−366	2.6†
b v. c.............	058	2.3	—	—	275	2.3	203	1.6
a v. c.............	022	0.6	—	—	−090	1.3	−163	1.6

B. Comparisons between Groups

	Sessions*					
	a		b		c	
Groups	Diff.	t	Diff.	t	Diff.	t
I v. II..................	514	7.2†	—	—	—	—
I v. II-a................	—	—	570	4.9†	—	—
I v. II-b................	—	—	050	1.1	272	2.0
I v. II-c................	—	—	180	1.9	329	1.8
II-a v. II-b.............	—	—	520	4.4†	—	—
II-a v II-c..............	—	—	390	2.7†	—	—
II-b v. II-c.............	—	—	130	1.3	572	0.3

* a—Sessions 1–5.
  b—Session 6 (last 60 min) and session 7.
  c—Sessions 11–12.
† Significant at a 5 percent level of confidence or better.

DISCRIMINATIVE AND REINFORCING PROPERTIES OF DIFFERENTIAL TRACE STIMULI[1]

Stephen B. Kendall
University of Western Ontario

Mabry (1965) and Meyers (1958) have investigated discrimination formation where a delay was interposed between the discriminative stimuli and primary reinforcement. In these experiments there was no difference between the exteroceptive stimulus conditions following $S+$ and $S-$. Following the delay period a reinforcer was delivered or not depending on the exteroceptive stimulus preceding the delay. In both experiments the reinforcer was response-contingent as was the change from either of the discriminative stimuli to the delay stimulus. Thus these experiments employed a pair of two-component Chains, one of which terminated in reinforcement and the other not. In both Chains exteroceptive stimulus conditions were the same during the terminal component.

In both of these experiments the focus of interest was on behavior in the presence of the positive and negative stimuli which comprised the initial members of the two Chains. Both found that response rates were lower in the initial member of the Chain which did not terminate in positive reinforcement.

Meyers (1958) reports data on behavior in the terminal member of the Chains (the delay interval). He found differential behavior in the presence of the delay stimulus only after the subjects had

[1] This research was conducted while the author was at the University of Alabama. I would like to express my gratitude to William Palya for his diligent assistance in conducting the experiments.

accomplished several discrimination reversals. At first the rates in the delay interval were the same regardless of whether the delay interval was preceded by $S+$ or $S-$. Following several discrimination reversals the rate in the delay stimulus following $S-$ was lower than the rate following $S+$. Mabry (1965) did not study behavior during the delay interval extensively, but he does comment that pauses were sometimes observed following the negative stimulus which were longer than those following the positive stimulus.

Since there is a delay between the discriminative stimuli and reinforcement, the discriminative stimuli in such a situation might be called "trace" discriminative stimuli. The present investigations were designed to inquire further into: (*a*) behavior following trace discriminative stimuli and (*b*) the reinforcing properties of trace discriminative stimuli.

EXPERIMENT 1

Experiment 1 was designed to study behavior following the differential trace stimuli. Instead of employing two Chain schedules as did Mabry (1965) and Meyers (1958), a procedure was used where a Mixed schedule occurred following stimuli which indicated which component of the Mixed schedule was to follow. The Mixed schedule consisted of two fixed-ratio schedules. If the smaller of the pair of *FR*s was due to occur, it was preceded by one stimulus and if the higher was due to occur it was preceded by a different stimulus. The occurrence of the Mixed schedule was not contingent on responding during the preceding period of time when the differential stimuli were present.

Meyers (1958) found that differential behavior occurred in the delay interval only after several discrimination reversals. In the present experiment we inquired into whether or not responding in the Mixed schedule would be differentially affected by the stimuli which predicted the component. In particular, we were interested in the pause time before responding in the Mixed schedule. In addition, we were interested in the question of whether or not several discrimination reversals were necessary in order to produce differential pausing in the different components of the Mixed schedule.

The subjects for all experiments were four experimentally naïve silver king pigeons. Their designations are P–91, P–28, P–152, and

P–155. The age and sex of the birds were unknown. The subjects for other experiments were chosen from these four birds.

The apparatus for all experiments consisted of a two-key pigeon chamber housed inside a large sound-attenuating chamber. The right key was designated the observing key and the left key the food key. A 15-watt light bulb stationed immediately above the work panel provided general illumination and indicated the beginning and end of the sessions.

Programming was accomplished with electromechanical devices and data were recorded on counters, running time meters, and a cumulative recorder.

Procedure

The birds were trained to peck the food key by successive approximation. During successive approximation training and subsequent fixed-ratio training the food key was illuminated by a yellow light and the observing key was dark. Following key training each subject was trained on a two-component Mixed fixed-ratio schedule (MIX *FR FR*). The values of the Mixed schedules used were MIX *FR* 10 *FR* 50 for P–91 and MIX *FR* 10 *FR* 100 for the other three birds. The two *FR*s appeared in an irregular sequence. Following at least five sessions on the terminal values of the Mixed schedule a 30-sec period was introduced following each reinforcement, during which neither the food key nor the observing key was operative. During the 30-sec period the food key was dark and the observing key was either green or blue. If the next programmed *FR* was *FR* 10 a green light was displayed on the observing key; if the next *FR* was *FR* 100 (*FR* 50 for P–91) a blue light appeared on the observing key. Following the 30-sec period the yellow light reappeared on the food key and either *FR* 10 or *FR* 100 was in effect. (See Figure 10.1.)

Thus in this procedure there was no difference in exteroceptive stimuli during *FR* 10 or *FR* 100 but the stimuli preceding the onset of the yellow light indicated which *FR* was to follow. A chaining procedure was not employed as in the previously mentioned studies by Meyers (1958) and Mabry (1965) so that the change from the conditions preceding the Mixed schedule to the Mixed schedule itself was not response-contingent.

Following the completion of an *FR* a 4-sec grain reinforcer was

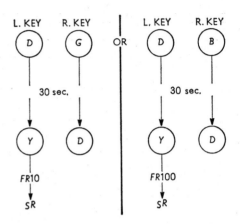

FIGURE 10.1. Representation of the procedure for Experiment 1. The stimulus on the right key indicated the schedule of reinforcement (*FR* 10 or *FR* 100) that was to be in effect on the left key. The letters in the circles represent colors on the keys: *D* is dark, *Y* is yellow, *G* is green, and *B* is blue.

delivered and a new 30-sec period was initiated with the appropriate light on the observing key. Pecks at the observing key had no scheduled consequences in this experiment.

Results

The dependent variable in this experiment was the pause time or latency in the *FR*s. If the stimuli preceding the *FR*s served as discriminative stimuli for *FR* performance we would expect a longer pause time preceding *FR* 100 than preceding *FR* 10.

Pause times in *FR* 10 and *FR* 100 are presented in Figure 10.2. These are average pause times for the last four sessions under this experimental condition. In all cases the pause times for *FR* 100 are greater than for *FR* 10. Two sets of bar graphs are presented for P–91 and P–152. The pair marked "R" is for pause times following discrimination reversal. Originally, blue had preceded *FR* 100 and green *FR* 10. In the reversal the relation between the colors and the schedules was reversed. In the reversal the pause time preceding *FR* 100 does not reach its previous value.

Unfortunately, distributions of pause times are not available so that it is not easy to tell whether the effect shown in Figure 10.2 is due to a few very long pauses preceding some *FR* 100s or whether the pause preceding *FR* 100 is stable. Examination of the daily cumulative records indicated that there were occasionally very long pause times preceding the large *FR* and that these might account for the effect. Other records seemed to show relatively consistent pauses prior to *FR* 100.

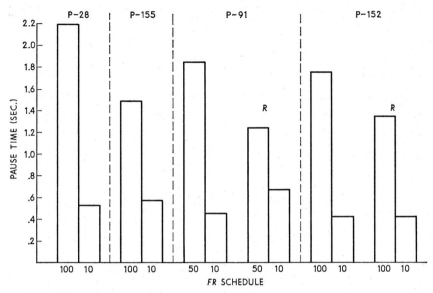

FIGURE 10.2. Pause time in the two components of the Mixed *FR* schedule for each of the four subjects. The "R" above the second pair of bars for P–91 and P–152 indicates pause times after discrimination reversal.

The data from this experiment support the hypothesis that the stimuli preceding a Mixed schedule take on discriminative properties for behavior in the presence of the Mixed schedule and thus can have two discriminative effects. The first discriminative effect is the one already reported by Mabry (1965) and Meyers (1958) for a somewhat different situation. The second is the one demonstrated here. Stimuli preceding a schedule may control behavior in that schedule, even though the stimuli are no longer present. In addition, this effect did not require several discrimination reversals to achieve, as had been reported by Meyers (1958).

EXPERIMENT 2

Experiment 1 demonstrated a discriminative effect of differential stimuli which preceded two different *FR* schedules when the *FR* behavior was emitted under constant exteroceptive stimulus conditions. In Experiment 2 we sought to demonstrate a reinforcing function of these differential stimuli by the observing-response technique (Wyckoff, 1952).

The subjects for this experiment were P–91, P–28, and P–155.

Before this experiment and after Experiment 1, P–91 was stabilized
on MIX *FR* 10 *FR* 100.

Procedure

The procedure consisted of removing the differential stimuli during the 30-sec periods preceding the *FR* schedules and making them
response-contingent. In order to get some initial behavior on the
observing key, it was illuminated yellow, the mixed stimulus color,

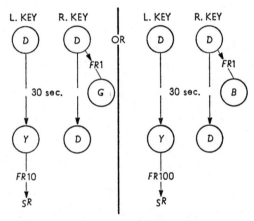

FIGURE 10.3.   Representation of the procedure for Experiment 2. The conditions are the same as in Experiment 1, except that the appearance of the stimuli on the right key is dependent on a response on that key. The letters in the
circles represent colors on the keys, as in Figure 10.1.

and a few grain reinforcements were presented for pecks to the
observing key. The yellow light was then removed and a few more
grain reinforcements were delivered for pecks at the dark observing key. Following this, the only consequence of pecks to the observing key became the illumination, for a maximum of 30 sec, of the
observing key with the color appropriate to the *FR* schedule that
followed on the food key. Thus the first peck to the observing key
during the 30-sec dark period produced a stimulus which lasted
until the Mixed schedule stimulus appeared. When the Mixed schedule stimulus appeared the observing key became inoperative and
the light on the observing key, if a prior observing response had
turned it on, was extinguished. (See Figure 10.3.)

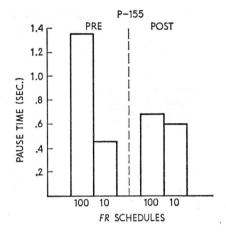

FIGURE 10.4. Pause times for P–155 before (PRE) and after (POST) the attempt to condition observing responses.

Results

Within a few days following the initial training to peck the observing key none of the birds was making responses to the observing key, although this method of training has been found successful in training observing responses in all other cases in which the author has tried it (*cf.*, Kendall, 1965a, b). The birds were allowed to continue on this procedure for several sessions, but there were only a few responses to the observing key.

Following this failure to obtain observing responses, automatic presentation of the differential stimuli during the 30-sec period preceding the MIX *FR FR* schedule was reinstated. This resulted in the only interesting data from this experiment. Unfortunately, these data are available for only one bird, because there were some procedural errors with the other two. These data are presented in Figure 10.4. The pause times preceding *FR* 100 and *FR* 10 are shown both before (PRE) and after (POST) the attempt to train observing responses. The PRE data are taken from the last four days before observing-response training and the POST data are taken from the first four days following observing-response training. It appears from these results that the previously developed discrimination had spontaneously deteriorated during the period when the discriminative stimuli were absent. This deterioration of the discrimination might be responsible for the failure to obtain observing responses.

EXPERIMENT 3

In Experiment 2, I speculated that the failure to produce and maintain observing responses was due to the breakdown of the previously formed discrimination during a period when the discriminative stimuli were absent. It appeared that a technique was needed which both maintained the discrimination and allowed opportunity for observing responses to be made. This experiment was aimed at that goal.

Procedure

The subjects were allowed to remain on the procedure where the differential stimuli were automatically presented in order to restabilize the discrimination. When this was accomplished they were reexposed to the response-contingent situation with a 30-sec presentation of one of the differential stimuli contingent on an observing response during the period preceding the MIX FR FR schedule. The major modification of the experiment was the addition of an 8-sec period just before the Mixed schedule, during which the differential stimuli were automatically presented. Thus if no observing responses occurred, there was a 30-sec period during which both keys were dark following reinforcement. Following this, the observing key was illuminated with the color appropriate to the next FR. Following the 8-sec period the food key was illuminated with the yellow light and one of the FRs was in effect. (See Figure 10.5.)

No special shaping was used to get the birds to peck the observing key.

Results

All three subjects learned to peck the observing key. After several sessions they were pecking it during almost every period during which both keys were dark (the 30-sec period following reinforcement). Thus the objective of the research had apparently been achieved.

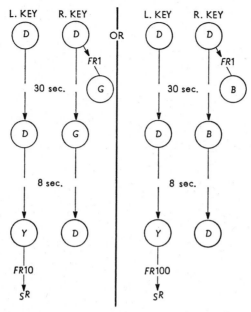

FIGURE 10.5. Representation of the procedure for Experiment 3. The conditions are the same as in Experiment 2, except that the stimuli appear on the right key for 8 sec before the two schedules of reinforcement go into effect. The stimuli are still response-produced in the initial 30-sec period. The letters in the circles represent colors on the keys, as in Figure 10.1.

In order to demonstrate that the stimuli were reinforcing because of their differential relation to the reinforcement schedules a nondifferential control procedure was initiated. The *FR* schedules appeared in an irregular sequence. During the nondifferential control procedure the green and blue lights were alternated. Thus these stimuli no longer bore any systematic relation to the schedules. Both response-contingent stimuli and the stimuli presented during the 8-sec period preceding the onset of the Mixed schedule were alternated so that neither predicted which component of the MIX *FR FR* schedule would follow.

The results of both the differential and nondifferential procedure are shown in Figure 10.6. The condition where the stimuli were differentially associated with the components of the MIX *FR FR* schedule is called "informative" and abbreviated *"I"* on the graph. The stimulus alternation procedure is called "noninformative" and labeled *"NI."* The results are presented in terms of an observing ratio which has been employed before (Kendall & Gibson, 1965).

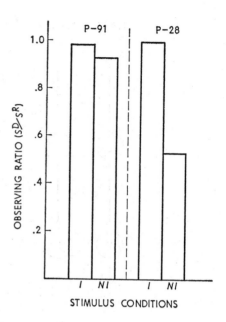

FIGURE 10.6. Observing ratios for P–91 and P–28 during the informative (*I*) and noninformative (*NI*) conditions. See text for explanation of labels.

Since the observing key schedule was CRF and since the resulting stimulus lasted the full available 30 sec there was opportunity for only one observing response per food reinforcement. Thus the maximum observing response output is 1.0 and the minimum is 0.

The results of the noninformative procedure were not satisfactory. P–91 and P–28 were selected for presentation because P–91 showed the least decline in observing ratio during the noninformative condition and P–28 showed the most. All bars Figure 10.6 represent the average of the last four sessions under a given condition. It can be seen that although the stimuli no longer bore a systematic relation to the *FR* schedules some observing behavior remained.

EXPERIMENT 4

Two hypotheses might explain the failure of the observing-response output to decline substantially when the nondifferential (noninformative) procedure was introduced in Experiment 3. One is that pecks to the observing key were occasionally adventitiously correlated with the onset of the yellow light. This would tend to maintain the behavior through superstitious chaining (Sidman,

1960b). The other hypothesis is that stimulus change might, in itself, have had enough reinforcing power to maintain responses to the observing key.

Several possibilities are available for checking these alternatives. In the present experiment we chose simply to replicate Experiment 3 with a shorter duration of the stimulus produced by the observing response. It has been shown that when the stimulus duration is 1 sec pigeons will make multiple observing responses in a MIX *FR* 30 *FR* 50 schedule (Kendall, 1968). Furthermore this effect might be enhanced in the present experiment since there is no concurrent food behavior to compete with the observing response (Kelleher, Riddle, & Cook, 1962; Kendall, 1965a, 1965b). Thus if more observing responses were being emitted, we would have the opportunity to measure a more substantial decline in observing response output during the nondifferential procedure.

Procedure

All three subjects were returned to the response-contingent informative procedure and the duration of the stimuli was gradually shortened over a period of time until a stimulus duration of 1 sec had been reached. (See Figure 10.7.) Following stabilization of behavior under these conditions the noninformative control procedure was reintroduced.

Results

During the informative phase all three subjects maintained key pecking during the 30-sec period following reinforcement. Since multiple observing responses were permitted during this interval the data are plotted in Figure 10.8 as response rate (responses per 30 sec). Response rates during the 30-sec interval are plotted separately for intervals preceding *FR* 10 and *FR* 100.

All three subjects yielded a higher response rate in intervals preceding *FR* 10 than in intervals preceding *FR* 100. Approximately twice as many observing responses were emitted in intervals preceding *FR* 10. Assuming that we had established both stimuli as conditioned reinforcers the stimulus preceding *FR* 10 would appear to have been the stronger.

The results of the nondifferential control are shown in Figure

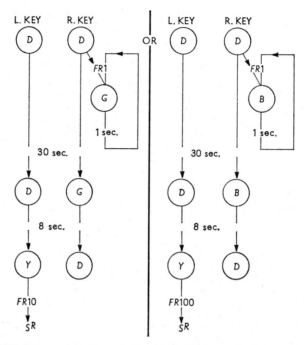

FIGURE 10.7. Representation of the final, "informative" procedure for Experiment 4. The conditions are the same as in Experiment 3, except that the response-produced stimulus on the right key lasts 1 sec, rather than up to the end of the initial 30-sec period. The letters in the circles represent colors on the keys, as in Figure 10.1.

The same procedure was used in Experiment 5, except the value of the FR on the right key was varied.

10.9. The nondifferential control was done in a different way for each of the three subjects. For P–91 the Mixed schedule was left in effect on the food key and observing responses produced alternately blue and green lights on the observing key. P–28 was placed on FR 10 in the presence of the yellow food key light and the stimuli alternated on the observing key. P–152 was placed on FR 100 on the food key and the stimuli alternated on the observing key.

The rationale for these differences in procedure is as follows. During the informative stimulus procedure the stimuli not only predicted the schedule to follow but automatic presentation of the stimuli for 8 sec preceded the onset of an FR schedule. Perhaps the reinforcing function of these stimuli derived not from the differential relation of the stimuli to the schedules but from the fact that the lights always preceded the schedules. In this event blue and

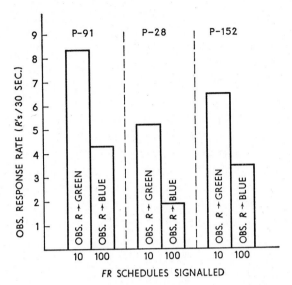

FIGURE 10.8.   Observing response rates for P–91, P–28, and P–152 rates are plotted separately for the periods preceding FR 10 and FR 100.

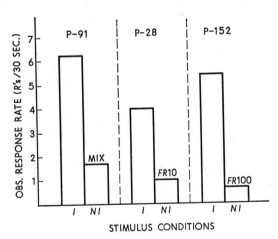

FIGURE 10.9.   Observing response rates for P–91, P–28, and P–152 during informative (I) and noninformative (NI) conditions. See text for complete explanation.

green should have an equivalent reinforcing effect during the non-informative phase for P–28, and P–152 because they always precede the same *FR* schedule. In fact, we might find an overall increase in observing response output for P–28 because the stimuli were paired with the lower *FR*. Similarly, an overall decrease in observing response rate might occur for P–152 because the stimuli were always paired with the higher *FR*. According to this logic no change in observing response rate should occur for P–91 since P–91 produced both stimuli in the nondifferential procedure. This hypothesis assumes that the stimulus-producing responses were not true observing responses, that is, they were not maintained because of the *differential* relation of the stimuli to the *FR* schedules. Simple pairing of the blue and green lights with the yellow light might serve to establish these stimuli as conditioned reinforcers.

It can be seen in Figure 10.9, however, that in all three cases there was a decline in the average observing response rate during the noninformative phase of the experiment. The response rates did not drop to zero, but the decline was substantial in all three cases.

This finding supports the hypothesis that either stimulus change or superstitious chaining was operating in Experiment 3 to maintain observing behavior during the noninformative condition. The finding that observing behavior was not completely eliminated in the present experiment makes it seem likely that the behavior was maintained primarily by stimulus change during the noninformative phase. If superstitious chaining were maintaining the observing behavior, the change from informative to noninformative should not have produced a very substantial decrease in observing behavior. The data from the present experiment strongly support the hypothesis that observing responses were maintained because of the differential relation of the stimuli to the schedules (their "informative" function).

EXPERIMENT 5

In Experiment 4, the reinforcing properties of trace discriminative stimuli were demonstrated. The rate of responding for the stimuli decreased when the stimuli were made nondifferential (or "noninformative"). To further assess the strength of these stimuli as conditioned reinforcers this experiment used small fixed-ratio schedules on the observing key.

Procedure

In Experiment 4, the subjects had been on a continuous reinforcement, i.e., FR 1, schedule for the trace discriminative stimuli. In the present experiment three other FR values were studied, FR 2, FR 4, and FR 8. (See Figure 10.7.) Two birds were given 15 sessions at each value. Two sessions of FR 6 were used to make the transition from FR 4 to FR 8. The stimulus duration remained at 1 sec.

Results

The results of this experiment are plotted in terms of the observing ratio in Figure 10.10. The average number of stimuli produced per food reinforcement is the dependent variable. Note the relatively large decrease in the number of stimuli produced in the PRE-FR 10 interval as opposed to the relatively small decline in the PRE-FR 100 interval. Nevertheless, the number of stimuli produced in the PRE-FR 10 interval always remains higher than in the PRE-FR 100 interval.

DISCUSSION

Experiment 1 demonstrated that two stimuli signaling different FR schedules can differentially affect behavior in the two correlated FR schedules, even though no differential stimuli are present while the FR schedules are in force. This is similar to the finding of Meyers (1958). Meyers' data differ, however, in that several discrimination reversals were required before the differential behavior in the Mixed schedule stimulus was obtained. In Experiment 1, differential behavior in the Mixed schedule stimulus was obtained without these reversals. There are several procedural differences between Experiment 1 and Meyers' study. Meyers employed Chain schedules in which the terminal component (Mixed schedule stimulus) did not appear unless there was responding in the initial component. Another difference is that Meyers used a MIX FI EXT schedule as the terminal component, whereas the present study employed MIX FR FR schedules.

The present study also bears some resemblance to studies of

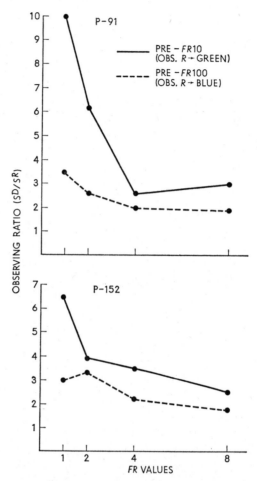

FIGURE 10.10. Observing ratios for P–91 and P–152 as a function of the fixed-ratio schedule on the observing key.

primed schedules (Ferster & Skinner, 1957). Ferster and Skinner studied a MULT *FR* primed *FI* schedule. During most of the *FI* component exteroceptive stimulus conditions were the same as in the *FR* component. A different stimulus was present during the initial portion of the *FI* component. When this stimulus was terminated the subjects continued to respond with the positively accelerated response rate typical of *FI*s even though the current exteroceptive stimulus conditions were identical with those of the *FR* component. In the *FR* component the subjects responded at a high steady rate typical of FRs. The difference between the present experiment and primed schedules is that, with primed schedules, the priming stimulus is in effect during part of the time that the schedule is in effect. In the present experiment the stimuli occurred before the Mixed schedule went into effect. Another difference is that Ferster and Skinner primed only one component of the Multiple schedule whereas the present experiment employed two separate stimuli, one for each component of the Mixed schedule.

Since the stimuli employed in Experiment 1 were shown to have a discriminative effect on later behavior it seems reasonable to inquire as to whether these stimuli may serve as conditioned reinforcers, since discriminative stimuli may usually be shown to have a reinforcing effect.

Experiment 2 was an attempt to demonstrate that the differential pre-schedule stimuli were conditioned reinforcers. None of the subjects learned the observing-response which would produce these stimuli. The results of one subject suggested that the stimuli had lost their discriminative function when removed and that some time was required for the reestablishment of the discrimination. If the stimuli had lost their discriminative functions, it is reasonable that they would not serve as conditioned reinforcers.

The question arising from Experiment 2 is why the stimuli should lose their discriminative properties simply by being removed for a short time from the situation. I have tried to replicate this finding in a simple discrimination situation where pigeons were reinforced in $S+$ and not in $S-$. When a discrimination had been formed they were exposed to a Mixed schedule in the presence of a third stimulus. Finally they were returned to the discrimination situation. It was found that discrimination was completely intact except for a small amount of "warm-up." One possibility is that the type of discrimination loss observed in Experiment 2 is a function of the complexity or difficulty of the discrimination.

In Experiment 3, a procedure was devised which permitted the discrimination to remain intact while still allowing opportunity for observing responses to occur. The subjects were easily conditioned to make the observing response, but when a nondifferential control was introduced, the level of observing behavior did not decrease appreciably for some of the subjects. It was speculated that either a superstitious chain had developed or that the subjects were reinforced by stimulus change regardless of the relation of the stimuli to the reinforcement schedules. Appel (1963) found that some behavior which is apparently reinforced simply by stimulus change will occur in an ordinary *FR* schedule. This behavior occurred during the pause after reinforcement typical of *FR*s. In my experiments there was an enforced pause after reinforcement (the food key was temporarily unlit and inoperative) and it is possible the reinforcement by stimulus change could account for the results of the nondifferential control of Experiment 3. If this is the case we are in doubt as to whether the responses conditioned in the informative or differential phase were true observing responses, i.e., were reinforcing because of differential relation of the stimuli to the reinforcement schedules.

Experiment 4 was similar to Experiment 3 except that the duration of the stimuli contingent on an observing response was shortened from 30 sec to 1 sec. It was hoped that a briefer stimulus would produce more behavior during the observing period and would clarify the results of Experiment 3. In Experiment 4 the results of the nondifferential control demonstrated that perhaps some behavior was maintained by stimulus change, but that there was a substantial decrease in the response rate from the differential condition. This decrease indicates that the stimuli were acting as conditioned reinforcers during the differential phase of Experiment 4.

Other results of Experiment 4 suggested that of the two stimuli, the one preceding *FR* 10 was the stronger conditioned reinforcer since the observing response that produced the PRE-*FR* 10 stimulus occurred at a higher rate than the observing response that produced the PRE-*FR* 100 stimulus.

Some theories of observing behavior propose that both positive and negative discriminative stimuli reinforce observing responses, since both are informative (Hendry, 1965; Schaub, Chapter 13; Schaub & Honig, 1967). Although the present experiments are quite different from either of these experiments, it should be noted that in one sense both stimuli produced by observing responses were negative stimuli. No pecks at the food key were ever reinforced in the presence of these stimuli. Pecks at the food key were only reinforced in the presence of the yellow key light. A discriminative effect of these stimuli was demonstrated in Experiment 1 but the behavior affected did not occur in the presence of either of the differential stimuli. Since the differential stimuli involved were negative stimuli for pecking at the food key in their presence, but positive discriminative stimuli for subsequent differential behavior on the food key, the present results do not definitively show that negative stimuli are reinforcing because of their information value.

There is one aspect of the data from Experiment 4 which seems to be relevant to the information theory of observing responses. It was noted above that the observing response rate was higher in the PRE-*FR* 10 period than in the PRE-*FR* 100 period. If observing responses are maintained solely because they provide information or reduce uncertainty there is no reason for this to be so. Even if the information theory is substantially correct, some factor other than information must be involved to produce different rates of responding for the two stimuli.

Experiment 5 was an attempt to further evaluate the strength of the trace stimuli as conditioned reinforcers by increasing the number of responses necessary to obtain them. Both subjects showed a sharp decline in observing response output during the PRE-*FR* 10 period as the observing response *FR* was increased, but showed only a moderate decline during the PRE-*FR* 100 period. One possibility for accounting for this finding is to note that the subjects had only 30 sec in which to make observing responses. This necessarily limited the number of stimuli which might be obtained per food reinforcement. Note, however, that there was a sharp decline in the number of stimuli obtained in the PRE-*FR* 10 period when the ratio was raised from *FR* 1 to *FR* 2. (Figure 10.10.) If time were the limiting factor a similar sharp decline ought to have occurred when the ratio was raised from *FR* 2 to *FR* 4 and from *FR* 4 to *FR* 8.

Perhaps a more plausible conclusion is that the PRE-*FR* 10 stimulus appears to be more sensitive to the increase in *FR* than the PRE-100 stimulus because there was more observing behavior in the PRE-*FR* 10 period to begin with. Both stimuli are probably weak-conditioned reinforcers and are sensitive to increases in the *FR* value, but the effect is greater in the PRE-*FR* 10 period because of the higher initial rate.

SUMMARY

Previous observing response experiments by the author have suggested that it is not necessary for the differential stimuli to be temporally contiguous with reinforcement in order for them to serve as conditioned reinforcers. When short stimulus durations are used the reinforcement is most often received in the presence of a stimulus common to both schedules (Kendall, 1965c).

The present research was specifically designed to remove the discriminative stimuli from reinforcement and to ensure that reinforcement was always received in the presence of a stimulus common to both schedules. Both the discriminative and reinforcing properties of such "trace" stimuli were dealt with.

The first experiment demonstrated that differential stimuli may have a discriminative effect on behavior which follows the stimuli (the Mixed schedule). Thus these stimuli may be termed "trace discriminative stimuli."

The second experiment failed to demonstrate a reinforcing effect of the trace stimuli, but suggested that the discrimination will spontaneously disintegrate if these stimuli are absent from situation for a period of time.

The third experiment, in which the trace stimuli were eventually produced automatically as well as by observing responses, initially suggested that the trace stimuli had acquired conditioned reinforcement value. A control procedure threw this conclusion into doubt when it was found that observing responses did not extinguish when the trace stimuli were nondifferentially associated with the two FR schedules. It was speculated that responses to the observing key were either maintained by superstitious chaining or simply by stimulus change.

The fourth experiment provided a more sensitive baseline against which to test the nondifferential control procedure since more observing behavior was generated with the 1-sec stimulus. It was concluded from this experiment that (a) the differential stimuli did develop into conditioned reinforcers since there was a sizable drop in observing response output when the nondifferential control was used, (b) the stimulus preceding FR 10 was a stronger conditioned reinforcer than the stimulus preceding FR 100, and (c) there is a possibility that a small amount of behavior may be maintained on the observing key by stimulus change alone, regardless of the relationship of the stimuli to the Mixed schedule.

The fifth experiment suggested that there was a differential sensitivity to the increase in the FR on the observing key. With a higher FR on the observing key the number of stimuli produced in the PRE-FR 10 period dropped more sharply than the number of stimuli produced in the PRE-FR 100 period.

chapter 11

A COMPARISON OF VARIOUS TYPES OF STIMULUS-CHANGE IN TWO ALTERNATING FIXED-RATIO COMPONENTS

E. K. Crossman

NASA–Ames Research Center

INTRODUCTION

From the literature on Chain schedules of reinforcement and conditioned reinforcement it is apparent that the enduring type of stimulus change which occurs in a Chain schedule has a different influence on behavior from that of the type of stimulus change which results when a stimulus is presented only briefly, e.g., a feeder light flash (cf., Kelleher, 1966a, b). The components which make up a Chain schedule are each associated with a different exteroceptive stimulus which remains in effect for the duration of the component. Stimuli appearing in the early components of a Chain suppress behavior when compared to the behavior observed on a comparable schedule of reinforcement (Tandem schedule) in which the same stimulus is present throughout all components (Gollub, 1958). On the other hand, momentary, rather than enduring, types of stimulus change may produce the opposite result. For example, brief flashes of the feeder light or houselights have been shown to increase the rate of responding if these stimuli were paired with unconditioned reinforcement (Findley & Brady, 1965; Zimmerman, 1963).

Rate of response has usually been the principal dependent variable in those experiments concerned with the two types of stimulus change. One exception is a study by Findley and Brady (1965).

These investigators trained a chimpanzee to respond on two alternating *FR* 4000 schedules. In one of the schedules a feeder light flash followed every 400 responses and was present during the reinforcement cycle which lasted 30 sec. In the other schedule the feeder light flashes were absent. Findley and Brady reported that response rates on the *FR* schedule with the feeder light flashes were higher than on the *FR* schedule without these flashes. Furthermore, the pause preceding the first response of the *FR* 4000 schedule that contained the feeder light flashes was shorter than the pause which preceded the other *FR* 4000 schedule. Thus, on the basis of both response rate and response latency, or pausing, Findley and Brady concluded that such brief flashes were conditioned reinforcers.

The technique of alternating two *FR* schedules containing different stimulus conditions and measuring the pause which occurs before each of the schedules is somewhat similar to the psychophysical method of constant stimuli (Woodworth & Schlosberg, 1954). This technique offers several possible advantages over other proce-

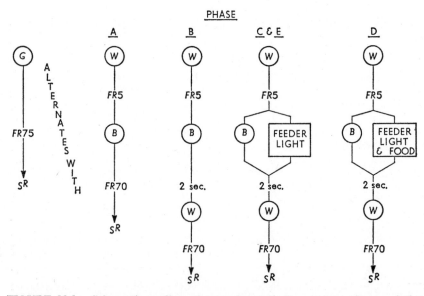

FIGURE 11.1. Schematic outline of procedures in the various phases of the experiment. The circles represent the response key and the letter represents its color; "G" is green, "W" is white, and "B" is blue. An *FR* 75 schedule with a green key was the constant condition in all phases that alternated with the other conditions, that differed in the phases as shown. The alternatives are all referred to as Chain schedules, though only the first (Phase A) is, strictly speaking, a Chain schedule, namely, CHAIN *FR* 5 *FR* 70. The nature and duration of the stimulus produced by the fifth response (*FR* 5) distinguish the various phases; the differences are described in the text.

dures for comparing two or more stimulus conditions. First, the animal is repeatedly and equally exposed to both stimulus conditions in close juxtaposition. This stands in contrast to the more usual procedure of presenting first one set of stimulus conditions for many sessions until some measure of behavioral stability is attained and then presenting another set for approximately the same period of time. Secondly, by scheduling all contingencies and stimulus conditions on a single key this procedure avoids the difficulties of controlling behavioral interactions which often occur in a multiple key situation.

The purpose of the present research was to further explore the usefulness of the alternating-FR-schedules technique for comparing both constant and momentary types of stimulus change. In each instance a simple FR schedule, in which no stimulus change occurred, was alternated with another FR schedule in which one of the two types of stimulus change was programmed. (See Figure 11.1.) Then, the pause lengths before each schedule were compared. As outlined above, something is already known about the properties of these types of stimulus change. It was hoped that the present technique would offer an independent means of confirming and perhaps elaborating on such properties.

METHOD: PHASES A–E

Two male White Carneaux pigeons, P–21 and P–22, served as subjects. These birds had previously been exposed to simple FR schedules. The chamber was a standard operant conditioning pigeon chamber and contained one translucent pecking key which was transilluminated by different colored lights. The aperture to the feeder hopper was located directly below the response key. During a reinforcement cycle, this hopper, which contained Purina pigeon chow, was elevated for 3 sec. Electromechanical systems controlled the programming and recording aspects of the experiment.

Each session was two hours long, and the birds obtained their entire supply of food reinforcement during sessions. On weekends, supplemental food was provided in lieu of the experimental session. The number of obtainable reinforcements per session was limited only by the time required to complete each schedule and by the session length itself.

The following five phases represent five separate experimental conditions, each of which lasted for 19 sessions. The basic schedule in each phase consisted of two alternating *FR* 75 schedules of food reinforcement. One schedule, a simple *FR* 75 schedule, contained a constant stimulus throughout. Initially, the other *FR* 75 schedule was a CHAIN *FR* 5 *FR* 70 schedule. During the remaining four phases various types of stimulus change were inserted during a 2-sec interval after the *FR* 5 component. Technically speaking, the schedules in these latter four phases were not Chain schedules (Ferster & Skinner, 1957). Nevertheless, to avoid confusion by renaming each schedule separately, all of these schedules will be referred to as Chains. The details of each schedule change and the corresponding results will be treated individually.

PHASE A

Procedure

Both P–21 and P–22 had been previously shaped to peck the key on a small *FR* schedule when the key was either red or green. In the present experiment, starting at *FR* 20 in the presence of a green key, the *FR* requirement was increased in steps of five per day until *FR* 75 had been reached. This *FR* 75 schedule was then alternated with a CHAIN *FR* 5 *FR* 70 schedule. Both schedules terminated in 3 sec of food reinforcement. During the first component of the Chain schedule, *FR* 5, a white light was projected on the key; a blue light was projected on the key during the second component, *FR* 70.

Results

Figure 11.2 shows the latency or pause preceding the first response on the *FR* 75 schedule as well as the pause before the first response on the Chain schedule for P–21 and P–22. The data in panel A of this figure represent the mean pause lengths for the last five sessions of Phase A.

During the last five sessions P–21 consistently paused longer before the CHAIN *FR* 5 *FR* 70 schedule than before the *FR* 75 schedule. The same was true of P–22, who showed an even greater separation in the two curves than P–21.

The actual mean running times, as measured from the first to last response, for both schedules are illustrated in Figure 11.3. Panel A of Figure 11.3 shows that for P–21, the time to complete

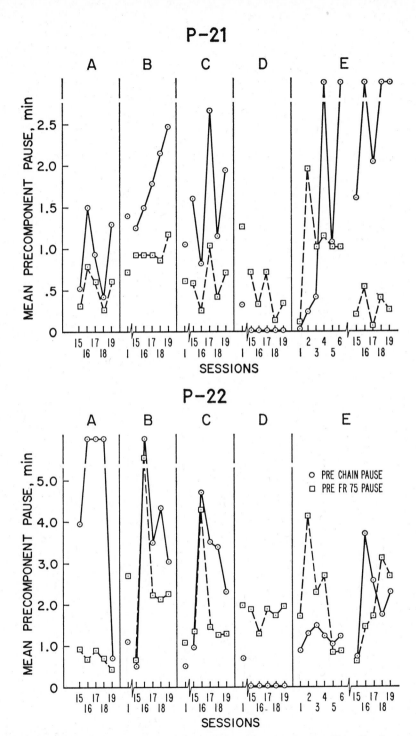

FIGURE 11.2. A comparison of the mean pause times preceding the first response of the *FR* 75 schedule and the first response of the Chain schedule. Letters at the top of each record correspond to the separate experimental phases (see Figure 11.1).

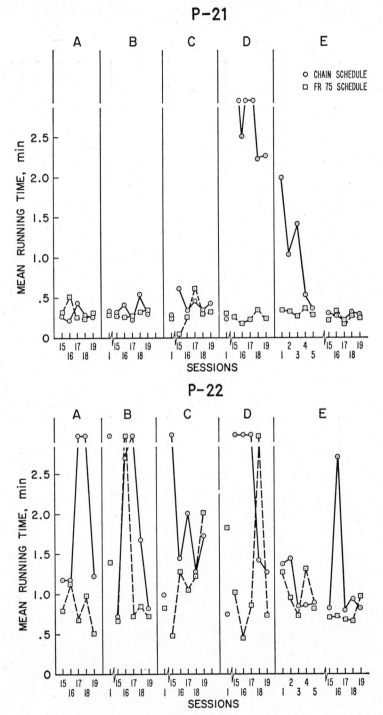

FIGURE 11.3. A comparison of the mean elapsed or running times between the first and last response of the *FR* 75 and Chain schedules. Letters at the top of each record correspond to the separate experimental phases (see Figure 11.1).

the FR 75 schedule did not reliably differ from the time taken to complete the Chain schedule. On the other hand, bird P–22, who paused for long periods prior to the Chain schedule, did take longer to complete the Chain schedule than the FR schedule.

PHASE B

Procedure

Because the pause preceding the Chain schedule had been found to exceed the pause before the FR 75 schedule, the stimulus conditions responsible for this result were of interest. In the FR 75 schedule the green light remained on the response key until the 75th response was completed. Immediately after this response, the key was darkened. Simultaneously the feeder light came on and the hopper was elevated. In the CHAIN FR 5 FR 70 schedule the blue stimulus, which was present during the FR 70 component, was also contiguous with the reinforcement cycle. However, the first stimulus of the Chain, the white light, terminated after the fifth response and was replaced by the blue light. Thus, the relatively longer pause observed in the presence of the white light preceding the first response of the Chain may have been caused by the separation in time between the white light and unconditioned reinforcement. The following procedure was designed to test this possibility.

In Phase B the CHAIN FR 5 FR 70 schedule was altered as follows. As during Phase A, the key remained white when the Chain schedule was in effect and until the fifth response on the Chain schedule had occurred. Then, the key was changed to blue. However, instead of remaining blue until the moment of reinforcement, the white light on the key was reinstated 2 sec later and remained on until the beginning of the 3-sec reinforcement cycle, at which point the key was darkened. Thus the stimuli present at the beginning of both the FR 75 schedule and the Chain schedule were also present in close temporal juxtaposition with the primary reinforcer. If this new procedure abolishes the critical difference between the two schedules observed in Phase A, the pauses before the two schedules in Phase B should be about equal.

Results

According to the data in panel B of Figure 11.2 for P–21, the mean pause before the Chain schedule (white key) was longer than the mean pause before the *FR* 75 schedule (green key) during the first session, as well as the last five sessions. This difference in the duration of pausing was even greater than that seen in panel A. However, for P–21 there was no consistent separation in the running times of the two schedules (see panel B, Figure 11.3).

It is also apparent in Phase B for P–21 that the absolute values of pauses have increased above their former values in Phase A (see Figure 11.2). An increase of this sort is probably a function of the number of schedules completed. Thus, if an animal completed 50 *FR* 75 schedules and 50 Chain schedules, the amount of time available for pausing would be much less than if only 5 of each type of schedule were completed. Accordingly, primary emphasis is placed upon the ratio of the durations of pausing before the different schedules *within each session*.

The procedural change in Phase B appears to have had a different effect on P–22. Whereas the pre-Chain pause was longer than the PRE-*FR* pause during Phase A (see Figure 11.2), this consistent difference was not maintained in Phase B. As shown in panel B, Figure 11.2, a reversal in the two mean pause times occurred during the 1st and 15th sessions. Also, the absolute values of the pre-Chain pauses were slightly lower than those recorded during Phase A, while the absolute values of the PRE-*FR* 75 pauses were generally higher.

A similar effect on the running times of this animal can be observed in Figure 11.3. Whereas in Phase A, P–22's running time for the Chain schedule always was higher than for the *FR* 75 schedule, this was not always the case in Phase B, as shown, for example, in session 16.

PHASE C

Procedure

In the previous phase, the strategy of attempting to reduce the size of the pre-Chain pause relative to the PRE-*FR* 75 pause by making the first stimulus in the Chain also the last stimulus in the Chain was not uniformly successful. Therefore, it was decided to supplement the existing stimuli in the Chain schedule with another stimulus thought to be a conditioned reinforcer. As in Phase B, the fifth response in the Chain schedule was followed by a brief stimulus change—a change in the key color from white to blue for 2 sec. In addition to this brief stimulus change, during Phase C the feeder light was turned on for the duration of the 2-sec. interval. Because the FR 75 schedule contained no stimulus of this kind, except at the completion of the schedule, the pre-Chain pause should have decreased below the value of the PRE-FR 75 pause if the feeder light were, in fact, a conditioned reinforcer.

Results

Because the effects of conditioned reinforcers of this type are sometimes quick to fade, the first session in which the feeder light was presented after the fifth response of the Chain schedule is of particular importance. However, the data for P–21 in Figure 11.2 (see panel C) indicate that, even in the first session, the mean pre-Chain pause continued to be elevated above the mean PRE-FR 75 pause. Also, the actual mean running times for the two schedules are, with one exception, higher for the Chain schedule than for the FR 75 schedule (see panel C, Figure 11.3).

The data for P–22 in panel C (Figure 11.2) resemble those shown in panel B for this bird. That is, the pre-Chain pause was sometimes longer and sometimes shorter than the PRE-FR 75 pause. The same comparison can be made of the actual running times of the two schedules shown in panel C of Figure 11.3. As in Phase B, the two running times were not consistently different.

PHASE D

Procedure

The interpolation of the feeder light in the Chain schedule during Phase C seemed to affect the pre-schedule pauses and the actual running times very little. This is particularly surprising because the feeder light has often been demonstrated to be a conditioned reinforcer. This discrepancy may be due to the insensitivity of the technique toward such stimuli or some peculiarity about the feeder light as a stimulus.

In more detail, the following aspects of the procedure in Phase C were considered as possible causes for the failure to obtain a conditioned reinforcing effect. First, after the FR 5 component of the

Chain schedule had been completed, during Phase C, the key changed from white to blue for 2 sec. At the same time the feeder light also came on for 2 sec. This complex of stimuli may have been discriminated by the birds from the presentation of the feeder light at the end of the Chain schedule, where the key changed from white to black for the 3-sec. reinforcement cycle. Secondly, the feeder light was always paired with food at the end of the Chain schedule but never at the beginning. If, on the basis of some unknown properties, the pigeons were able to discriminate the beginning of the Chain schedule from the latter part of this schedule, these same properties may have been utilized in the discrimination of the feeder light following the fifth response from the feeder light at the end of the schedule. Thus, the effectiveness of the early feeder light as a conditioned reinforcer would be nullified.

Therefore, during Phase D, the feeder hopper was elevated during the 2-sec interval following the fifth response of the Chain schedule. Also during this 2-sec. interval the key changed from white to blue and the feeder light was illuminated as before. This deliberate pairing should have accomplished two things. First, it should have demonstrated the sensitivity of the technique to a strong reinforcing stimulus, such as food; and secondly, pairing food with the other stimuli at this early point in the schedule should impart conditioned reinforcing properties to these other stimuli. This latter effect was tested during the last phase (Phase E).

Results

From the data in Figure 11.2, it is apparent that presenting food for 2 sec after the fifth response in the Chain schedule had a dramatic and immediate effect on both birds. As shown in panel D, the pre-Chain pause dropped well below the PRE-*FR* 75 pause, even within the 1st session, and by the 15th session the mean value of the pre-Chain pause was only 1–2 sec for every session. Although the pre-Chain pause had been reduced, the actual running time for the Chain schedule, as shown in Figure 11.3 (see panel D) had increased for both birds. During the last five sessions, with one exception (session 18, P–22) the running time for the Chain schedule was substantially longer than the time required to complete the *FR* 75 schedule.

The manner in which the running time for the Chain schedule came to exceed the running time for the *FR* 75 schedule is of particular interest. Figures 11.4 and 11.5 represent cumulative records of the performance for P–21 during the last session of Phases C and D, respectively. The data for P–22 are quite similar. In Figure 11.4 the only stimuli presented during the 2-sec. interval following the fifth response on the Chain schedule (note diagonal pip) were the blue key light and the feeder light. Under these conditions the pre-Chain pause on the average can be seen to be longer than the PRE-FR 75 pause, as was verified quantitatively in panel C of Figure 11.2. Furthermore, with few exceptions (e.g., see "a") the two components of the Chain schedule, FR 5 and FR 70, appear to act as a unitary schedule with little pausing between these components. As shown in Figure 11.5, however, the addition of the feeder hopper to the 2-sec interval fractionates the Chain response pattern. A long pause has developed prior to the first response on the FR 70 component of the Chain (PRE-FR 70 pause). It is also apparent in Figure 11.5 that following the FR 75 schedule, there is little delay in completing the FR 5 component. Because the running time for the Chain schedule was calculated from the first response of the FR 5 component, the appearance of the long PRE-FR 70 pauses produced an increase in the running time attributed to the Chain schedule. The increase in the running time for the Chain is directly verified in Figure 11.3, panel D, for both birds. However, the running time for the FR 75 schedule during Phase D was about the same as during Phase C.

Further examination of Figure 11.5 suggests that the PRE-FR 70 pause was actually longer than the PRE-FR 75 pause during the final session of Phase D. While this relation was firmly established for P–21 during all of the last five sessions of this phase, the same finding was not consistently true for P–22.

The development of the transition in which the two components of the Chain schedule were separated from one another is shown in Figure 11.6 for P–21 and in Figure 11.7 for P–22. These figures illustrate the changes which occurred in the individual pre-Chain pauses and the PRE-FR 70 pauses when food was introduced (or withdrawn, Phase E) following the FR 5 component. (The pre-Chain pause could be referred to as the PRE-FR 5 pause, but to preserve consistency this substitution will not be made.) Each plotted point represents a single pause, and these points are shown in the order in which they occurred.

During the last session of Phase C the pre-Chain pause was long and variable but the PRE-FR 70 pause was both shorter and less

P-21

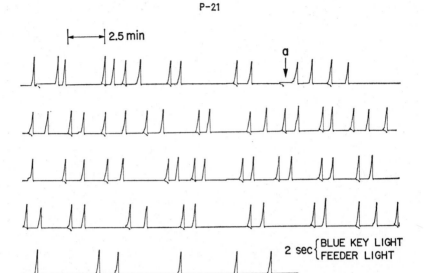

FIGURE 11.4. Cumulative record of last session during Phase C. The Chain schedule performance is identified by the diagonal pip, which occurred after the fifth response. Pen resets to base line after 75th response on both schedules.

P-21

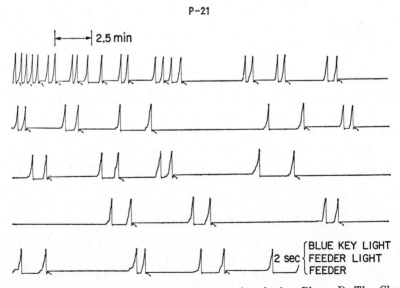

FIGURE 11.5. Cumulative record of last session during Phase D. The Chain schedule performance is identified by the diagonal pip, which occurred after the fifth response. Note the long pauses which precede the *FR* 70 component of the Chain. Pen resets to base line after 75th response on both schedules.

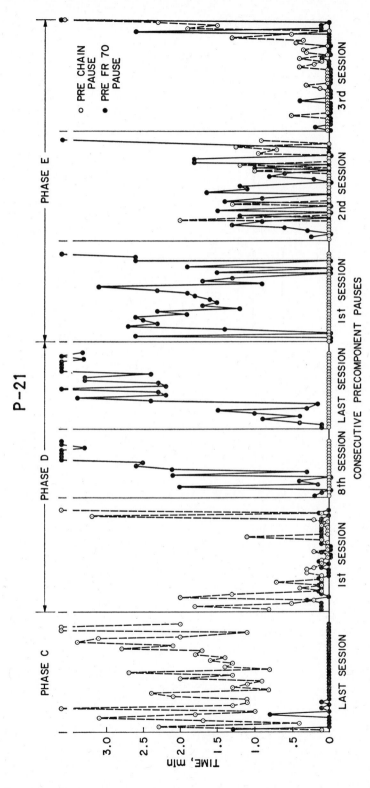

FIGURE 11.6. Selected sessions illustrate transitional characteristics of the pre-Chain and PRE-*FR* 70 pauses when food was introduced after the fifth response of the Chain (Phase D) and subsequently withdrawn (Phase E).

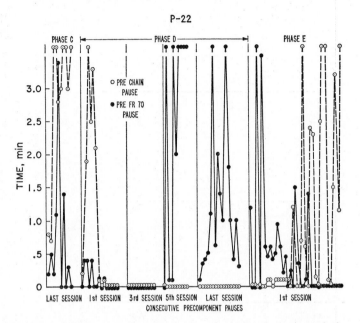

FIGURE 11.7. Selected sessions illustrate transitional characteristics of the pre-Chain and PRE-*FR* 70 pauses when food was introduced after the fifth response of the Chain (Phase D) and subsequently withdrawn (Phase E).

variable for P–21 (Figure 11.6) and P–22 (Figure 11.7). When the feeder was elevated following the *FR* 5 component (Phase D) the pre-Chain pause dropped to a low, stable value within the first session for both birds. The PRE-*FR* 70 pause, on the other hand, had not yet begun to increase. Not until the fifth session did P–22 begin to pause for long periods preceding the *FR* 70 component (see Figure 11.7) and a total of eight sessions was required before the same phenomenon could be observed in P–21's performance (see Figure 11.6). In other words, the initial effect of the introduction of reinforcement was to reduce the pre-Chain pause without substantially altering the PRE-*FR* 70 pause. Then, some sessions later, the PRE-*FR* 70 pause lengthened.

PHASE E

Procedure

In order to determine the effects of having presented food concurrently with the feeder light and the blue key in Phase E, the feeder hopper was no longer elevated during the 2-sec. interval after the *FR* 5 component. Thus, the experimental conditions in Phases C and E were essentially alike.

Results

According to Figure 11.2, withholding food after the fifth response produced a gradual increase in the pre-Chain pause. By the fifth session for P–22 and the fourth session for P–21, this pause had exceeded the PRE-*FR* 75 pause. During the last five sessions of Phase E, there was either no consistent difference in the lengths of the pre-Chain and PRE-*FR* 75 pauses (P–22), or the pre-Chain pause actually was longer than the PRE-*FR* 75 pause (P–21).

In Figure 11.3, the running time for the Chain schedule during the last five sessions of Phase E was appreciably reduced over that recorded during Phase D, but the running time for the *FR* 75 schedule showed little change when compared to Phase D. As might be suspected, the reduction in the running time for the Chain schedule primarily resulted from a decrease in the PRE-*FR* 70 pause.

Figures 11.6 and 11.7 confirm this expectation. During the last session of Phase D, the pre-Chain pause was extremely short, about 1–2 sec, and the PRE-*FR* 70 pause was long for both birds. The first effect of removing the food after the fifth response of the Chain appears to be a sudden reduction in the PRE-*FR* 70 pause (note the first several PRE-*FR* 70 pauses in the first session of Phase E of Figures 11.6 and 11.7). Subsequently the PRE-*FR* 70 pause increased and then gradually declined. For P–22 (Figure 11.7) the decline in the PRE-*FR* 70 pause appears to have run its course within the first session of Phase E. The transition is somewhat slower for P–21 (Figure 11.6), and although the PRE-*FR* 70 pause generally declined during the first session of Phase E, it is only in the third session that the PRE-*FR* 70 pause reaches a stable low value. Reference to Figures 11.6 and 11.7 shows that following the initiation of the decline in the PRE-*FR* 70 pause, the pre-Chain pause began to increase. This occurred in the first session of Phase E for P–22 and in the second session for P–21. Careful examination of Figures 11.6 and 11.7 shows that the increase in the pre-Chain pause during Phase E did not occur as quickly as did the decrease in this pause which took place during the first session of Phase D. For example, for P–22 the pre-Chain pause was reduced to near asymptotic value after only 7 repetitions of the food-reinforced FR 5 component (see first session, Phase D), but about 17 repetitions of the unreinforced FR 5 component were required before the pre-Chain pause substantially increased (see first session, Phase E). This effect was even more pronounced in P–21's data.

Thus, in Phase E, the temporal order in which the various pauses changed their length was reversed from the order observed in Phase D. When food was presented after the fifth response of the Chain (Phase D), the pre-Chain pause was affected immediately and was reduced to a low value; then the PRE-FR 70 pause increased. When food was removed after the fifth response of the Chain (Phase E) the PRE-FR 70 pause was the first pause to be affected, and it gradually decreased. Subsequently, the pre-Chain pause increased.

DISCUSSION

Various investigators have compared the performance of pigeons on Chain FI schedules and Tandem FI schedules composed of the same number of components (Kelleher, 1966a). The consistent finding is that response rates in the early components of the Chain schedule are lower than in the Tandem schedule, and that the FI scallop does not develop in the first link of the Chain. This finding appears to be applicable only to "extended" Chain schedules consisting of three or more components.

During Phase A of the present experiment the same sort of comparison was made, but with a two-component Chain. It was noted that response rates, or actual running times, were not consistently different for the Chain and FR 75 schedules (the FR 75 could be called TAND FR 5 FR 70). However, the behavioral suppression was greater in the Chain schedule if the relatively longer pause before the first response on this schedule is taken to represent suppression.

The relation of the stimuli in the Chain to primary reinforcement has been explored in order to discover the conditions responsible for the suppression. It seems to be generally accepted that the early stimuli in a chain derive their aversive properties from their correlation with the absence of primary reinforcement. Accordingly, Kelleher and Fry (1962) varied the sequence of stimuli in CHAIN FI 90 sec FI 90 sec FI 90 sec. In the varied sequence, each stimulus was randomly paired with food one third of the time. Although food was still delivered only after every third component, the pauses seen in the Chain schedule with a fixed sequence of stimuli disappeared in the variable Chain. Taking a slightly different approach, Findley (1962) varied the length of the Chain instead of the sequence in which stimuli were presented. For example, in a five component, *FI* 15 sec Chain schedule, Findley reported low response rates in the early components. Positively accelerating response rates could be maintained in the early components, Findley found, by presenting food, in a random fashion, after each of the components. Thus, sometimes food would follow the first component, sometimes the second component, etc. However, the sequence of stimuli was fixed. The first stimulus in the sequence reappeared after every delivery of food.

The results from these two experiments suggest that the rate of response in the presence of a stimulus can be increased if that stimulus is paired, at least intermittently, with unconditioned reinforcement. It is somewhat surprising, therefore, that during Phase B of the present experiment, the pairing of the white key with food at the end of the Chain failed to reduce the pre-Chain pause relative to the PRE-*FR* 75 pause for P–21. Apparently, the white key *preceding* the 2-sec. interval during which the key changed to blue, was discriminated by this bird from the white key *following* the 2-sec stimulus change.

Also, the failure to demonstrate a consistent conditioned reinforcing effect during Phase C, even in the first session, was unexpected in view of the large number of studies which have indicated that the feeder light flash is a conditioned reinforcer in other reinforcement schedules (cf., Kelleher, 1966a). Even after food was paired for 19 sessions with the feeder light flash during the 2-sec. interval (Phase D) the pre-Chain pause remained shorter than the PRE-*FR* 75 pause for only five sessions after the food was withdrawn (Phase E). In the study by Findley and Brady (1965), in which an *FR* 4000 schedule was alternated with another *FR* 4000 schedule containing a feeder light flash after ever 400th response, the pauses preceding the schedule with the feeder light flashes were consistently shorter than those preceding the simple *FR* 4000 schedule over 31 sessions. Why Findley and Brady's schedule was able to maintain this difference in duration of pauses for so long, in contrast to the results of the present experiment, is not clear. The larger *FR* schedule, different species of organism, or the more frequent appearance of the feeder light flashes within the *FR* schedule itself represent some possible causes for the discrepancy in the two sets of data.

Another possibility, however, derives from procedural details in the present study. The blue key light accompanied the feeder light flash during the 2-sec interval following the first five responses of the Chain, but at the end of the Chain the key was white up until the beginning of the reinforcement cycle. Then the key darkened. Thus, the pigeons may have discriminated "blue-key-feeder-light-flash" from "dark-key-feeder-light-flash." However, since food was actually paired with both stimulus combinations (Phase D) and continued to be paired with "dark-key-feeder-light-flash" in Phase E, the failure to obtain a more enduring conditioned reinforcing effect suggests that either the feeder light flash was a very weak conditioned reinforcer, or that the present technique was simply too insensitive.

An increase in the reinforcement probability associated with a particular operant produces a more rapid change in behavior than a comparable decrease. This is tantamount to claiming that conditioning proceeds at a more rapid rate than Extinction. Skinner (1938, pp. 69, 75) has shown that response rate may increase abruptly after the first reinforcement of a bar press. When bar presses are no longer reinforced, however, response rate usually decreases at a much slower rate. This asymmetrical relation is perhaps relevant to the changes in the pre-Chain pauses during the early sessions of Phases D and E. As mentioned in the results, when the reinforcement frequency for the *FR* 5 component was increased from 0 percent to 100 percent (Phase D) the pre-Chain pause decreased more rapidly than it increased when the reinforcement frequency for the *FR* 5 component was decreased from 100 percent to 0 percent (Phase E).

One observation should be mentioned in regard to the decrease in the PRE-*FR* 70 pause during Phase E. The first few times the birds completed the *FR* 5 component without reinforcement, there was no pausing at all before the *FR* 70 component. This sudden decrease in the PRE-*FR* 70 pause is reminiscent of the "frustration effect" reported by Amsel and Roussel (1952). These investigators trained rats to traverse a two-stage straight runway. Initially the rats were reinforced at the midpoint and at the end of the runway. However, when the percentage of reinforcement at the midpoint was reduced from 100 percent to 50 percent, the rats increased their running speed in the terminal stage. In the present experiment, this sudden reduction in the PRE-FR 70 pause was only temporary, although the PRE-FR 70 pause did eventually return to a very low value.

Base-line schedules of reinforcement are seldom composed entirely of FR components when an attempt is made to measure the effects of moderate or weak conditioned reinforcers. The reasoning behind this exclusion is based on the insensitivity of the running rate on this schedule. The present experiment demonstrates that the dependent variable of the latency or pausing between the various FR components, rather than running rate, can be consistently influenced by certain types of stimulus change, as well as changes in the absolute or relative rates of reinforcement associated with the various components.

SUMMARY

Large discriminative effects of Chain stimuli were produced, without appreciable reinforcing effects. A fixed-ratio schedule (FR 75) was compared with various Chain schedules with the same response requirements. CHAIN FR 5 FR 70 produced longer pre-Chain latencies than FR 75. Longer pauses were produced with a brief stimulus after FR 5 than with CHAIN FR 5 FR 70. When a conditioned reinforcer (feeder light) was presented along with the brief stimulus, the pre-Chain pause continued to be elevated, and the mean running time was longer than for the simple FR 75. Primary reinforcement presented along with the brief stimulus, however, produced a rapid drop in pre-Chain latency, and a gradual increase in latency following the brief stimulus.

chapter 12

REINFORCING VALUE OF INFORMATION: FIXED-RATIO SCHEDULES[1]

Derek P. Hendry

University of Illinois, Chicago Circle

INTRODUCTION

Much of the burden placed by behavior theorists on the learning and remembering of animals may be assumed by essentially unmotivated perceptual processes. The Gestalt psychologists argued, with many demonstrations and examples, that the brain imposed upon the data of sense an order that was something over and above the elements of sense that were organized. Behaviorists, on the other hand, attributed development of skills to a process of learning by associating the arbitrarily selected coincidences and sequences of sense, or of sense and behavior. A view which is consistent with most if not all of the evidence and which embraces the fundamental tenets of both the Gestalt and Behaviorist traditions is that the perceptual apparatus of animals detects invariant relations in the data of sense (e.g., Gibson, 1966). These invariances are not imposed by the brain—they are for ordinary perception inherent in the environment and determined by the laws of physics. For example, the visual apparatus contains detectors for macroscopic abstracted features of the environment (e.g., Hubel, 1963; Hubel & Wiesel, 1962; Lettvin, Maturana, McCulloch, & Pitts, 1959).

[1] The author is grateful for the assistance of Mary Bailey Gruber, Robert Abele, Barry Jacobs, William J. Lennon, Ralph Pipitone and Lana Schiller. The work reported was partially supported by grant No. GM 14221 from USPHS and grants from the Smith Klein and French Foundation, and the General Research Support Fund of the Presbyterian–St. Luke's Hospital and the University of Illinois Research Board.

These detectors are in general detectors of certain spatial and temporal sequences. For example, certain cells detect edges by being responsive to higher order derivatives of reflectances of adjacent regions in the visual field. An edge is a particular kind of sequence among spatially ordered elements. Other cells detect movement by being responsive to changes in the reflectance of the "same" parts of the visual field. Movement is a particular kind of sequence among spatially and temporally ordered elements. Such new discoveries in physiology and psychology have divested many of the old Gestaltist demonstrations of their mystery, if not of their fascination. For example, if the visual system contains components that are responsive to both increase and decrease in illumination (Hartline, 1938), and if we make the plausible assumption that such "on-off" cells are implicated in the detection of movement, the phi phenomenon becomes perfectly understandable—indeed, predictable. The phi phenomenon has been called a "movement illusion." Movement was perceived, even though nothing in the environment was moving. We see now that this was a fundamentally false description, because we accept that all perceived movement must be produced by a temporal sequence of neural states in sets related in a particular way. Thus a rotating spiral phenomenally expands (or contracts) whether the spiral itself or a "motion picture" of static images of it is viewed.

Let us take as settled (which it is not) that the sensory apparatus of animals operates to detect invariances. From this point of view casual observation of human behavior reveals sensitivity to invariances even where the transformation rules are arbitrary and unlike any transformation found in the natural environment. For example, one can identify a sentence written in Clarendon or Gothic type, in English, or in French, spoken or written. This kind of capacity led logicians to the paradoxically idealist view that there was such a thing as a "proposition" over and above, or separate from, any particular realization or representation of the proposition. Clearly, it is hopeless to look for similarities among the various "stimuli" so long as these stimuli are expressed as momentary distributions of energy. Yet there is such a thing as the *meaning* of a sentence, which does not change when it is written rather than spoken. We conclude from this example and from many similar cases that men are able to detect invariances at a very high level of abstraction when the sequences of the fundamental sense-data are arbitrary (but repeated). Another way of expressing this is to say that men are sensitive to the information in the environment. Do lower animals have a similar capacity? From general evolutionary arguments it is a plausible assumption that animals are sensitive to information, though they clearly must have more severe limits in this capacity than men. At all events, let us again assume that animals are sensitive to information.

Sensitivity to information implies that animals can learn; that is to say, they are not prescient. This in turn implies that the registration of information is reinforcing. This in turn suggests that the opportunity to engage in behavior which obtains information is reinforcing. A "new" environment is one to whose structure, or relations of sequences, the animal has never been exposed. The process of extracting the new information requires repeated exposure to the strange structure. To say that the environment loses its strangeness is to say that perceptual effects of behaving in certain ways become predictable. The behavioral effects of the sensitivity to information is an indication of "learning."

Important aspects of the information available in experimental environments are referred to as "contingencies of reinforcement." Since these are relations between behavior and certain important sensory consequences, the concept can also be applied in perception. For example, a man looking at a table around which he is walking may be said to be exposing himself to a set of contingencies. There are determinable relations between his perceptual behavior (walking and looking) and the perspective changes in the rhomboid discontinuities of reflectance that we have learned to call the "surface of the table." An animal producing food by pecking a key is exposed to a set of contingencies in a way that may be regarded as the same in principle.

The experiments to be described were devised in the context of the quite well-defined hypothesis that events which are "informative" reinforce the perceptual exploratory behavior of organisms. Our reasoning followed the arguments of Berlyne (1957, 1960). A condition of uncertainty may be said to exist when a Mixed (un-cued) schedule contains two (or more) schedules that the animal could discriminate if given the opportunity. This uncertainty should be a motivating condition and reduction of the uncertainty should be a reinforcing event. Uncertainty is reduced by cues correlated with specific probabilities of future events or current contingencies. Such cues give information, we say, or are informative.

Because informative cues acquire their (putative) reinforcing function as a result of arbitrary experienced correlations they apparently qualify as "conditioned reinforcers." However, they do not derive their reinforcing value in the ordinary way from some unconditioned reinforcer, such as food. They are not necessarily associated, in the sense of being contemporaneous, with an unconditioned reinforcer. They would be reinforcing even if uncorrelated with, say, food, so long as their relation to food was systematic or regular. When one of the components of the Mixed schedule is Extinction (as in the original experiments of Wyckoff, Chapter 9), it is always possible to treat the reinforcing effect of the informative cues as derived from the association of *one* of them with food. For that reason I avoided Extinction as a component in the Mixed schedule. Consequently, *both* cues are associated with food.

Fixed-ratio (FR) schedules were chosen as the components. There are several especially interesting features of Mixed FR schedules. In the first place, the amount of "work" done is proportional to the ratio, so different schedules can be compared. Secondly, a typical performance is easy to identify. Thirdly, we know that FR schedules are discriminable (Pliskoff & Goldiamond, 1966). Fourthly, there is no reason to suppose that a Multiple FR schedule is preferred to the corresponding Mixed FR schedule, unless information is reinforcing.

Typical procedures which involve observing behavior have affinities with Concurrent schedules. One way of arranging Concurrent schedules is to have the different schedules available on a single operandum, and have the schedule be selected by performance of some other changeover (CO) response. CO requirements are usually symmetric—i.e., the same for both directions of transition between schedules. The common type of observing-response procedure may be regarded as a special case of Concurrent schedules with asymmetric, unidirectional CO requirements; a CO response changes Schedule 1 to Schedule 2, but not vice versa. The Concurrent schedules are a Mixed schedule and the corresponding Multiple schedule. The observing response effects the change from the Mixed to the Multiple schedule, but the transition from the Multiple to the Mixed schedule is usually not under the subject's control.

A two-key Concurrent schedule may also represent typical observing-behavior experiments. Here, instead of having a response whose only function is to produce signals, a schedule without signals is offered for one response and the same schedule with signals is offered for an alternative response. These are Concurrent schedules, but the animal may be described as observing when he consistently chooses the schedule with the signals.

We conducted two series of experiments. In series A the procedure can be described as a single-key Concurrent schedule with a unidirectional CO key. In series B, the procedure was a two-key Concurrent-Chains schedule.

The subjects in all the experiments were pigeons, maintained at 75–80 percent of undeprived weight. A two-key chamber was used. Contingencies were controlled in some cases by solid state timing and switching circuits in the same room, and in some cases by a remote GE 225 digital computer.

SERIES A

Experiment A1

In Experiment A1, two different FR schedules were presented on the left key, which was white. A given number of responses on the

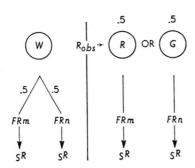

FIGURE 12.1. Representation of the procedure for Experiment A1. An observing response (R_{obs}) converted MIX $FR\ m\ FR\ n$ with a white (W) key to MULT $FR\ m\ FR\ n$ with a red (R) or green (G) key. The schedule of primary reinforcement was on the left key and the schedule of R_{obs} was on the right key.

right (dark) key would turn both keys red if the smaller FR were in effect and green if the larger FR were in effect. Thus, responses on the right key converted the Mixed schedule into the corresponding Multiple schedule. The procedure is represented in Figure 12.1.

Observing behavior was somewhat elusive, and the FR components of the Mixed schedule were changed several times to larger and more discrepant values. A few birds, whose performance will not be further described here, never sustained observing behavior. With FR 10 and FR 40, two birds learned to make observing responses and their performance was sustained for several sessions when the observing key schedule was raised to FR 4. Observing responses were almost always emitted after the magazine operated and before responding resumed on the food key. However, observing behavior eventually disappeared with MIX FR 10 FR 40. Observing behavior was restored for a few sessions with MIX FR 20 FR 60. With MIX FR 20 FR 80 observing behavior was again restored and this time proved to be reasonably stable in the case of three birds. Observing behavior was also sustained with MIX FR 20 FR 100.

Figure 12.2 shows performance of birds identified as P–1, P–2 and P–3, selected to show an intermediate amount of observing behavior. When the red or green lights are not on, the recorder pen is deflected downwards and the food reinforcements appear as upward displacements of the trace. When the lights are on, the pen is up. The pen goes down at the end of reinforcement and stays down until the red or green lights are turned on again. Thus the maintenance of consistent observing behavior immediately after reinforcement results in a cumulative record of conventional appearance, with downward pips at reinforcement. Figure 12.2 shows that this was the predominant behavior. The observing ratio is run off rapidly, if at all, just after reinforcement. There are very few cases of incomplete observing ratios. When red is obtained, 20 responses on the food key are promptly emitted. When green is obtained there is an initial pause of variable length before the 80 food key responses are emitted. When neither red nor green is obtained the initial pause on the food key is very short, whether the current ratio is 20 or 80. One consequence of the initial pause in green is a considerably higher rate of reinforcement when stimuli are not observed than when they are. Observing behavior is maintained in spite of its unfavorable effect on rate of reinforcement.

Later parts of the records for P–1 and P–2 in Figure 12.2 show the absence of observing behavior (no event marker deflections and recording pen down except for upward pips). In both these cases there is a sharp transition from obtaining almost every cue to obtaining almost none. This all-or-none characteristic of observing behavior was typical, though it did not obscure the emergence of orderly results.

The probability of observing behavior declined as the observing fixed-ratio schedule was raised. Figure 12.3 and 12.4 show the results of this procedure.

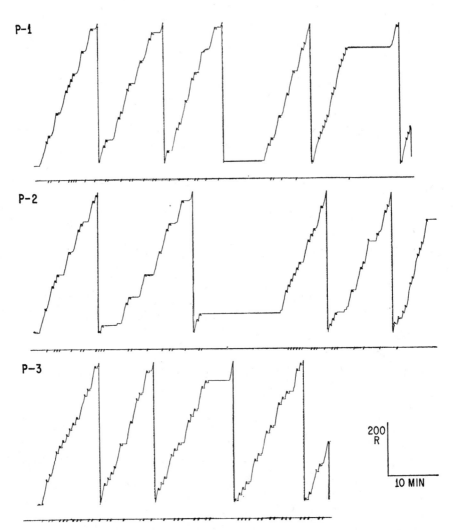

FIGURE 12.2. P–1, P–2, and P–3. Performance for a complete session, showing an intermediate amount of observing behavior. The cumulative records show food key responses reinforced on *FR* 20 or *FR* 80. When the food key is white (signifying either *FR* 20 or *FR* 80) the recording pen is down, and reinforcements appear as upward deflections. When both keys are green (signifying *FR* 80) or red (signifying *FR* 20) the recording pen is up, makes a downward pip at the start of reinforcement, and goes down again after reinforcement, when the food key is again white. Duration of the pen in the down position shows how long the food key remained white before observing responses produced either red or green. The occurrence of each observing response, reinforced on the schedule *FR* 4, is shown by deflections of the event marker on the lower trace.

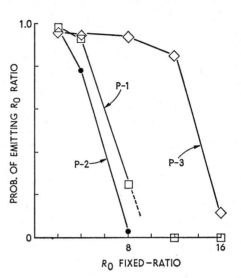

FIGURE 12.3. Birds P–1, P–2 and P–3. Probability of emitting the observing response (R_0) fixed ratio as a function of the size of that ratio. R_0 obtained the cues associated with FR 20 and FR 80. The values are the means of the last four sessions at each point.

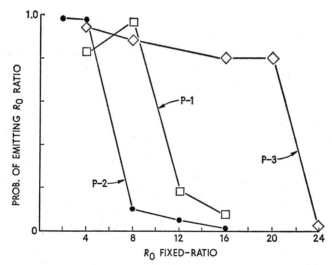

FIGURE 12.4. Birds P–1, P–2 and P–3. The same functions as shown in Figure 12.3, except that the Mixed schedule components were FR 20 and FR 100.

Distribution of observing responses. Observing behavior usually occurred immediately after reinforcement or not at all, except in the case of MIX FR 20 FR 100. With MIX FR 20 FR 100 the exceptions were frequent enough to reveal a clear pattern. The distribution of observing behavior of birds 1, 2 and 3 in representative sessions is shown in Figure 12.5. Actually plotted are the probability

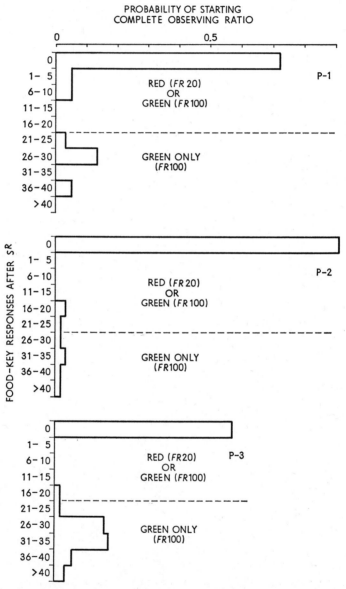

FIGURE 12.5. Distribution of complete *FR* runs of observing responses. Observing responses converted MIX *FR* 20 *FR* 100 to MULT *FR* 20 *FR* 100. The graph shows the probability of starting a complete observing ratio as a function of how many food key responses had been emitted since the last reinforcement. For P-1, P-2, and P-3 the observing response schedules were respectively *FR* 4, *FR* 4, *FR* 8.

distributions of the "starting positions" of reinforced runs of observing responses. If the *FR* of observing responses occurred immediately after primary reinforcement the starting position would be zero; if 20 responses on the food key occurred first, the starting position would be 20. There were no cases where observing response *FR* runs were broken by intervening responses on the food keys, and there were very few incomplete observing response runs.

Figure 12.5 shows that observing behavior was most likely to occur immediately after primary reinforcement. Observing response runs were sometimes initiated after 20 or more food key responses. This behavior was most marked in the case of P–3. These runs, of course, always produced the green signal, yet there was no tendency for such late runs to diminish with continued exposure to MIX *FR* 20 *FR* 100. This result argues against the green signal's being aversive and implies instead that it was reinforcing. The distributions, especially in the case of P–3, are similar to those of Kendall's (1965a) bird, P–4B, in that many observing responses occurred just after the point at which reinforcement would have occurred on the shorter *FR* component of the Mixed schedule. This aspect of the distribution may be taken to reveal relative strengths of competing food-reinforced responses and observing responses.

From another point of view, the persistence of late runs of observing behavior, which always produce the same signal (green), is puzzling. Assuming that the birds distinguish late observing behavior from observing behavior emitted immediately after primary reinforcement, one must conclude that late observing behavior gives no information. At best one might interpret the late observing behavior as serving to "confirm" that the long ratio was in effect, but on the face of it the late observing behavior presents a difficulty for the information interpretation.

Experiment A2

Either signal (red or green) gives all the information (i.e., 1 bit). Therefore, the two signals should not differ in their conditioned reinforcing value if the value depends only on reduction of uncertainty. In fact, red and green separately do not have, independently of their signaling function, any conditioned reinforcing value. It is only the Hullian formulation (see Chapter 1) that makes one think that red and green separately should be conditioned reinforcers, because red and green are present before and during reinforcement.

There are several ways that one might attempt to measure conditioned reinforcing value of each signal separately. One method that looks promising but turns out to have difficulties involves using the signals to reinforce a new response. This is like adding a new link to an established Chain. If the original schedule of primary reinforcement is continued differences in performance may be attributed to the schedules of primary reinforcement rather than the signals for them. Thus, in the test situation,

a) $R_{new} \longrightarrow$ red, FR 20 $\longrightarrow S^R$
b) $R'_{new} \longrightarrow$ green, FR 100 $\longrightarrow S^R$

a stronger R_{new} than R'_{new} would only indicate a stronger reinforcing effect of FR 20 than FR 100.

Alternatively, if primary reinforcement is not continued, thus,

a) $R_{new} \longrightarrow$ red, FR 20 $\longrightarrow$ no S^R
b) $R'_{new} \longrightarrow$ green, FR 100 $\longrightarrow$ no S^R

any reinforcing value of the signals will presumably decline gradually and measured effects in this unstable situation will be very difficult to interpret.

Another way to measure reinforcing value of each signal is through measuring preferences for one signal over the other. However, again, the actual measurement would amount to adding a new link to a Chain, and would therefore encounter all the objections raised against the new-response method.

There is one method of comparing the effectiveness of each signal in maintaining observing behavior which does not involve adding a new link, and therefore avoids the objections to the new-response method. In this method one tests whether observing behavior was reinforced specifically by the informative nature of its consequences by retaining the same consequences in physical or sensory terms and eliminating their informative character. We did this by switching from MIX FR 20 FR 100 to FR 20 or FR 100, leaving other conditions unchanged.[2] What should happen? As the

---

[2] While our procedure may lead to extinction of the observing response, it differs from other procedures described as Extinction. In the Extinction procedure most commonly used to evaluate conditioned reinforcing value the pri-

animal learns that there is only a single set of contingencies and zero uncertainty, the frequency of observing behavior should gradually decline. It should not necessarily decline faster when FR 20 or FR 100 is in effect. Any difference between the rates of decline should be a result of differences in the time required for the bird to "notice" that the conditions have changed and that there is now zero rather than maximal uncertainty.[3] Note that with this method we are not "changing the rules." Each signal retains the significance it previously had.

If one does not appeal to the concept of information, no unequivocal prediction can apparently be made. The information interpretation is that the signals reinforce by reducing uncertainty; alternative interpretations assume that the signals reinforce by virtue of their association with reinforcement. Now, when the schedule is

---

mary reinforcement is discontinued. A specified response may then produce the signal previously associated with the more favorable schedule, the signal previously associated with the less favorable schedule, or no signal. Such a procedure may be criticized because it presents the animal with an essentially new problem, since the response-produced stimuli no longer have the same significance. However, it has not been an uncommon finding with such a procedure that the less-favorable or "negative" stimulus maintains more behavior than the more favorable or "positive" stimulus. Such a result constitutes a difficult paradox if the behavior is considered to be maintained by the residual conditioned reinforcing effect of the stimuli. However, such a result is to be expected according to the information interpretation. The test procedure is not symmetrical with respect to the two stimuli. When the negative stimulus is S^Δ (no primary reinforcement) the testing procedure ensures that the S^Δ retains its significance. On the other hand, the S^D loses its significance during the test procedure. A recent experiment by Myers and Morningstar (1968) used the relevant procedures in a straightforward way and gave quite clear results. Children pushed a button to produce S^D and candy or S^Δ and no candy. In Extinction most responding was sustained by S^Δ, less by S^D, and least by no stimulus. A similar result was obtained in an earlier, well-controlled study by Bitterman, Feddersen and Tyler (1953). Rats ran an alley to distinctive baited or unbaited goal boxes. Running to the previously unbaited goal box was more resistant to Extinction (comparison of Groups II–N and II–S).

[3] This interpretation is different from, though related to, the "discrimination hypothesis" of conditioned reinforcement. According to the discrimination hypothesis, responses attributed to conditioned reinforcement are emitted because the testing situation is similar to the situation which sustains the primarily reinforced behavior. The persistence of the relevant behavior in the test situation depends upon the degree of similarity of the test situation and the training situation. This hypothesis applies to the interpretation of data about conditioned reinforcement obtained after the withdrawal of primary reinforcement. When primary reinforcement is continued, as in our test procedures, there is no firm basis to predict from the discrimination hypothesis whether or not observing behavior will be sustained. The information interpretation demands that observing behavior decline, and we may guess that its rate of decline, reflecting a behavioral process, will depend upon how easily detectable is the change in condition.

changed from MIX *FR* 20 *FR* 100 or MULT *FR* 20 *FR* 100 to *FR* 20 (or *FR* 100) the association of the optional stimulus with reinforcement is just what it was before and there is no change in the schedule of reinforcement of the observing response. Therefore, there should be no change in observing behavior. Observing behavior is sometimes reinforced by a red signal (*FR* 20) and sometimes by a green (*FR* 100). According to the traditional reinforcement-theory interpretation red is more reinforcing than green. In the Mixed schedule the strength of the observing behavior represents some kind of average of the reinforcing effect of red and green. Therefore, when the schedules are used singly rather than mixed, the observing behavior should be even stronger in one component (presumably in the case of *FR* 20). It must be noted, however, that none of those predictions from reinforcement theory is clearly implied by the theory. Only the information interpretation gives a clear prediction.

We pursued the implications of this reasoning by alternating MIX *FR* 20 *FR* 100 with *FR* 20 and *FR* 100 with P–1 and P–2 in an extended session. In one case we made *FR* 20 the first single schedule, and in the other case *FR* 100. The changes in the probability of observing behavior are shown in Figure 12.6. The results show:

1. A decline in the probability of observing behavior when *FR* 20 or *FR* 100 is in effect.
2. A rise in the probability of observing behavior when MIX *FR* 20 *FR* 100 is restored.
3. An apparently faster decline in the probability of observing behavior during *FR* 20 than during *FR* 100.

The third point is brought out more clearly in Figure 12.7, which shows the cumulated frequency of completed observing ratios in the sessions of *FR* 20 or *FR* 100 rather than the Mixed schedule. Clearly, observing behavior is less persistent when it always produces the red stimulus (*FR* 20) than when it always produces the green stimulus (*FR* 100). We do not conclude from this that the signal for *FR* 100 is more reinforcing than that for *FR* 20. Instead, we conclude that the change from MIX *FR* 20 *FR* 100 to *FR* 20 is more quickly detected than is the change to *FR* 100. With *FR* 20 or *FR* 100 on the left key the key colors produced by responses on the right key have the character of irrelevant stimuli, not signals, since they carry no information. The inference that *FR* 20 is more easily

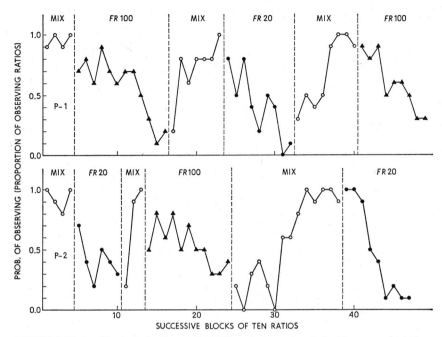

FIGURE 12.6. Changes in the probability of observing behavior as a function of the schedule of primary reinforcement. Observing behavior produced the stimuli associated with *FR* 20 (red) or *FR* 100 (green). Either the Mixed schedule was in effect, or *FR* 20 only, or *FR* 100 only. The observing-response schedule was *FR* 8 for P–1 and *FR* 4 for P–2.

discriminable from MIX *FR* 20 *FR* 100 than is *FR* 100 is a secondary point. The most important result is the demonstration that the signals for *FR* 20 and *FR* 100 can sustain observing behavior much more reliably in the context of the Mixed schedule (MIX *FR* 20 *FR* 100) than they can separately. In no way can one average the value of *FR* 20 and *FR* 100 signals to produce a higher value for the Mixed case. Thus, the basic assumption of the reinforcement-theory interpretation is untenable.

SERIES B

All the experiments in this series used a two-key Concurrent-Chain procedure. The first link in both Chains was always *FR* 10 and both response keys were always white during the first link. The second-link schedules were various combinations of ratio schedules, selected for particular purposes.

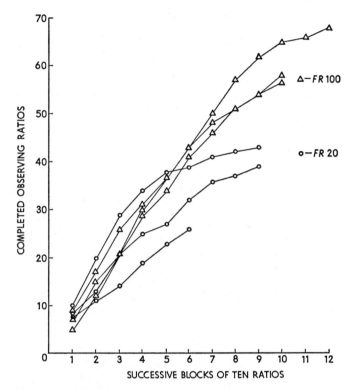

FIGURE 12.7. The cumulated completed observing ratios after three transitions from MIX *FR* 20 and three transitions
from MIX *FR* 20 *FR* 100 to *FR* 100. The data are taken from
Figure 12.6.

Two adult, male pigeons, previously untrained, were exposed to
all procedures in Experiments in Series B. Each session lasted for
50 reinforcements.

Experiments B1, B2, and B3

The second links in Experiments B1, B2, and B3 were designed
to vary in the degree of uncertainty that they represented for the
birds. The procedures are diagrammed in Figure 12.8. The left
white key represents minimal uncertainty since the condition that
follows (*FR X*) is fixed (where *X* is the same number for a large
number of sessions). In Experiment B1 the right white key represents most uncertainty, since one of two schedules is equally likely

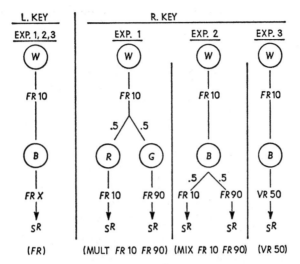

FIGURE 12.8. Representation of the procedures for Experiments B1, B2, and B3. All procedures were two-key Concurrent Chains. Minimal uncertainty was induced for left key responding, in the sense that the second link had fixed contingencies. On the right key maximal uncertainty was induced, in the sense that the second link in the Chain had variable contingencies. The uncertainty on the right key was reduced in Experiment B1, by having signals in the second link; and not reduced in Experiments B2 and B3, by having no signals in the second link. The letters in the circles represent colors on the keys: W is white, R is red, G is green and B is blue. In all experiments the choice between the left and right keys was exclusive. The 10th peck of the white, left (right) key changed its color and darkened the right (left) key. Responses on the dark key had no effect. Both keys turned white again following reinforcement.

to follow. The situation is exactly the same in Experiment B2, except that the different schedules are not signaled (by red and green keys), so uncertainty is not reduced. Before considering Experiment B3, note that the Experiments, through variation of X in $FR\ X$, were designed to determine a preference function, rather than simply a single value of preference. We expected that the difference between preference functions for Experiments B1 and B2 would indicate the value of reduction of uncertainty in the second link during Experiment B1. However, the preference functions for Experiments B1 and B2 were remarkably similar, and this result prompted us to do Experiment B3. We reasoned that in MIX $FR\ 10\ FR\ 90$ the birds could obtain all the information by the occurrence or nonoccurrence of reinforcement after 10 pecks. In Experiment B3, therefore, we replaced the MIX $FR\ 10\ FR\ 90$ schedule with $VR\ 50$. The $VR\ 50$ was obtained by reinforcing every

10th response with a probability of 0.2. The *VR* 50 schedule required the same mean number of responses per primary reinforcement (50) as the Mixed schedule of Experiment B2 and the Multiple schedule of Experiment B1, but the occurrence of reinforcement could not be predicted from the previous nonoccurrence of reinforcement. That is, even if the animal could count 10 responses he could not thereby reduce the uncertainty about reinforcement for the next 10 responses.

One general feature of the results in Series B Experiments should be mentioned: by using an *FR* 10 schedule as the initial link we were successful in making the bird's choice of one key or the other definite and unequivocal. On very few occasions did a bird initiate responding on one key and then switch to the other key. Once responding began the initial *FR* 10 was run off rapidly. This performance contrasts with what we could expect if the initial link had been a variable-interval (*VI*) schedule. With an initial *VI* there would have been fairly rapid switching from one key to another (rather than exclusive choice of one key), probably because such behavior incurs no penalty and tends to maximize reinforcements (stimulus changes) per response.

Figure 12.9 shows the preference functions relating choice of MULT *FR* 10 *FR* 90 (Experiment B1), MIX *FR* 10 *FR* 90 (Experiment B2), and *VR* 50 (Experiment B3) to *FR X*, the size of the *FR* in the other option. The *FR* schedule equivalent to (50 percent preference) MULT *FR* 10 *FR* 90 (Experiment B1) is about *FR* 20 and that equivalent to MIX *FR* 10 *FR* 90 (Experiment B2) is also about *FR* 20. It was this result that prompted Experiment B3. Experiments B1 and B2 were designed to differ maximally in the informative consequences of responding on the right key and yet the preference functions were very similar. As noted, we thought that the birds' own behavior might have a signaling relation to the two ratio components on the left key and we eliminated this source of uncertainty-reduction by using the *VR* 50 schedule. Note that the *VR* 50 schedule is also a Mixed schedule, containing *FR* 10, *FR* 20, *FR* 30, etc., rather than only *FR* 10 and *FR* 90. The *FR* schedule equivalent to *VR* 50 is about *FR* 30. To evaluate the difference between preference functions we ranked the preferences (percentage values) for various values of *FR X* over the Multiple or Mixed schedules and tested the hypothesis that these ranks were from the same population. The results showed that the preference for *FR X*

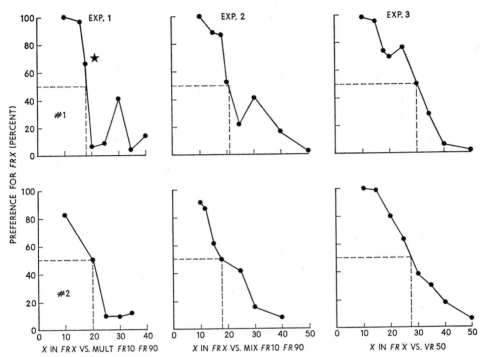

FIGURE 12.9. P–1 and P–2. Experiments 1, 2, and 3, Series B. *FR X* v. MULT *FR* 10 *FR* 90 (Experiment 1), MIX *FR* 10 *FR* 90 (Experiment 2), and *VR* 50 (Experiment 3). Preference for *FR X* as a function of *X*. Means of last 3–4 sessions (150–200 reinforcements). The starred point represents the mean of two determinations with *X* ascending (100 percent) and descending (32 percent).

over the Mixed schedule (Experiment B2) was not different from the preference for the *FR X* over the Multiple schedule, but the preference for *FR X* over the *VR* schedule (Experiment B3) was greater than the preference for *FR X* over the Multiple schedule. That is, in Figure 12.9 the curve for Experiment B3 as compared with Experiment B1 is reliably displaced to the right. This indicates that MULT *FR* 10 *FR* 90 is more "attractive" or reinforcing than it would be on the basis of reinforcement frequency alone, supporting the original hypothesis that the signals in MULT *FR* 10 *FR* 90 are a source of reinforcement through reduction of uncertainty.

The rate of reinforcement in *FR X* and in MULT *FR* 10 *FR* 90 are compared for birds 1 and 2 in Figure 12.10 and 12.11, respectively. Both birds maintained a near-constant response rate in the

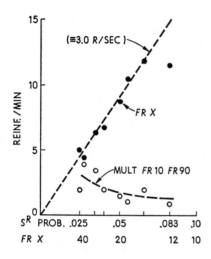

FIGURE 12.10. P–1. Experiment B1. *FR X* v. MULT *FR* 10 *FR* 90. Rates of primary reinforcement as a function of *X*. The rates for *FR* X and for MULT *FR* 10 *FR* 90 are given. The abscissa is linear with respect to reinforcements per response, so that constant response rate plots as a straight line.

FR X (about 3.0*R*/sec for P–1 and 2.5 *R*/sec for P–2), resulting in a reinforcement rate directly proportional to $1/X$. The reinforcement rate (the total number of occasions *FR* 10 or *FR* 90 was obtained divided by total duration of *FR* 10 or *FR* 90) in the Multiple schedule was always lower than in *FR X*. With smaller *FR X*, longer initial pauses appeared during green (*FR* 90), producing a lower overall response rate and a lower overall reinforcement rate.

It should be noted from comparisons of Figures 12.9, 12.10, and 12.11 that the birds showed a strong preference for the Multiple

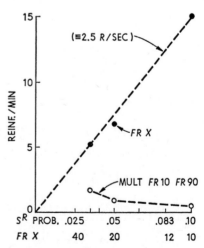
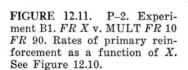

FIGURE 12.11. P–2. Experiment B1. *FR X* v. MULT *FR* 10 *FR* 90. Rates of primary reinforcement as a function of *X*. See Figure 12.10.

schedules even to values of *FR X* which produced a considerably higher reinforcement rate.

Experiment B4

Experiments B1 and B2 had failed to show a clear preference for MIX *FR* 10 *FR* 90 or MULT *FR* 10 *FR* 90, as measured by their equally preferred *FR* schedules. In Experiment B4 these schedules were directly compared, with the procedure diagrammed in Figure 12.12. The main result was a marked preference, ranging from 75

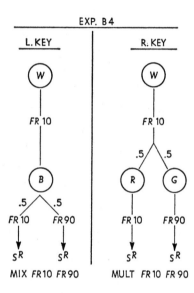

FIGURE 12.12. Representation of the procedure for Experiment B4. Conventions as for Figure 12.8.

percent–100 percent over many sessions, for the Multiple schedule. Figure 12.13 shows, for bird P–1, that the Multiple schedule was preferred (left bars), that it controlled, in the initial *FR* 10 link, a higher response rate (middle bars), but that it produced a lower reinforcement rate (right bars). On the extreme right of Figure 12.13 the reinforcement rate on the Multiple schedule is shown broken down into the reinforcement rates in the two components (*FR* 10 and *FR* 90).[4] Cumulative records of performance are shown in Figures 12.14 and 12.15.

---

[4] The results for P–2 were similar. However, in most sessions P–2 chose the Multiple schedule almost 100 percent of the time, giving too few data in the other Chain to furnish comparable statistics of response rates and reinforcement rates. The data that were obtained, in scattered sessions, did conform to the pattern of results shown in Figure 12.13.

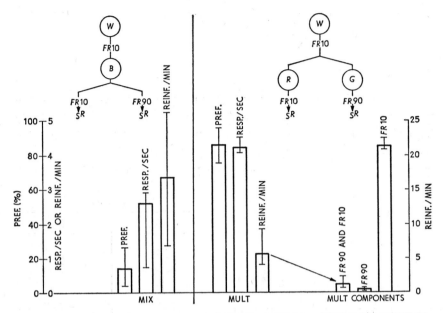

FIGURE 12.13. P–1. Experiment B4. MIX *FR* 10 *FR* 90 v. MULT *FR* 10 *FR* 90. Preference, response rate in the initial link leading to each option, and reinforcement rate in each option. The bars give the medians of the means of criterion sessions, and the vertical lines give the ranges of the means. The three measures for the Mixed schedule are shown on the left, and for the Multiple schedule on the right. The reinforcement rate in the Multiple schedule is shown on the extreme right on a different scale broken down into the reinforcement rate in *FR* 10 and *FR* 90 separately. The response rate was calculated by averaging the reciprocal of interresponse-times. The reinforcement rate was calculated as the reciprocal of the mean duration of the second link in the Chain schedule.

The results of Experiment B4 conflict with those of Experiments B1 and B2. The three experiments seem to go counter to the rule: Things equal to the same thing are themselves equal. Both MIX *FR* 10 *FR* 90 and MULT *FR* 10 *FR* 90 are equally preferred to approximately *FR* 20 (Experiments B1 and B2) but MIX *FR* 10 *FR* 90 and MULT *FR* 10 *FR* 90 are not themselves equally preferred (Experiment B4). Perhaps this is simply another example of the nontransitivity of preferences; perhaps it is due to some idiosyncrasy of our experimental methods. However, I wish to draw attention to the conflict in a cautionary spirit, and identify it as of secondary importance. If Experiment B3 was not completely satisfactory in accounting for the failure of a difference to emerge in Experiments B1 and B2 between the reinforcing value of Mixed and Multiple

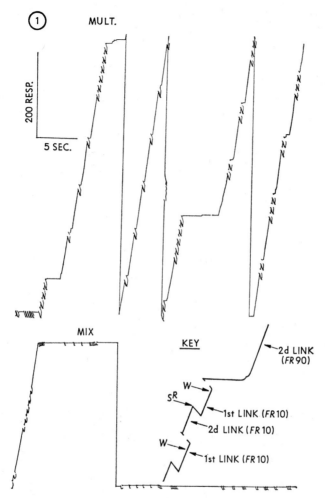

FIGURE 12.14. P–1. Experiment B4. Mixed ratios versus Multiple ratios. Typical cumulative records of final performance. The key at lower right shows how to interpret the records. The upper record, labeled MULT, shows performance on the right key (CHAIN *FR* 10 MULT *FR* 10 *FR* 90) and the lower record shows performance on the left key (CHAIN *FR* 10 MIX *FR* 10 *FR* 90). Both pens offset together to distinguish first and second links.

schedules, the results of Experiment B4 leave no doubt that the MULT *FR* 10 *FR* 90 is more reinforcing than MIX *FR* 10 *FR* 90. The Multiple schedule is strongly preferred, and responses reinforced by the appearance of the Multiple schedule are emitted at a higher rate (Figure 12.13). These results are in accordance with expectations derived from our original suppositions about the con-

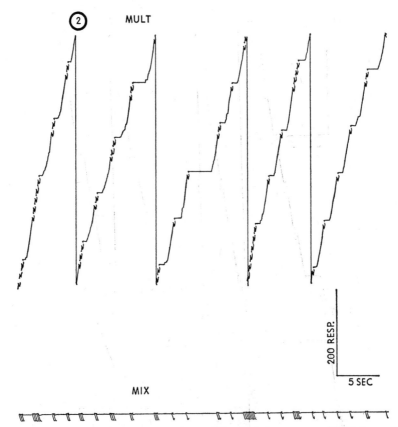

FIGURE 12.15.   P–2. Experiment B4. Mixed ratios versus Multiple ratios. Typical cumulative records of final performance. See Figure 12.14. Note that the CHAIN *FR* 10 MIX *FR* 10 *FR* 90 was never chosen in this session.

ditions that may generate uncertainty and the reinforcing effect of reduction of uncertainty.

Experiment B5

In Experiment B4 it could just conceivably be argued that the birds preferred red and green to blue key lights. The procedure in Experiment B5, shown in Figure 12.16, represents a final step in reducing the physical and sensory differences between the contingencies on the two keys, while retaining differences in terms of the informative consequences of responding on them. The consequences of responding on the two keys are identical, except that red and

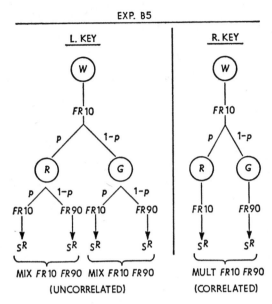

FIGURE 12.16. Representation of the procedure for Experiment B5. Conventions as for Figure 12.8. Performance was stabilized with $p = 0.2$, 0.5, and 0.8.

green on the right are correlated with the schedules of reinforcement, while red and green on the left key are not.

In this experiment, for reasons explained below, the proportion of short ratios (p) was set at 0.2, 0.5 and 0.8, performance being allowed to stabilize at each value.

The results are shown in Figures 12.17 and 12.18. Here again there was a very strong preference for the Multiple schedule (upper panel), irrespective of the proportion of short ratios. The scaling of the abscissa was devised so that a constant response rate would produce a linear plot in the lower panel of Figures 12.17 and 12.18. Thus, distances on the abscissa from 0.2–0.5 and 0.5–0.8 are in the ratio 13:37. The lower panels of Figures 12.17 and 12.18 show a close fit to a linear scale for the Mixed or *uncorrelated* schedule. This agrees with the observation (see cumulative records in Figures 12.19 and 12.20) that the birds responded at a fairly steady rate on the uncorrelated key up to the delivery of reinforcement. The large range of reinforcement rates on the uncorrelated schedule was not due to a variation in response rate, but was due to

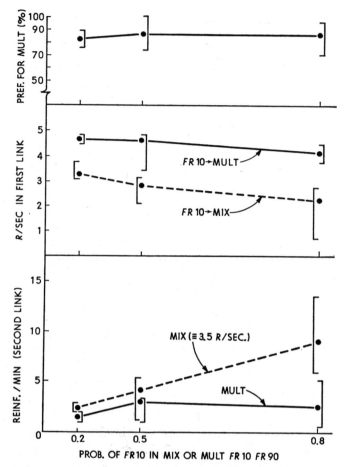

FIGURE 12.17.   P–1. Experiment B5. Mixed ratios versus Multiple ratios. Preference for Multiple ratios, response rate in the initial link leading to Mixed or Multiple ratios, and reinforcement rate in the final link (Mixed or Multiple), all as functions of the probability of *FR* 10 in the Mixed and Multiple schedule. The points are the medians of values obtained in 5–10 criterion sessions, and the brackets are the ranges of the values. The abscissa is scaled to yield a linear reinforcement rate in the bottom panel, given a constant response rate.

the (random) variability in the proportion of long and short *FR*s from session to session. The number of times the uncorrelated schedule was chosen was so small that the actual proportion of shorts *FR*s obtained in a session ranged from 100 percent to 0 percent.

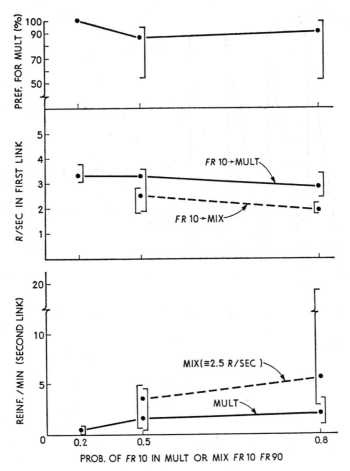

FIGURE 12.18. P–2. Experiment B5. Mixed ratios versus Multiple ratios. See Figure 12.17.

The preference for the Multiple schedule was again reflected in the response rates in the initial *FR* 10 link, shown in the middle panel of Figures 12.17 and 12.18.

Figures 12.19 and 12.20 show representative cumulative records of performance in Experiment B5.

Further attempts to relate performance to rates of reinforcement

It has recently been found that preference (relative rates in the first links of Concurrent Chains) can be better predicted from rela-

MULT

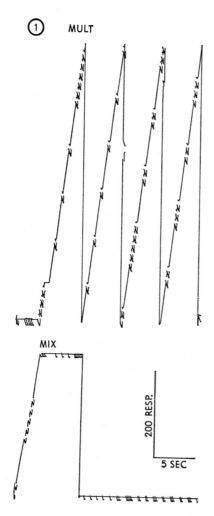

FIGURE 12.19. P–1. Experiment B5. Mixed ratios versus Multiple ratios. Typical cumulative records of final performance. See Figure 12.14 for key.

MIX

200 RESP.

5 SEC

tive rates of reinforcement in the second links when every occurrence of the second link is taken to represent a rate of reinforcement; it is these rates that are averaged to give average rate of reinforcement (Killeen, 1968). This has been referred to as the "harmonic" rate of reinforcement. That is, if the duration of a second link is d_i, the harmonic rate of reinforcement is:

$$1/n \sum_{i=1}^{n} 1/d_i$$

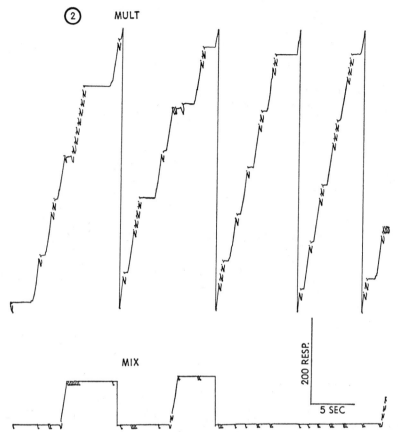

FIGURE 12.20.   P–2. Experiment B5. Mixed ratios versus Multiple ratios. Typical cumulative records of final performance. See Figure 12.14 for key.

as opposed to the arithmetic mean, which is:

$$n \,\bigg|\, \sum_{i=1}^{n} d_i$$

What would be the effect of using these different averages for the present results? Let us consider the second links, which were always ratio schedules. For purposes of analysis, let us assume a constant rate of responding (R responses per sec.) in the second links. Let us denote rate of reinforcement by "r," and indicate with subscripts "A" and "H" whether the rate is an arithmetic or harmonic mean. A second subscript, "X," "10," "90," "MIX," or

"MULT" indicates the schedule whose average rate of reinforcement is being considered.

Where the schedule is $FR\ X$,

$$r_{A,X} = R/X$$

Where the schedule is equally often $FR\ 10$ and $FR\ 90$,

$$d_{10} = 10/R$$

and

$$d_{90} = 90/R$$

Therefore,

$$r_{A,\text{MULT}} = r_{A,\text{MIX}} = 2/(10/R + 90/R)$$
$$= R/50$$

The two second links are equal in reinforcement rate (A.M.) when,

$$R/X = R/50$$

or

$$X = 50$$

This result is intuitively obvious; but the corresponding result using r_H is perhaps not so obvious.

For $FR\ X$,

$$r_{H,X} = 1/n \sum_{i=1}^{n} (R/X)_i$$

$$= 1/n(nR/X)$$
$$= R/X$$

since all $(R/X)_i$ are equal, on the assumption that R is constant. That is, the A.M. and H.M. of a set of constant values are equal. For $FR\ 10$ or $FR\ 90$,

$$r_{H,\text{MIX}} = r_{H,\text{MULT}}$$
$$= (R/10 + R/90)/2$$
$$= R/18$$

The two second links are equal in reinforcement rate (H.M.) when,

$$R/X = R/18$$

or

$$X = 18$$

These analytic relations are shown in Figure 13.21. The figure shows that rate of reinforcement:

a) in *FR X* is proportional to $1/X$ for both A.M. and H.M.

b) in *FR* 10 or *FR* 90 is a constant equal to the value of FR 50 for the A.M. and *FR* 18 for the H.M.

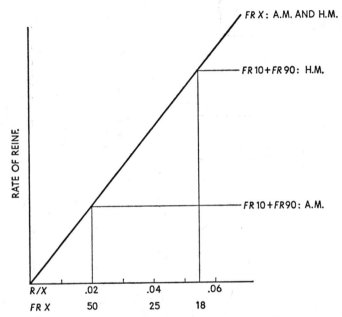

FIGURE 12.21. The effect of different ways of computing average rate of reinforcement, assuming a constant response rate. The arithmetic mean reinforcement rate for a fixed ratio is proportional to X, the number of responses per reinforcement. The value of the harmonic mean is the same. In the case of MIX *FR* 10 *FR* 90 the arithmetic mean is equal to that for *FR* 50, while the harmonic mean is equal to that for *FR* 18.

Complete data for calculation of these different averages were available for Experiment B2 (*FR X* v. MIX *FR* 10 *FR* 90) and Experiment B3 (*FR X* v. *VR* 50.)

   Experiment B2 (*FR versus MIX*). The average reinforcement rates in the second link for Experiment B2, both arithmetic means and harmonic means, are given in Figures 12.22 and 12.23. Briefly, the results conform quite well to the assumption of a constant response rate. For both birds the assumption is best met for the *FR X* second link where the A.M. and H.M. practically coincide and lie very close to the straight line that represents a constant

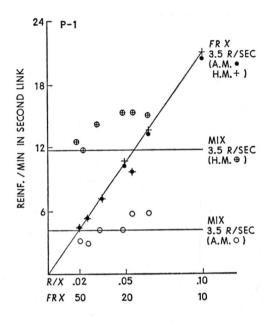

FIGURE 12.22. P–1. Experiment B2. The rates of reinforcement in the second link (arithmetic means and harmonic means). The second links were *FR X* or MIX *FR* 10 *FR* 90. The response rate was calculated from the straight line fitted to the arithmetic reinforcement rates for *FR X*. Data points were omitted where the schedule was chosen too infrequently to give reliable estimates of reinforcement rate.

response rate. The same rate in the MIX schedule would have produced points lying on the lower constant line for A.M. and the higher constant line for H.M. The obtained points do, in fact, lie reasonably close to those lines.

The intersection of the functions for H.M., as already explained,

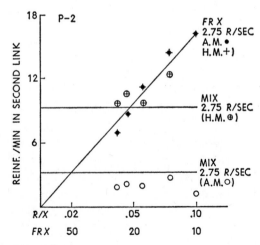

FIGURE 12.23.   P–2. Experiment B2. See Figure 12.22.

give an estimate of the FR equivalent in reinforcement rate to MIX FR 10 FR 90. This turns out to be FR 18 if the analytic function is used. If the best fits to the actual data points in Figures 12.22, and 12.23 are used, the values are about FR 15–20 for both birds. Referring back now to Figure 12.9, we see that the FR X and MIX FR 10 FR 90 are equally chosen when $X = 21$ for P–1 and $X = 18$ for P–2.

It is clear that the harmonic mean reinforcement rates in the second link predict the indifference point for FR X v. MIX FR 10

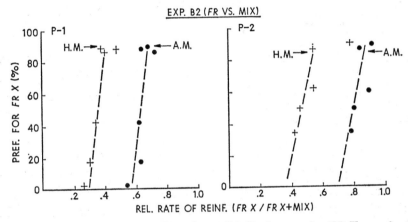

FIGURE 12.24. P–1 and P–2. Experiment B2. Preference for FR X as a function of relative reinforcement rates in the final links. Relative reinforcement rates were calculated from arithmetic means (A.M.) and harmonic means (H.M.) of reinforcement rates. The straight lines were fitted to the data points by inspection.

FR 90 much better than the arithmetic mean. How well does the relation between harmonic means of reinforcement rate match the preference for the schedules over all values of X? This is shown in Figure 12.24. Clearly, preference for FR X does not vary appreciably according to relative reinforcement rate, whether based on arithmetic or harmonic means. The effect of taking harmonic means, rather than arithmetic, is to lower all reinforcement rates by a constant factor, as would be expected if response rates were constant.

Similarly, relative response rates in the initial links (FR 10) were fairly constant, and showed no relation to relative reinforcement rates in the final links. This result is shown in Figure 12.25.

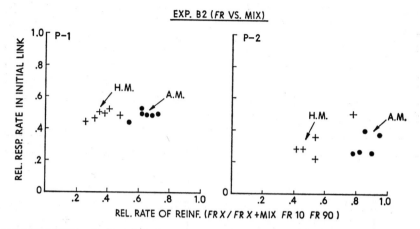

FIGURE 12.25. P-1 and P-2. Experiment B2. Relative response rates in initial links (*FR* 10) as a function of relative reinforcement rates in final links (*FR X* or MIX *FR* 10 *FR* 90). For the relative response rates in the initial links the rate of the initial link leading to *FR X* is the numerator. Relative reinforcement rates were calculated from arithmetic means (A.M.) and harmonic means (H.M.) of reinforcement rates.

Experiment B3 (FR versus VR). The arithmetic mean of the *VR* schedule used in Experiment B3 is $(1/0.2)\,10 = 50$. The *VR* schedule actually consists of *FR* 10, 20, 30, 40,—etc. which occur in the respective proportions $0.8^{n-1}(0.2)$, $(N = 1, 2, 3, \text{etc.})$, or 0.2, 0,16, 0.128, etc.

The harmonic mean rate of reinforcement, assuming a constant response rate, is the average of 1/10, 1/20, 1/30, etc., weighted in the proportion 0.2, 0.16, 0.128, etc.
That is,

$$r_{H,VR} = \left[\sum_{n=1}^{\infty} \frac{0.8^{n-1}(0.2)}{10n} \right]^{-1}$$

The expression converges, and

$$r_{H,VR} = 25$$

Figure 12.26 and 12.27 show the reinforcement rates for Experiment B3. P-1 has somewhat higher response rates in the *VR* schedule (therefore higher reinforcement rates) than the rate (2.9 *R*/sec) in *FR X*. Nevertheless, the reinforcement rates of both birds are fairly constant and the actually obtained harmonic mean

FIGURE 12.26. P–1. Experiment B3. The rates of reinforcement in the second links (arithmetic means and harmonic means). The second links were *FR X* or *VR* 50. The response rate was calculated from the straight line fitted to the arithmetic reinforcement rates for *FR X*.

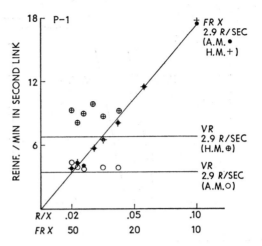

reinforcement rates of *FR X* and *VR* 50 are equal when X $\simeq$ 25. This would imply (if the birds were sensitive to harmonic rate of reinforcement) that *VR* 50 would be equivalent to about *FR* 25, rather than about *FR* 50 on the basis of arithmetic rate of reinforcement.

Figure 12.28 corresponds to Figure 12.24 and shows how preference for the *FR X* second link is related to relative arithmetic and harmonic mean reinforcement rates. As in the case of Experiment B2, preference does not vary appreciably according to relative

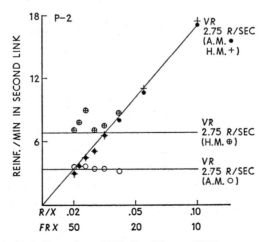

FIGURE 12.27. P–2. Experiment B3. See Figure 12.26.

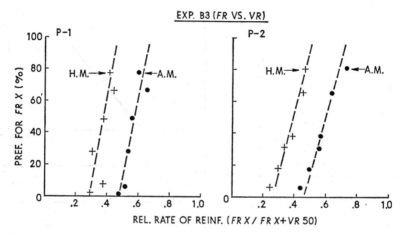

FIGURE 12.28.   P–1 and P–2. Experiment B3. Preference for *FR X* as a function of relative reinforcement rates in the final links. Relative reinforcement rates were calculated from arithmetic means (A.M.) and harmonic means (H.M.) of reinforcement rates. The straight lines were fitted to the data points by inspection.

reinforcement rate, and the effect of taking harmonic means, rather than arithmetic, is to lower all reinforcement rates by a constant factor, as would be expected if response rates were constant.

Again, as shown in Figure 12.29, relative response rates in the initial links (*FR* 10) were fairly constant, and showed no relation to relative reinforcement rates in the final links. Some of these rather complex relations are summarized in Table 12.1, which shows the reinforcement rates of MIX *FR* 10 *FR* 90 and *VR* 50, calculated on the assumption of a constant response rate. The estimates of the obtained reinforcement rates are essentially possible predictions of the equivalent *FR X* schedule, since the arithmetic and harmonic mean reinforcement rates are always the same for any value of *FR X*. The values of *FR X* actually found to be equivalent to the MIX and *VR* schedules are at the bottom of the table. These values are closer to the predictions based on harmonic means. However, this relative closeness of prediction may be misleading if it is not also noted that preference varied over its whole range with very small changes in relative reinforcing rate, as shown in Figure 12.24 and 12.28. Therefore, in spite of the fact that harmonic reinforcement rates came closer to predicting the value of *FR X* equivalent to MIX *FR* 10 *FR* 90 and *VR* 50, we have to

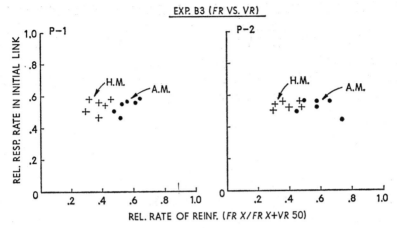

FIGURE 12.29. P–1 and P–2. Experiment B3. Relative response rates in initial links (*FR* 10) as a function of relative reinforcement rates in final links (*FR X* or *VR* 50). For the relative response rates in the initial links the rate of the initial link leading to *FR X* is the numerator. Relative reinforcement rates were calculated from arithmetic means (A.M.) and harmonic means (H.M.) of reinforcement rates.

conclude that relative reinforcement rate, whether based on arithmetic or harmonic means, is a poor predictor of preference in these experimental situations.

The calculated values in Table 12.1 were produced on the assumption of a constant response rate. The results in fact showed this to be a reasonable assumption. However, that assumption in

TABLE 12.1

Reinforcement Rates and Equivalent *FR X* Values for MIX *FR* 10 *FR* 90 (Experiment B2) and *VR* 50 (Experiment B3)

	MIX *FR* 10 *FR* 90			*VR* 50		
		Obtained (Est.)			Obtained (Est.)	
	Calculated	P–1	P–2	Calculated	P–1	P–2
Reinforcement rate (A.M.)..........50		50*	50†	50	40§	50″
Reinforcement rate (H.M.)..........18		15-20*	15-20†	25	25§	25″
Equiv. *FR X*........		21¶	18¶		30¶	27¶

* From Figure 12.22.   § From Figure 12.26.   ¶ From Figure 12.9.
† From Figure 12.23.   ″ From Figure 12.27.

the context of ratio schedules is equivalent to working with probabilities rather than reinforcement rates. Thus, we recall that for $FR\ X$, $r_{A,x} = R/X$. But, of course, $FR\ X$ is a probability of reinforcement of $1/X$, or $K(R/X)$, with K and R two constants. Therefore, every calculated value of reinforcement rate, whether arithmetic or harmonic, is also a value of probability of reinforcement, without any assumptions concerning response rate. We have no data to indicate whether rate or probability of reinforcement is the more effective variable in these experiments; we can say with fine impartiality that neither variable predicts preference or response rate in the initial links of the Concurrent Chain schedules we used.

Experiment B5 (*MIX versus MULT*). The Results of Experiment B1 showed a strong preference for the Multiple FR schedule over a single FR schedule with the same mean value. There seems to be a strong preference for variable contingencies no matter what the components are (e.g., Fantino, 1967; Herrnstein, 1964b; Logan, 1960). However, the results of Experiment B4 showed that the preference for the Multiple schedule was not a preference simply for a variety of contingencies; the birds preferred the cued variable contingencies to the same contingencies uncued.

Experiment B5 has conceptual affinities with a procedure used by Wyckoff (see Chapter 9). In his experiment periods of Extinction alternated unpredictably with periods of FI 30 sec and observing responses produced cues correlated with the two components. The observing response was performed when the cues were correlated with the component schedules (MULT FI EXT), but extinguished when the cues were uncorrelated (MIX FI EXT). Wyckoff assumed that probability of reinforcement in the presence of a cue determined its conditioned reinforcing value. Wyckoff therefore concluded (see Wyckoff, 1959) that the preference for the Multiple schedule implied that the function relating conditioned reinforcing value to probability of reinforcement was positively accelerated over part of its range. His reasoning, also essentially followed by Bower, McLean and Meacham (1966), can best be illustrated by reference to Figure 12.30. Figure 12.30 shows a finite value for the reinforcing value of FI 30 sec (or any other value of FI) and zero value for Extinction. These two values have to be averaged for MULT FI EXT and the average value has to be higher than the value corresponding to MIX FI EXT, in order to produce a preference for the Multiple schedule. Hence the conclusion of a positively accelerated curve.[5]

If one accepts Wyckoff's assumptions, mainly that, in the situation of the kind used in these experiments, conditioned-reinforcing value is a function of probability of reinforcement, then, indeed, one cannot escape Wyckoff's inference, or something closely resembling it, on the basis of his results, or those of Kelleher (1958a) who found that a "cued" combination of VR 100 and Extinction was preferred to the same combination uncued, or those of Experiment B1 in this study. There are many more studies whose results

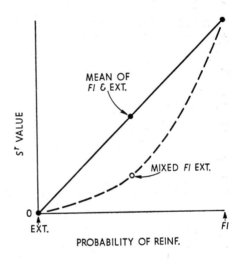

FIGURE 12.30. Illustration of the basis of Wyckoff's inference that the function relating conditioned reinforcing (S^r) value of a cue to the probability of reinforcement in its presence is positively accelerated over some of its range. (See text.)

would lead to the same inference (e.g., Bower, McLean, & Meacham, 1966; Fantino, 1967; Kelleher, Riddle, & Cook, 1962; Kendall, 1965a, 1965b; Lutz & Perkins, 1960; Mitchell, Perkins, & Perkins, 1965; Prokasy, 1956; Wehling & Prokasy, 1962). The generality of the preference for variable contingencies over fixed contingencies suggests, by Wyckoff's reasoning, that incentive as a

---

[5] Note that this argument assumes an arithmetic averaging rule for the values of cues associated with different components in a Multiple schedule. This assumption is itself unrealistic and arbitrary. Preference (in relative terms) for Multiple over Mixed schedules can be explained on the basis of any averaging rules that make one kind of average greater than another. One can then assign the rule that gives the lower average to the case of the Mixed schedule. The only justification for such a tactic is the generality of its success. Further observations on Wyckoff's assumptions are made in Chapter 14.

function of probability of reinforcement is positively accelerated over *all* of its range. Such a conclusion is unpalatable because other incentive functions are negatively accelerated. Wyckoff's objective was to derive the effect of a combination of cues from the properties they may be expected to have when isolated. This takes no account of the possibility that combinations of things may have emergent properties that the things separately do not have. It should be clear on reflection that information is something that can be given by one of at least a pair of events. It would be ludicrous, not to say mathematically incorrect, to search for the informative function of an event out of the context in which it serves that function. Information cannot be a property of an isolated event. The unit of information, one bit, implies two possible events.

Even though the results (Figure 12.13) showed that the preferred Multiple schedule provided a *lower* reinforcement rate than the nonpreferred Mixed schedule, some new averaging rule might be found to reverse this result, such that the average reinforcement rate would turn out higher for the Multiple schedule.

Experiment B5 was designed with a view to distinguishing between our information analysis of the preference for a Multiple schedule and interpretations that appealed to advantages of the Multiple schedule in terms of differential primary reinforcement, no matter how the effects of the components were averaged. We knew that the proportion of short FRs would probably affect the mean reinforcement rate in Multiple and Mixed schedules differently, conferring a different degree of advantage on the Mixed schedule in terms of reinforcement rate. On the other hand, according to the information interpretation, changing the proportion of short FRs would affect the initial uncertainty and, therefore, the reinforcing effect of the cues, in a known way.

Our reasoning can be understood by reference to Figure 12.31. Varying the proportion of FR 10 in the Mixed and Multiple schedules did differentially affect the reinforcement rates (reinforcements per minute) in the two schedules. This can be seen in the bottom panel of Figures 12.17 and 12.18. With more FR 10s the difference in reinforcement rate favoring the Mixed schedule increases; this increase (transformed) is shown as the broken line in Figure 12.31. The unbroken line in Figure 12.31 represents the information given by the cues in the Multiple schedule (or the uncertainty in the absence of the cues), which, of course, depends only on the proportions of the two components. Therefore, according to a "differential primary reinforcement" interpretation, the preference for the Multiple schedule in Experiment B5 should have been greater the more infrequent the *FR* 10 no matter what the averaging rule was, *so long as the same rule were applied to both the Mixed and Multiple schedules.* According to the information interpretation, preference for the Multiple schedule should have been greatest when *FR* 10 and *FR* 90 were equally likely.

Figure 12.17 and Figure 12.18 show a more or less constant

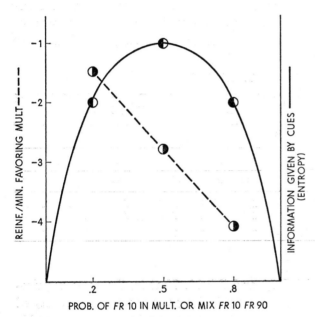

FIGURE 12.31. Comparison of two bases for assessing the relative attractiveness of Mixed and Multiple schedules as a function of the probability of one component. The direction of the left scale was chosen for ease of comparison with the top sections of Figures 12.17 and 12.18. (See text.)

preference for the Multiple schedule, a result which supports neither interpretation. Perhaps the range of variation of *p* was insufficient to produce variations of preference.

We may extend our previous analysis in terms of reinforcement probability, applied to Experiments B2 and B3, to the case of Experiment B5, to determine whether the obtained preference relations might reflect conditioned reinforcing values of cues associated with particular probabilities. The mean probability of reinforcement of *FR* 10 and *FR* 90 is $(1/10 + 1/90)/2 = 1/18$. By this computation the *FR* equivalent to MIX *FR* 10 *FR* 90 is *FR* 18, not *FR* 50, the mean of the ratios. For Experiment B5, however, there are various ways of calculating probabilities of reinforcement depending on the relative frequency of FR 10 and the correlation of key color with component FR schedules.

Table 12.2 gives various calculated probabilities of reinforcement in the experiment. The overall probability of reinforcement is, of course, the same on both keys, so that must be an irrelevant variable with no effect in determining preference. To explain the observed preference, then, one must discover an appropriate rule for averaging the probabilities of reinforcement of the red and green cue separately. One cannot combine probabilities of reinforcement of cues at the most basic level, exposure-by-exposure, because by that method both sides are identical, containing the

TABLE 12.2

Two Calculations of Probability of Reinforcement As a Function of Probability of FR 10 in a Combination (MIX or MULT) of FR 10 and FR 90. (Experiment B5)

Probability of FR 10	Overall Prob. of S^R (both keys) $\left(\dfrac{\text{Total } S^R}{\text{Total Resp.}}\right)$	Color-by-Color Probability of S^R					
		Right Key (MULT)			Left Key (MIX)		
		Red	Green	Mean	Red	Green	Mean
0.2.........0.013		.10	.011	.055	.029	.029	.029
0.5.........0.020		.10	.011	.055	.055	.055	.055
0.8.........0.039		.10	.011	.055	.082	.082	.082

same proportions of FR 10 and FR 90. That is, the ratio requirements are the same on both sides. Ruling our overall probability of reinforcement and exposure-by-exposure probability as possible measures, one is left only with what one may call color-by-color probabilities. Reinforcements per response on the left red key and the left green key is sometimes 0.10 and sometimes 0.011. The mean of these is 0.055. Weighting 0.10 according to the probability of occurrence of the short ratio gives 0.029 ($p = 0.2$) and 0.082 ($p = 0.8$), as shown in columns 6 and 7 of Table 12.2.

Comparison of columns 5 and 8 of Table 12.2 does not look promising in accounting for the results. Preference did not vary according to any simple transformation of these sets of numbers. If one weighted the Multiple schedule components according to relative frequency of occurrence of the components one would end up with the same probabilities as for the Mixed schedule in column 8. In short, there appears to be no simple way of accounting for the preference for MULT FR 10 FR 90 over MIX FR 10 FR 90 by averaging the probabilities of reinforcement represented by the contingencies. Results of Series A experiments led to a similar conclusion.

We revert to our explanation that the red cues and green cues reduced uncertainty in Experiment B5 when they appeared on the right (MULT) key but not on the left (MIX) key. Although this explanation seems the only one able to account for most of the observed preferences it does so in only a gross way because it stands in need of precise quantitative expression. Moreover, this explanation suffered two notable failures. In Experiment B5 it falsely predicted changes in preference for MULT FR 10 FR 90 as a function of probability of FR 10. In Experiment A2, observing behavior persisted when it had no informative effect (Figure 12.5). These failures, however, are not so complete and fundamental as the failure of the concept of differential food-reinforcement to account for the results.

SUMMARY

Uncertainty was established by programming a large and a small fixed-ratio schedule in an unpredictable sequence. In some cases, the subjects (pigeons) reduced uncertainty by observing responses which produced identifying signals on a fixed-ratio schedule. Observing behavior was sustained at considerable cost in terms of frequency of primary reinforcement. In other cases subjects avoided uncertainty by choosing fixed contingencies or the same variable contingencies with identifying signals.

Analysis of the experimental data revealed no possibility of deriving the conditioned reinforcing value of the pair of cues associated with the two FRs from the conditioned reinforcing value of each cue in isolation. The results are interpreted in terms of a reinforcing effect of reduction of uncertainty.

chapter 13

RESPONSE-CUE CONTINGENCY AND CUE EFFECTIVENESS[1]

Ronald E. Schaub

State University of New York at Buffalo

Stimuli associated with primary reinforcement in an instrumental learning situation are known to have what is called discriminative stimulus (S^D) properties. Furthermore, if such stimuli can be produced by an animal, these stimuli may then become reinforcers (S^r). Indeed, the response contingency may be the only characteristic which separates these two functions (Keller & Schoenfeld, 1950). But what about stimuli associated not with primary reinforcement but instead with extinction (EXT). We know that such EXT stimuli will serve to suppress responding in their presence. This is the familiar S^Δ function. Suppose cues associated with EXT were now produced by some response of the animal. It would be reasonable to suppose that such cues would have a suppressive function, and that they would act as conditioned punishers (S^p).

The empirical question as to whether indeed such an S^p function can be developed is still open, as Leitenberg (1965) has pointed out. At any rate, there would be little reason to suppose that cues correlated with EXT components are *reinforcing*. Nevertheless, there is considerable indirect evidence which suggests that this might be true. For example, a number of observing response studies have shown that animals will maintain substantial rates of

[1] The research reported in this paper is based on a doctoral dissertation submitted in partial fulfillment of the requirements for the Ph.D. degree, department of psychology, Dalhousie University, Halifax, Nova Scotia. This research was supported by Grant APB-102 from the National Research Council of Canada to W. K. Honig. The author wishes to thank W. K. Honig for his generous assistance and encouragement throughout the course of this research.

responses that produce cues associated with EXT (Kelleher, 1958b; Kelleher, Riddle, & Cook, 1962; Schaub & Honig, 1967; Wyckoff, 1952). In fact, Kelleher's study showed that, under certain conditions, the rate of observing (cue-producing) behavior was higher in EXT than in positive components. It appears reasonable to assume that the EXT cues in these experiments had reinforcing rather than punishing effects.

These findings suggest that an alternative hypothesis is required which includes a reanalysis of the traditional "associative" functions. We might begin with the observation that conditioned reinforcers derive their power from two correlated but distinct mechanisms. One such mechanism may be associative; the neutral stimulus through contiguity with the primary reinforcer may itself become reinforcing. Such a mechanism should also result in aversive characteristics for stimuli associated with EXT. On the other hand, these same contingencies may result in the stimuli acquiring informative value, and the production of information may be in itself reinforcing. Considering informative value, it does not matter whether a cue is correlated with reinforcement or EXT components, as long as its occurrence reduces uncertainty (Berlyne, 1957). Thus, both kinds of cues may be positively reinforcing when made response-dependent. This latter function can be recognized as an extension of the information hypothesis (Egger & Miller, 1962, 1963) and has previously been suggested as an explanation of the observing-response kind of experiment (Schaub & Honig, 1967; Hendry, 1965; Hendry & Coulbourn, 1967).

The following series of experiments represents an attempt to separate the functional roles of brief intermittent cues by varying the response-cue contingency. The paradigm is similar to that previously reported by Schaub and Honig. Briefly, pairs of birds were trained on a discrimination in which periods of intermittent food reinforcement (*VI* 1) alternated unpredictably with periods of EXT. The duration of the separate components varied from 2 to 10 min in such a way that each made up one half of the session. By pecking at the food-producing key, one member of each pair—designated the master bird—could also change the illumination of that key from white to red or green for 1.5 sec on a *FR* 3 schedule. (Red and green were correlated with the two components of the schedule in a counterbalanced order). When the color changed on the master bird's key, an identical color change occurred for the second member of each pair—the yoked bird. Thus, for the master bird, the cues could serve discriminative and reinforcing (or punishing) functions since they were both response-dependent and systematically related to the availability of food reinforcement. For the yoked birds, the cues could serve only a discriminative function since they were not response-dependent but still related in the same way to the availability of reinforcement. The first experiment was primarily a replication of the Schaub and Honig (1967) study with some variations in procedure detailed below.

EXPERIMENT 1a

Four pairs of subjects were used. Master birds produced both positive (VI) and EXT cues for themselves and their partners. The procedure described above was continued for 25, 1-hour sessions. The performance is described in terms of a discrimination ratio (DR) which represents the proportion of total responses per session made during the EXT components. If there is no difference in the rate of response between the positive and EXT components the DR is 0.50. If birds show perfect discrimination (no responding during EXT) the ratio is 0.00. Discrimination ratios were calculated for each bird for each session. The results are represented in Figure 13.1. While the mean DR for both master and yoked groups is less than 0.50 after this training (indicating fewer responses during EXT) it is clear that the yoked subjects responded proportionately less in EXT components than master birds. This difference was apparent in all four pairs of birds.

It is conceivable that the higher DR for the master birds simply represents poorer discriminative control. In order to determine whether the master birds were distinguishing the colors, the response rate when the key was red or green was calculated for each component for the 25 sessions. These results are seen in Figure 13.2. Both master and yoked groups show good discrimination between VI and EXT cues with insufficient difference between the groups to account for the differences in DRs shown in Figure 13.1. Thus the differences in overall discriminative performance (DRs) must be due in part to differences in the responding to the white key.

Furthermore, the pattern of responding was distinctive for the two groups. An example of cumulative recordings for master and yoked birds is seen in Figure 13.3. During EXT components (indi-

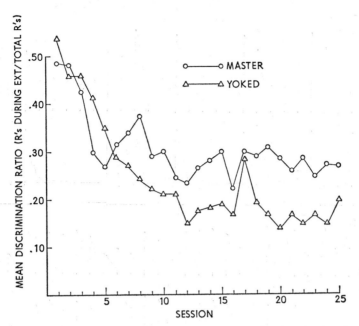

FIGURE 13.1. Mean discrimination ratios for master and yoked groups as a function of training session.

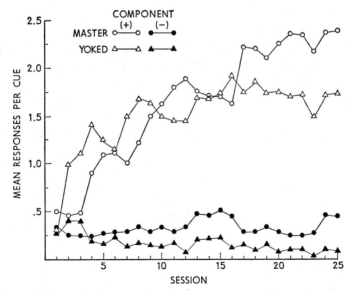

FIGURE 13.2. Mean number of responses per cue for master and yoked groups as a function of component and session.

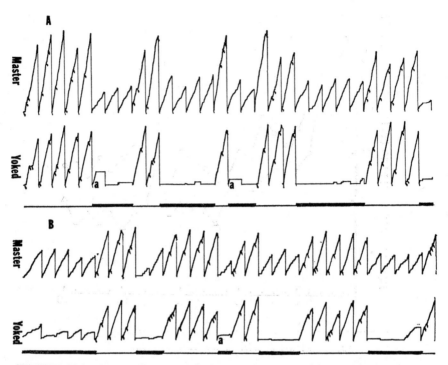

FIGURE 13.3   Cumulative records for master-yoked pair at asymptotic performance. The dark bar shows when periods of EXT were in effect. The pen reset every 2 min.

cated by the dark bar) master birds responded in a steady pattern. In contrast, yoked birds either responded at the same rate as during the *VI* component or ceased responding altogether. Since the amount of discriminative "information" was equal for both groups, the results suggested that the production of the EXT cue reinforced the master bird's responding in EXT. One reason for the failure of the yoked birds to show perfect discrimination can also be seen in the cumulative records. At the beginning of many of the EXT components, yoked birds continued responding after the presentation of the first EXT cue (marked "a"). Apparently a number of such cues was required before yoked birds ceased responding.

EXPERIMENT 1b

In order to test the degree of stimulus control exerted by the *VI* and EXT stimuli respectively, either the *VI* or EXT cues were systematically withheld for a single session (in a counterbalanced order) without changing the schedules of reinforcement. The results of this procedure are represented in Figure 13.4, which compares the session during which only a single cue was available (Test) with the mean *DR* of the immediately preceding session (Pre-test). (Since it might be expected that the withholding of cues during one component for the master bird would alter its response

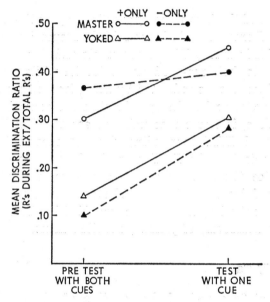

FIGURE 13.4. Mean discrimination ratios for pre-test (both cues) and test (single cue) sessions.

rate in both components, the resulting effects on the cues received by the yoked bird would be twofold. [1] There would be no cues during one component. [2] The frequency and distribution of cues in the second component would vary. Since, for the yoked birds, we were only interested in the effect of the former operation, the frequency and distribution of the remaining cues was kept constant by "artificially" programming them. This was achieved by tape recording cue signals from master birds during "regular" sessions, and using these tapes to program cues for the yoked birds during the "test" session.) All subgroups showed a reliable increase in *DR* on the test session except master birds receiving the EXT cue only.[2] Thus it appeared that EXT component behavior for master birds was directly attributable to characteristics of the EXT cues. The withholding of the *VI* cue had little effect on the overall distribution of responses in the two components, suggesting that it had acquired little stimulus control.

Discussion

The results of the first study appear to support those reported by Schaub and Honig (1967). Master birds respond at higher rates than yoked birds during EXT components and this difference must be attributed to their cue-producing behavior while the key light is white. Furthermore, as indicated by Experiment 1b, master birds' performance was under the specific stimulus control of the EXT cues. Therefore, it seems reasonable to assume that these specific cues reinforced EXT responding for the master birds. Since, through association, the EXT cues should acquire only aversive characteristics, the effectiveness of these cues as reinforcers must be determined by other factors. The reinforcing properties are possibly determined by information provided by the cues about the arrival (or nonarrival) of primary reinforcement.

EXPERIMENT 2a

Experiment 2a examined the question of whether the level of behavioral control observed in the first study could be established using only a single cue (*either* positive [*VI*] or negative [EXT]). One theoretical explanation of the reinforcing effectiveness of EXT cues has been that they derive their power from some averaged reinforcing effectiveness of positive and EXT cues taken together (Bower, McLean, & Meacham, 1966; Kelleher & Gollub, 1962; Wyckoff, 1959). In other words, the conditioned reinforcing effect of cues associated with primary reinforcement "spreads" to the EXT cues. If, however, cues were available only, for example, during the EXT component and still effectively reinforced EXT

---

[2] The changes in the *DR* due to the dropping of cues do not result from the omission of the lower response rate during the EXT cue. Analyses of the data, not reported here, show that *DR* differences are reliably a function of the rate of responding to the white key light.

responding, the "average-cue-effectiveness" explanation would appear inappropriate.

Method and results

Four pairs of birds were trained on the *VI* 1 EXT discrimination, where master birds could produce only *VI* cues—otherwise,

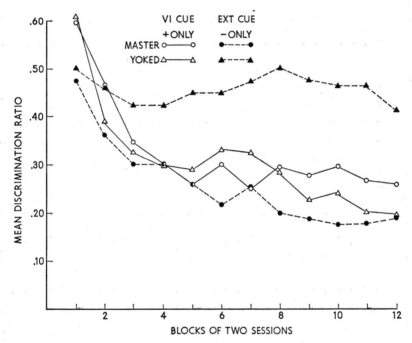

FIGURE 13.5.   Mean discrimination ratios for master and yoked groups in the single cue condition as a function of blocks of two sessions.

the procedures were identical to Experiment 1. Similarly, four pairs of birds were trained with EXT cues only. The results for 24 sessions are presented in Figure 13.5. As the figure suggests, there is a significant interaction between the cue component (*VI* or EXT) and cue contingency (master or yoked). When the master birds produced the *VI* cues only, they showed proportionately more EXT component responding than their yoked partners. However, when the master birds produced only EXT cues, their EXT component responding was proportionately *less* than that of their yoked

partners. These differences are almost entirely due to the performance of the yoked birds. The master birds' *DR*s did not differ
significantly from those of the master birds in Experiment 1a.
Examples of the cumulative recordings for the four conditions can
be seen in Figure 13.6. In the upper frame are the records for a

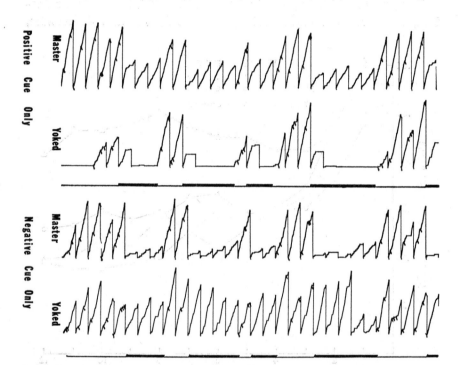

FIGURE 13.6   Cumulative records of performance of two pairs of birds in
Experiment 2a. The birds in the upper records received the positive cue only
and the birds in the lower records received the negative cue only. The dark bar
shows when periods of EXT were in effect. The pen reset every 2 min.

master-yoked pair with only the *VI* cue available. Again, the master
bird responds at a steady rate throughout the EXT component. The
yoked bird, in contrast, shows only a limited number of responses
at the beginning of each EXT component. The performance of a
master-yoked pair when only the EXT cue is available is seen in the
lower panel of Figure 13.6. The EXT response rate of the master
bird is somewhat lower in this condition (this is the most extreme
example) while the yoked bird shows little evidence of discrimination. Thus, a picture is seen similar to that observed in the analysis
of the *DR*s.

The master-yoked relation seen in the first study appears to be supported only in the case where only the *VI* cue is available. As suggested previously, the reversal in the relation when only the EXT cue was available was largely due to the failure of the yoked birds to show any discrimination between *VI* and EXT periods. The obvious explanation for this behavior is that the cue "density" was insufficient to establish good discriminative control. In the following continuation of the present study, this possibility is examined.

EXPERIMENT 2b

If the yoked birds receiving only EXT cues received insufficient cues to establish discriminative control, then increasing cue density should have an immediate effect of decreasing the *DR*. Accordingly, the yoked group receiving negative cues only was given six more sessions during which the "cue density" was artificially manipulated. (Again, tape-recorded signals from master birds' cue-producing behavior were employed. By recording from birds in different conditions cue frequencies were available from 4.4 to 8.2 cues per minute.) These results are represented in Figure 13.7. It can be seen that increasing the cue density had the effect of immediately

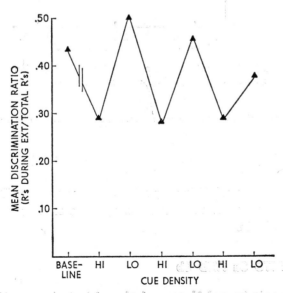

FIGURE 13.7. Mean discrimination ratios for yoked birds receiving negative cues only as a function of cue density. Cue densities were 8.2 per minute (high) and 4.4 per minute (low).

lowering the *DR* and that this effect was reversible. Thus, it appeared that the degree of discriminative control in the yoked birds was a direct function of the cue density.

The asymptotic performance levels (sessions 22–25) for all groups in Experiments 1a and 2a are summarized in Figure 13.8. The apparent interaction between cue conditions and cue contingency is highly significant. The trend in the *DR*s of the yoked subgroups can be attributed to differential cue densities. For the

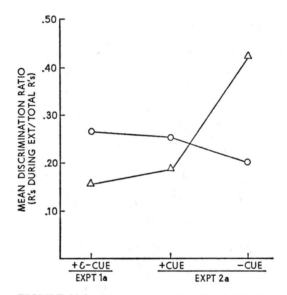

FIGURE 13.8. Mean asymptotic discrimination ratios for groups in Experiments 1a and 2a.

master birds, the results of Experiment 2a suggest that the actual presence of the EXT cue leads to proportionately lower EXT component responding. This may indicate that the negative cue may, in fact, also have a suppressive effect on negative component responding. However, this effect is very slight and the relative EXT component performance for master birds appears similar regardless of the cues available.

EXPERIMENTS 3a AND 3b

Experiments 3a and 3b were designed to test a specific hypothesis regarding the "informative" value of the response-produced cues. As Egger and Miller (1962, 1963) have suggested, the informative value of cues may be the identifying characteristic of (conditioned) reinforcers. If, therefore, the information provided by the cue is made redundant, the cue should lose its reinforcing effectiveness. Again, four pairs of birds were used as in Experiment 1a. While the birds were designated "master" and "yoked," and could obtain *VI* and EXT cues as in Experiment 1, both groups independently received the same program of *VI* and EXT cues provided for the yoked birds of Experiment 1a. (Cue signals were tape-recorded, thus maintaining identical numbers and distributions.) Since the tape-recorded cues were sufficient to establish good discriminative control, as shown in Experiment 1, the additional response-produced cues were redundant for the master birds in this study. If the master birds ceased responding in the EXT component, this would suggest that the EXT cues had informative value in Experiment 1a. If, however, the master birds maintained a high level of responding during the EXT component, it would suggest that the reinforcing function was derived from some associative relation. The results are represented in Figure 13.9. The performance of neither the master nor the yoked groups differed

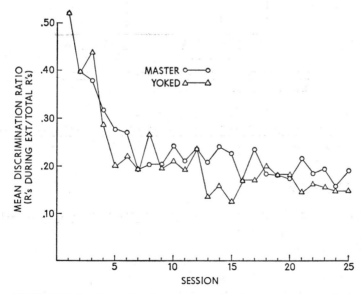

FIGURE 13.9. Mean discrimination ratios for master and yoked groups with added tape-recorded cues as a function of training session.

from the yoked group of Experiment 1. Thus the information interpretation was supported.

In a continuation of this experiment, the tape-recorded cues were eliminated, and the birds performed for another 25 sessions. The results, comparing the asymptotic performance levels (sessions 22–25) to those with the added cues, are represented in Figure 13.10. As can be seen, the master birds showed a significant increase in the rate of negative component responding suggesting

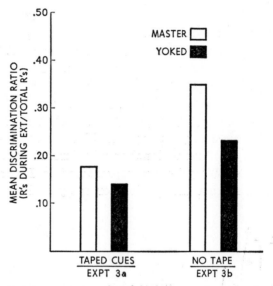

FIGURE 13.10. Mean asymptotic discrimination ratios for experiments 3a and 3b.

that the response-produced cues *acquired* informative value when they were no longer redundant.

CONCLUSIONS

The general results of these studies indicate that cues correlated with EXT can be reinforcing and this is probably due to their informative value. Secondly, the data suggest that EXT cues also have suppressive effects on responding during EXT. Considering these results and others in the literature, it is proposed that a two-factor model is necessary to explain the findings. Reward value may be derived (for both positive and negative cues) from the information that response-produced cues provide. Associative factors, however, provide reward value only for the positive cue; negative cues acquire aversive values. The final value, therefore, is determined for positive and negative cues by the sum of the two factors. A schematic model is presented in Figure 13.11.

While the two-factor model fits the present data and can be used to explain a wide variety of other research, this kind of analysis is not completely satisfying. Clearly, with two factors representing opposite polarities, any result can be explained. At the same time,

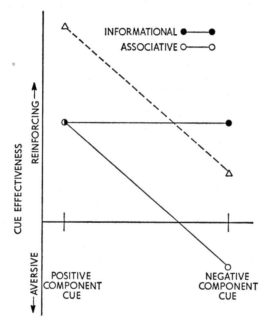

FIGURE 13.11.   Schematic model representing cue effectiveness as a function of component and Associative-Informative source. Final cue effectiveness is represented by the broken line.

however, we are not prepared to abandon either the associative or informative mechanism. There seems to be adequate support in these data for both factors.

SUMMARY

Cues correlated with Extinction can reinforce observing responses, and the effect is probably due to the informative value of the stimuli. The cues correlated with Extinction also have suppressive effects on responding during Extinction components. Reinforcing value of a cue may be interpreted as having two additive components: informative value, which refers to the biological significance of positive and negative cues, and associative value, which increases the reward effectiveness of positive cues, but tends to make negative cues aversive.

chapter 14

DIFFERENTIAL REINFORCING EFFECTS OF STIMULI ASSOCIATED WITH THE PRESENCE OR ABSENCE OF A SCHEDULE OF PUNISHMENT[1]

James A. Dinsmoor, Garry A. Flint,[2] Richard F. Smith,[3] and Neal F. Viemeister[4]

Indiana University

INTRODUCTION

"The relationships of importance always involve three things: the situation, call it the stimulus if you like; the behavior, call it the response if you like; and the consequences, the reinforcers." The speaker is B. F. Skinner, in an interview published in *Psychology Today* for September, 1967 (pp. 23 and 68). What is usually studied in a conditioning experiment is one response, sandwiched between the stimulus which precedes it and the stimulus which follows it. But what is studied in the paradigm to which Wyckoff (see Chapter 9) gave the name "observing response" is a stimulus or stimuli sandwiched between two items of behavior, the response which produces them and the response which follows their production. Both responses may be studied simultaneously and their relationship examined. Thus, the observing paradigm lies at the interface of two of our most important behavioral processes, that

[1] This investigation was supported by a research grant (MH 10474) from the National Institute of Mental Health, Public Health Service. We would also like to acknowledge the technical assistance of Eunice M. King.

[2] Now at the Langley Porter Neuropsychiatric Institute.

[3] Now at the University of Utah.

[4] Now at the University of Washington.

commonly known as secondary or conditioned reinforcement and that known as stimulus control or discrimination.

To produce a difference in the tendency to respond under two stimulus conditions, it is necessary to sustain responses under one or to suppress responses under the other. Since the first of these processes has been much more fully explored, we are particularly interested in the second. The outstanding mystery of this form of discrimination is why the organism continues to make contact with, i.e., observe, the negative stimulus, the one that is associated with the punishment of subsequent behavior. According to the accepted laws of stimulus pairing, a stimulus that is associated selectively with a primary aversive event, such as the receipt of shock, should itself take on aversive properties. It should become a stimulus to be avoided rather than produced, a stimulus which suppresses rather than strengthens observing behavior. Since we know that an organism does, in fact, learn a discrimination based on punishment (e.g., Azrin, 1956; Brethower & Reynolds, 1962; Dinsmoor, 1952; Honig & Slivka, 1964; Rachlin, 1966), it appears that some compensating factor must either transform the character of this stimulus or outweigh its negative effects.

For the understanding of discriminative behavior, the observing response provides an important conceptual tool; for understanding conditioned reinforcement, it provides a useful measure. Like the more conventional chaining paradigm, the observing paradigm offers what biological investigators have called a "chronic preparation." That is, the reinforcing power of the stimulus is maintained over long periods of time, so that it may be measured while successive parametric manipulations are performed on the controlling variables. But what distinguishes the observing response from responses in the first component of a two-component Chain, for example, is its relation to the final reinforcer. The chained response serves both to produce the next stimulus and to initiate the contingency that accompanies it. But in the observing paradigm the contingency is initiated by the experimenter on a schedule which is independent of the subject's behavior and is merely "revealed" by the observing response. That is, the observing response produces the stimulus but has no effect on the contingency. In work performed with the chaining paradigm, two relations are confounded. Unless special precautions are taken (Dinsmoor & Clayton, 1963, 1966), effects attributed to the conditioned reinforcer are susceptible to more direct interpretation in terms of the temporal relationship between the response and its more distant, but more potent, final reinforcer (see McDiarmid & Rilling, 1965). The contingencies for these two events can be separated, however, by resorting to the observing paradigm.

Until recently, the conditions under which a stimulus acquired the power to reinforce behavior seemed to be relatively restricted, and it could be hoped that they would soon be subsumed under a relatively simple formula, such as temporal association with an already reinforcing event. Recent data, however, have suggested that the list of sufficient conditions is much too broad to be subsumed under any simple unitary formula. If there is, indeed, a unifying principle, it must lie at some higher level of abstraction. We will not attempt to wrestle with such a difficult problem in the present paper.

In most of the previous work conducted specifically with the observing response, the stimuli produced have been those necessary for a discrimination based on positive reinforcement. The fact that these stimuli do maintain the observing response has posed a problem for straightforward associationistic accounts of conditioned reinforcement. If the frequency of primary reinforcement in the presence of the positive stimulus is averaged with the frequency in the presence of the negative stimulus, the resulting value is no higher than the frequency of reinforcement when these stimuli are absent.

Two general types of interpretation have been advanced to account for the advantage gained by the discriminative stimuli. One of these formulations suggests that something other than simple association is the critical variable. Wyckoff's original suggestion, for example, was that "exposure to discriminative stimuli has a reinforcing effect on the observing response to the extent that the subject has learned to respond differently to these discriminative stimuli (see Chapter 9)." That is, the reinforcing effect is based on the efficacy of these stimuli in controlling subsequent behavior or on their utility in making it possible to adjust this behavior more appropriately to the prevailing contingencies.

A more recent variant of this approach is the "information" hypothesis (e.g., Hendry, 1965; Hendry and Coulbourn, 1967; Schaub & Honig, 1967), which ascribes reinforcing properties to stimuli predictive of biologically important events. Thus far, this hypothesis has been worded with sufficient vagueness to encompass a wide variety of empirical findings, but a reasonable implication for the present work is that a stimulus that predicts the possibility of punishment may have positively reinforcing properties. Recent work by Knapp, Kause, and Perkins (1959), Lockard (1963), and Perkins, Levis, and Seymann (1963) has been interpreted as supporting such a formulation.

The second type of interpretation makes a quantitative assumption designed specifically to account for the observed result. This may be illustrated by Wyckoff's later suggestion (1959) that the function relating the potency of a stimulus to the frequency of primary reinforcement in its presence need not be rectilinear but may be positively accelerated. That is, constant increments in frequency produce increasingly larger increments in the effectiveness of the stimulus. (Such an assumption, incidentally, does not seem to be in accord with the data arising from studies involving two-component Chain and Concurrent schedules of reinforcement; for example, the results of Herrnstein (1964a) show a negative rather than a positive acceleration.) Under this assumption, the attractiveness of the two alternative stimuli produced by the observing response is asymmetrical with respect to the attractiveness of the stimulus associated with an intermediate frequency of reinforcement, i.e., the stimulus which is present before the subject makes the observing response. Thus, the net effect of producing one of these stimuli half of the time and the other half of the time would be a gain in reinforcing value.[5] There is plenty of slippage at other points in the system, of course, which would permit the same result. It has not been established, for example, that the suppressive effects of stimuli accompanied by decrements in reinforcement frequency are comparable to the postive effects of stimuli accompanied by increments in the frequency of reinforcement.

Formulations of this type have been entirely arbitrary; they have not been based on any broader rationale. However, they do have the virtue of being relatively specific and therefore potentially subject to experimental test. A similar function could be suggested for the case in which the discrimination is based on punishment rather than on positive reinforcement. In this case, it would be necessary to assume that the reinforcing effect of the stimulus

---

[5] This argument is illustrated in Figure 12.30. [Ed.]

associated with the absence of punishment is greater than the suppressive effect of the stimulus associated with the presence of punishment. Such an asymmetry would be somewhat surprising, intuitively, since it is the negative stimulus that is associated most immediately and directly with the effective event. Moreover, the necessary rule relating the effect of the stimulus to the frequency of punishment would be opposite in direction to the rule postulated to account for the positive case. In the negative case, constant increments in the frequency of punishment would have to be assumed to produce smaller and smaller, rather than larger and larger, increments in the punishing effect of the stimulus.

So far, the speculations concerning these matters have run far ahead of the data. Some attempts have been made, however, by such investigators as Kendall and Gibson (1965), Schaub and Honig (1967), and Schaub (1967) to separate and evaluate independently the conditioned reinforcing effects of stimuli associated with alternative schedules of positive reinforcement. Our interest, on the present occasion, is to describe and interpret similar data that we have obtained using stimuli associated with the presence or absence of a punishment contingency. These data have been extracted from a much larger body of material collected during the early stages of a broader investigation of the entire pattern of behavior involved in this type of relation.

At the beginning of our work, we found that it was very difficult to establish substantial and reliable observing performances in the case of some of our birds (Dinsmoor & Smith, 1966). Consequently, much of the work we have been doing smacks more of "find out" than of "show that" research. When you have to locate appropriate parameters as quickly as possible, you cannot afford some of the usual luxuries of experimental design. In the initial stages, at least, and even during some of our current work, we have been more concerned with the problem of guessing, at a very modest level of confidence, the effects of various parameters, in order to carry on our work, than with the problem of confirming effects in such a way that all bystanders must find our conclusions inescapable. Our objectives have been to develop suitable techniques for gaining control over a complex pattern of behavior and to form some tentative conclusions which might stimulate fresh analyses of what is going on. You may think of our activities, if you wish, as a glorified set of pilot experiments, which would probably not be acceptable to the editors of our more "archival" journals. Nevertheless, we have found this approach far more fruitful and exciting than a succession of meticulously controlled experiments which show that under certain well-specified circumstances—nothing much happened.

The data that we will offer in the present paper will speak for themselves. We will not provide detailed histories of the successive procedures previously employed with each of our birds. Such descriptions would be much too cumbersome for present purposes. Our major findings have been replicated, despite differences in the history of individual birds, and this indicates that they are generalizable characteristics of the final performance and not dependent on the vagaries of individual history. We will first describe the standard experimental routine in concrete detail and the general pattern of behavior that results. Then we will go on to a presentation of some data relevant to the central issue to which this paper is addressed, together with specifications of any alterations in the parameters under which these data were obtained.

BASIC PROCEDURE AND RESULTS

The basic procedure we have used in our work to date is diagrammed in Figure 14.1. A pigeon is maintained at a constant body weight, about 70 percent of his undeprived weight, and tested in daily sessions of 90 min duration in a chamber manufactured by Lehigh Valley Electronics. Two keys are available.

The key on the bird's right is known as the food key. When this key is white, the bird is on a Mixed schedule. Two components, each varying in duration, are presented in alternation. The duration of each component is determined by presenting input pulses every 9 sec to a random probability generator set at $\frac{1}{5}$. The lower limit is therefore 9 sec, and the upper limit has arbitrarily been set at 234 sec (26 pulses). Under each of these components independently, reinforcement, in the form of $2\frac{1}{2}$ sec of access to grain, is made available on a variable-interval schedule for pecking the key. The successive intervals between reinforcements are determined by presenting input pulses every 10 sec to another probability generator set at $\frac{1}{12}$. In this case, the lower limit is 10 sec and the upper limit has been set at 240 sec (24 pulses).

The difference between the two components is that in one of them a 0.1-sec shock is programmed for each completion of a fixed number of responses. When the schedule shifts to the no-punishment component, the count is retained until the return of the punishment component. In our current work this ratio is normally set at either 20 or 35. The shock is delivered via implanted electrodes (Azrin, 1959) through a 10,000 ohm resistor. The intensity ranges from 50 to 300 volts for a given bird on a given block of sessions. This is one of the parameters we are currently exploring with some of our birds, although the results are as yet incomplete.

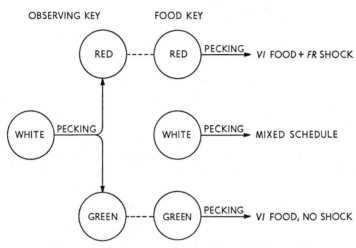

FIGURE 14.1.   Procedural diagram. Under the standard routine, a peck on the left or "observing" key produces a display of red or green both on this key and on the right or "food" key for a fixed period of time. During this period, when the schedule on the food key includes the production of shock, the keys will be red; when it does not include the production of shock, the keys will be green.

The only consequence programmed on the key on the bird's left, known as the observing key, is the substitution on both keys of red or green illumination for white. When the bird pecks the observing key during the punishment component the keys turn red. Red means "danger" or "stop." When the bird pecks during the no-punishment component the keys turn green. Green means "go." In most of our training, the duration for which these colors remain on the keys has been set at 60 sec following each peck. If the schedule changes in the meantime, the color of the keys changes along with it. If the bird pecks the observing key again while it is red or green, the period of observation is extended for another 60 sec, timed from this peck. At other times during the session both keys remain white, except for a blackout during reinforcement. The keys are also dark before and after the session.

Substantial observing performances have been established in five birds under this procedure. In each case, the bird was first trained to discriminate between red and green by presenting them, as appropriate, throughout the session. The observing key was inoperative, and very few responses were recorded—for some birds a mode of zero—during the session. (For our first few birds, the observing key was dark, but the lighted key was later added as a control procedure.) After a number of such sessions, during which the shock was introduced at a low level and then increased in intensity, and during which the bird's rate of pecking on the food key when it was green reached a ratio of at least three times the rate when it was red, the observing procedure was instituted. The keys were white at the beginning of the session, and the bird was required to peck the observing key to produce green or red.

Two of our birds developed the observing performance on the first such session, without further assistance. Three others required from 188 to 267 more sessions, during which such special procedures as retraining the discrimination, withholding shock, and withholding food reinforcement in white were sometimes employed to facilitate the establishment of the desired performance. The first two birds began their observing performances at shock intensities of 175 volts (P–340) and 250 volts (P–2761). The other three first achieved persistent performances at 100 (P–1582), 100 (P–5890), and 150 volts (P–2903), after failure at higher voltages. In all of these cases, the ratio of responses to shocks during the punishment schedule was set at 35. In three cases, the period of observation was set at 60 sec, and in the other two cases, at 30 sec. Finally, another three birds, which failed to establish an observing performance under the standard procedure, were transferred to a procedure known as green only, which will be described later.

The pattern of performance, when it was finally established, was essentially the same for each of these birds. An example is presented in Figure 14.2. The lower half shows what is happening on the observing key. An upward displacement is superimposed on the cumulative record when the bird is observing, that is, when red or green is present. Although our procedure permits the bird to extend the period of observation by pecking the key again while red or green is present, this hardly ever happens: the upward displacements of the record are quite regular in width. The normal pattern of performance on the observing key is a single peck, followed by a 60-sec wait until the white reappears, then another peck a few seconds later. Occasionally, however, the bird allows the keys to remain white for a more extended period.

Responding on the food key when it is white is shown in the upper left portion of the figure, responding when it is red or green

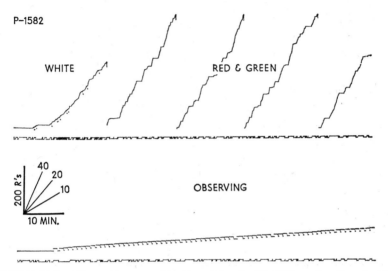

FIGURE 14.2.   Illustrative records of pecking by P–1582 under the standard procedure (session 460). The upper half shows the performance on the food key. The record to the left was obtained when the key was white, the record to the right when it was red or green (base line down or up, respectively). The lower half shows the performance on the observing key. Vertical displacements of the cumulative record show when the keys were red or green. Each display lasted 60 sec. The shock ratio was 35 and its intensity 100 volts.

in the upper right. The difference between the red and the green performance is evident in the slope of the record. The color on the key is also marked by the position of the pen along the base line. When the pen is down, the key is red. Occasional vertical strokes mark occasions when shock is delivered. When the pen is up, the key is green.

We would like to call attention to the asymmetry of the rates of responding on the food key in the presence of red, green, and white. White may be thought of as a neutral stimulus, or halfway point, between red and green. The contingencies are mixed. About half of the time the schedule is the same as that for red; during the other half it is the same as that for green. We might expect, then, that the rate of pecking during white would fall halfway between that for red and that for green. This is not the case, however. As may be seen in the upper half of Figure 14.2, the average rate in red and green is higher than that in white. Perhaps the bird's preference for seeing red and green, as expressed by his tendency to peck the observing key, is related to the preference for red and green expressed by his performance on the food key.

Let us now consider each color individually. Numerical records of pecking on the food key for this session (460) show the rate in white to be 12 pecks per minute. The rate in green is considerably higher, 45.3 pecks per minute. But the rate in red is only slightly lower, 5.2 pecks per minute. This asymmetry has been replicated several hundred times. It is characteristic of all sessions and of all birds. In other words, green is a much more favorable situation but red only a slightly less favorable situation for responding on the food key than white. It would be interesting if this preference function should prove predictive of the effects of these stimuli as consequences of pecking the observing key. If the relation holds, green should be highly reinforcing but red only slightly punishing.

PREFERENCE FOR RED OR FOR GREEN

Some indication of the relative contribution of seeing red and seeing green to the reinforcement of the observing response can be obtained under our standard observing procedure. To a degree, the color that will be produced by the next peck on the observing key can be predicted from the color previously seen, provided that too long an interval has not elapsed. As we have seen, switching between the punishment and no-punishment schedules, which determine which color will be produced, is governed by a random probability generator. For the present work, the probability of switching has been set at a value considerably less than one half, i.e., one in five. This means that the schedule is more likely to remain the same after one input pulse to the generator (9 sec), or even after two or three, than it is to change. When the color last seen was red, the color produced by the next peck is likely to be red, and when the color last seen was green, the color produced by the next peck is likely to be green. Therefore, presentations of red or green can serve as discriminative stimuli not only for the contingency on the food key but also for the color that will be produced by the next peck on the observing key. The relation is similar to that analyzed by Dinsmoor (1952, pp. 31–33) for a procedure in which all responses during certain segments of time were followed by shocks but no responses during other segments were followed by shock. (See also Azrin & Holz, 1966; Jenkins, 1965; Pierrel & Blue, 1967.)

One way of analyzing the resulting discrimination is to record the latency of the next peck on the observing key each time white reappears following the display of red or of green. Since we had arranged for the coding and punching of the time and character of all experimental events on paper tape, the necessary information was at hand. The data were analyzed by computer and plotted as conditional frequency distributions for the latency of pecking when red was the color last seen and when that color was green. An example of such a pair of distributions, accumulated for 10 sessions of P–2902's performance at 100 volts, is presented as Figure 14.3. A complicating factor is that red and green are discriminative also for the performance on the food key, and the higher rates that are sometimes observed on this key following green may interfere with pecking the observing key. One bird (P–2761) consistently pecks sooner following red. In most cases, however, this factor has been overridden and the expected performance has been shown, as illustrated by Figure 14.3. In the distributions presented, the primary difference is that the frequency of pecking the observing key soon after (2–3 sec) the reappearance of white is approximately three times as great following observation of green as following observation of red.

But computer analysis of 10-session blocks is a somewhat cumbersome method for obtaining results of this sort. The process may be speeded by reducing the length of time red or green is displayed following a peck on the observing key. Many more responses are then available within a single session. Pecking when green is scheduled can be cumulated on one recorder and pecking when red is scheduled on another. A pair of records obtained from P–5890 during a session when the period of observation was only 5 sec, rather than 60, is presented as Figure 14.4. In this instance, the bird did not begin pecking the observing key until more than 24 minutes had elapsed. The difference in the lengths of the initial

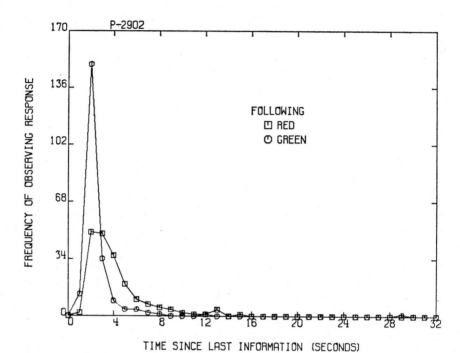

FIGURE 14.3. Frequency distributions for P–2902, cumulated for 10 sessions, of the latency in seconds of the peck on the observing key following its return to white. The squares show the distribution when the color last displayed was red, the circles when it was green. The shock ratio was 35 and its intensity 100 volts.

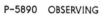

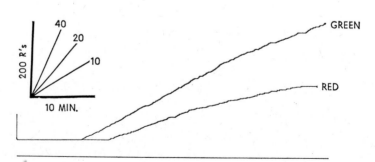

FIGURE 14.4. Separate cumulative records of P–5890's pecking on the observing key when this produced red or green for 5 seconds (session 303). The shock ratio was 35 and shock intensity 100 volts.

horizontal segments may reflect merely the vagaries of random allotment of time to the alternative schedules, but the difference revealed by the increasing divergence of the two records is behavioral. The bird pecks more frequently when pecking produces green than when it produces red. The same result has been replicated for session after session and for several different birds.

It is clear, then, that our birds prefer seeing green to seeing red. In other words, the stimulus indicating that it is safe to peck the food key is more reinforcing than the stimulus indicating that such responses may lead to shock. But this does not measure the absolute reinforcing value of red. It does not tell us whether red: (1) is merely a less-effective reinforcer which nevertheless makes some positive contribution to the maintenance of the observing behavior; (2) is a neutral stimulus, which is produced inadvertently, so to speak, but has no effect; or (3) is a conditioned punisher, the negative effects of which are overcome by the positive effects of sometimes producing green.

GREEN-ONLY AND RED-ONLY PROCEDURES

In order to get some indication of the absolute values of red and green as consequences of pecking the observing key, we have used two modifications of our standard observing procedure. These are compared with the standard procedure in Table 14.1. The first modification has been labeled "green-only." Under this procedure, red can no longer be produced. When the bird pecks the observing

TABLE 14.1

A Comparison of Three Observing Procedures

Observing Procedure	Food Key Schedule	
	Punishment	No Punishment
Green-only.................	No change	Green
Red-green.................	Red	Green
Red-only.................	Red	No change

key during the punishment schedule nothing happens. The keys remain white. There is no change in stimulation. But when he pecks the observing key during the no-punishment schedule he produces green, in the usual manner. The second procedure, now labeled "red-green," is our standard observing procedure. Either red or green may be produced, depending on which schedule is in effect on the food key. The third procedure has been labeled "red-only." In this case, green can no longer be produced. When the bird pecks the observing key during the punishment schedule, he produces red, as usual. But when he pecks during the no-punishment schedule, nothing happens. There is no change in key color.

The first bit of evidence we would like to present concerning the effectiveness of red or green by itself in reinforcing the observing response comes from our efforts to establish an observing performance in each of our birds. As was mentioned earlier, five of our birds eventually acquired a substantial and persistent observing performance under the standard red-green procedure, although in three of these cases this required a relatively lengthy search for appropriate parametric values. With no bird have we given up the attempt to establish observing behavior. In three cases, however, we finally turned in desperation to the green-only procedure. In all three cases, we were successful in establishing the observing performance within a relatively small number of sessions. Since the intensity of the shock was set at 300 volts and each of these birds had had previous training, the comparison is not rigorously controlled. We were more interested in obtaining some behavior to work with at this point than in testing unambiguously the rate of acquisition. However, in the light of our previous failure with these same birds, the results are quite suggestive. What they indicate is that green alone, even when delivered only half of the time and for considerably less than half of the pecks on the observing key, is more effective than the combination of red and green, delivered as alternative consequences for a given peck. Not only does red appear to carry little of the load of maintaining the observing response but it may, instead, exercise an inhibitory effect. An example of one bird's performance under the green-only procedure is presented in Figure 14.5. As before, a cumulative record of the bird's performance on the food key when it is white is presented in the upper left portion of the figure; its performance in green is presented in the upper right. In the lower half of the figure, we have presented its performance throughout the session on the observing key. Whenever the bird sees green, the pen is deflected upward. In this case, the width of each period of observation is not constant, since the schedule usually reverts to punishment before the full 60 sec are up.

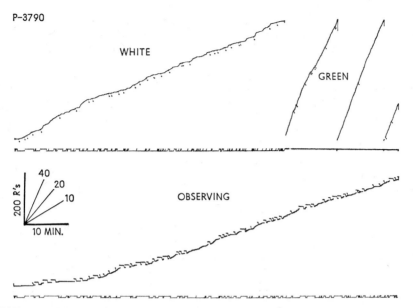

FIGURE 14.5. Illustrative records of pecking by P–3790 under the green-only procedure (session 329). The upper half shows the performance on the food key. The record to the left was obtained when the key was white, the record to the right when it was green. The lower half shows the performance on the observing key. Upward displacements of the cumulative record show when the keys were green. Although the display of green sometimes lasted for a full minute, it was terminated whenever the punishment schedule returned on the food key. The shock ratio was 20 and its intensity 300 volts.

Note that quite a few responses occur when there is no change in stimulation. Green appears to be relatively effective as an intermittent reinforcer.

REDUCING THE PERIOD OF OBSERVATION

When a full 60-sec period of red or green is presented as a consequence of pecking the observing key, the rate of pecking is severely limited. As soon as the color appears, the bird stops pecking. Even though our standard procedure permits the bird to extend the length of the period of observation by pecking again in the presence of red or green, this hardly ever occurs. Under these conditions, no true rate emerges. The most we can obtain is a distribution of latencies between the reappearance of white and the next peck on the observing key. Since the presentation of red or green interrupts the pecking and the bird may require additional time before he detects the reappearance of white, these latencies are not comparable to the interresponse times between successive pecks when no change in stimulation occurs. When the bird pecks the observing key and nothing happens, he is free to peck it again immediately. The way is open for relatively high rates of responding.

In an attempt to minimize this factor, we have trained some of our birds to peck the observing key for relatively brief periods of observation. Our greatest success to date has been with P–3031. This happens to be a bird which had failed, initially, to develop a stable observing performance under the red-green procedure. Accordingly, we resorted to the green-only procedure, which we suspected might be more effective. After we had succeeded in establishing a reliable performance for a 60-sec maximum of green as a reinforcer, we began progressively reducing the length of the period of observation, allowing a number of sessions for the bird to stabilize at each value. As in the case of other birds with which we have tried this procedure, the performance seemed to be well maintained at 30- and 15-sec durations. Some difficulty was encountered at 5 sec, however, and our initial attempts were unsuccessful at 2 sec. A possible source of our difficulty is that throughout most of our work we have maintained a 2-sec changeover delay following the production of red or green. That is, reinforcement does not become available for pecking the food key, even if otherwise scheduled, until 2 sec have elapsed following the peck on the observing key. Otherwise, as Kelleher (1958a) has pointed out, interruption of food key pecking by pecking on the observing key would lead, under an interval schedule, to an increment in the probability or reinforcement for the next peck on the food key. This might lead, we feared, to superstitious chaining, and thereby to a spurious source of reinforcement for pecking the observing key. However, it would be difficult to choose a length of delay which would precisely counterbalance this factor. As the length of the period of observation is reduced, this delay may serve as an increasingly severe penalty for observing responses, since it occupies an increasing portion of the red or green time. At extreme values, when the period of observation is less than the length of the delay, the bird can never produce food in the presence of red or green.

The way in which P–3031 solved this problem is of some interest.

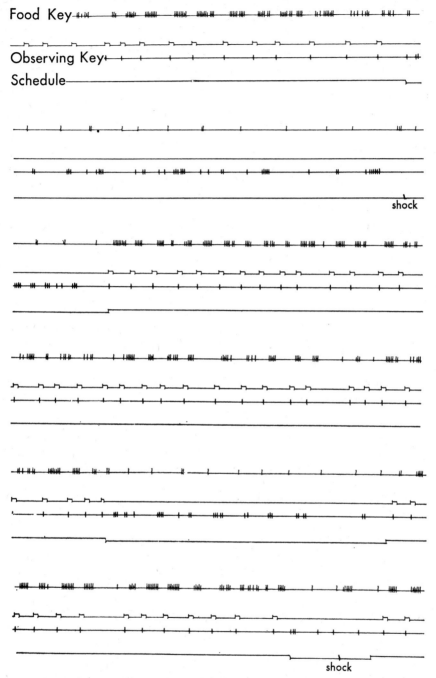

FIGURE 14.6. Successive segments, totaling 9 min, from a four-pen operations record of the performance of P–3031 on session 314. The top pen recorded pecking on the food key, the second 1-sec presentations of green, the third pecks on the observing key, and the fourth periods when no punishment was programmed on the food key. Two points at which shock was delivered are also indicated. The shock ratio was 20 and its intensity 300 volts.

A detailed representation of his performance under the green-only procedure, reproduced from an operations record, is presented in Figure 14.6. Six successive segments of time are presented, each lasting a little over 90 sec. In each segment, the pips on the top line represent pecks on the food key, the 1-sec displacements of the second line represent periods when the keys are green, the pips on the third line represent pecks on the observing key, and upward displacement of the fourth line indicates periods when there can be no punishment. At two points, which are appropriately labeled, the occurrence of shock is indicated by pips on the record.

The pattern of performance represented in this figure was extremely stable. When no-punishment is scheduled on the food key, the characteristic performance is as follows: the bird pecks the observing key, producing 1 sec of green; while the green is present, he pauses; after the green disappears, he typically pecks from five to nine times on the food key; he then returns to the observing key and initiates the next cycle. In other words, the 1-sec presentation of green serves as what we might call a "trace discriminative stimulus." The bird does not peck in the presence of this stimulus but pecks the food key at a relatively high rate immediately following each presentation.

During the punishment schedule, when shocks are programmed for every 20 pecks on the food key, the pattern of performance is quite different. The bird may peck the observing key once or several times, in rapid succession; then he pecks the food key. Responding on each key appears, in some sense, to be "spaced out"; that is, relatively long intervals appear without a peck. An item which may be worthy of note, however, is the series of pecks which is sometimes observed on the food key following a shock. In their study of fixed-ratio punishment, Azrin, Holz, and Hake (1963) reported a uniform distribution of pecking in the interval between successive shocks. Most of our birds have shown no conspicuous departure from this finding, but P–3031 did. Since the shock is delivered for a fixed number of pecks, receipt of a shock can serve as a discriminative stimulus indicating that the next few responses on the food key will not be followed by shock. In other words, shock can serve the same function as seeing green. Apparently P–3031 was sensitive to this contingency, since in many cases a flurry of food key responses occurred following the receipt of shock.

SOME QUANTITATIVE COMPARISONS

At this point, we ask the reader to review Table 14.1 again. Comparisons can be made horizontally, between the bird's performances under any two cells within the same row. These are comparisons within the same session or sessions between the performance during the punishment schedule and performance during the no-punishment schedule. Comparisons can also be made vertically, between adjacent cells within the same column. These comparisons are sequential, and may be affected by changes in such day-to-day parameters as temperature, handling, electrical resistance, and deprivation, but we have always provided P–3031 with at least 10 sessions under each procedure, in addition to the transition session, in order to permit an evaluation of variability due to these factors. Note that procedural differences between the successive rows in the table involve in each case only one change, a change either in what follows pecking of the observing key during the punishment schedule or what follows during the no-punishment schedule.

Under the green-only procedure, the rate of pecking on the observing key is typically higher when no change is produced than when pecking produces green. This may not have been obvious in the operations record, but more substantial evidence will be presented later, in Figure 14.8. Two factors are probably responsible. First, even though the keys now turn green for only 1 sec, this interrupts the performance on the observing key, limiting it to a single peck on each occasion. The bird does not peck again, once the green had appeared. In other words, even limitation of the period of observation to 1 sec does not provide an entirely fair basis of comparison. Second, as we have seen from the operations record, following each exposure to green the bird pecks several times on the food key, which interferes with his return to the observing key. These two factors limit the rate of observing during the no-punishment schedule, when green is produced.

One might be tempted to analyze these data by treating the occurrence of a peck on the observing key followed by no change in stimulation as a compound stimulus which provides the same information as was formerly provided by the production of red. This compound stimulus might then be interpreted as a source of reinforcement. However, this interpretation would require that the same stimulus compound be effective under the red-only procedure, when it would provide the information previously provided by the production of green. But as subsequent data will show, observing is not maintained under the red-only procedure.

Therefore, in analyzing the present green-only data, it seems more reasonable to attribute pecking of the observing key during the punishment schedule to the reinforcing effects of producing green at other times, during the no-punishment schedule. Technically speaking, the green only procedure can be classified as a mixed CRF-Extinction schedule of conditioned reinforcement for pecks on the observing key. During some periods pecking produces no change in key color, during others it consistently produces a green stimulus for 1 sec. The implication of this interpretation is quite important: it indicates that the reinforcing effects of green are sufficient to account for all pecks that occur on the observing key, whether they occur under green-only or under the standard red-green procedure. In other words, the production of red makes no contribution to the maintenance of the observing performance.

Cumulative records of P–3031's performance during the first transition from green-only to the standard red-green procedure are presented in Figure 14.7. The record in the upper half of the figure shows performance on the food key. The strokes represent deliveries of food. The rate shifts abruptly when the contingency changes from punishment to no-punishment and vice versa. After 45 min of green only, the procedure is shifted to red-green for the second half of the session, at the point marked by the heavy vertical line. No change is apparent in the bird's pattern of performance on the food key.

In the lower half of the figure, the excursion on the left shows the bird's performance on the observing key during those segments of the session when it is programmed to produce green. This recorder operated only when the no-punishment schedule was programmed on the food key. The rate is extremely regular throughout the session; again, this performance is not affected by the change in procedure from green-only to red-green observing, which is marked by the heavy vertical line.

Finally, the excursion on the right, taken from another recorder, shows the bird's performance on the observing key during those segments of the session when a punishment contingency is programmed on the food key. During the first half of the session, when

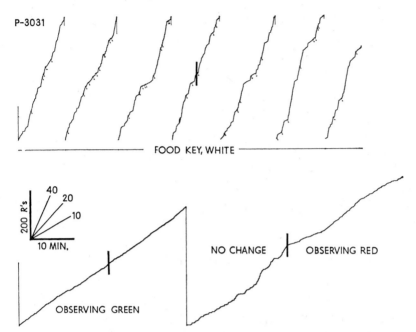

P-3031

FOOD KEY, WHITE

200 R's

40
20
10
10 MIN.

NO CHANGE

OBSERVING RED

OBSERVING GREEN

FIGURE 14.7. Cumulative records of P–3031's performance during transition session 288, when the procedure was changed from green only to red-green. The point at which the change occurred is marked on each record by a heavy vertical line. Pecking on the food key is recorded in the upper half of the figure, pecking on the observing key in the lower half. For the observing key, pecking during the no-punishment schedule, which produced green, is recorded to the left; pecking during the punishment schedule, which before the transition produced no change but later produced red, is recorded to the right. The shock ratio was 20 and its intensity 300 volts.

no change in stimulation is produced, the rate is irregular. An average rate only slightly higher than that for green, in this instance, is produced by the occurrence of relatively high rates during some portions of the record. Overall, a positive acceleration is evident as the session progresses. When the procedure is changed, at the heavy vertical line, so that pecking the observing key produces red during the punishment contingency, the immediate effect is a substantial reduction in rate, followed by recovery to a fairly stable rate that nevertheless remains lower than when no change was produced in the color of the key.

We will now consider records of P–3031's rate of pecking on the observing key, session by session, to obtain a more complete and authoritative picture of his performance. In Figure 14.8, the daily

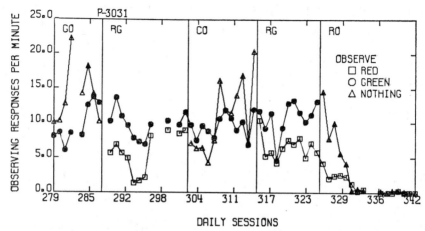

FIGURE 14.8. Successive daily rates of pecking the observing key by P–3031 under three different procedures. The panel headings indicate whether the pecking produced green only (*GO*), both red and green (*RG*), or red only (*RO*). The rates were computed from latencies when the color last presented was red (squares) or green (circles) and from interresponse times when no change was produced (triangles). When the observing occurred during the no-punishment schedule on the food key the symbols are solid. The stimulus display lasted one sec. The shock ratio was 20 and its intensity 300 volts. Cumulative records for transition session 288 have been presented in Figure 14.7.

rates of pecking following red are plotted as squares, following no change as triangles, and following green as circles. To facilitate comparison, all rates during the no-punishment schedule are plotted as solid (black) symbols, all rates during the punishment schedule as open (white) symbols. These rates are taken from the last half (45 min) of each session, to eliminate possible random effects of the warm-up which often appeared at the beginning of the session. Also, times when the keys were red or green have been eliminated in making these computations. In other words, latencies have been treated as interresponse times. Data were lost on some sessions due to difficulties with the paper tape punch.

The first panel (*GO*) shows the final training sessions on the one-sec green only procedure. As we saw in the operations record and the cumulative curves, the rate is generally higher when no change is produced (triangles) than when pecking produces green (circles). The reasons for this have already been discussed.

The second panel (*RG*) shows the performance on a subsequent block of red-green sessions. By and large, the bird pecks at a lower rate when this produces red (squares) than when it produced no change in key color. This might be taken to indicate that seeing red serves as a conditioned punisher, but it must be remembered that one of the same artifacts is still present that we used to account for limitation of the rate for green: when the keys turn red, this interrupts the pecking on the observing key, limiting it to a single peck until after the keys return to white again. No opportunity is given for multiple pecks to occur. Therefore, the reduction in observing rate when red is produced is not conclusive. Moreover, if the production of red had a severely punishing effect, we might expect it to drive the rates to much lower levels. Some indication of such a phenomenon is given in sessions 293 to 295, but the subsequent recovery to a much higher level makes it difficult to decide whether this was a systematic effect or merely the result of some temporary fluctuation in background parameters.

Continuing in our search for a punishing effect of red, we might take note of the trends within each block of sessions. In the first panel, the rate of observing when no change is produced (open triangles) fluctuates in a seemingly haphazard fashion. When red is substituted in the second panel (open squares), the rate drops after a few sessions, but subsequently recovers. When the green-only procedure is replicated, as shown in the third panel, the rate of responding when no change is produced (open triangles) begins at a relatively low value and rises. Finally, when red is programmed again, in the fourth panel, the rate is fairly high on the first session, but drops and remains low on subsequent sessions. Again, the data are suggestive, but by no means conclusive.

We know from previous data (Dinsmoor, 1952) that continuous production of a potent punisher, like shock, during some parts of a session, affects the rate of response during other parts of the session, when punishment is not delivered. If red were a potent form of punishment under our present procedure, we would expect it to have some effect on the rate of pecking during other parts of the session, when green is produced. The data we are now tracing are the solid black circles, as they run across successive panels. Comparing this rate under the green-only procedure (first and third panels) with the corresponding rate under the red-green procedure (second and fourth panels), we can see no evidence for a systematic effect.

It would be possible to argue, of course, that responding for green is entirely independent of what happens following the response at other times during the session, i.e., that under present conditions the discrimination is so good that there is no induction between the two performances. But there is ample evidence of induction in the other direction. Intermittent production of green maintains a substantial rate during other parts of the session when pecks on the observing key produce no change in stimulation (green only procedure). And intermittent production of green maintains a substantial rate during other parts of the session when pecks on the observing key produce red (red-green procedure). And yet intermittent production of red, the stimulus associated with punishment on the food key, seems to have no effect on the rate of responding when pecking produces green. If red has a punishing effect, it does not appear to be a powerful one.

In view of the importance of these comparisons, we have replicated the same sequence of procedures with another bird, P–4667, using in this case a 5-sec period of observation. The first transition to red-green following green only led progressively, over four sessions, to a complete collapse of the observing performance. After four sessions of retraining on green only, however, the second transition to red-green led to a sustained performance. As with P–3031, the rate for red was lower than when pecking the observing key produced no change in stimulation, but the rate for green did not seem to be affected.

The final panel in Figure 14.8 shows the effects of changing the procedure to red only. Under this procedure, you will recall, pecking the observing key produces 1 sec of red when the punishment contingency is in effect on the food key but produces no change in stimulation during the no-punishment schedule. P–3031 has had quite a bit of exposure to the contingencies associated with red, and begins this last series of sessions with a relatively high rate on the observing key. This seems to offer a highly favorable test situation for demonstrating any possible reinforcing effects of producing red. All that is necessary is for red to maintain a previously established performance. But this it fails to do.

After eight more sessions of red only, which are not shown in Figure 14.8, we attempted to reestablish observing with 1-sec displays of both red and green. This was not successful. We then reestablished the response, using 30-sec displays of green only, and established a new base line with 5-sec displays of both red and green. On six occasions thereafter, we tested the effects of the red-only procedure, each time finding that the rate of observing dropped to a near-zero level. Each time, we reestablished the observing performance by restoring green to the procedure. The last two of these tests are shown in Figure 14.9.

To make sure that these results did not reflect some idiosyncrasy of P–3031 or of his conditioning history, we also performed a

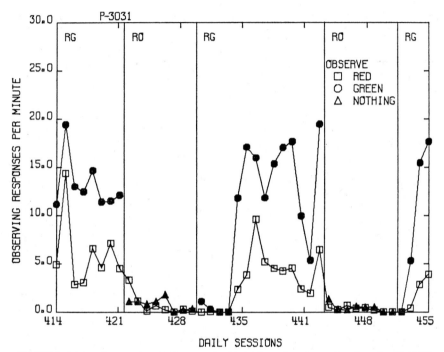

FIGURE 14.9. Successive daily rates of pecking the observing key by P–3031 under the red-green (*RG*) and red only (*RO*) procedures. The rates were computed from latencies when the color last presented was red (squares) or green (circles) and from interresponse times when no change was produced (triangles). When the observing occurred during the no-punishment schedule on the food key the symbols are solid. The stimulus display lasted 5 sec. When programmed, shocks of 300 volts were delivered following every 20th response on the food key.

similar series of tests on P–2761. During the second of these tests, at a 30-sec duration of display, we included four sessions in which grain could be secured only during red. This "priming" procedure established a substantial rate of observing, but when the selective food reinforcement was discontinued, the rate quickly dropped back again to its usual level. Our last two tests with P–2761 are shown in

Figure 14.10. Again, the production of red alone, without the accompaniment of green, fails to sustain the observing performance. We have also conducted brief tests with other birds, but have never succeeded in maintaining the response.

Since our birds readily make the transition to green only, following red-green, and maintain relatively high rates of responding, the failure to maintain the observing performance under the red only procedure seems to confirm our previous conclusion that red is not

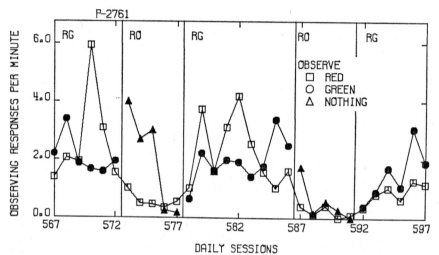

FIGURE 14.10. Successive daily rates of pecking the observing key by P–2761 under the red-green (*RG*) and red only (*RO*) procedures. The rates were computed from latencies when the color last presented was red (squares) or green (circles) and from interresponse times when no change was produced (triangles). When the observing occurred during the no-punishment schedule on the food key the symbols are solid. (This bird pecked the food key at a higher rate following green than following red, and the competing activity may have delayed the corresponding peck on the observing key.) The stimulus display lasted 30 sec. When programmed, shocks of 200 volts were delivered following every 35th response on the food key.

an effective reinforcer. In all of our data, we have been able to find no evidence of a positive effect. Whether red is actually punishing is at this point difficult to say. Perhaps more sensitive techniques can be found which will answer this question; it is possible, for example, that birds will peck to remove red from the keys. The most we have been able to do with our present techniques is to bracket the range within which the effect of red must lie. But if red had severe suppressive effects, these should have shown up in a difference between the performance under the green-only procedure and the performance when red was added. There are some suggestions of temporary deterioration, but the data are far from conclusive.

Clearly, our data do not support the suggestion that the observing response is maintained because it provides useful information concerning the consequences of subsequent behavior. On the other hand, the large magnitude of the reinforcing effect of green and the small magnitude of the punishing effect, if any, of red do not seem wholly in accord with what would be expected on the basis of the association between these stimuli and the delivery of shock. The two effects are far from symmetrical. It is possible that they represent an algebraic summation of two different sources of strength. By association, green should be positively reinforcing and red punishing. As information, both should be positively reinforcing. Empirically, green appears to be highly reinforcing and red almost neutral in its effect.

SUMMARY

The purpose of this study was to find out why pigeons observe stimuli indicating whether subsequent behavior may be punished. Two general formulations were considered: (a) that these stimuli are reinforcing because they provide useful information; (b) that the effect of each stimulus is based on its temporal association with the punishment.

The pigeons were tested under variations of a standard procedure in which pecking an "observing" key changed the illumination of this key and an adjacent "food" key from white to red or green. When the keys were green, pecking the food key produced access to grain on a variable-interval schedule averaging a little less than 2 min. When the keys were red, pecking not only produced grain on an identical schedule but also produced 0.1-sec shock following every 20th or every 35th response. Switching between these schedules was controlled by a random probability generator and occurred, on the average, about every 2 min. When the pigeon did not peck the observing key, the two schedules continued to alternate as usual but were not accompanied by differential stimulation; that is, the keys remained white.

As would be expected, a discriminative performance was maintained on the food key. The rate of pecking was high in the presence of green, intermediate in the presence of white, and low in the presence of red. When the keys turned white, the pigeon pecked the observing key.

In order to assess the contribution of red and the contribution of green to the maintenance of the observing performance, two special procedures were employed. When only the green stimulus was available, the bird produced it as often as before and frequently pecked the key when this produced no change in stimulation. When only the red was available, the bird stopped pecking the observing key.

Since the production of red did not maintain the observing performance, it is clear that the effects of these stimuli on the observing response cannot be explained wholly in terms of the information they convey to the subject. Some other factor must be involved. On the other hand, since there was little evidence that the production of red suppressed the observing performance when green was also available, there is some question whether the effects of these stimuli can be explained wholly in terms of their temporal association with the shock. It is possible that information and association summate algebraically to make green highly reinforcing and red approximately neutral in its effect.

chapter 15

CONCLUDING COMMENTARY

Derek P. Hendry
University of Illinois
Chicago Circle

REMARKS ON FINDINGS

Previous work on second-order schedules, reviewed by Marr in Chapter 2, verifies in a convincing and elegant fashion that temporal association with a primary reinforcer has a strong effect on conditioned reinforcing value of stimuli. Stimuli paired with the final primary reinforcer are capable of sustaining second-order performances indefinitely. These results do not show, however, that the absence of a close temporal association with reinforcement will prevent a stimulus from becoming a conditioned reinforcer.

Several contributors show that the scheduling of conditioned reinforcement may have very powerful effects, overriding the control normally exerted by the schedule of primary reinforcement. Thomas (Chapter 4) pitted the demands of the schedule of conditioned reinforcement against the demands of the schedule of primary reinforcement. The schedule of primary reinforcement favored a low- (or zero) response rate, while the schedule of conditioned reinforcement favored a high-response rate. A high-response rate was maintained, so conditioned reinforcement was obtained at the cost of primary reinforcement. Further evidence of a sustained effect of the schedule of conditioned reinforcement largely independently of the primary reinforcer, was provided by Zimmerman (Chapter 5). Performance was sustained for an indefinite time after the primary reinforcer had been discontinued. From a strictly operational point of view Zimmerman's results demonstrate functional autonomy in the pigeon—the ultimate in durability of a conditioned reinforcer.

When performance is sustained by cues associated with primary reinforcement it is tempting to construe this as simply another case of intermittent reinforcement, because occasionally the conditioned reinforcer "keeps its promise" and the primary reinforcer follows. This point of view, so congenial because it excuses us from theoretical exertions, is made quite implausible by the results obtained by Thomas (Chapter 4). He showed that performance would be sustained by a feeder light flash even when this contingency occurred under conditions discriminable from those in which a response produced the primary reinforcer. To put it differently, the animal "knew" that responding on a green key never produced the primary reinforcer, and that the "promise" of the feeder light flash was never fulfilled when the key was green. Nevertheless, the feeder light flash still reinforced pecking the green key. Thomas showed that the animals could readily discriminate the condition of the key being green, and they could distinguish a feeder light flash from a neutral stimulus.

The results of Kendall (Chapter 10) and Hendry (Chapter 12) agree in showing that various mixed-ratio schedules generate sufficient uncertainty to sustain observing behavior reinforced by signals for the component ratios. In Kendall's experiments the cues signaled the forthcoming ratio and in Hendry's experiments the current ratio.

Kendall's first experiment shows that a detected signal need not give any indication of being a conditioned reinforcer. We know that the signals were detected by their orderly and consistent effect on behavior. There was a delay between the brief stimulus and the primary reinforcer. The original definition of discriminative stimulus, as we have noted in Chapter 1, required a reinforced response to occur during or perhaps just after the stimulus. Therefore, to retain the terminology for cases like Kendall's, it is necessary to invent the concept of *trace discriminative stimulus*. (*cf.*, Dinsmoor, *et al.*, Chapter 14; Hendry & Dillow, 1966). Insofar as the results of Kendall and others show that trace discriminative stimuli may be conditioned reinforcers, they weaken the whole basis of the traditional approach to conditioned reinforcement. What Kendall's result brings into question is the tenet, fundamental to associationist learning theory, that *contiguity* of the stimulus with a primary reinforcer is necessary for the stimulus to become a conditioned reinforcer. Well-known effects of Chain schedules of reinforcement have weakened the claim that contiguity of a stimulus with primary reinforcement is necessary for the stimulus to become reinforcing. Consider a three-component Chain schedule. The stimulus (S_2) associated with the middle component is never closely associated with primary reinforcement and signifies its delay rather than its imminence. Yet the maintenance of performance in the first component is taken to show a conditioned reinforcing effectiveness of S_2. To tailor our definitions better to the body of knowledge, a discriminative stimulus has to be regarded as a stimulus in whose presence a particular response occasionally produces a reinforcer —*either primary or conditioned*. Thus, in a Chain, the stimulus (S_1) in the final component is a discriminative stimulus and may also be expected to be a conditioned reinforcer. Given that, S_2 must be a discriminative stimulus—and so on, conceivably, *ad infinitum*. The pity is that this more inclusive definition of discriminative stimulus does not allow us to retain the simple generalization that all discriminative stimuli are conditioned reinforcers. In the context of Chain schedules the generalization implies that every stimulus in the Chain will become a conditioned reinforcer. This is a patently false implication since performance is suppressed, often for several hours, in the early links of extended chains (*cf.,* Kelleher & Gollub, 1962). The fact that all stimuli in a Chain are not conditioned reinforcers implies that there is at least one stimulus that is a discriminative stimulus and is not a conditioned reinforcer.

Crossman's experiment (Chapter 11) depended heavily on the assumption that a conditioned reinforcing effect within a Chain will show up as a reduction in the latency of initiating the Chain. Whether this is so or not may depend in a complex way on the conditions. In Crossman's procedure the interspersed brief cue is analogous to a checkpoint in a countdown. In a 75-step countdown (FR 75) arrival at fifth position (5 down, 70 to go) is not the most exciting event, though it may have clear signaling properties.

Crossman's procedures are similar to those of Farmer and Schoenfeld (1966), who used interval, rather than ratio, schedules. The procedures are compared in Figure 15.1.

The effect on the reinforced response of the interspersed stimulus differs systematically according to its position in a temporal sequence (Farmer & Schoenfeld, 1966). Does its effect vary also according to its position in a response sequence? Crossman's results are similar to Farmer and Schoenfeld's, in that a cue available long before the scheduled primary reinforcer has little effect on the reinforced response. It may be that the significance of the cue (indicating the relative remoteness of reinforcement in time or responses) overrides any conditioned reinforcing effect it might have by virtue of its occasional pairing with the primary reinforcer. Crossman's results are more consistent with a punishing,

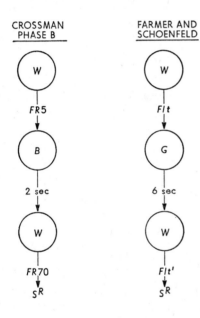

FIGURE 15.1. Comparison of two procedures in which a stimulus marks a "distance" from reinforcement. Circled letters represent key colors: W is white, B is blue, G is green. $t + t' = 54$ sec. (See text.)

rather than with a reinforcing, effect of the added stimulus, insofar as the animals waited longer after a reinforcement before initiating the schedule containing the added stimulus.

According to a general interpretation of the Information Hypothesis, a stimulus that reduces uncertainty is a conditioned reinforcer. A situation which may contain periods of reinforcement or periods of nonreinforcement represents greater uncertainty for the animal than one which contains only periods of reinforcement or only periods of nonreinforcement. This implies that under certain conditions, in experiments like those of Wyckoff (Chapter 9) and Steiner (see Chapter 1), for example, S^Δ will be a conditioned reinforcer. This implication is clearly at odds with traditional reinforcement theory, as embodied, for example, in Autor's law, according to which S^Δ should have zero reinforcing value.

Several investigations have been directed to this implication of the idea that animals are sensitive to information. Hendry and Coulbourn (1967) showed that S^Δ became a conditioned reinforcer if it also predicted the delivery of food. Schaub (see Chapter 13) showed that S^Δ can sustain observing behavior in a situation where S^Δ reduces uncertainty.

To assess the reinforcing effect of a stimulus one arranges for it to follow a carefully measured test response. When there are only two possible conditions, signified by S^D and S^Δ, all the available information (1 bit) is given by S^D or S^Δ. This is the basis of the inference that S^Δ should be reinforcing. However, in the test for a conditioned reinforcing effect, if the test response produces S^D as well as S^Δ, the test response can be interpreted as partially reinforced (by S^D). On the other hand, there are two arguments against having the test response produce only S^Δ. One argument is that S^Δ signifies Extinction and while S^Δ may be reinforcing, it controls not-responding. Thus, the discriminative action of S^Δ may be misinterpreted for a nonreinforcing or a punishing effect. Secondly, if the S^D is simply omitted, but unsignaled primary reinforcement still occurs, failure of S^D to follow the test response may be a distinctive enough event to function as a new S^D.

It is therefore difficult to make a convincing case for a reinforcing effect of S^Δ by the usual tests. One way of determining how effective in the generation of conditioned reinforcement is the informative value of a cue, is to discover the effects of varying informative value directly.

Steiner (1967) varied the redundancy of the observing-response-produced cues by varying the discriminability of the ("free") nonresponse-produced cues. The more discriminable the cues, the weaker the observing behavior. Another example of eliminating the observing-response-produced cues by making them redundant is shown in Figure 15.2. A three-link Tandem *FI* schedule was programmed on the food key, and the current link could be determined (i.e., signaled) by observing responses on another key. Note in Figure 15.2 that observing behavior is usually absent for the 15 sec that any cue signifying a component is on, and is eliminated completely when the cues are turned on continuously. This result was obtained when the appropriate cue was displayed on the food key or on the observing key. In the former case the physical effects of observing responses were not changed, only the context in which observing could take place. It was the change in context that made the observing-response-produced cues redundant.

The informative value of cues may also be varied by varying the initial probability of each cue, or each condition that the cues signify or predict. This technique was used by the present author in Chapter 12 (without a satisfactory result) and previously. In one

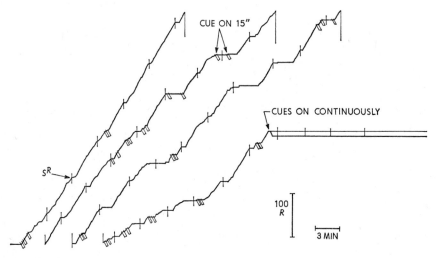

FIGURE 15.2.   Effect on observing FI 1 key performance when observing responses occasionally (VI 3) produce the cues (for 15 sec) associated with Chain 3(FI) and when the cues are presented continuously. Unpublished results of experiments reported by Hendry and Dillow (1966).

experiment (Hendry, 1965), a chimpanzee made observing responses to produce the cues (S^D and S^Δ) that distinguished periods of VR 100 from periods of Extinction. Observing response rate varied as a function of the probability of obtaining S^D, as shown in Figure 15.3. The function has the rough shape of the entropy of a two-event system, namely

$$H = -[p \log p + (1 - p) \log (1 - p)]$$

where p is the probability of one of the events. Finding out whether VR 100 or Extinction is in effect is most reinforcing, as indicated

by observing response rate, where the two schedules are equiproba-
ble or nearly so. When one of the schedules—no matter which
one—is highly probable, finding out which one is in effect is not
reinforcing. Likewise, it was shown in Chapter 12 that making a
particular schedule occur with probability 1.0, rather than 0.5,
eliminated observing behavior.

Explanations of maintained observing behavior by differential
positive reinforcement are ruled out in cases where the cues to be

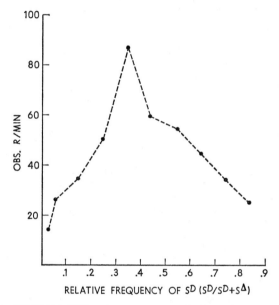

FIGURE 15.3. Average rate of observing responses as a function of the likelihood of obtaining S^D [from Hendry (1965)].

observed signal differential contingencies of punishment. By this
method Dinsmoor *et al.* (Chapter 14) show that information about
impending punishment is reinforcing. In the context of differential
contingencies of punishment the stimuli corresponding to S^D and S^Δ
may be called *danger signal* and *safe signal*. Dinsmoor *et al.* found
that the safe signal was reinforcing when used alone, but not the
danger signal.

The inequality of the reinforcing effects of the safe and danger
signals apparently shows that these reinforcing effects are not
wholly derived from their informative function. A similar conclu-

sion arises in the case of discriminations based on positive reinforcement. Thus, from experiments in which birds could produce
the cues for either favorable or unfavorable states of the environment, both Dinsmoor and Schaub arrive at the conclusion that the
reinforcing value of such cues is derived from a combination of
associative and informative factors.

REINFORCEMENT THROUGH PUNISHMENT

No attempt has been made in this book to deal with the phenomena of learned reward based upon escape from an aversive situation, commonly attributed to the reduction of "fear" or "anxiety."
The only systematic treatment of this subject appears to be that of
Miller (1951). An integration of these effects into the several
conceptual schemes outlined in this book remains a task for the
future. For the present, however, prompted by the results of Chapter 14 by Dinsmoor and his colleagues, I wish to consider the extension of concepts of information to the case of aversive control. It
turns out that some of the relevant experimental results have very
general implications.

The Estes-Skinner procedure

Signals related to an aversive event have complex effects that
depend upon the past experience of the animal and the schedule of
reinforcement upon which the signal is superimposed. In the simple
case of the Estes-Skinner procedure, where a signal (CS)-shock
(US) combination is superimposed on a base line of positively
reinforced responding, performance is first suppressed during the
signal (e.g., Estes & Skinner, 1941). As the procedure is continued,
a graded effect appears during the signal, with suppression eventually being confined to the later part of the signal (e.g., Sidman,
1960a) and response facilitation often occurring during the early
part (e.g., Hendry & Van Toller, 1965).

The effects of the signal for shock on performance that has been
or is being maintained by an avoidance schedule are the same but
opposite in direction. The initial increase in rate gives way to a
graded effect similar to "scalloping" in fixed-interval schedules of
reinforcement (Kelleher, Riddle, & Cook, 1963; Sidman, Herrnstein, & Conrad, 1957; Waller & Waller, 1963). The rate maintained in the absence of the signal is eventually suppressed at the

beginning of the signal and enhanced at the end. This is clearly shown for the individual signals in cumulative records of performance (Kelleher, Riddle, & Cook, 1963; Sidman, Herrnstein, & Conrad, 1957) and in numerical data of average response rates (Rescorla, 1967, 1968).

The emergence of two opposite effects of a stimulus preceding shock can be explained by its signaling properties, or the correct predictions that it may afford the animal. Thus, after long exposure to the situation, the onset of a stimulus at least several seconds long signals absence of shock. The longer the stimulus stays on the more it signals the imminence of shock. These two functions of the stimulus may be referred to as those of a safe signal and a danger signal. When the duration of the signal is made random, its status as a combination of a safe signal and danger signal should be eliminated and the grading of response rate should be abolished. This is what happens (Millenson & Hendry, 1967).

The concepts of safe signal and danger signal can be validated to some extent by arranging the appropriate contingencies between shock and two stimuli, explicitly making one stimulus a signal for shock and the other a signal for absence of shock. The effects are clear-cut—a relative suppression of positively reinforced responses in the danger signal and their maintenance or enhancement in the safe signal (Ayres, 1966; Hammond, 1965; Hendry, 1967; Hendry, Yarczower, & Switalski, 1966; Ray & Stein, 1959). Likewise, there is a relative enhancement of the rate of avoidance responses during the danger signal and suppression during a safe signal arranged as a Pavlovian CS^- or as a Pavlovian conditioned inhibitor paired with the CS (Rescorla & LoLordo, 1965).

The effectiveness of the signaling properties of a preshock stimulus is consistent with the effects of varying its duration. The shorter the signal, the more difficult it must be to resolve a safe duration. Thus, shorter durations of the signal produce more conditioned suppression (Stein, Sidman, & Brady, 1958).

Response-produced signals for aversive stimuli

In spite of all the complexity of effects of signals related to an aversive event, there has been very little inquiry into the effects of such signals on responses which produce them. This is probably because widely held ideas about punishment seem to assume what these effects are, so that we do not recognize our ignorance about them. For example, the CS in the Estes-Skinner procedure often elicits fear as defined by a number of objective criteria, and some of the respondents elicited by the US. Accordingly, the CS is identified as a "conditioned aversive stimulus," whose removal is assumed to be reinforcing. This reinforcing effect is used in the explanation of avoidance behavior. It seems to follow that the CS must be an effective punisher, reducing the probability of response that produce it. Of course, that does not follow at all, even if the CS is aversive in the sense of reinforcing escape responses. The conclusion that the CS is a punisher is an example of a fallible inference from the functions a stimulus has when it is present to the functions it has when it is response-produced. Whether the CS is a punisher or not is an empirical question. Under the proper conditions, if it reduced uncertainty, we would expect the CS to be a positive reinforcer. A case in point is the preference of rats for a predictable shock (a stimulus followed by shock) over an unpredictable shock (shock followed by the stimulus, or accompanied by the stimulus or randomly related to the stimulus) (e.g., Lockard, 1963, 1965; Perkins, Seyman, Levis, & Spencer, 1966).

It follows that a stimulus may be both positively and negatively reinforcing. The objection to this conclusion is that "if the stimulus is the same it must have the same effect." However, though the positively and negatively reinforcing stimulus is the same, the test conditions for positive and negative reinforcement are different. In one case the stimulus is turned off by the experimenter and turned on by the animal; in the other case the stimulus is turned on by the experimenter and off by the animal. It may be possible to have the stimulus turned both on and off by the animal, showing a positive and negative reinforcing effect of the same stimulus. One such case is reported by Bower and Miller (1958) where the stimulus was electrical stimulation of the medial forebrain bundle of the hypothalamus. A general case of a stimulus apparently having both positive reinforcing and aversive effects is news that turns out to be bad. Even those whose experience is that only bad news comes by telegram nevertheless open and read telegrams. It is a mundane but important observation that this performance presupposes an appropriate history; young children show little interest in telegrams. An experimental analog of "bad news" is a signal for EXT (S^Δ). After an appropriate experimental history, S^Δ may become a positive reinforcer (Schaub, Chapter 13.)

One notable study (Hake & Azrin, 1965) showed more clearly than previous similar studies a punishing effect of a signal for shock, and a suppressive effect, while the signal was on, on positively reinforced performance. This is an interesting result because one might have expected the signal for shock to be reinforcing rather than punishing for one of two reasons: Either the signal, which lasted 15 sec when terminated with shock, predicted the shock, or its onset was a safe signal, associated with absence of shock. However, somewhat different conditions might have made the signal a conditioned reinforcer. In the absence of the signal there was no uncertainty about the occurrence of shock, because it occurred only at the end of the signal. If the shock had occurred unsignaled when response rate was low and preceded by the response-produced signal when response rate was high, a conditioned reinforcing effect of the signal might have resulted. This result would be consistent with the demonstrated preference for signaled over unsignaled shock.

Another study that allows us to make some statements about the conditioned reinforcing or punishing effect of signals related to shock showed that a safe signal in the form of a conditioned inhibitor of conditioned suppression could reinforce a new response (Hendry, 1967). There was also a suggestion that the danger signal itself raised the rate of the test response, but so little that it might be interpreted as an effect of stimulus-change or some other irrelevant process.

Shock as a positive reinforcer

One very puzzling behavioral phenomenon may be interpreted in terms of a reinforcing effect of a safe signal. If a squirrel monkey has a history of making a particular response in a situation in which he is occasionally shocked, the response can be brought under the control of the shock by presenting the shock on a fixed-interval schedule for responding. The final performance resembles the pattern of accelerated responding typical of fixed-interval schedules of positive reinforcement. The monkey persists, apparently indefinitely, in emitting at relatively high rates responses whose only effect is the periodic production of electric shock. (Morse, Mead, & Kelleher, 1967; Stretch, Orloff, & Dalrymple, 1968). No shocks would be received if the monkey stopped responding completely.

The clue to the explanation of this behavior may be that the probability of response is initially high enough to ensure some shocked responses and some unshocked responses in an experimental session. That is a condition of uncertainty, the animal being unable to predict when a response will be shocked, or, in other words, it is a situation with no effective stimulus that signals shock. Given that the probability of response is not reduced to zero by this initial condition, it must happen that responses immediately after a shocked response are never shocked. In fact, the conditions of training in the reports cited are such as to ensure that, initially, the highest probability of a response is immediately after shock. We may assume that the monkeys discriminate these contingencies of punishment. It follows that, given always that the probability of response is not zero, the only safe signal is the shock itself. The shock alone initiates a fixed period when no shocks can be received. Therefore, the shock itself should become a conditioned reinforcer.

Working in the department of pharmacology at Harvard medical school, C. B. Smith made one of the earliest uses of a second-order schedule procedure, to determine whether an electric shock could be made a conditioned reinforcer.[1] Smith used FR $(FI:P)$, where P was a brief electric shock. That is, completion of several FI shock schedules was reinforced with food. This schedule produced the typical fixed-interval acceleration (or scallop) between shocks, and this development of schedule control is evidence for a positive reinforcing value of the shock. The scallops disappeared and the response rate declined in a control condition in which the shock was eliminated.

Smith's study is reminiscent of the demonstrations of discriminative control of responding by punishment (Holz & Azrin, 1961, 1963). Holz and Azrin showed that the rate of punished responding could be made to depend predominantly on the schedule of reinforcement for punished responding, when punishment served as a positive discriminative stimulus. In addition, the suppressive effect of electric shock was eliminated or reduced when it signaled the imminence of positive reinforcement in a fixed-interval schedule.

Positive discriminative stimuli are usually conditioned reinfor-

---

[1] This investigation was described at the 71st Annual Convention of the American Psychological Association at Philadelphia in 1963, but no description has appeared in print.

cers. Therefore, we would expect the electric shock in Holz and Azrin's studies, since it served as S^D, to be a conditioned reinforcer, as was the case in Smith's experiment. The results of Holz and Azrin (1963) do contain some data that could be interpreted as showing a reinforcing effect of electric shock. When every response in the third quarter of FI 4 was punished, the responding showed two scallops—up to the first punished response, then after punishment up to the food reinforcement. The procedure bears obvious similarities to Smith's and the results are also similar. Both experiments suggest a conditioned reinforcing effect of electric shock when it occurs in a systematic relation to positive reinforcement.

Holz and Azrin's procedure was unlike that of Smith in that the electric shock was given only in the third quarter of FI 4 and not also in association with the food reinforcement. The interpretation we favor is that the shock was acting as a timing stimulus, and was informative by virtue of coming at a more or less fixed time in relation to reinforcement. Pairing the stimulus with a reinforcer is not necessary to make that stimulus a conditioned reinforcer, though it may make it a more effective conditioned reinforcer. Unfortunately Holz and Azrin did not, for purposes of comparison, schedule a response-produced neutral stimulus in the third quarter of FI 4. However, in a similar procedure (see Figure 15.3) Farmer and Schoenfeld (1966a, 1966b) have shown fixed-interval schedule control, and thus a presumptive reinforcing value, of a neutral stimulus placed at intermediate positions in FI 1, but not necessarily in close association with the primary reinforcer.

Temporal and informative relations in extensions of the Estes-Skinner procedure

We have already drawn attention to the informative interpretation of the effect of duration of the CS in the Estes-Skinner procedure. We discuss here further observations on relations of temporal and informative factors in conditioned suppression. This discussion is relevant to the application of an information analysis to conditioned suppression both directly through the concepts of safe signal and danger signal, and indirectly through the interpretation of conditioned suppression as subject to the laws of classical conditioning, and therefore to analyses in terms of information.

Both Seligman (1966) and Ayres (1966) found that a redundant predictor of shock and a 50 percent reliable predictor suppressed the positively reinforced base-line performance, though Seligman found (and Ayres did not) that a 100 percent reliable predictor of shock produced even more suppression. The results as a whole seemed to indicate a very limited relevance of the concept of information to conditioned suppression. However, in both these experiments the animals were exposed to only 10 or 20 presentations of the relevant combinations of stimuli. In information analysis the speed with which informative functions of stimuli are learned has not been made explicit. There are two extreme possibilities. One is that the detection of an informative relation is almost entirely a perceptual matter, with a negligible learning component. The other possibility is than an informative function is essentially a learned discrimination and that speed of learning the discrimination will depend on its difficulty. Of course, detection of an informative relation could require any combination of degrees of perceptual and learning capacities. The effects of the Estes-Skinner procedure described above show that detection of informative relations takes a long time to develop. For tens or hundreds of CS-US pairings performance is uniformly suppressed throughout the CS. Graded response rate during the CS develops gradually (Hendry & Van Toller, 1965; Millenson & Hendry, 1967). In one sense, the informative relations override the temporal relations between stimuli, but, in another sense, given a sufficiently dynamic, relational conception of "stimulus," the informative relations and temporal relations between stimuli are mutually consistent.

The results of Wagner, Logan, Haberlandt, and Price (1968), in contrast to those of Seligman and Ayres, are in accordance with the view that the effect of a stimulus is in the long run determined by its informative relation to the reinforcer (shock in the Estes-Skinner procedure). In this study two compound sound-light stimuli were used, A_1L and A_2L. A_1L was a reliable predictor of the reinforcer (analogous to S^D or S^+ or CS^+) and A_2L was a reliable predictor of its absence (analogous to S^Δ or S^- or CS^-). In some conditions A_1L and A_2L predicted the reinforcer with 50 percent reliability. The effects of presenting the components were determined, but, in this case, after several hundred presentations of the compounds. The performance of the animals was dominated by the signaling properties of the compounds and components. Thus, even though L was a 50 percent reliable predictor of the reinforcer in all conditions, in the main experimental conditions it was redundant, since it was always paired with a better predictor. Accordingly, L was behaviorally ineffective. On the other hand, in the control conditions, where A_1L and A_2L were both 50 percent reliable predictors, L was as effective as, or more effective than, A_1 and A_2. These results held in the case of the Estes-Skinner procedure which we have been considering, but also in the case of classical aversive conditioning of eyelid closure and in the case of signaled positive reinforcement in an operant discrimination. The generality of the result gives considerable encouragement for experimental analysis in terms of concepts of information.

To summarize the view that we have been discussing, it seems likely that, in the case of conditioned suppression at least, temporal association of stimuli dominates what animals learn initially about "what-leads-to-what," but that performance eventually comes under the influence of more complex, informative relations in the environment. Indeed, learning associations may be necessary to ensure exposure, in common situations, to the relevant, more complex relations that are finally learned.

General implications

The generality of the results of Wagner *et al.*, applying to both classical and instrumental conditioning situations, have been remarked. In instrumental learning, the process of going from responsiveness to simple temporal relations to responsiveness to informative relations is seen perhaps most clearly in the case of matching-to-sample (e.g., Ferster, 1960). Suppose the target choices are red and green side keys with sample on a center key. Pecking a green side key is occasionally reinforced and pecking a red side key is occasionally reinforced, and the bird learns to peck the (center) sample key to produce a red side key and a green side key, by the ordinary process of chaining. This keeps the bird exposed to the relevant sequences, which are: (1) Peck red center key, peck red side key, food sometimes. (2) Peck green center key, peck green side key, food sometimes. (3) Peck red center key, peck green side key, food never. (4) Peck green center key, peck red side key, food never.

The bird initially pecks red and green side keys rather indiscriminately, his performance being dominated by the simple temporal (probabilistic) relation between these side-key colors and the reinforcing stimulus. Thus the bird continues to be exposed to the four sequences above. That the bird is sensitive to the differences between these sequences is shown by the fact that his performance comes to be controlled by them (e.g., Ferster, 1960). To discriminate the relations between stimuli, the bird has to be exposed repeatedly to various relations, and this is accomplished by the initial effectiveness of simple S-R (or S-S) association.

The foregoing is a fairly speculative theory suggested by strictly behavioral phenomena. The similarity of this theory to aspects of Hebb's (1949) theory of brain function is especially striking because Hebb's theory was suggested by and designed to deal with quite a different kind of phenomena. Part of Hebb's theory was that in ontogenesis symbol-manipulation and higher mental processes had to be preceded by the organization of sensory systems by an association (S-R or S-S) process. The higher mental processes simply consist of the development of concatenations and transformations of neural representations of the associated elements. The separate but merging processes of association and creation of higher order relations that Hebb postulated for ontogenesis, we postulate as part of the organism's ordinary commerce with the environment. Here we resist the temptation to speculate further, for example, about species differences and the relevance of the theory to educational practice.

If our theory is near the mark, it is obviously futile to try to decide whether learned behavior incorporates or is controlled only by associations (S-R or R-S) on the one hand; or whether it may be determined, on the other hand, by the more complex relations that we have called informative. These are not exclusive alternatives. For the same animal in the same physical circumstances, performance may be determined at one time by associations and at another time by more complex informative relations, or, perhaps, at still another time, by both. More specifically, in a given situation the stimulus most effective in controlling behavior may at one time be the stimulus most closely associated with the reinforcer; at another time it may be the stimulus that most reliably predicts the reinforcer, or a stimulus with a cue function; at another time, both kinds of stimuli may be effective. Also, the effectiveness of a stimulus may be determined partly by its associations and partly by the information it conveys, as proposed by Schaub (Chapter 13).

NOTE ON TERMINOLOGY

We suffer from certain deficiencies in referring to phenomena that come under the heading of conditioned reinforcement. There exists a rather vague concept of "strength" or "effectiveness" of a stimulus, referring to the effect the stimulus has on responses that produce it. This is not the same as reinforcing strength, but is akin to the precise concept of *stimulus control.* All the stimuli impinging on an animal at a given moment vary in their effectiveness with respect to a particular operant. The degree to which the probability of an operant varies with the presence/absence of a discriminative stimulus is referred to as the degree of *stimulus control* exerted by the stimulus. What is needed is a term that refers to the degree to which the emission of an operant can be controlled by a response-produced stimulus. This was formerly referred to as the strength of the conditioned reinforcer. However, there seems to be a need to refer to the effectiveness of the stimulus without the normal implications of calling it a reinforcer. Let us call it a *maintaining stimulus;* in second-order schedules :S is a maintaining stimulus. The strength of a maintaining stimulus is the degree to which the probability of some response or pattern of responses depends upon whether the response produces the stimulus. This parallels the definition of strength of a controlling stimulus. Thus *effective* stimuli are either *controlling* stimuli or *maintaining* stimuli. The class of maintaining stimuli includes reinforcing stimuli.

The need to distinguish a maintaining from a reinforcing function comes partly from the fact that a response-produced stimulus that maintains one operant may not maintain a similar, but different operant, as shown, for example, by Keehn (1962), whose experiment is described in Chapter 8. A primary reinforcer is said to be "trans-situational," effective in maintaining an arbitrary operant. Since the effectiveness of a conditioned reinforcer is notoriously difficult to demonstrate in a different environment from the one in which it was established, it seems more prudent and objective to avoid the connotations of the word "reinforcer" by a liberal use of the term "maintaining stimulus" in place of "conditioned reinforcer." Another particular result which argues against calling a maintaining stimulus a reinforcer is Schuster's demonstration (Chapter 8) that a schedule of maintaining stimuli with a schedule of primary reinforcement is not preferred to the schedule of primary reinforcement alone. Clearly, the maintaining stimulus did not add any incentive value to the option in which it figured even when it was associated with the primary reinforcer. On the other hand, both Marr (Chapter 2) and De Lorge (Chapter 3) comment on a case in which a stimulus *not* associated with the primary reinforcer was nevertheless quite an effective maintaining stimulus in a second-order schedule.

The need for a term like "maintaining stimulus" became apparent only in going over all the contributions in this book. Therefore, I have placed this note on terminology at the end of the book, where some readers may never find it. This will minimize the risk of confusion from defining a term that is never used. If it has any merit, it will presumably survive.

REFERENCES

REFERENCES

Amsel, A.   The role of frustrative non-reward in noncontinuous reward situations. *Psychological Bulletin,* 1958, 55, 102–119.

Amsel, A. and Hancock, W.   Motivational properties of frustration: III. Relation of frustration effect to antedating goal factors. *Journal of Experimental Psychology,* 1957, 53, 126–131.

Amsel, A. and Roussel, J.   Motivational properties of frustration: I. Effect on a running response of the addition of frustration to the motivational complex. *Journal of Experimental Psychology,* 43, 363–368.

Appel, J. B.   Aversive aspects of a schedule of positive reinforcement. *Journal of the Experimental Analysis of Behavior,* 1963, 6, 423–428.

Armus, H. L. and Garlich, M. M.   Secondary reinforcing strength as a function of schedule of primary reinforcement. *Journal of Comparative and Physiological Psychology,* 1961, 54, 56–58.

Autor, S. M.   "The strength of conditioned reinforcers as a function of frequency and probability of reinforcement." Doctoral dissertation, Harvard University, 1960.

Ayres, J. J. B.   Conditioned suppression and the information hypothesis. *Journal of Comparative and Physiological Psychology,* 1966, 62, 21–25.

Azrin, N. H.   Some effects of two intermittent schedules of immediate and non-immediate punishment. *Journal of Psychology,* 1956, 42, 3–21.

Azrin, N. H.   A technique for delivering shock to pigeons. *Journal of the Experimental Analysis of Behavior,* 1959, 2, 161–163.

Azrin, N. H.   Time-out from positive reinforcement. *Science,* 1961, 133, 382–383.

Azrin, N. H. and Holz, W. C.   Punishment. In E. K. Honig (Ed.), *Operant behavior: areas of research and application.* New York: Appleton-Century-Crofts, 1966.

Azrin, N. H., Holz, W. C. and Hake, D. F.   Fixed-ratio punishment. *Journal of the Experimental Analysis of Behavior,* 1963, 6, 141–148.

Badia, P., McBane, B., Suter, S. and Lewis, P.   Preference behavior in an immediate versus variably delayed shock situation with and without a warning signal. *Journal of Experimental Psychology,* 1966, 72, 847–852.

Badia, P., Suter, S. and Lewis, P.   Rat vocalization to shock with and without a CS. *Psychonomic Science,* 1966, 4, 117–118.

Baron, J.   An EEG correlate of autonomic discrimination. *Psychonomic Science,* 1966, 4, 255–256.

Berlyne, D. E.   Attention, perception and behavior theory. *Psychological Review*, 1951, 58, 137–146.

Berlyne, D. E.   Uncertainty and conflict: a point of contact between information theory and behavior theory concepts. *Psychological Review*, 1957, 64, 329–333.

Berlyne, D. E.   *Conflict, Arousal and Curiosity*, New York: McGraw-Hill, 1960.

Bersh, P. J.   The influence of two variables upon the establishment of a secondary reinforcer for operant responses. *Journal of Experimental Psychology*, 1951, 41, 62–73.

Bitterman, M. E., Fedderson, W. E. and Tyler, D. W.   Secondary reinforcement and the discrimination hypothesis. *American Journal of Psychology*, 1953, 66, 456–464.

Bloomfield, T. M.   Behavior contrast and relative reinforcement frequency in two multiple schedules. *Journal of the Experimental Analysis of Behavior*, 1967, 10, 151–158.

Blough, D. S.   Delayed matching in the pigeon. *Journal of the Experimental Analysis of Behavior*, 1959, 2, 151–160.

Borasin, G.   "An experimental investigation of backward, forward and strictly simultaneous conditioning of fear." Master's Thesis. Kent State University, 1952.

Bower, G. and Grusec, T.   Effect of prior Pavlovian discrimination training upon learning an operant discrimination. *Journal of the Experimental Analysis of Behavior*, 1964, 7, 401–404.

Bower, G. and Miller, N. W.   Rewarding and punishing effects from stimulating the same place in the rat's brain. *Journal of Comparative and Physiological Psychology*, 1958, 51, 669–674.

Bower, G., McLean, J. and Meacham, J.   Value of knowing when reinforcement is due. *Journal of Comparative and Physiological Psychology*, 1966, 62, 184–192.

Brady, J. V., Porter, R. W., Conrad, D. G., & Mason, J. W.   Avoidance behavior and the development of gastroduodenal ulcers. *Journal of the Experimental Analysis of Behavior*, 1958, 1, 69–72.

Brethower, D. M. and Reynolds, G. S.   A facilitative effect of punishment on unpunished behavior. *Journal of the Experimental Analysis of Behavior*, 1962, 5, 191–199.

Broadbent, D.   *Perception and Communication*, Pergamon, New York, 1958.

Brogden, W. J., Lipman, E. A. and Culler, E.   The role of incentive in conditioning and extinction. *American Journal of Psychology*, 1938, 51, 109–117.

Bugelski, B. R.   Extinction with and without sub-goal reinforcement. *Journal of Comparative Psychology*, 1938, 26, 121–134.

Byrd, L. D.   "Stimulus functions in extended chain schedules." Doctoral dissertation, University of North Carolina, 1967.

Catania, A. C.   Concurrent performances: A baseline for the study of reinforcement magnitude. *Journal of the Experimental Analysis of Behavior,* 1963, 6, 299–300.

Catania, A. C. Concurrent operants. In Honig, W. K. (Ed.), *Operant behavior: areas of research and application.* New York: Appleton-Century-Crofts, 1966, 213–270.

Catania, A. C. and Reynolds, G. S. Behavioral contrast with fixed-interval and low-rate reinforcement. *Journal of the Experimental Analysis of Behavior,* 1961, 4, 383–386.

Chung, S. H. and Herrnstein, R. J. Choice and delay of reinforcement. *Journal of the Experimental Analysis of Behavior,* 1967, 10, 67–74.

Church, R. M. The varied effects of punishment on behavior. *Psychological Review,* 1963, 70, 389–402.

Cook, J. O. and Barnes, L. W., Jr. Choice of delay of inevitable shock. *Journal of Abnormal and Social Psychology,* 1964, 68, 669–672.

Crossman, E. K. Pause relationships in multiple and chained fixed-ratio schedules. *Journal of the Experimental Analysis of Behavior,* in press.

D'Amato, M. R. and Gumenik, W. E. Some effects of immediate versus randomly delayed shock on an instrumental response and cognitive processes. *Journal of Abnormal and Social Psychology,* 1960, 60, 64–67.

D'Amato, M. R., Lachman, R. and Kivy, P. Secondary reinforcement as affected by reward schedule and the testing situation. *Journal of Comparative and Physiological Psychology,* 1958, 51, 737–741.

DeLorge, J. Fixed-interval behavior maintained by conditioned reinforcement. *Journal of the Experimental Analysis of Behavior,* 1967, 10, 271–276.

Dewey, J. The reflex arc concept in Psychology. *Psychological Review,* 1896, 3, 357–370.

Dinsmoor, J. A. A quantitative comparison of the discriminative and secondary reinforcing functions of a stimulus. *Journal of Experimental Psychology,* 1950, 40, 458–472.

Dinsmoor, J. A. A discrimination based on punishment. *Quarterly Journal of Experimental Psychology,* 1952, 4, 27–45.

Dinsmoor, J. A. and Clayton, Marilyn H. Chaining and secondary reinforcement based on escape from shock. *Journal of the Experimental Analysis of Behavior,* 1963, 6, 75–80.

Dinsmoor, J. A. and Clayton, Marilyn H. A conditioned reinforcer maintained by temporal association with the termination of shock. *Journal of the Experimental Analysis of Behavior,* 1966, 9, 547–552.

Dinsmoor, J. A. and Smith, R. F. Punishment discrimination and the reinforcement of observing behavior. Paper presented at the meeting of the American Association for the Advancement of Science, Washington, D.C., December, 1966.

Egger, M. D. and Miller, N. E. Secondary reinforcement in rats as a function of information value and reliability of the stimulus. *Journal of Experimental Psychology,* 1962, 64, 97–104.

Egger, M. D. and Miller, N. E. When is reward reinforcing?: an experimental study of the information hypothesis. *Journal of Comparative and Physiological Psychology*, 1963, 56, 132–137.

Ehrenfreund, D.   An experimental test of the continuity theory and discrimination learning with pattern vision. *Journal of Comparative Physiological Psychology*, 1948, 41, 408–422.

Estes, W. K.   Discriminative conditioning II. Effects of a Pavlovian conditioned stimulus upon a subsequently established operant response. *Journal of Experimental Psychology*, 1948, 38, 173–177.

Estes, W. K.   Toward a statistical theory of learning. *Psychological Review*, 1950, 57, 94–107.

Estes, W. K. and Skinner, B. F.   Some quantitative properties of anxiety. *Journal of Experimental Psychology*, 1941, 29, 390–400.

Fantino, E.   Some data on the discriminative stimulus hypothesis of secondary reinforcement. *Psychological Review*, 1965, 15, 409–415.

Fantino, E.   Preference for mixed- versus fixed-ratio schedules. *Journal of the Experimental Analysis of Behavior*, 1967, 10, 35–43.

Fantino, E. and Herrnstein, R. J.   Secondary reinforcement and number of primary reinforcements. *Journal of the Experimental Analysis of Behavior*, 1968, 11, 9–14.

Farmer, J. and Schoenfeld, W. N.   The effect of a response-contingent stimulus introduced into a fixed-interval schedule at varying temporal placement. *Psychonomic Science*, 1966a, 6, 15–16.

Farmer, J. and Schoenfeld, W. N.   Varying temporal placement of an added stimulus in a fixed-interval schedule. *Journal of the Experimental Analysis of Behavior*, 1966b, 9, 369–375.

Ferster, C. B.   Sustained behavior under delayed reinforcement. *Journal of Experimental Psychology*, 1953, 45, 218–224.

Ferster, C. B.   Control of behavior in chimpanzees and pigeons by time out from positive reinforcement. *Psychological Monographs*, 1958a, 72, Whole No. 461, 38.

Ferster, C. B.   Intermittent reinforcement of a complex response in a chimpanzee. *Journal of the Experimental Analysis of Behavior*, 1958b. 1, 163–165.

Ferster, C. B.   Intermittent reinforcement of matching to sample in the pigeon. *Journal of the Experimental Analysis of Behavior*, 1960, 3, 259–272.

Ferster, C. B., Holtzman, E. P. and Leckrone, W. R.   A response key for use with projection-type display units. *Journal of the Experimental Analysis of Behavior*, 1962, 5, 322.

Ferster, C. B. and Skinner, B. F.   *Schedules of reinforcement.* New York: Appleton-Century-Crofts, 1957.

Findley, J. D.   "Rates of response in a two-member chain as a function of mean variable-interval schedule of reinforcement on the second member." Doctoral dissertation, Columbia University, 1954.

Findley, J. D.   Preference and switching under concurrent scheduling. *Journal of the Experimental Analysis of Behavior*, 1958, 1, 123–144.

Findley, J. D.   An experimental outline for building and exploring multi-operant behavior repertoires. *Journal of the Experimental Analysis of Behavior*, 1962, 5, 113–166.

Findley, J. D. and Brady, J. V.   Facilitation of large ratio performance by use of conditioned reinforcement. *Journal of the Experimental Analysis of Behavior*, 1965, 8, 125–129.

Galambos, R. and Griffin, D. R.   Obstacle avoidance by flying bats: The cries of bats. *Journal of Experimental Zoology*, 1942, 89, 475–490.

Galambos, R., Sheatz, G. and Vernier, V. G.   Electrophysiological correlates of a conditioned response in cats. *Science*, 1956, 123, 376–377.

Gibson, J. J.   *The senses considered as perceptual systems*. Boston: Houghton Mifflin, 1966.

Gilbert, R. (Ed.)   *Discrimination Learning*. University of Aberdeen, Aberdeen, Scotland, 1967.

Gollub, L. R.   "The chaining of fixed-interval schedules." Doctoral dissertation, Harvard University, 1958.

Guthrie, E. R.   *The Psychology of Learning*, Revised. New York: Harper, 1952.

Hake, D. F. and Azrin, N. H.   Conditioned punishment. *Journal of the Experimental Analysis of Behavior*, 1965, 8, 279–293.

Hall, J. F.   Studies in secondary reinforcement: I. Secondary reinforcement as a function of the frequency of primary reinforcement. *Journal of Comparative and Physiological Psychology*, 1951, 44, 246–251.

Hall, Mary H.   An interview with "Mr. Behaviorist," B. F. Skinner. *Psychology Today*, 1967, 1, *No. 5*, 20–23 and 68–70.

Hamm, H. D. and Zimmerman, J.   The "frustration effect" in operant studies: A necessary control procedure. *Psychonomic Science*, 1967, 9, 253–254.

Hammond, L. J.   Increased responding to *CS* in differential *CER*. *Psychonomic Science*, 1965, 5, 337–338.

Hartline, H. K.   The responses of single optic nerve fibers of the vertebrate eye to illumination of the retina. *American Journal of Physiology*, 1938, 121, 400–415.

Hebb, D. O.   *The organization of behavior*. Wiley, New York, 1949.

Held, R. and Freeman, S. J.   Plasticity in human sensorimotor control. *Science*, 1963, 142, 455–462.

Hendry, D. P.   Reinforcing value of information. NASA Technical Report 65–1, Space Research Laboratory. University of Maryland, 1965.

Hendry, D. P.   Conditioned inhibition of conditioned suppression. *Psychonomic Science*, 1967, 9, 261–262.

Hendry, D. P. and Coulbourn, J. N.   Reinforcing effect of an informative stimulus that is not a positive discriminative stimulus. *Psychonomic Science*, 1967, 7, 241–242.

Hendry, D. P. and Dillow, P. V.   Observing behavior during interval schedules. *Journal of the Experimental Analysis of Behavior*, 1966, 9, 337–349.

Hendry, D. P. and Van Toller, C.   Alleviation of conditioned suppression.

Journal of Comparative and Physiological Psychology, 1965, 59, 458–460.

Hendry, D. P., Yarczower, M. and Switalski, R. W. Discrimination training and generalization of conditioned suppression. NASA Technical Report No. 66–3, Space Research Laboratory, University of Maryland, 1966.

Hernández-Peón, R., Scherrer, H. and Jouvet, M. Modification of electrical activity in cochlear nucleus during "attention" in unanesthetized cats. *Science,* 1956. 123, 331–332.

Herrnstein, R. J. "Behavioral consequences of the removal of a discriminative stimulus associated with variable-interval reinforcement." Doctoral Dissertation, Harvard University, 1955.

Herrnstein, R. J. Some factors influencing behavior in a two-response situation. *Transactions of the New York Academy of Science,* 1958, 21, 35–45.

Herrnstein, R. J. Relative and absolute strength of response as a function of frequency of reinforcement. *Journal of the Experimental Analysis of Behavior,* 1961, 4, 267–272.

Herrnstein, R. J. Secondary reinforcement and the rate of primary reinforcement. *Journal of the Experimental Analysis of Behavior,* 1964a, 7, 27–36.

Herrnstein, R. J. Aperiodicity as a factor in choice. *Journal of the Experimental Analysis of Behavior,* 1964b, 7, 179–182.

Herrnstein, R. J. Superstition: A corollary of the principles of operant conditioning. In W. K. Honig (Ed.), *Operant Behavior: Areas of Research and Application.* New York: Appleton-Century-Crofts, 1966, 33–51.

Herrnstein, R. J. and Morse, W. H. A conjunctive schedule of reinforcement. *Journal of the Experimental Analysis of Behavior,* 1958, 1, 15–24.

Hodos, W. and Valenstein, E. S. An evaluation of response rate as a measure of rewarding intracranial stimulation. *Journal of Comparative and Physiological Psychology,* 1962, 55, 80–84.

Holz, W. C. and Azrin, N. H. Discriminative properties of punishment. *Journal of the Experimental Analysis of Behavior,* 1961, 4, 225–232.

Holz, W. C. and Azrin, N. H. A comparison of several procedures for eliminating behavior. *Journal of the Experimental Analysis of Behavior,* 1963, 6, 399–406.

Holz, W. C., Azrin, N. H. and Ulrich, R. E. Punishment of temporarily spaced responding. *Journal of the Experimental Analysis of Behavior,* 1963, 6, 115–122.

Honig, W. K. and Slivka, R. M. Stimulus generalization of the effects of punishment. *Journal of the Experimental Analysis of Behavior,* 1964, 7, 21–25.

Houliham, J. and Renner, K. E. The role of generalization and delay on the relative aversiveness of inevitable shock. Paper read at Midwestern Psychological Association Meeting, Chicago, May, 1967.

Hubel, D. H.   Integrative processes in ventral visual pathways of the cat. *Journal of the Optical Society of America,* 1963, 53, 58–66.

Hubel, D. H. and Wiesel, J. N.   Receptive fields, binocular interaction, and functional architecture in the cat's visual cortex. *Journal of Physiology,* 1962, 160, 106–154.

Hull, C. L.   *Principles of Behavior.* New York: Appleton-Century-Crofts, 1943.

Hull, C. L.   Simple qualitative discrimination learning. *Psychological Review,* 1950, 57, 303–313.

Hull, C. L.   *Essentials of Behavior.* New Haven: Yale University Press, 1951.

Jenkins, H. M.   Measurement of stimulus control during discriminative operant conditioning. *Psychological Bulletin,* 1965, 64, 365–376.

Jenkins, W. O.   A temporal gradient of derived reinforcement. *American Journal of Psychology,* 1950, 63, 237–243.

Keehn, J. D.   The effect of post-stimulus conditions on the secondary reinforcing power of a stimulus. *Journal of Comparative and Physiological Psychology,* 1962, 55, 22–26.

Kelleher, R. T.   Conditioned reinforcement in chimpanzees. *Journal of Comparative and Physiological Psychology,* 1957, 49, 571–575.

Kelleher, R. T.   Stimulus-producing responses and attention in the chimpanzee. *Journal of the Experimental Analysis of Behavior,* 1958a, 1, 87–102.

Kelleher, R. T.   Fixed-ratio schedules of conditioned reinforcement with chimpanzees. *Journal of the Experimental Analysis of Behavior,* 1958b, 1, 281–289.

Kelleher, R. T.   Schedules of conditioned reinforcement during experimental extinction. *Journal of the Experimental Analysis of Behavior,* 1961, 4, 1–5.

Kelleher, R. T.   Chaining and conditioned reinforcement. In W. K. Honig (Ed.) *Operant Behavior: Areas of research and application.* New York: Appleton-Century-Crofts, 1966a, 160–212.

Kelleher, R. T.   Conditioned reinforcement in second-order schedules. *Journal of the Experimental Analysis of Behavior,* 1966b, 9, 475–486.

Kelleher, R. T. and Fry, W.   Stimulus functions in chained fixed-interval schedules. *Journal of the Experimental Analysis of Behavior,* 1962, 5, 167–173.

Kelleher, R. T., Fry, W. T. and Cook, L.   Adjusting fixed-ratio schedules in the squirrel monkey. *Journal of the Experimental Analysis of Behavior,* 1964, 7, 69–77.

Kelleher, R. T. and Gollub, L. R.   A review of positive conditioned reinforcement. *Journal of the Experimental Analysis of Behavior,* 1962, 5, 543–597.

Kelleher, R. T., Riddle, W. C. and Cook, L.   Observing responses in pigeons. *Journal of the Experimental Analysis of Behavior,* 1962, 5, 3–13.

Keller, F. S. and Schoenfeld, W. N.   *Principles of Psychology.* New York: Appleton-Century-Crofts, 1950.

Kendall, S. B. Competing behavior and observing responses. *Psychonomic Science*, 1965a, 3, 279–280.

Kendall, S. B. An observing response analysis of fixed-ratio discrimination. *Psychonomic Science*, 1965b, 3, 281–282.

Kendall, S. B. The distribution of observing responses in a mixed *FI-FR* schedule. *Journal of the Experimental Analysis of Behavior*, 1965c, 8, 305–312.

Killeen, P. On the measurement of reinforcement frequency in the study of preference. *Journal of the Experimental Analysis of Behavior*, 1968, 11, 263–269.

Klein, R. M. Intermittent primary reinforcement as a parameter of secondary reinforcement. *Journal of Experimental Psychology*, 1959, 58, 423–427.

Knapp, R. K., Kause, R. H. and Perkins, C. C., Jr. Immediate versus delayed shock in T-maze performance. *Journal of Experimental Psychology*, 1959, 58, 357–362.

Lawrence, D. H. Acquired distinctiveness of cues: I. Transfer between discriminations on the basis of familiarity with the stimulus. *Journal of Experimental Psychology*, 1949, 39, 770–784.

Lawrence, D. H. Acquired distinctiveness of cues: II. Selective association in a constant stimulus situation. *Journal of Experimental Psychology*, 1950, 40, 175–188.

Leckrone, W. R., Zimmerman, J. and Hanford, P. V. A pigeon magazine shutter for preventing unprogrammed grain reinforcement. *Psychonomic Science*, 1966, 6, 239–240.

Leitenberg, H. Is time-out from positive reinforcement an aversive event? *Psychological Bulletin*, 1965, 64, 428–441.

Leitenberg, H. Conditioned acceleration and conditioned suppression in pigeons. *Journal of the Experimental Analysis of Behavior*, 1966, 9, 205–212.

Lettvin, J. Y., Maturana, H. R. McCulloch, W. S. and Pitts, W. H. What the frog's eye tells the frog's brain. *Proceedings of the Institute of Radio Engineers*, 1959, 47, 1940–1951.

Levis, D. J. and Perkins, C. C., Jr. Acquisition of observing responses (R_o) with water reward. *Psychological Reports*, 1965, 16, 114.

Lockard, Joan S. Choice of a warning signal or no warning signal in an unavoidable shock situation. *Journal of Comparative and Physiological Psychology*, 1963, 56, 526–530.

Lockard, J. A. Choice of warning signal or none in several unavoidable shock situations. *Psychonomic Science*, 1965, 3, 5–6.

Logan, F. A. *Incentive*. New Haven: Yale University Press, 1960.

Logan, F. A. Decision making by rats: Delay versus amount of reward. *Journal of Comparative and Physiological Psychology*, 1965a, 59, 1–12.

Logan, F. A. Decision making by rats: Uncertain outcome choices. *Journal of Comparative and Physiological Psychology*, 1965b, 59, 246–251.

Logan, F. A. and Wagner, A. R. *Reward and punishment*. Boston: Allyn and Bacon, 1965.

Lott, D. F. Secondary reinforcement and frustration: A conceptual paradox. *Psychological Bulletin,* 1967, 67, 197–198.

Lutz, R. E. and Perkins, C. C., Jr. A time variable in the acquisition of observing responses. *Journal of Comparative and Physiological Psychology,* 1960, 53, 180–182.

Mabry, J. H. Discriminative functions based on a delay in the reinforcement relation. *Journal of the Experimental Analysis of Behavior,* 1965, 8, 97–103.

Mackintosh, N. J. Selective attention in animal discrimination learning. *Psychological Bulletin,* 1965, 64, 124–150.

Marr, M. J. "The conditioned reinforcing property of chain schedule stimuli." Doctoral dissertation, University of North Carolina, 1965.

Marr, M. J. A sequence schedule of reinforcement. Paper presented at Southeastern Psychological Association Convention. Roanoke, Virginia, 1968.

Marr, M. J. and de Lorge, J. O. Maintenance of behavior: Conditioned reinforcer *vs.* a neutral stimulus. Paper presented at Southeastern Psychological Association, New Orleans, La., April, 1966.

Marx, M. H. and Knarr, F. A. Long-term development of reinforcing properties of a stimulus as a function of temporal relationship to food reinforcement. *Journal of Comparative and Physiological Psychology,* 1963, 56, 546–550.

McDiarmid, C. G. and Rilling, M. E. Reinforcement delay and reinforcement rate as determinants of schedule preference. *Psychonomic Science,* 1965, 2, 195–196.

Mechner, F. Probability relations with response sequences under ratio reinforcement. *Journal of Experimental Analysis of Behavior,* 1958, 1, 109–121.

Mechner, F. A notation system for the description of behavioral procedures. *Journal of the Experimental Analysis of Behavior,* 1959, 2, 133–150.

Meehl, P. E. On the circularity of the law of effect. *Psychological Bulletin,* 1950, 47, 52–75.

Meyers, J. L. The effects of delay of reinforcement upon an operant discrimination in the pigeon. *Journal of Experimental Psychology,* 1958, 55, 363–368.

Miles, R. C. The relative effectiveness of secondary reinforcers throughout deprivation and habit-strength parameters. *Journal of Comparative and Physiological Psychology,* 1956, 49, 126–130.

Millenson, J. R. *Principles of Behavioral Analysis.* New York: McGraw-Hill, 1967.

Millenson, J. R. and Hendry, D. P. Quantification of response suppression in conditioned anxiety training. *Canadian Journal of Psychology,* 1967, 21, 215–224.

Miller, N. E. Learnable drives and rewards. In S. S. Stevens (Ed.), *Handbook of Experimental Psychology.* New York: Wiley, 1951. 435–472.

Miller, N. E. and Carmona, A.   Modification of a visceral response, salivation in thirsty dogs, by instrumental training with water reward. *Journal of Comparative and Physiological Psychology*, 1967, 63, 1–6.

Miller, N. E. and DiCara, L.   Instrumental learning of heart rate changes in curarized rats: Shaping and specificity to discriminative stimulus. *Journal of Comparative and Physiological Psychology*, 1967, 63, 12–19.

Mitchell, K. M., Perkins, N. P., and Perkins, C. C., Jr.   Conditions affecting acquisition of observing responses in the absence of differential reward. *Journal of Comparative and Physiological Psychology*, 1965, 60, 435–437.

Morse, W. H.   Intermittent reinforcement. In W. K. Honig (Ed.), *Operant Behavior: Areas of Research and Application*. New York: Appleton-Century-Crofts, 1966, 52–108.

Morse, W. H., Mead, R. N., and Kelleher, R. T.   Modulation of elicited behavior by a fixed-interval schedule of electric shock presentation. *Science*, 1967, 157, 215–217.

Mowrer, O. H.   *Learning Theory and Behavior*. New York: Wiley, 1960.

Mowrer, O. H. and Aiken, E. G.   Contiguity versus drive-reduction in conditioned fear: Temporal variations in conditioned and unconditioned stimulus. *American Journal of Psychology*, 1954, 67, 26–38.

Mowrer, O. H. and Jones, H. M.   Habit strength as a function of the pattern of reinforcement. *Journal of Experimental Psychology*, 1945, 35, 292–311.

Myers, J. L.   Secondary reinforcement: A review of recent experimentation. *Psychological Bulletin*, 1958, 55, 284–301.

Myers, N. A. and Morningstar, M.   The role of the approach response in secondary reinforcement. *Psychonomic Science*, 1968, 10, 77–78.

Myers, N. A. and Myers, J. L.   Effects of secondary reinforcement schedules in extinction on children's responding. *Journal of Experimental Psychology*, 1962, 64, 586–588.

Nagaty, M. G.   The effect of reinforcement on closely following S-R connections: II Effect of food reward immediately preceding performance of an instrumental conditioned response on extinction of that response. *Journal of Experimental Psychology*, 1951, 42, 333–340.

Neuringer, A. J.   Effects of reinforcement magnitude on choice and rate of responding. *Journal of the Experimental Analysis of Behavior*, 1967, 10, 417–424.

Neuringer, A. J. and Chung, S.   Quasi-reinforcement: Control of responding by a percentage reinforcement schedule. *Journal of the Experimental Analysis of Behavior*, 1967, 10, 45–54.

Nevin, J. A. and Shettleworth, S. J.   An analysis of contrast effects in multiple schedules. *Journal of the Experimental Analysis of Behavior*, 1966, 9, 305–315.

Notterman, J. M.   Force emission during bar pressing. *Journal of Experimental Psychology*, 1959, 58, 341–347.

Notterman, J. M.   A study of some relations among aperiodic reinforcement, discrimination training, and secondary reinforcement. *Journal of Experimental Psychology*, 1951, 41, 161–169.

Pavlov, I. P. *Conditioned Reflexes*. (Translated and edited by G. V. Anrep.) London: Oxford University Press, 1927.

Perkins, C. C., Jr. A conceptual scheme for studies of stimulus generalization. In Mostofsky, D. I. (Ed.), *Stimulus Generalization*. Stanford: Stanford University Press, 1965, 38–54.

Perkins, C. C., Jr. The stimulus conditions which follow learned responses. *Psychological Review*, 1955, 62, 341–348.

Perkins, C. C., Jr., Levis, D. J., and Seymann, R. Preference for signal-shock *vs.* shock-signal. *Psychological Reports*, 1963, 13, 735–738.

Perkins, C. C., Jr., Seymann, R. G., Levis, D. J., and Spencer, H. R., Jr. Factors affecting preference for signal-shock over shock-signal. *Journal of Experimental Psychology*, 1966, 72, 190–196.

Pierrel, R. and Blue, S. Antecedent reinforcement contingencies in the stimulus control of an auditory discrimination. *Journal of the Experimental Analysis of Behavior*, 1967, 10, 545–550.

Pliskoff, S. S. and Goldiamond, I. Some discriminative properties of fixed-ratio performance in the pigeon. *Journal of the Experimental Analysis of Behavior*, 1966, 2, 1–9.

Premack, D. Reinforcement theory. In D. Levine (Ed.), *Nebraska Symposium on Motivation*. Lincoln, Nebraska: University of Nebraska Press, 1965.

Prokasy, W. F., Jr. The acquisition of observing responses in the absence of differential external reinforcement. *Journal of Comparative and Physiological Psychology*, 1956, 49, 131–134.

Rachlin, H. The effect of shock intensity on concurrent and single-key responding in concurrent-chain schedules. *Journal of the Experimental Analysis of Behavior*, 1967, 10, 87–93.

Rachlin, H. Recovery of responses during mild punishment. *Journal of the Experimental Analysis of Behavior*, 1966, 9, 251–263.

Randolph, J. J. and Sewell, W. R. Competitive conditioned reinforcement during differential reinforcement of low rates. *Psychonomic Science*, 1965, 3, 411–412.

Randolph, J. J., Thomas, J. R., and Sewell, W. R. Performance enhancement of low rate behavior by conditioned positive reinforcement. *Journal of the Experimental Analysis of Behavior*, in press.

Ratner, S. C. Reinforcing and discriminative properties of the click in a Skinner box. *Psychological Reports*, 1956, 2, 332.

Ray, O. and Stein, L. Generalization of conditioned suppression. *Journal of the Experimental Analysis of Behavior*, 1959, 2, 357–361.

Rescorla, R. A. Predictability and number of pairings in Pavlovian fear conditioning. *Psychonomic Science*, 1966, 4, 383–384.

Rescorla, R. A. Inhibition of delay in Pavlovian fear conditioning. *Journal of Comparative and Physiological Psychology*, 1967, 64, 114–120.

Rescorla, R. A. Probability of shock in the presence and absence of *CS* in fear conditioning. *Journal of Comparative and Physiological Psychology*, 1968, 66, 1–5.

Rescorla, R. A. and LoLordo, V. M.   Inhibition of avoidance behavior. *Journal of Comparative and Physiological Psychology*, 1965, 59, 406–412.

Rescorla, R. A. and Solomon, R. L.   Two-process learning theory: Relationships between Pavlovian conditioning and instrumental learning. *Psychological Review*, 1967, 74, 151–182.

Reynolds, G. S.   Behavioral contrast. *Journal of the Experimental Analysis of Behavior*, 1961a, 4, 55–71.

Reynolds, G. S.   Attention in the pigeon. *Journal of the Experimental Analysis of Behavior*, 1961b, 4, 203–208.

Reynolds, G. S.   Potency of conditioned reinforcers based on food and on food and punishment. *Science*, 1963a, 139, 838–839.

Reynolds, G. S.   On some determinants of choice in the pigeon. *Journal of the Experimental Analysis of Behavior*, 1963b, 6, 53–59.

Reynolds, G. S.   Temporally spaced responding by pigeons: Development and effects of deprivation and extinction. *Journal of the Experimental Analysis of Behavior*, 1964, 7, 415–421.

Reynolds, G. S. and Catania, A. C.   Behavioral contrast with fixed-interval and low-rate reinforcement. *Journal of the Experimental Analysis of Behavior*, 1961, 4, 387–391.

Saltzman, I. J.   Maze learning in the absence of primary reinforcement: A study of secondary reinforcement. *Journal of Comparative and Physiological Psychology*, 1949, 42, 161–173.

Schaub, R. E.   Informational and associative functions of response-produced cues. Paper presented at the Eastern Psychological Association Convention, Boston, 1967.

Schaub, R. E. and Honig, W. K.   Reinforcement of behavior with cues correlated with extinction. *Psychonomic Science*, 1967, 7, 15–16.

Schoenfeld, W. N., Antonitis, J. J., and Bersh, P. J.   A preliminary study of training conditions necessary for secondary reinforcement. *Journal of Experimental Psychology*, 1950, 40, 40–45.

Seligman, M.   *CS* redundancy and secondary punishment. Paper presented at Eastern Psychological Association Convention, New York, 1966.

Seymann, R. G.   The effect of preparatory responses on running speed. Paper presented at Psychonomic Society, Chicago, October, 1965.

Sharpless, S. K. and Jasper, H. H.   Habituation of the arousal reaction. *Brain*, 1956, 79, 655–680.

Sidman, M.   Avoidance conditioning with brief shock and no exteroceptive warning stimulus. *Science*, 1953, 118, 157–158.

Sidman, M.   Normal sources of pathological behavior. *Science*, 1960a, 132, 61–68.

Sidman, M.   *Tactics of Scientific Research*. New York: Basic Books, 1960b.

Sidman, M., Herrnstein, R. J., and Conrad, D. G.   Maintenance of avoidance behavior by inavoidable shocks. *Journal of Comparative and Physiological Psychology*, 1957, 50, 553–557.

Skinner, B. F. *The Behavior of Organisms*. New York: Appleton-Century-Crofts, 1938.

Skinner, B. F. Are theories of learning necessary? *Psychological Review*, 1950, 57, 193–216.

Skinner, B. F. *Science and Human Behavior*. New York: MacMillan, 1953.

Solomon, R. L. Punishment. *American Psychologist*, 1964, 19, 239–258.

Solomon, R. L., Kamin, L. J., and Wynne, L. C. Traumatic avoidance learning: The outcomes of several extinction procedures with dogs. *Journal of Abnormal and Social Psychology*, 1953, 48, 291–302.

Spence, K. W. The nature of discrimination learning in animals. *Psychological Review*, 1936, 43, 427–449.

Spence, K. W. *Behavior Theory and Conditioning*. New Haven: Yale University Press, 1956.

Spence, K. W. *Behavior Theory and Learning*. Englewood Cliffs, New Jersey: Prentice-Hall, 1960.

Spooner, A. and Kellogg, W. N. The backward conditioning curve. *American Journal of Psychology*, 1947, 60, 321–334.

Spradlin, J. E., Girardeau, F. L., and Hom, G. L. Stimulus properties of reinforcement during extinction of a free operant response. *Journal of Experimental Child Psychology*, 1966, 4, 369–380.

Staddon, J. E. R. Some properties of spaced responding in pigeons. *Journal of the Experimental Analysis of Behavior*, 1965, 8, 19–27.

Stein, L. Secondary reinforcement established with subcortical stimulation. *Science*, 1958, 127, 466–467.

Stein, L., Sidman, M. and Brady, J. V. Some effects of two temporal variables on conditioned suppression. *Journal of the Experimental Analysis of Behavior*, 1958, 1, 153–162.

Steiner, J. Observing responses and uncertainty reduction. *Quarterly Journal of Experimental Psychology*, 1967, 19, 18–29.

Stretch, R., Orloff, E. R., and Dalrymple, S. D. Modulation of responding by fixed-interval schedule of electric shock presentation in squirrel monkeys. *Science*, 1968, 162, 583–586.

Stubbs, A. Competitive conditioned reinforcement and efficient differential reinforcement of low rate performance. *Psychonomic Science*, 1967, 8, 299–300.

Terrace, H. S. Stimulus control. In W. K. Honig (Ed.), *Operant Behavior: Areas of Research and Application*. New York: Appleton-Century-Crofts, 1966.

Thomas, J. R. Multiple baseline of stimulus functions in an *FR* chained schedule. *Journal of the Experimental Analysis of Behavior*, 1964, 7, 241–245.

Thomas, J. R. and Stubbs, A. Enhancement of fixed-ratio performance by briefly presented conditioned reinforcing stimuli. *Psychonomic Science*, 1966, 5, 329–330.

Thomas, J. R. and Stubbs, A.   Stimulus control of temporally-spaced responding in second-order schedules. *Journal of the Experimental Analysis of Behavior,* 1967, 10, 175–183.

Thompson, D. M.   Escape from S^D associated with fixed-ratio reinforcement. *Journal of the Experimental Analysis of Behavior,* 1964, 7, 1–8.

Thorndike, E. L.   *Animal Intelligence.* New York: MacMillan, 1911.

Tolman, E. C. and Brunswik, E.   The organism and the causal texture of the environment. *Psychological Review,* 1935, 42, 43–77.

Trowill, J. A.   Instrumental conditioning of the heart rate in the curarized rat. *Journal of Comparative and Physiological Psychology,* 1967, 63, 7–11.

Verhave, T.   Towards an empirical calculus of reinforcement value. *Journal of the Experimental Analysis of Behavior,* 1963, 6, 525–536.

Wagner, A. R.   Conditioned frustration as a learned drive. *Journal of Experimental Psychology,* 1963, 66, 142–148.

Wagner, A. R., Logan, F. A., Haberlandt, K. and Price, T.   Stimulus selection in animal discrimination learning. *Journal of Experimental Psychology,* 1968, 76, 171–180.

Waller, M. B. and Waller, P. F.   The effects of unavoidable shocks on a multiple schedule having an avoidance component. *Journal of the Experimental Analysis of Behavior,* 1963, 6, 29–37.

Wehling, H. F. and Prokasy, W. F.   Role of food deprivation in the acquisition of the observing response. *Psychological Review,* 1962, 10, 399–407.

Weiner, H.   Response cost and the aversive control of human operant behavior. *Journal of the Experimental Analysis of Behavior,* 1963, 6, 415–421.

Weissman, N. W. and Crossman, E. K.   A comparison of two types of extinction following fixed-ratio training. *Journal of the Experimental Analysis of Behavior,* 1966, 9, 41–46.

Wike, E. L.   *Secondary Reinforcement: Selected Experiments.* New York: Harper and Row, 1966.

Wilson, M. P. and Keller, F. S.   On the selective reinforcement of spaced responses. *Journal of Comparative and Physiological Psychology,* 1953, 46, 190–193.

Woodworth, R. S. and Schlosberg, H.   *Experimental Psychology.* New York: Holt, Rinehart and Winston, 1954.

Wyckoff, L. B., Jr.   The role of observing responses in discrimination learning. Part 1. *Psychological Review,* 1952, 59, 431–442.

Wyckoff, L. B., Jr.   Toward a quantitative theory of secondary reinforcement. *Psychological Review,* 1959, 66, 68–78.

Zimmerman, D. W.   Durable secondary reinforcement: Method and theory. *Psychological Review,* 1957, 64, 373–383.

Zimmerman, D. W.   Sustained performance in rats based on secondary reinforcement. *Journal of Comparative and Physiological Psychology,* 1959, 52, 353–358.

Zimmerman, D. W.   Intermittent reinforcement of discriminatively controlled responding and runs of responses. *Journal of the Experimental Analysis of Behavior,* 1960, **3**, 83–91.

Zimmerman, J.   Technique for sustaining behavior with conditioned reinforcement. *Science,* 1963, **142**, 682–684.

Zimmerman, J. and Hanford, P. V.   Sustaining behavior with conditioned reinforcement as the only response-produced consequence. *Psychological Reports,* 1966, **19**, 391–401.

Zimmerman, J. and Hanford, P. V.   Differential effects of extinction on behaviors maintained by concurrent schedules of primary and conditioned reinforcement. *Psychonomic Science,* 1967a, **8**, 103–104.

Zimmerman, J. and Hanford, P. V.   Sustained mismatching performance in pigeons with chronically maintained conditioned reinforcement. *American Psychologist,* 1967b, **22**, 534. (Abstract)

Zimmerman, J. and Hanford, P. V.   Differential effects of food frequency on behaviors maintained by concurrent schedules of primary and conditioned reinforcement. Paper presented at the American Psychological Association Convention, San Francisco, 1968.

Zimmerman, J., Hanford, P. V., and Brown, W.   Effects of conditioned reinforcement frequency in an intermittent free feeding situation. *Journal of the Experimental Analysis of Behavior,* 1967, **10**, 331–340.

GLOSSARY

GLOSSARY

This is not an exhaustive glossary, but covers mainly new terms, old terms with new meanings and terms which have a history of being misunderstood and misused. Short explanatory commentaries have been included where they seemed appropriate. For the sake of clarity, in a few cases, the Mechner/Millenson notation is used. (See Mechner, 1958; Millenson, 1967.)

Aversive Stimulus. Same as negative reinforcing stimulus. A stimulus whose removal is reinforcing. The aversive stimulus most commonly used in experiments is electric shock.

Avoidance. A procedure in which an operant is maintained by its effect in preventing delivery of a stimulus, usually electric shock. In a different situation an operant that has the effect of terminating the stimulus will usually be learned. The stimulus is, therefore, a negative reinforcer or aversive stimulus. However, most experimenters do not provide an independent demonstration that the stimulus to be avoided is, in fact, aversive. In a common avoidance procedure a stimulus, say a tone, precedes the scheduled delivery of shock. This procedure is often called *discriminated avoidance.* In that case the animal may make the required response to avoid the shock and thereby terminate the tone. Since termination of the tone appears to maintain the operant, the tone is referred to as an aversive stimulus; and, since this function of the tone depends on experience, it is called a *conditioned aversive stimulus (CAS).* However, under many circumstances the animal fails to make a response during the tone and the scheduled shock is delivered. In these cases the tone does not qualify as an aversive stimulus, and some doubt is thereby thrown on the usefulness of considering the tone an aversive stimulus in cases where the animal does *not* fail to make the avoidance response during the tone. At the present time it is not possible to give an operational specification of conditioned aversive stimulus that is satisfactory in the sense that the stimulus so defined will always have the same behavioral effect.

Active avoidance is a name given to procedures in which nondelivery of the aversive stimulus depends on the emission of some operant.

In *passive avoidance* nondelivery of an aversive stimulus depends on the nonemission of some operant; passive avoidance is, therefore, another name for punishment (*q.v.*).

Sidman avoidance is a procedure in which an operant postpones an unsignaled shock, usually for a fixed time. The schedule is specified by the response-shock interval (*RS*) and the repetition rate of shocks (*SS*). A schedule, *RS* 30, *SS* 5 would deliver shocks every 5 sec if no response occurred for 30 sec, thus:

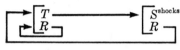

Originated by Sidman (1953).

Behavioral Contrast. An effect on performance on an unchanged schedule of reinforcement due to a change in another schedule of reinforcement to which the animal is exposed. For example, if MULT *VI* 1 *VI* 1 is changed to MULT *VI* 1 EXT, response rate increases in the periods of *VI* 1. This is called positive behavioral contrast because the effect is an enhancement of the difference in rate that the two schedules would control in isolation. Alternatively, the contrast may be considered positive because the direction of change of response rate in the constant component is opposite to that in the changed component. A decrease in the response rates in the unchanged *VI* 1 would be referred to as negative behavioral contrast or induction. Positive behavioral contrast may be produced by punishment in one component of a Multiple schedule; in that case the rate in the unpunished component increases. The concept may also apply to more complex behavior like traversing an alley. When a rat is intermittently reinforced in the goal box of alley A, then traverses alley B, response speed in alley B eventually becomes higher on those occasions following nonreinforcement in alley A. This is referred to as the frustration effect, but might also be called positive behavioral contrast insofar as the response speed in alley B is increased by an operation in alley A that would reduce response speed in alley A.

Chain Schedule or Chained Schedules (CHAIN). A schedule in which responding during one stimulus is reinforced on a given schedule by the production of a second stimulus, during which responding is reinforced on a given schedule by the production of a third stimulus, and so on, up to final primary reinforcement. A Chain schedule resembles a Multiple schedule (*q.v.*) except that reinforcement occurs after only the final component, not after each component. A Chain schedule resembles a Tandem schedule (*q.v.*) except that each component is signaled by a distinctive stimulus. For example, in CHAIN *FI* 2 *FR* 5 a response after 2 min in one distinctive stimulus would produce a second distinctive stimulus, during which the fifth response would produce the reinforcer.

Changeover Delay (COD). In Concurrent schedules the specification that a minimum time must elapse before a response is effective in schedule B after the previous response in schedule A (or vice versa). The operants in A and B have to be distinguishable, as when A and B are scheduled on different keys.

We may clarify *COD* procedures by referring to the probability of reinforcement for a B response, or the probability of reinforcement for a B interresponse time, after an A response, as a function of time since the last A response. Suppose the probability of reinforcement for the next response or interresponse time (*IRT*) were related to the time since the last A response as follows:

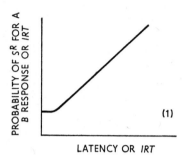

A *COD* would change the above relation as follows:

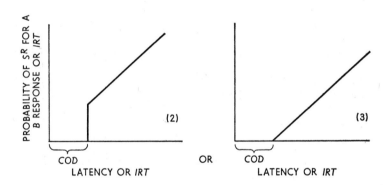

When the *COD* is initiated by the last A response, the abscissae, above, are latencies of the first B response. When the *COD* is initiated by the first B response, the abscissae are magnitudes of the first *IRT*. Whether the relation shown in (2) or that shown in (3) (or some other form) actually obtains depends on details of programming. The essential effect of the *COD* is a zero probability or reinforcement for a period after a switch from one schedule to another.

A third method is to have the *COD* initiated by a separate switching operant, such as a response on a third key. The zero in the abscissae of (1) and (2) and (3) would then be the time of occurrence of the switching response on the third key.

The purpose of the *COD* is generally to enhance the independence of performance on each schedule and to prevent rapid switching between two schedules that may result from the greater probability of reinforcement for AB and BA than for AA and BB response sequences.

Changeover Response. A switching from one schedule to another in Concurrent schedules, either from one key to another (as in two-key Concurrent schedules) or via another operant (the changeover or switching operant). For example, suppose FR 50 and VR 10 are scheduled concurrently on two keys, A and B. The number of changeover responses is the number of times the animal makes a response on key A followed by a response on key B, and vice versa. Use of a switching operant would require a different response(s), say five pecks on a third key, before the schedule switched into became operative and the schedule switched out of became inoperative.

Clock. A series of stimuli that is correlated with the passage of time. For example, changing key colors every minute constitutes a clock.

Clock Cues. A series of stimuli which are correlated with the passage of time and which exert control of behavior.

Clue. A stimulus that precedes a reinforcer by a fixed time, as a delayed CS or a trace CS.

Clue Hypothesis. Part of the information hypothesis. The hypothesis that clues are conditioned reinforcers.

Concurrent Operants. Two or more distinguishable operants capable of being executed with little mutual interference at the same time or in rapid alternation, under the control of separate programs. For example, pecks on one key might be reinforced according to an FR 5 schedule, pecks on another key according to an FI 2 schedule, and depression of a foot pedal according to an FR 50 schedule. In that situation there would be three concurrent operants.

Concurrent Schedules ($CONC$). Schedules which are in effect simultaneously, or which can follow one another in rapid succession. (See Concurrent Operants.)

Conditioned Response (CR). The response, resembling the unconditioned response, elicited by a conditioned stimulus after repeated pairing of conditioned stimulus and unconditioned stimulus in classical conditioning. (See Conditioning, Classical.)

Conditioned Stimulus (CS). In the context of a classical conditioning procedure, an arbitrary (neutral) stimulus that is to be paired with an unconditioned stimulus and that does not at the beginning of the experiment elicit the unconditioned response. Also "conditional stimulus." (See Conditioning, Classical.)

Conditioned Suppression. A reduction in rate of an operant in the presence of an originally neutral stimulus which has repeatedly preceded an aversive stimulus. The originally neutral stimulus is sometimes called a conditioned aversive stimulus (CAS), and the suppression is sometimes called a conditioned emotional response (CER). The terms "anxiety" and

"fear" refer less to the suppression of an operant and more to the inferred classically conditioned autonomic effects of the aversive stimulus.

Conditioning, Classical. Also called respondent conditioning, type S conditioning and Pavlovian conditioning. The establishment and strengthening of a conditioned reflex through the roughly simultaneous presentation
of unconditioned and conditioned stimuli. For example, a puff of air (unconditioned stimulus) to the cornea elicits a reflex blink (unconditioned
response). If the puff of air is repeatedly preceded (by an interval of up
to a few seconds) by another stimulus, say a tone, the blink will come to
be elicited by the tone itself. The tone is referred to as the conditioned
stimulus and the response it comes to elicit as the conditioned response.
Introductory texts give many of the variables controlling this process,
such as intensity of the unconditioned and conditioned stimuli, the temporal relation of conditioned and unconditioned stimuli, the number and
frequency of presentations of the two stimuli, and the probability that
the unconditioned stimulus will follow the conditioned stimulus. (See
Conditioning, Operant.)

Conditioning, Instrumental. See Conditioning, Operant.

Conditioning, Operant. Also called Type R conditioning and instrumental conditioning. The strengthening of an operant by the occurrence
of a reinforcer after emission of the operant. For example, producing a
high rate of barking by giving a hungry dog food after it barks is a
case of operant conditioning. Similarly, a high probability of saying
"please" can be produced by giving a hungry child food after the child
says "please." Giving food to a hungry pigeon after it has pecked a response key is a prototype of operant conditioning procedures. Introductory
texts give many of the variables that control the rate and pattern of
responding in operant conditioning, such as the schedule of reinforcement,
the amount or intensity of the reinforcer and the delay between a response
and the reinforcer.

Instrumental conditioning refers to the procedure of making a reinforcer depend upon a particular piece of behavior, and, therefore, includes
operant conditioning. However, in studies of operant conditioning, as the
term is generally used, the instrumental response is distinguished by the
fact that its instrumental function in producing the reinforcer is negli-
gibly limited by the speed with which one operant can be emitted. This
character of the instrumental response, together with the experimental
situation, is sometimes acknowledged by calling the operant a *free* operant. The operant is free in the sense of being unrestricted and capable
of being emitted at a high rate.

Traversing a maze or alley (toward food in the goal box) is thus an
instrumental response, but not a free operant. It takes a relatively long
time (at least several seconds) and cannot be repeated without some intervening operation. In contrast, pecking a response key takes a small
fraction of a second and making one peck does not in any physical way
limit the possibility of making another peck. Thus, the main dependent

variable in (free) operant conditioning is some variant of rate or probability of responding, measures which characterize a large segment of behavior comprising hundreds or thousands of instances of the operant. In other cases of instrumental behavior, such as maze running, the main dependent variable is response speed or latency, measures that refer to a single (average) instance of the instrumental response.

Conditioning, Pavlovian.   See Conditioning, Classical.

Conditioning, Respondent.   See Conditioning, Classical.

Conditioning, Type R.   See Conditioning, Operant.

Conditioning, Type S.   See Conditioning, Classical.

Contingencies of Reinforcement (or Punishment).   The actual relations among responses, time, stimuli, and reinforcement (or punishment), as distinct from the (limiting) conditions specified by the schedule of reinforcement (or punishment).

Continuous Reinforcement (*CRF*).   Reinforcement of every instance of an operant. For example, the arrangement of the program so that every key peck operates the feeder. Thus, *CRF* is equivalent to *FR* 1.

Contrast.   See Behavioral Contrast.

Control (as in "Stimulus Control").   An observed tendency for a probability or rate of responding to vary with the value of a variable (e.g, wavelength of a visual stimulus; presence or absence of a given visual stimulus).

Counter.   Some dimension of a stimulus which varies systematically with number of responses emitted, counted from the preceding reinforcement or some other event.

Cue.   Any stimulus which, when presented, is known to exert control of an operant, in the sense of reliably affecting its probability of occurrence. See Discriminative Stimulus.

Cue Hypothesis.   Part of the information hypothesis. The hypothesis that cues are conditioned reinforcers.

Danger Signal.   A stimulus associated with an aversive event, or one that predicts an aversive event, as, for example: a tone that sounds for 30 sec before delivery of an electric shock; a tone that sounds for 10 sec from 20 to 30 sec before delivery of an electric shock; a tone that sounds when a schedule of intermittent punishment by electric shock is in effect, even though no shocks are delivered.

An animal may distinguish the onset of, or the initial part of, a signal of long duration that precedes shock, in which case the onset or short durations of the pre-shock signal would signal no shock and would therefore act as *safe signals* (*q.v.*). The behavioral relevance of these definitions is discussed in Chapter 15.

Delayed Conditioned Reflex. A classically conditioned reflex with a conditioned stimulus of unusually long duration (more than a few seconds), so that an appreciable time elapses between onset of the conditioned stimulus and presentation of the unconditioned stimulus. See Trace-Conditioned Reflex.

Differential Reinforcement of High Rates (DRH). A procedure in operant conditioning according to which reinforcement is made contingent upon response rate exceeding some specified value. As a schedule, *DRH* may be used as the principal condition, or as an added condition in conjunction with some other schedule. As a schedule, *DRH* is usually accomplished by specifying a maximum interval between successive responses as a condition for reinforcement, thus:

$$R \rightarrow \begin{bmatrix} T \\ R \end{bmatrix} \longrightarrow S^R$$

Differential Reinforcement of Low Rates (DRL). A procedure in operant conditioning according to which reinforcement is made contingent upon the response rate being below some specified value. As a schedule, *DRL* may be used as the principal condition, or an added condition in conjunction with some other schedule. As a schedule, *DRL* is usually accomplished by specifying a minimum interval between successive responses as a condition for reinforcement, thus:

$$\overline{R_t} \longrightarrow R \longrightarrow S^R \quad \text{or} \quad \begin{bmatrix} T \\ R \end{bmatrix} \rightarrow R \longrightarrow S^R$$

Differential Reinforcement of Other Behavior (DRO). A procedure in operant conditioning according to which reinforcement is made contingent upon the nonoccurrence of the response of interest. The same as *DRL* except that the reinforcer is contingent on the absence of a response rather than on a delayed response. As a schedule, *DRO* is always used in conjunction with some other schedule. *DRO* is usually accomplished by specifying that the reinforcer will be delivered after a given period has elapsed since the last response, thus:

$$\overline{R_t} \longrightarrow S^R$$

Differential Reinforcement of Paced Responding (DRP). A procedure in operant conditioning according to which reinforcement is made contingent upon the response rate falling between specified limits. As a schedule, *DRP* is usually accomplished by specifying a minimum and a maximum interval between successive responses as a condition for reinforcement, thus:

$$\begin{bmatrix} T_{min} \\ R \end{bmatrix} \rightarrow \begin{bmatrix} T_{max-min} \\ R \end{bmatrix} \longrightarrow S^R \quad \text{or} \quad R \rightarrow \begin{bmatrix} T_{max} \\ \overline{R_{T_{min}}} \end{bmatrix} \rightarrow R \rightarrow S^R$$

Differential Reinforcement of Rate. A procedure in operant conditioning according to which reinforcement is made contingent upon response rate meeting a given criterion.

Discriminanda. See Discrimination.

Discrimination. This word is used in two main senses, as the *operation* of discrimination and as the *process* of discrimination. These two senses might be distinguished as "discrimination training" and "discrimination learning."

Operation. (discrimination training). Arranging different conditions of reinforcement in two (or more) situations that are the same in some respects and different in some respects. The respects in which the situations differ are called *discriminanda*. For example, the schedule of reinforcement might be arranged to be *FR* 20 with a blue response key and *FI* 5 with a yellow response key. Such a situation would constitute discrimination training and the blue and yellow key colors would be the discriminanda.

Process. (discrimination learning). The change in performance culminating in stimulus control by the discriminanda. In the example, discrimination learning would be the development of a high, uniform response rate with a blue key and a low, accelerated rate with a yellow key.

Discriminative Stimulus (S^D). Formerly, a stimulus in whose presence a particular operant was reinforced. Now, any of the members of a set of stimuli correlated one-to-one with different schedules of reinforcement. Both these definitions are operational, and do not make any reference to behavior.

Originally, a discriminative stimulus was defined as a stimulus that "set the occasion" for a particular operant (Skinner, 1938), with the implication that the operant would be emitted with a high probability in the presence of the stimulus. Thus, there were two cardinal features of a discriminative stimulus: (1) It was a stimulus in whose presence a particular operant was reinforced; (2) It was a stimulus in whose presence a particular operant had a high probability of emission. The first part is a purely operational specification and the second part is a purely behavioral criterion.

Because of the confusing history of the term discriminative stimulus (see Chapter 1), the term *cue*, precisely understood, is added to the lexicon and substitutes for "discriminative stimulus" in some of its usages. The term cue is preferred in much of the exposition in this book. A cue is a stimulus which, when presented, controls the probability of an operant or its pattern of emission. Whether or not a reinforcer occurs in connection with a cue need not be and is not specified. The term discriminative stimulus is restricted to its operational definition as given above.

Discriminative stimuli may be cues and cues may be discriminative stimuli. A reason for distinguishing cues is that only cues, since they control performance, give evidence of reducing uncertainty, which is reinforcing according to the information hypothesis.

Effective Stimulus. A stimulus that controls the probability of some response. Where the presentation of the stimulus controls the probability of a subsequent operant, the effective stimulus is referred to as a cue (or, more loosely, a discriminative stimulus). Where the stimulus controls the probability of an operant that precedes it, the effective stimulus may be referred to as a *maintaining stimulus* (*q.v.*). A cue or discriminative stimulus typically lasts for a long time (seconds or minutes) and a maintaining stimulus typically lasts a short time (fractions of a second or seconds). The concept of an effective stimulus also applies to classical conditioning, though that meaning is not considered here.

It has been accepted as a general rule that effective stimuli are conditioned reinforcers, but there are sufficient exceptions to sustain theoretical interest in the functions of effective stimuli.

Estes-Skinner Procedure. A procedure in which occasional unavoidable shocks, preceded by an exteroceptive stimulus, such as a light or tone, are superimposed on a schedule of positive reinforcement. This is a standard technique, originated by Estes and Skinner (1941), for studying a "conditioned emotional response" (*CER*). Various changes in behavior, said to have an emotional base, may be observed to develop during the originally neutral exteroceptive stimulus.

The Estes-Skinner procedure is often described in classical conditioning terms. Thus, the exteroceptive stimulus is the *CS*, the shock is the *US*, and an emotional response elicited by the *US* is the *UR*, and when elicited by the *CS* is the *C(E)R*. In these terms the contingencies of the Estes-Skinner procedure were first used by Watson and Rayner (1920), who established emotional behavior (*UR* and *CER*) to the stimulus of a rabbit (*CS*) by having the sight of the rabbit followed by the loud sound of a gong (*US*).

Extinction. This word is used in three main senses, as the *operation* of Extinction, the *effect* of Extinction, and the *process* of Extinction.

Operation. The withholding of a reinforcer previously contingent upon an operant. Thus, an experimenter might be said to introduce Extinction by disconnecting the feeder. This operation is a schedule, abbreviated EXT.

Effect. The result of withholding a reinforcer, namely, a decrease in the probability of the previously reinforced operant. Thus, it is commonly said that a response had undergone extinction, or extinguished, when its probability had reached a very low level during the operation of extinction.

Process. The process of weakening or making less probable the previously reinforced operant, as a consequence of repeated unreinforced responding. Thus, a response may be said to extinguish *slowly*.

First-Order Schedule. A component of a second-order schedule. See Second-Order Schedule.

Fixed-Interval Schedule (*FI*). A schedule in which reinforcement is produced by the first response emitted after a certain time has elapsed since the last reinforcement, thus:

$$T \longrightarrow R \longrightarrow S^R$$

The time (T) in minutes, unless noted, is indicated in the notation, as in "*FI 2*," "*FI 4.5*," "*FI 40 sec*," etc.

Fixed-Ratio Schedule (*FR*). A schedule of reinforcement in which a response is reinforced upon completion of a fixed number of responses counted from the preceding reinforcement. ("Ratio" refers to the ratio: responses/reinforcement.) Thus:

$$nR \longrightarrow S^R$$

The number of responses (n) is indicated in the notation, as in "*FR 22*," "*FR 100*," etc.

Functional Autonomy. The indefinite survival of instrumental behavior after the reinforcer used to establish the behavior has been withdrawn. Thus, functional autonomy could be described as infinite resistance to Extinction. The application of this concept has been mainly to human affairs. It has been proposed that the instrumental behavior acquires motivating and reinforcing properties. This idea is expressed in the tenet, "mechanisms become drives." There are no uncontested examples of functional autonomy in animals (but see Chapter 5).

Generalized Reinforcer. See Reinforcer, Generalized.

Higher Order Conditioning. Conditioning in which a previously established conditioned stimulus is used as the unconditioned stimulus in conditioning the response to a new stimulus. For example, suppose a tone had been established as a conditioned stimulus for an eye blink originally elicited by the pairing of the tone with a puff of air. Then if another stimulus, say a light, is paired with the tone without delivering the puff of air, sometimes the light develops the power to elicit the blink. Higher order conditioning is sometimes appealed to in the explanation of the maintenance of extended behavior Chains. See Conditioning, Classical.

Information, Uncertainty, Entropy, or Unpredictability. These words are closely interrelated. They are used in some contexts as synonyms and in other contexts as antonyms.

Consider a "situation," defined as a set of mutually exclusive events E_1, $E_2, \ldots E_n$, with probabilities of occurrence of $p_1, p_2, \ldots p_n$. The entropy of the situation is defined as:

$$H = -\Sigma p_i \log p_i$$

This may also be said to be the information or uncertainty in the situation. In this manner of speaking, entropy, information and uncertainty all refer to the disorderliness or unpredictability of the situation. The best prediction will be most often wrong when $p_i = $ constant, that is, when every possible event is equally likely. This is also the condition when H is a maximum.

When one is interested in one event, the next one, uncertainty may be determined before the event occurs. However, after the event occurs, there is no longer, in ordinary language, any uncertainty. Uncertainty has been reduced by the occurrence of the important event, or, one says, information has been obtained. However, the entropy of the situation is unchanged —the probability of the next event, E_i, is unchanged.

As mathematical or engineering concepts, information and uncertainty are equivalent to entropy, and the occurrence of events of interest is irrelevant to the meaning or use of information or uncertainty. In contrast, for events of interest most relevant to the psychological concepts of information and uncertainty, the amount of information given by an event is equal to the amount of uncertainty reduced by an event, which is assumed to be equal to the entropy of the situation.

Information Hypothesis. The hypothesis that conditioned reinforcing power is a property of informative stimului. Two versions of this hypothesis have been distinguished (Egger & Miller, 1962). According to the strong form, only an informative stimulus can become a conditioned reinforcer; according to the weak form, a noninformative stimulus may become a conditioned reinforcer, though a less-effective one than an informative stimulus.

Two methods of making a stimulus informative have been distinguished (see Chapter 1). One method is to have the stimulus occur at a relatively fixed time before the reinforcer. In that case the stimulus is called a "clue." Another method is to have the stimulus exert control of an operant in the sense of reliably affecting its probability of occurrence. In that case the stimulus is called a "cue."

The reinforcing effectiveness of both clues and cues are postulated to be derived from their function in reducing uncertainty.

Instrumental Conditioning. See Conditioning, Operant.

Interresponse Time (IRT). The time elapsing between two successive responses. The reciprocal of rate of responding. For example, a regular rate of 10 responses per minute would correspond to IRTs of 6 sec.

Interval Schedules. Schedules of reinforcement in which reinforcements are programmed by a clock, of the form:

$$T \longrightarrow R \longrightarrow S^R$$

Interval schedules are mainly fixed interval (q.v.) and variable interval (q.v.) but any interval involving a clock, such as a differential reinforcement of rate (q.v.) may be referred to as an interval schedule.

Irrelevant Stimulus. A stimulus that is associated with both the presence and absence of reinforcement. For example, in a wavelength-discrimination problem, the shape of the response key is an irrelevant stimulus. Note that, to qualify as "irrelevant" the stimulus must be "received" during or just before a reinforced response. The term is introduced because such a stimulus could be said to be a "discriminative stimulus" in a literal interpretation of the original definition of that term. See Discriminiative Stimulus.

IRT. Interresponses time (q.v.).

Maintaining Stimulus. A stimulus that controls the probability of responses that precede it. A subcategory of *effective stimulus*. A new term to replace "conditioned reinforcer" in some cases. The important use of the term *maintaining stimulus* would be in second-order schedules to refer to the efficacy of :S in maintaining patterns of behavior appropriate to the schedule of presentation of :S (i.e., the first-order schedule). See Effective Stimulus; :S.

Matching-to-sample. An experimental procedure in which reinforcement is contingent upon emitting a response controlled by a stimulus that is the same as ("matches") another stimulus. In a simple case response keys on the left and right of the chamber would be red and green (one red and one green), and another key in the center would sometimes be red and sometimes be green. Responses on the red (green) side key would be reinforced when the center key was red (green). The condition for reinforcement is usually a number (*FR* or *VR*) of correct matches.

A slightly different procedure is called "mismatching-to-sample," where responses on the red (green) side key would be reinforced when the center key was green (red).

In "delayed-matching-to-sample" responses to the side keys would be reinforced only after the sample on the center key had been removed.

A common programming method is to make the illumination of the side keys contingent on a response on the center, sample key.

Thus, for example, when reinforcement depends upon $n + 1$ correct red or green matches:

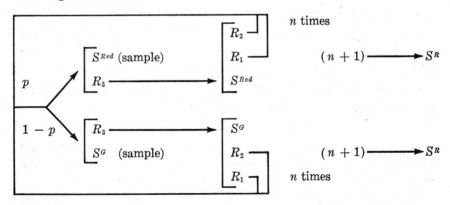

Where S^{Red} and S^{G} are red and green keys, and R_1 and R_2 are responses on a red and green key respectively, and R_3 is a response on the center, sample key.

Mixed Schedule (MIX). A schedule in which reinforcement is programmed by two or more component schedules alternating, usually at random. Same as a Multiple schedule except that exteroceptive stimuli are not used to signal when the different components are in force. The components are not signified by a different stimuli. For example, MIX *FI* 2 *FI* 3 represents a schedule in which a reinforcement becomes available either 2 min in one component or 3 min, in the other, after the last reinforcement.

Multiple Schedule (MULT). A schedule in which reinforcement is programmed by two or more schedules alternating, usually at random, each schedule being accompanied by an appropriate stimulus as long as the schedule is in force. Same as Mixed schedule except for the presence of exteroceptive stimuli signalling each component. For example, MULT *FI* 2 *FI* 3 represents a two-component schedule in which reinforcement becomes available either 2 min or 3 min after the last reinforcement, each component being signaled by a different stimulus.

Negative Conditioned Stimulus. (S^-) In the context of a classical conditioning procedure, a stimulus which is repeatedly presented without being followed by reinforcement. It tends to reduce or inhibit conditioned responses.

Observing Response. A response whose only direct consequence is the production of stimuli related to the contingencies of reinforcement. For example, if *FR* 20 or *FI* 2 are (unpredictably) scheduled on key A and a peck on key B produces a red stimulus if *FR* 20 is in effect and a blue stimulus if *FI* 2 is in effect, the peck on key B is an observing response. In this situation the observing response converts a Mixed schedule into the corresponding Multiple schedule.

Operant. A response whose probability of emission is under the control of its reinforcing consequences. See Conditioning, Operant.

Operandum. The part of the environment that is directly "operated upon" by each instance of a particular operant. In typical experiments the response-key that a pigeon pecks and the bar that a rat presses are operanda. The term was suggested by Skinner, to replace the anthropomorphic term "manipulandum."

Pavlovian Conditioning. See Conditioning, Classical.

Post-Reinforcement Pause. The period after a reinforcement during which no responses occur. In fixed-ratio schedules there is usually a sharply defined post-reinforcement pause before responding is resumed at a characteristically high rate. This is referred to as a "break-and-run" performance.

Pre-Aversive Stimulus. A stimulus that repeatedly precedes an aversive stimulus, such as electric shock.

Pre-Reinforcement Stimulus. A stimulus that repeatedly precedes a positive reinforcer, such as food.

Program. A set of reinforcing conditions, including schedules, stimuli, response specifications, and the relations among these.

Punisher. The opposite of reinforcer (*q.v.*). A stimulus whose presentation usually results in the decrease in probability of an operant that closely preceded the stimulus. Punishers may be scheduled in the same ways as reinforcers. When using schedules of punishment it is necessary to sustain performance with a concurrent schedule of reinforcement. The interaction of punishing and reinforcing effects sometimes leads to new phenomena and new problems of experimental analysis, but in many situations punishers and reinforcers seem to have antagonistic, additive effects. However, schedules of punishment have been much less extensively and intensively studied than have schedules of reinforcement.

In spite of the straightforward effects of punishment in many situations, there are other situations the description of which poses problems. A particular operation may qualify as a punisher in one situation, but not in another. For example, turning off all chamber lights and disconnecting all response keys is a punisher under some schedules of reinforcement and a reinforcer under other schedules. Likewise, whether electric shock is a punisher or a reinforcer depends on the schedule of its presentation and the animal's past experience with the schedule. Even food is a reinforcer only in certain circumstances. In brief, it is more prudent to identify a punisher (or reinforcer) by its behavioral effects in a given situation than by physical attributes or through *a priori* assumptions.

Punishment. Generally, a procedure in which the probability of an operant is reduced by a stimulus that follows the operant.

Ratio Schedules. Schedules in which reinforcements are programmed according to the number of responses emitted by the organism.

Ratio strain. Performance on high ratio schedules is said to exhibit ratio strain when there is a disintegration of the regular break-and-run pattern of responding. The common feature of ratio strain is the appearance of pauses in responding of several seconds and longer. Several such pauses per reinforcement may occur, separated by bursts of responding at the typical high rate produced by the ratio schedule.

Redundant. Refers to a message that provides no information or reduction of uncertainty.

In the context of communication theory:

$$\text{redundancy} = 1 - \frac{\text{actual entropy}}{\text{max. entropy of the system}}$$

In the context of the analysis of behavior, a redundant message is a stimulus that predicts or announces an event when a different stimulus having the same function has already been presented. For example, suppose that the schedule of reinforcement is *FR* 20 when the response key is blue and *FI* 5 when the response key is yellow, and that a 1,000 *Hz* tone sounds after 10 responses on the blue key and a 4,000 *Hz* tone sounds after 10 responses on the yellow key. The tones are redundant. However, suppose the bird turns away from the key, so that it is not receiving the key color, but still receiving the tone. Whether or not the tones are then redundant in the sense of not reducing uncertainty raises unresolved questions about the bird's "memory" and "attention."

When events occur in a relatively fixed sequence, or, in other words, when they exhibit strong sequential dependencies, the *sequence* is said to be highly redundant. In the case of a sequence of stimuli, those *stimuli* that appear later may be said to be redundant insofar as they are predicted by those appearing earlier. These are slightly different uses of the term redundant. However, we may say that a later stimulus in a redundant sequence provides no information. Therefore, in a classical conditioning situation, only the first stimulus in a fixed sequence of stimuli preceding the reinforcer should be informative. The different behavioral effects of the various stimuli in such a fixed sequence have not been sufficiently studied to yield simple generalizations. The Information Hypothesis (*q.v.*) implies that only the (first) informative stimulus will acquire a reinforcing capacity. See Information.

Reinforcement. This word is used in three main senses, as the operation of reinforcement, the effect of reinforcement, and the process of reinforcement.

Operation. The act of delivering a reinforcer (*q.v.*), or the occurrence of a reinforcer, or the specification that a response will, according to some schedule, be closely followed by a reinforcer.

Effect. The result of presenting a reinforcer, namely, making more probable a particular response which preceded the reinforcer.

Process. The process of strengthening or making more probable a response by (repeatedly) presenting a reinforcer after the response.

Reinforcement, as defined above, is sometimes called "operant reinforcement" as distinguished from "respondent reinforcement." See Reinforcement, respondent.

Reinforcement, Respondent. Presenting a conditioned and an unconditioned stimulus at approximately the same time.

Reinforcer. An operation, usually presenting a stimulus, that eventually results in the increase in probability of an operant that closely preceded the operation. The whole situation also serves to define the operant, as that class of responses more or less uniformly affected by a reinforcing effect. A reinforcer is sometimes said to be effective, given the appropriate conditions, in increasing the probability of any operant, though there are probably limits on this generalization.

In the definition given above, the reinforcer is understood to be "positive," as opposed to "negative." A negative reinforcer is an aversive stimulus, whose removal is reinforcing.

"Reinforcer" and "reinforcement" are also used to refer to the physical substance that is presented, such as food.

Reinforcer, Conditioned (S^r). A reinforcer whose reinforcing effect depends upon a history of training.

Reinforcer, Generalized. A conditioned reinforcer established and strengthened under more than one condition of deprivation. For example; pecking a green light might give access to food when the bird was hungry and water when it was thirsty. When performance had come under the control of the green light, it (presumably) would be a generalized reinforcer. For human beings, money, being an important element of contingencies involving presentation of many different reinforcers, is a generalized reinforcer. Other reinforcers, peculiar to human society, such as fame and power, may be regarded as generalized reinforcers, though it is difficult to point with assurance at the evidence for the appropriate histories of deprivation.

Reinforcer, Negative. A reinforcer (*q.v.*) for which the operation is removal of a stimulus; hence, an aversive stimulus.

Reinforcer, Primary (S^R). A reinforcer whose reinforcing effect does not depend upon a history of training. For example, food, water and sexual stimulation are regarded (under certain appropriate circumstances) as primary reinforcers.

Reinforcer, Secondary. Same as conditioned reinforcer. See Reinforcer, Conditioned.

Respondent. A response which is elicited by a particular stimulus, and hence is to be distinguished from an operant (*q.v.*). Respondent and operant are terms introduced by Skinner (1938).

Respondent Conditioning. Same as Classical Conditioning. See Conditioning, Classical.

Response Strength. 1. A theoretical construct abstracted from measures such as response frequency, latency, magnitude, vigor, resistance to extinction, etc.
2. In operant conditioning, response strength is usually equivalent to response probability.

:S. A brief stimulus at the end of a first-order component in a second-order schedule (*q.v.*).

S^Δ ("ess delta"). Also called "negative discriminative stimulus" and "S^-." A stimulus during which the primary reinforcer being used to sustain the performance being studied is not delivered. That is, a stimulus that signifies Extinction.

S^D ("ess dee"). Also called "discriminative stimulus," "positive discriminative stimulus," and "S^+." Any of the members of a set of stimuli correlated one-to-one with different schedules of reinforcement, such that a given stimulus signifies a given schedule. See Discriminative Stimulus.

Safe Signal. A stimulus associated with the absence of or delay of an aversive event. For example, if a 1,000 *Hz* tone is sometimes terminated with shock and a 4,000 *Hz* is never terminated with shock, the 4,000 *Hz* tone is a safe signal. See Danger Signal.

Scallop. Positively accelerated portion of a cumulative record, usually between successive reinforcement in interval schedules, or sometimes in ratio schedules.

Schedule Control. When performance appropriate to a particular schedule is generated by a stimulus which is not a primary reinforcer, the stimulus may be said to exert schedule control. For example, if a response 2 min after the last reinforcement produces a brief red light, and a response 2 min after that produces food, the behavior that emerges may not be distinguishable from that which emerges with an ordinary *FI* 2 schedule of reinforcement in which only food is produced. That is, response rate may show 2-min scallops (*q.v.*). The double scallop between reinforcements would disappear if the scheduled brief red light were eliminated. The brief red light in such a case would be said to exert schedule control. It may also be referred to as a maintaining stimulus and is notated "*:S*", as in TAND *FI* 2 *:S; FI* 2, in the example given. The occurrence of schedule control is prima facie evidence for the stimulus being a conditioned reinforcer.

Second-Order Schedule. A schedule in which the behavior specified by one schedule is reinforced according to another schedule. Thus, a second-order schedule is a schedule of schedules. A component schedule in a second-order schedule may be called a *first-order schedule*. In the notation for a second-order schedule, the first-order schedule is in parentheses, thus: (*FR* 5), and the second-order contingency is indicated before the parentheses, thus: *FR* 10 (*FR* 5). The second-order schedule *FR* 10 (*FR* 5) would be indistinguishable from *FR* 50. The second-order schedule *FR* 2 (*FI* 3) would be indistinguishable from TAND *FI* 3 *FI* 3. It is common to terminate each first-order component with a brief stimulus. The brief stimulus is referred to in general as "*:S*," and is inserted immediately after the first-order schedule, thus: *FR* 10 (*FI* 5*:S*). *FR* 10 (*FR* 5*:S*) requires 50 responses for reinforcement, but, in addition, a brief stimulus, such as a feeder light flash, follows every fifth response.

Sidman Avoidance. See Avoidance.

Signal. A stimulus that gives information to the organism. Thus, a signal is equivalent to an informative stimulus, and may be a clue (*q.v.*) or a cue (*q.v.*). The word signal is used because it is a short word whose meaning in ordinary English and in communication theory is close to the technical meaning intended in the context of the analysis of behavior.

Stimulus. Any condition of the internal or external environment that may be implicated in the control of behavior. Most stimuli used in behavioral research are exteroceptive; lights and sounds, either unpatterned or patterned, singly or in combination, controlled in intensity and time of presentation by the experimenter.

Occasionally, in accounting for some aspect of operant behavior, appeal is made to stimuli that are not directly controlled by the experimenter and/or not directly measured. A prominent example of stimuli implicated in the control of behavior but not actually observed or controlled are those produced by execution of a response, such as stimuli arising in muscles and joints and changes in retinal locus of a given visual stimulus by head movements. Other examples are the stimuli arising from activity of the autonomic nervous system, which causes such effects as widespread changes in cardiovascular function, secretion of epinephrine, elimination, and alertness. Such appeals to inferred stimuli are usually made with caution and received with skepticism. Extensive experimental verification, ideally resulting in establishing experimental control of the stimulus, is necessary to render acceptable an explanation in which these stimuli prominently figure.

While inferred stimuli are certainly appealed to more often than the subsequent experimental verification is actually pursued, the existence and importance of stimuli originally inferred has been convincingly shown in several notable cases. For example, according to one theory, sensory feedback from motor activity was essential for the normal development of perceptual capacity in young animals. Such feedback effects were known to exist, but were too complex and ill-defined to measure directly and were not definitely known to have an essential role in the development of the senses. A large number of studies employing partial control of the stimulus by altering or eliminating the motor-sensory feedback has shown its functional importance in the development and maintenance of normal motor coordination (c.f., Held & Freedman, 1963). Another well-known example comes from the case of echolocation in bats. It was originally thought on the basis of indirect evidence that bats avoided obstacles by receiving echos from them. These echos were inferred stimuli and their functional role in bat navigation was also inferred. Experiments that employed partial control of the stimulus (echo) by changing the nature of the obstacle and by interferring with the bats' audition subsequently confirmed the original hypothesis. (cf. Galambos and Griffin, 1942).

Stimulus Control.   The extent to which the rate, pattern, topography, or probability of occurrence of an operant is determined by the value of a stimulus variable.

Stimulus Generalization.   1. The tendency of a conditioned response elicited by a conditioned stimulus at a given value of a physical variable to occur in response to stimuli at other values of the variable.

2. The tendency of an operant reinforced under one set of conditions to be emitted under "similar" conditions.

Superstitious Behavior.   Behavior strengthened through effective reinforcing conditions created by the behavior itself, and not explicitly arranged by the experimenter. The reinforcer is not contingent upon the animal's behavior, but is scheduled arbitrarily. Thus it occurs to some extent independently of the organism's behavior. (The behavior that may occur and be reinforced is consequently, from a much wider class than the behavior that is actually emitted and reinforced.) Regular presentations of a reinforcer, about every minute, often produces easily observed superstitious behavior. For example, the bird may turn around several times between presentations of the reinforcer. This behavior then comes under the control of the reinforcer with the result that the behavior is emitted with an increasing probability as the fixed interval progresses. The fact that the behavior is emitted with highest probability just before reinforcement tends to stabilize performance, by reinforcing the superstitious behavior. A similar set of conditions may help explain human superstitions. For example, the longer the drought, the more frequent and vigorous will probably be "rainmaking" behavior, such as rain dances. The end of the drought in normal temperate climates would then become more and more likely to follow the behavior, thereby reinforcing the superstition.

Where the behavior is accompanied by a systematic sequence of stimuli up to reinforcement, so that individual stimuli come to control different patterns or rates of responding, the behavior is called "superstitious chaining."

Tandem Schedule (TAND). A schedule of reinforcement in which a single reinforcement is programmed by two or more schedules acting in succession without correlated stimuli. For example, in TAND *FI* 10 *FR* 25 a reinforcement occurs when 25 responses have been executed after an interval of 10 min has elapsed since the last reinforcement.

Time-Out (TO). A situation in which an Extinction schedule is in effect, and the organism characteristically does not engage in the behavior being studied. With pigeons a *TO* is conveniently arranged by turning off all lights in the chamber and disabling the response keys. Since pecking is visually guided, pigeons do not peck in the dark. Even if they did, however, the Extinction schedule would quickly reduce the probability of pecking. Sometimes enough light gets into the chamber to allow a bird accurately to peck the key, and the Extinction schedule might in that case assume more importance.

Topography, Response. The particular form of behavior, usually defined physically, that qualifies as a response, as distinguished from its operational definition, such as "switch closure for 10 msec." Thus, response topography if often appealed to in accounting for individual differences, unstable or irregular behavior, etc.

Trace-Conditioned Reflex. A conditioned reflex established by presenting a *CS* followed by a delay between termination of the *CS* and presentation of the *US*. Similar but not identical to delayed conditioned reflex (*q.v.*).

Uncertainty. In the context of the analysis of behavior, a condition in which contingencies are mixed or variable in response requirements and/or are temporally irregular. See Information.

Unconditioned Response (UR). A respondent reliably elicited by an unconditioned stimulus, without special training so far as the experimenter knows. See Conditioning, Classical.

Unconditioned Stimulus (US). A stimulus that reliably elicits a respondent at the beginning of an experiment, without special training so far as the experimenter knows. For example, acid in the mouth is a *US* for salivation, electric shock is a *US* for the galvanic skin response, light on the retina is a *US* for pupillary contraction, etc. The *US* is also called a reinforcer or reinforcement. See Conditioning, Classical.

Variable-Interval Schedule (VI). The same as fixed-interval schedule (*q.v.*), except that the time from a reinforcement to the availability of the next reinforcement is variable, thus:

$$\tilde{T} \longrightarrow R \longrightarrow S^R$$

The mean time (of $\tilde{T}$) is given in minutes, as in "*VI* 1," "*VI* 3," etc.

Variable-Ratio Schedule (VR). The same as fixed-ratio schedule (*q.v.*) except that the number of responses required for each reinforcement is variable, not fixed, thus:

$$\tilde{n}R \longrightarrow S^R$$

The mean number of responses per reinforcement is given, as in "*VR* 10," "*VR* 50," etc.

Warm-Up. A higher or lower, or more irregular response rate at the start of a session before the level of performance characteristic of the bulk of the session is attained.

Yoked Boxes. Boxes in which reinforcements for one subject in one box (*Y*) are determined by the performance of another subject in another box (*X*). This is a way of controlling temporal distribution of reinforcements independently of performance. For example, if the schedule of reinforcement in box *X* were *FR* 100, after 99 responses in box *X* reinforcement might become available in *both* boxes. Thus, the distributions of interreinforcement times would be virtually identical in the two boxes, though the schedules of reinforcement were quite different, one being a ratio schedule and the other an interval schedule.

Yoked boxes may be used to control the temporal distribution distribution of punishments. For example, an avoidance schedule may be in effect in Box *X*, with the unavoided shocks being delivered to the animals in *both* boxes. Thus, the number and pattern of shocks would be identical in the two boxes but the behavioral effects may be different. (cf. Brady, Porter, Conrad and Mason, 1958.)

INDEX

INDEX

*This book has been set in 10 point Century
Expanded leaded 3 points, and 9 point Century Expanded leaded 2 points. Section
numbers are 42 point and Section titles are
18 point Helvetica Regular; chapter numbers are 24 point and chapter titles are 14
point Helvetica Regular. The size of the
type page is 27 by 45½ picas.*